CHICAGO PUBLIC LIBRARY
HAROLD WASHINGTON LIBRARY CENTER

R0002423301

R00024 23301

Y0-BGW-731

LB 2336 .W36 c.1

Warren, Paul B. 1938-

The dynamics of funding

DATE		

CHICAGO PUBLIC LIBRARY
SOCIAL SCIENCES AND HISTORY
400 S. STATE ST   60605

© THE BAKER & TAYLOR CO

THE DYNAMICS OF FUNDING

an educator's guide to effective grantsmanship

PAUL B. WARREN
Boston University

ALLYN AND BACON, INC.
Boston   London   Sydney

*To Norma, William, and Carolyn
and to
Ruth Bay, in memoriam*

Copyright © 1980 by Allyn and Bacon, Inc., 470 Atlantic Avenue, Boston, Massachusetts 02210. All rights reserved. No part of the material protected by this copyright notice may be reproduced or utilized in any form or by any means, electronic or mechanical, including photocopying, recording, or by any information storage and retrieval system, without written permission from the copyright owner.

Library of Congress Cataloging in Publication Data

Warren, Paul B   1938–
   The dynamics of funding.

   Bibliography: p.
   Includes index.
   1. Endowments—United States. I. Title.
LB2336.W36   379'.12   79-15710
ISBN 0-205-06681-X

Production Editor: Robine Storm van Leeuwen
Manufacturing Editor: Linda Card

Printed in the United States of America

Contents

Foreword vi

Preface x

Acknowledgments xiv

1   **The Funding System: Setting the Stage**   1

Historical Overview 1 / The Proposal and the Funding System 6 / Characteristics of the Funding System 8 / Assumptions Governing Response to the System 12 / Elements Shaping Project Development 12 / Conflict and the Funding System 13 / An Approach to Conflict Resolution 18 / Summary 22 / Endnotes 23 /

2   **The Dynamics of the System**   25

Variables Affecting Program Definition 25 / Project Development and the Nature of Change 26 / School Desegregation, Teacher Centering, and the Funding System 27 / The Boston Response to the Racial Imbalance Act of 1965 and Educational Amendments of 1974 (Chapter 636): An Overview 28 / Desegregation Program Societal and Legislative Definition: The National Perspective 29 / Desegregation Program Societal and Legislative Definition: The Local Perspective 31 / Teaching Centers: Societal and Legislative Definition 34 / Generalizations Applicable to Other Funding Settings 38 / Variables Affecting Agency and Institution Definition Setting: Boston and Chapter 636 39 / Phase I—Local Education Agency Response to the Funding Agency Request 41 / Phase II—Variables Affecting University and Community Response 44 / The Community Setting 45 / Application of the Model to a Less Complex Setting: Head Start Program 47 / Summary 50 / Endnotes 51 /

iv   *The Dynamics of Funding*

3   **The Proposal Request: From Authorization to Solicitation   53**

Problem Definition: From Legislation to Rules and Regulations Publication   54   /   The Legislative Birth of a Program   55   /   The Appropriation-Setting Process   59   /   Agency Definition of the Problem   61   /   The Regulation-Setting Process   62   /   Regulation Setting: Events in the Public Domain   63   /   Regulation Setting: Events in the Private Domain   77   /   Functions of the Program Office   78   /   Time Lines Governing Decision Making   84   /   The Public-Private Interface   85   /   Summary   86   /   Endnotes   87   /

4   **The Proposal Document: A Political and Programmatic Statement   89**

The Nature of the Document   90   /   The Structure of the Proposal   91   /   Data Gathering, Analysis, and Assessment Tasks   95   /   Formulation and Development Tasks   97   /   Management and Assessment Tasks   101   /   Proposal Writing: Process as Content   107   /   A Strategy for Linking Process and Content   109   /   Summary   112   /   Endnotes   113   /

5   **The Response to the Proposal Request   115**

Analysis of the Proposal Request   116   /   Application of the Decision-Tree Analysis Approach   118   /   Planning for Proposal Development   144   /   A Systems Management Approach to Proposal Development   144   /   The Application of the Systems Approach   147   /   Characteristics of the Proposal Development Process: Implications for Planning   158   /   Summary   159   /   Endnotes   160   /

6   **The Writing of the Proposal Document   163**

The Proposal Format   163   /   Characteristics of Individual Components of the Proposal   169   /   Abstract   172   /   Introduction or Background   175   /   Problem Statement and/or Assessment of Need   179   /   Program Objectives   186   /   Program Activities or Methods and Procedures   195   /   Program Evaluation   204   /   Project Management   213   /   Project Management Samples   215   /   Budget   220   /   Appendices   229   /   Summary   231   /   Endnotes   231   /

7   **From Paper to Program**   233

   Procedural Factors Affecting Project Implementation 234 / Late Funding and Project Implementation 242 / Legislative Response to Late Funding Problems 248 / Design and Institutional Factors Affecting Project Implementation 249 / Institution Environmental Factors Contributing to Program Slippage 255 / Responding to the Conditions of Implementation 263 / Endnotes 268 /

8   **Strategies for Responding to the Funding Environment**   271

   Forecasting the Funding Environment 272 / General Characteristics 272 / Organizational Characteristics 274 / The Proposal Document and the Funding Environment 287 / The Submitting Institution and the Funding Environment 290 / Institutional Strategies for Responding to the Funding Environment 291 / Summary 303 / Endnotes 304 /

Postscript   307

Appendices:

A   Locating Sources of Federal Funding through Government Publications   311

B   Researching Foundations   319

C   Locating Federal and Foundation Funding Information through Nongovernmental Publications   331

D   Department of Health, Education and Welfare Regional Headquarters Offices   335

E   Federal Assistance Forms and Instructions for Completion   337

Glossary and Acronyms   351

Bibliography   354

Index   *359*

Foreword

The tradition that has shaped the giving of commissions, grants, stipends, and funded contracts is as old as the city states of ancient Greece. Kings, princes, popes, and priestly orders, with increasing frequency over the centuries, have given their consent or permission, coupled with a gift of money, to artisans, poets, philosophers, musicians, scholars, and explorers to execute projects and performances for the benefit of the court or state, or for the glorification of God. By the time of the Renaissance, grants in support of culture and higher learning had become a precise system of contractually based acts of patronage enabling the arts and sciences, pure and applied alike, to enhance the interests of competing power elites.

In the years between 1400 and 1900, the customs and laws affecting acts of patronage were elaborated and extended to include the establishment of scientific research institutes; normal schools for the training of teachers; infant, grammar, and high schools; and laboratories and conservatories. Grants from the state, from churches, and from wealthy benefactors became the stimuli for an explosion of knowledge production and the creation of teaching and learning environments. Five and one-half centuries of evolutionary development of the mechanism of grant awards, however, did not equal the impact of World War II. In mathematics and the pure sciences, for example, the modern era began in the twelfth century; yet more than half of those people who have worked in the modern era have worked during the decades since 1930!

Paul Warren's book documents comprehensively for social and educational research and development in particular but for all applied sciences and professions in general, the postwar *bureaucratization* of secular patronage for higher learning over the past quarter of a century. During this era, grants and contract awards from government agencies and foundations evolved at a rate so swift and with a volume so vast as to stagger the imaginations of even the most confident of scholars, scientists, educators, and artists. His book documents the extension of grants to the farthest reaches of public education—the three-year-old preschool children of Headstart—and shows how all aspects of human services delivery have been transformed through the political dynamics of funding.

The contemporary era, however, spans only the last forty years. My mentor in sociology, Ernest W. Burgess, used to reminisce about his first government grants in social research, which came in the early years of the New Deal. It was his newfound ability to employ dozens of statistical clerks at the expense of the government, he maintained, that made American sociology a *survey* enterprise. According to Burgess, urban sociology at the University of Chicago in the 1930s came to be defined as the science through which to spend $64,000 to locate a brothel (Burgess called it "the red light district") through demographic and ecological mapping, when a dollar tip to a cab driver would get a sound answer to the same question.

As recently as the 1950s, research grants could be obtained by social scientists and others simply by writing a six-page letter or memorandum explaining one's prospective inquiry to a foundation or government agency officer. Even late in the fifties, contracting arrangements were vague and universities kept poor records of who was carrying what awards in order to conduct studies, publish monographs, or experiment freely with political and social inventions for inducing change. I can recall another younger mentor, James Coleman, complaining bitterly about the red tape involved in conducting his field study of a sample of high schools under the funding auspice of the U.S. Office of Education. That agency had the audacity to require elaborate and intrusive accountability from principal investigators. Sociologists used to match notes on which sponsors were least bothersome and probative. Most professors still did their work without external funding. No distinction was made between their unfunded enterprises and those of the rising ranks of grantsmen. By the close of the 1950s, some tendencies to envy those who had freed themselves from normal teaching loads were discernible among social science and education faculties; but patterns of envy and conflict were reserved primarily for medicine, agriculture, engineering, and, above all, physics and chemistry, where the experiences of World War II had made the dynamics of funding converge totally with the dynamics of scientific inquiry. For other fields, save perhaps for rising stars in the conservatories and performing arts, grant-getting remained optional.

In 1962, when Washington, D.C., was Camelot and the Lancelots from Harvard rode high along Pennsylvania Avenue and in most executive departments, I participated in mounting and then managing a research grants program for the U.S. Social Security Administration. Here was a comparatively established agency that had relied for twenty-five years on the research advice of welfare economists without launching external awards or looking for ways to get into the fashionable federal competition for agency prestige through funding. Even this late in the postwar era, however, the procedures were simple and informal in contrast to developments after 1965. Researchers simply wrote a proposal and attached a budget, and the staff sifted out promising entries to pass along to an external review board for approval or rejection. I remember passing along a ten-page proposal from anthropologist Oscar Lewis, for example, that said little more than that he planned to study families on site in Puerto Rico, in order to perfect his concept of the culture of poverty. It was approved by the review board, with staff encouragement, because several of us thought that Lewis had done seminal work in Mexico and could probably be counted on to extend his achievement with agency funding.

What a far cry from the era ushered in, as Paul Warren describes in depth, by Robert MacNamara and the Department of Defense: milestones, PERT charting, PPBS, and sometimes even three-dimensional pop-up models, became the requisites for all proposals! Between 1965 and 1978, with the help of precedents from weapons research and medical studies during World War II and the Korean War, every science, discipline, profession, and sector of the arts became industrialized and bureaucratized simultaneously around the construct of the sponsored and funded project. Warren's book helps us to understand how a once occasional and elitist act of state patronage became an ever more elaborately developed system of competition for funds and thus for prestige, influence, and power.

Warren offers meticulously detailed case studies and inventories of tactics and procedures on the sound premise that the quest for project support has become a serious game that anyone can play—anyone, that is, who is prepared to shed amateurism in exchange for the knowledge and skills essential to success. The more democratic the project funding process has become, the more cross-pressured, technical, intense, and professional are the rules. As Warren demonstrates, the support staff required to service the still evolving rules has become mammoth. Washington, D.C., is surrounded by mediating and lobbying agents specializing in obtaining grant and contract awards. At home in hospitals, universities, school districts, corporate offices and cultural and social agencies, cadres of thousands of men and women have become specialists in grant and contract review and development.

Warren puts in vivid perspective the educator, academician, or program developer standing isolated on the darkling plain of this competition—the individual with an idea, an hypothesis, or a better footnote, who needs money or auspice to further creative production. He or she is aware, moreover, that the process no longer requires a lone inventor, for the government's request for a proposal may in itself prescribe nearly all that is to be accomplished, thus calling for a complex series of echoing playbacks of legislative or executive answers to what the educator or scientist is convinced is the wrong question. Warren's depiction also extends to cases in which the proposer's task is to attach a local or institutional need to the rumbling wagon of a federal grant announcement that was intended to head in an entirely different direction. With painstaking documentation, Warren shows the range of paradoxes and ambiguities that crop up across that darkling plain to confound earnest and cynical, innocent and corrupt inventors alike.

Midway through his treatise, Warren uses the metaphor of dramaturgy to elaborate on the dynamics of funding. He writes, "In the same manner in which any producer of a proposal for a play or film assesses the tastes and size of the potential market prior to making the decision to mount a production, and in the same manner any director makes adjustments in a script appropriate for the intended audience, those responsible for determining the feasibility of securing funding . . . must take equivalent steps in planning and writing the proposal document." Paul Warren and I have worked together for six years to stimulate and improve the project development activities of a university faculty. I came to this task after nearly twenty years of work as a researcher and administrator in centers, institutes, bureaus, and laboratories. Together, we have concluded that the metaphor of the theater characterizes the contemporary dynamics of funding most aptly. As Warren's comment above hints, however, the effect of contemporary forces is to inject business management—consumer research, market analysis, and accounting—into the creative process of playwriting, casting, and production.

The results, at least in the soft sectors of the behavioral and social sciences and the arts and humanities, have been to multiply fraudulence and chicanery and to add imitation and dullness at rates that threaten to undermine the essential value of the funding process. (I suspect the same may be said for grants and contracts in the hard sectors of science and technology; I am simply unqualified to verify the suspicion.) The value of Warren's book, however, lies beyond this inference of despair. He counsels hope and patience. His message presupposes an inventor, change-agent, or inspired "Hound of Heaven," in quest of reasonable support to sustain study and to foster widespread sharing in the public interest.

I applaud Warren's counsel of hope. The creative process has always included producing a thousand unworthy plays as the price of underwriting a single great one. The years from 1959 through 1968, similarly, will go into the annals of educational research, development, and practice as the era when sound alternatives to conventionally stupid pedagogies were generated at public expense. The shelves and files of the new library at the National Institute of Education now groan with the products and learning of that fertile period. Those products range from tons of unsifted, junky nonsense to small deposits of knowledge, insight, and clinical possibilities that will gradually be winnowed out and converted into a base for effective teaching and learning. The process is identical, essentially, with that to be found in the National Institutes of Health, the National Science Foundation, and a dozen other public agencies of open inquiry and project development in medicine, engineering, and the hard sciences.

Warren's book should contribute to rendering the somewhat manic and depressive cycling of the project funding process not only intelligible, but also saner and more accessible to citizen participation, and more reasonably governable by civil servants and foundation officers. His message, I believe, invites us to extend the cultural frontiers of the Renaissance: to risk openly the search for change and the quest for understanding, however absurd or freighted the voyage often becomes, and to fling wide the gates that bar the way to higher learning.

Robert A. Dentler
Dean of Education
Boston University

Preface

This book is intended for educators who are interested in improving the skills and understanding necessary to secure grants. Strategies for identifying funding sources, methods of analyzing agency guidelines, and writing of the proposal document are, of course, chief concerns. But securing a grant is not an isolated endeavor; it is part of a larger process that begins with social and educational needs, and ends, one hopes, with a successfully implemented project. This process is examined closely in the belief that a thorough understanding of it is essential to effective grantsmanship.*

It is possible to trace the history of the grant in America with a fair degree of precision. It is more difficult, however, to identify precisely when the skills associated with securing grants become sufficiently important to justify their consideration distinct from the academic specialization or particular need of an individual or institution seeking support for a project. With the rapid expansion of foundation and federal support for health, education, and welfare programs in the mid-1960s, however, the old tradition of securing private and government support for educational and human service programs was transformed by the entry of the "grantsman." Unlike the earlier scholars, artists, or social reformers, the goals and skills of the grantsman did not necessarily extend beyond the identification of funding sources, the writing of the proposal, and the securing of the award. These skills were packaged under the label "grantsmanship."

Despite the changing patterns of funding in the 1970s and the leveling off of appropriations, the role of the grantsman has not diminished in importance. The grantsman clearly meets a need of organizations seeking private and government support for program development: program staff do not necessarily

---

*Although *The Dynamics of Funding* is designed to enable the reader to understand the many variables contributing to the final form of a proposal request, and the implications of these variables for implementing the funded project, it is recognized that some readers may need to prepare a proposal immediately. Chapters 4 through 6 meet the needs of individuals confronting this dilemma. Chapter 4 provides an overview of both the organizational and technical qualities of the proposal document; chapter 5 identifies the strategies appropriate for planning the proposal development process; and chapter 6 serves as a manual enabling the submitter to write a proposal appropriate to the requirements set by the funding agency.

possess the skills and time needed to become familiar with legislation, priorities of funding agencies, and technical requirements for proposal development and submittal. Grantsmanship, however, has come to be associated too frequently with one goal, to get grants, and with one set of skills, to write proposals or to engage in whatever activities are necessary to win the approval of agents who make awards. The term, as commonly used, fails to address the intent of securing funding, that is, the conduct of research, the operation of programs, or the delivery of services.

The author's experience as a proposal writer, project director, proposal reader, and, for the past five years, research and development officer in a major university's school of education, has indelibly shaped both the form and substance of this work. *The Dynamics of Funding* attempts to transform these direct experiences in a way that provides the reader with the skills to use the proposal document as a tool to secure funding and as a strategy to affect his or her institution or agency, or those served by the institution or agency. Although there is no necessary relationship between the securing of federal, state, or foundation funds and the bringing about of change (or even the desire to bring about change), the author primarily is addressing readers who wish to use a grant or contract to affect a program or to carry out an activity that depends on external funding. The work, therefore, is designed to assist those seeking to use a project to implement new programs, and it focuses on the quest for competitive awards, rather than entitlements or formula grants.

Given the background of the writer, much of the discussion and most of the examples used to illustrate points are drawn from the experiences of educational and human service institutions in securing funding from federal, state, or foundation sources. The experiences of universities and colleges, public school systems, and community agencies seeking support for educational and human service programs provide the basis for analyses and recommendations presented. A concentrated effort has been made to select illustrations that apply to the widest range of activities and institutions, without sacrificing the specificity that will enable readers to apply these concepts and strategies to their particular settings.

Approaching funding as a complex process, the book synthesizes the discrete treatment of those elements of the process that are available in proposal writing manuals, directories, registries, and the perodical literature with the research findings examining the success and failure of funded programs. Observations of people who have participated in shaping educational legislation, in developing program guidelines, in writing proposals, and in managing funded projects complement observations already in print. Reference works that are particularly helpful to the writer and/or manager in acquiring the skills necessary to secure funding and to carry out the funded project successfully are also used as information sources. *The Dynamics of Funding* is thus both a reference work for the professional person first approaching the quest for external funding and for the more experienced, a text that encourages the systematic analysis of past experiences and the reassessment of future strategies.

The organization of the book and its title represent a conscious attempt to bring order to the author's experiences with government or foundation supported projects. The biases that surface, despite efforts to test general impressions against objective data, reflect the prevailing social and political climate at the time the writer was introduced to grants and contract administration. Perception of reality and how things might be are shaped unavoidably by setting the decade of the 1970s against that of the 1960s.

The decade of the 1960s included the New Frontier, the Great Society, and the War on Poverty; it was a decade in which federal aid to education reached a new high water mark before dramatically receding in the political and economic backwash of Vietnam. It was a period in which alphabet agencies in the area of education were spun out by executive fiat at a rate second only to that of F.D.R.'s first term as President. Of equal import, the 1960s was a decade of hope during which many believed that flaws in the social and moral fabric of the nation could be addressed and remedied. The nation was seduced by the notion of Camelot; but as the dreams were disrupted by day-to-day events and the actors removed from the stage, the dream quickly ended. There was to be no room for dreams in the 1970s. Historian Henry Steele Commager in a telephone conversation with the author (January 9, 1979) has gone as far as to call the boundary between the 1960s and 1970s "a great divide—the divide of disillusionment."

The decade of the 1960s was unique in that a host of international and domestic political events were complemented by domestic pressures for change growing out of the civil rights movement. Simultaneously, new levels of prosperity in the United States permitted the nation the luxury of placing dollars behind statements of belief embodied in the legislation. Serendipity also contributed. The charisma of John F. Kennedy and Martin Luther King, and the political acumen of Lyndon B. Johnson, a former school teacher, provided timely vehicles for translating and transforming the social conditions into legislation, with accompanying appropriations of unprecedented magnitude. The environment conducive to the birth of grantsmanship was set during these years.

Despite the death of the dream and the changed social, political, and economic climate of the 1970s, which encouraged program management terminology (cost effectivensss, performance specifications, milestone charting, process/product evaluation) and discouraged program development and the special reform jargon of the 1960s, neither the prestige of the grantsman nor the level of appropriations has declined.

With 1980 ushering in an apparent era of austerity, priorities have changed, however, and the competition for securing funding has increased. The New Frontier and Great Society provided a training ground for obtaining grants by staffs of schools and human service agencies; the New Austerity will rigorously test the ability of the grantsman to apply the lessons of the 1960s.

The history of the past fifteen years forms the backdrop against which this book has been developed. It is not the intent of this work, however, to examine the range of political, social, and economic factors that contributed to the failure of government, school, and community agencies to realize the expectations implicit in the New Frontier and Great Society policy pronouncements; many fine works examining this period and the years that followed have been written. Rather, this work draws on events of the past that are directly relevant to understanding events that shape the formulation of proposal requests; the response by institutions or agencies competing for funds; the evaluation of proposals by review panels, and the implementation of the project by the submitting institution, should funding be secured.

Collectively considered, these elements constitute the process of funding; the nature of the interaction between these elements shapes the form and substance of the specific proposal and the chances for success of the specific project. Because events that define each element of the process may change from month to month, from year to year, and from setting to setting, it is an understanding of the process that permits individuals to apply the skills to succeed in securing funding and mounting a successful project. The dynamics of the process give funding its definition.

The writer hopes that a better understanding of the dynamics of funding will provide those responsible for initiating steps that lead to authorizing legislation and program guidelines with a clearer understanding of the conflicts built into the funding system. Without the necessary adjustments at the source, attempts to adjust farther downstream will only be palliative. It is also hoped that, by analyzing the factors shaping the responses of institutions and community groups to funding opportunities, administrators, teachers, and human service personnel will understand better the factors that contribute to the success or failure of their funding endeavors.

This book, then, is intended first and foremost for individuals, whatever their position in the hierarchy of organizational units participating in the funding process. For them, the writing and funding of the proposal are the means to meet the challenge of bringing about change. Regardless of the organizational and social reforms that may occur in the forseeable future, the proposal will remain the means to complete the transaction between program sponsor and program recipient. The proposal will serve to set expectations and to delineate specifications for those providing funds, those responsible for the project, and those who need to be served. The proposal thus will remain at the core of the funding process.

Paul B. Warren

Acknowledgments

In the course of developing *The Dynamics of Funding* from the point of conceptualization to the drafting of the final document, the thinking and skills of many individuals have contributed to the form and substance of the work. Experiences and insights of program officers in federal and state agencies, directors, staff and trainees or clients in funded projects, and university colleagues have been distilled and are represented in the text. Although it is impossible to extend my gratitude to all of these individuals personally, particular thanks are owed the following individuals: Ted Parker and Lou Simonini of the Region I Equal Education Opportunity Program Office; Richard Stirling of the Region I Administration for Children, Youth, and Families; and Charles MacMillan, a program officer in the Massachusetts Bureau for Equal Education Opportunity Office at the time of writing. All listened and responded constructively to the approach taken by the author. Alan Schmeider and Matt Judson of the Washington, D.C. Teacher Center Office and Dustin Wilson and Myrtle Bond of the Consumer Education Office provided invaluable perspectives on the funding process; Marie Barrie of Teacher Corps also provided the benefit of her experience in several program offices of the Department of Health, Education and Welfare; Tom Keys assisted in untangling the variables that contributed to the evolution of the Right-to-Read Program; and Ted Sky in the Office of the General Counsel, U.S. Office of Education, aided in identifying the administrative maze that leads to the ultimate request for proposals. Sam Halperin and George Kaplan of the Washington-based Institute for Educational leadership assisted in synthesizing much of the material through the planning that went into an IEL-sponsored seminar.

William Van Til and Samuel Keys, who first introduced me to the world of funding while I was a doctoral student in the mid 1960s, are owed special thanks. Dr. Keys's introduction in the 1960s was followed up with assistance from Washington, D.C. during the writing of the book. Jorie Mark, the project officer for the first project on which I served as director also provided insights at critical stages of the book's development. Robert Dentler, Dean of the Boston University School of Education, has simultaneously been my best critic and supporter; his influence on the book extends significantly beyond the material included in the text.

With the transformation of ideas to paper, the services of others helped me to escape, for the most part, from the convoluted prose too often the trademark of the academic. Margaret Oliver tackled the initial editing and transformation of handwritten manuscript to type; Victoria Sands assisted in tracking down elusive documents and organizing the proposal-specific material. The skill and patience of Dorothy Howells, Grace Sheldrick, and Janet Goldman, who served as manuscript editors, taught me to appreciate fully those people who stand between the author's manuscript and the typesetter.

P.B.W.

1

The Funding System: Setting the Stage

HISTORICAL OVERVIEW

Until recently, writing proposals to obtain support for research or for delivering social and educational services was the responsibility of groups of people constituting a relatively small and isolated subculture in government agencies, foundations, and educational and social institutions. Many organizations responsible for the delivering of educational and social services relied on federal, state, and foundation assistance for support. Until the late 1950s, however, grants and contracts to these institutions remained essentially the province of government officials, education and social service administrators, and the few scholars whose research interests caught the eye of a benefactor. The formulation of legislation, the setting of program guidelines, and an institution's response to funding opportunities usually merited the attention of only the institutional officers directly concerned with obtaining institutional support. Other people made the decisions, and individuals or institutions who reaped the benefits—or paid the costs—were recipients rather than participants in the funding process.

The origin of the grant in the United States can be traced to 1842, when Congress made an award of $30,000 to Professor Samuel Morse to test the feasibility of public use of the telegraph. Support for educational and service delivery programs, however, came from general aid and enabling statutes that earmarked tax dollars for program support. With the passage of the Morrill Act in 1862, the proposal became a vehicle for transmitting money to educational institutions for specified programs of research, training, or development. This act, which supported the establishment of colleges of agricultural and mechanical arts, set precedents for the contemporary dynamics of funding: (1) higher education was recognized as an instrument for national development; (2) the federal government, during a period of national crisis (the Civil War), authorized monies to meet a national need by developing a system to increase the agricultural strength of the nation; and, (3) an initial tentative step was taken toward "categorical" or "problem-specific" support to aid specific groups.

The main purpose of the Morrill Act was ". . . to promote the liberal and *practical education* of the *industrial classes*" [italics added]. Specific educational needs of segments of the population, not being met by the private colleges and universities, were to be addressed. (If we substitute "public schools of the nation" or "community organizations and private nonprofit organizations" for "colleges and universities," we have a statement of intent appropriate for contemporary federally and state-authorized appropriations for educational development.)

In many ways, the precedents set by the Morrill Act represented logical extensions of the authority and purpose of the Old Deluder Satan Act of 1647 and the Ordinance of 1787. The Old Deluder Satan Act was the first instance of state-ordered instruction and was a response to a perceived threat. The Ordinance of 1787 granted knowledge a role in meeting the needs of the nation, stating: "Religion, morality and knowledge being necessary for good government and the happiness of mankind, schools and the means of education shall forever be encouraged."[1]

The notion that education can serve as a tool of national development was made more explicit during World War I. The Smith-Hughes Act of 1917 addressed the nation's need for technically trained manpower. This act, more than earlier education legislation, was a direct congressional response to "suddenly discovered" educational needs and set a critical precedent for understanding the dynamics of funding: external events, unrelated directly to the state of education, often precipitate the drafting of legislation to address educational or social needs long present but not formally acknowledged. Draft boards discovered at the outbreak of World War I that nearly 25 percent of the draftees were illiterate, that many draftees did not speak English, and that many of those found physically unfit for service possessed physical defects that could have been remedied if diagnosed during their school years. These discoveries created an "educational crisis" calling for action.

National crises continued to precipitate government support for educational and human service program development. The use of federal funding to remedy specific societal problems identified by Congress increased during World War II and flourished in the defense-minded sociopolitical climate that followed. The 1940 National Defense Training Program provided funding to train defense workers; the G.I. Bill of Rights (Serviceman's Readjustment Act of 1944) enabled approximately four million veterans to participate in vocational and other education programs below college level. In addition to providing college tuition support for veterans, the National Defense Training Act of 1958 provided substantial financial assistance for programs to improve instruction in science, mathematics, and foreign languages. It was signed into law, not coincidentally, less than one year after the Soviet Union launched Sputnik.

The importance of crisis in precipitating congressional debate and action, and its relevance for the program developer, cannot be underestimated. As Munger states:

> The depression forced emergency aid to education in the 1930s. The severe postwar teacher shortage stimulated the federal aid proposals of the late 1940s. The baby-boom of the 1950s—abetted by suburban sprawl—generated the school construction bills of the same decade. Impacted areas legislation followed one national defense crisis, while the National Defense Education Act was called into existence by the Cold War crisis that followed the launching of Sputnik.[2]

Anyone who is tempted to postulate a causal model to project future availability of funding, using the single variable of national crisis, should, however, resist the temptation. Crisis is only one variable that affects projections of future funding.

The National Defense Education Act of 1958, and the solicitation of grant proposals from universities, colleges, and school systems, allowed new groups to participate in the development of programs to secure grants. In the past, aid had been distributed to institution officers or eligible individuals largely through legislatively defined allocation formulas; NDEA provided participants in the funded projects the opportunity to establish the training content and strategies consistent with criteria set by the legislation and the National Science Foundation (responsible for administration of the program). This trend accelerated dramatically during the late Kennedy and early Johnson administrations.

Although President Kennedy was unable to achieve a breakthrough in aid to elementary and secondary education, efforts of his administration led to passage of the Elementary and Secondary Education Act in 1965, during the Johnson administration. The power of the executive branch to create a climate conducive to the passage of education legislation, even without a clearly defined crisis directly related to the problem, was demonstrated briefly during the Kennedy administration. During that period, the executive branch was active in identifying educational and social needs and in offering strategies to meet them. As Moynihan states: "President Kennedy brought to Washington as office holders, or consultants or just friends, a striking echelon of persons whose profession might justifiably be described as knowing what ails societies and whose art is to get treatment underway before the patient is especially aware of anything noteworthy taking place."[3] Bailey and Mosher, in their excellent study of the factors contributing to passage of the Elementary and Secondary Education Act, observe that: ". . . the phoenix of new ideas and directions could be discerned in the very ashes of defeat"[4] of the various Kennedy-sponsored bills.

The Kennedy period is particularly important in that it dramatically increased the extent to which securing grants and contracts became part of the public consciousness. The ideas and directions generated by his administration were transformed into legislation that aided President Johnson's "War on Poverty." Programs supported by legislation directly involved teachers, social service workers, community representatives, parents, and even the recipients of services in both the planning and implementation of projects. During this period hundreds of thousands succeeded or failed in mounting educational and social service programs. Education and social service personnel, en masse, were directly affected by legislative and funding decisions; millions of young people were affected by the outcomes of programs in operation; and the population at large watched to see whether expectations could be met.

With the 1964 landslide election of Lyndon Johnson, the social and political environment was ready for the distribution of massive federal aid to education and social service agencies. Elected on a strong education and equal opportunity platform, President Johnson claimed a mandate for his programs. A large majority of new Democratic congressmen provided key support on critical legislative committees. President Johnson's good working relationship with Congress and his experience in steering legislation through the intricate network of congressional obstacles provided the necessary political acumen to assure legislative action.

These political factors were augmented by social and political forces at work in society. A favorable climate existed, at least temporarily, for waging war on poverty. The education-related components of the Civil Rights Act of 1964, providing presidential and congressional authority to carry out the Supreme Court desegregation mandate of 1954, simultaneously increased the federal role in education and largely isolated the race-related controversies that had contributed to the demise of previously proposed, general educational legislation. During the Kennedy administration, legislation had been passed to upgrade the skills of the unemployed in urban and depressed rural areas. The nation's poor, as a result of the political climate set by the administration and of unrest in the cities, became a major political concern. The Economic Opportunity Act of 1964, which authorized the Job Corps, Neighborhood Youth Corps, Adult Basic Education programs, and Community Action programs and created the Office of Economic Opportunity, established strategies to address vocational needs far beyond previous vocational training legislation.

The magnitude of funding and broad scope of activities created a self-renewing public awareness. The participation of new populations in program formulation at the local level, even before passage of ESEA, involved hundreds of thousands of people in the development and management of proposals and programs that conformed to legislative and funding agency guidelines. Projects increasingly became a way of life for many seeking to realize the "Great Society."

During the 1965-66 period, the amount of federal funds allocated for education programs almost tripled.* *Grantsmanship* became a widely used term.

---

*Appropriations rose from $890,685,000 in 1965 to $2,408,209,000 in 1966.

The tradition of securing private and federal support for research, training, and facility construction was transformed by *grantsmen.* "They generally had but one goal—to get grants—and one set of skills—to write proposals or engage in whatever activities were necessary to win the approval and attention of agents who allocated grants. . . . Neither their goal nor their skills were highly associated with the intent of the legislation or with effective educational innovation."[5]

ESEA's significance for those seeking funds for federally authorized programs fortunately extends beyond its spawning of grantsmen. The bill was a political masterpiece that paid homage to the political axiom, "All in the game win." Benefits were extended to various parties and were tightly interfaced; any major amendment would have damaged the total program seriously. ESEA broke the logjam of federal aid to elementary and secondary schools:

> Passage of ESEA, and a host of subsequent federal aid statutes, permanently ended the impasse over the legitimacy of federal intervention on the school scene. While school aid fights during the subsequent decade (1965–1975) have been abundant, they have all revolved about what kind and how much federal aid to offer and how best to construct a workable federal/state partnership, rather than over the continuity of the ESEA itself.[6]*

Despite varying assessments of the impact of several titled and competitive programs authorized by ESEA,† everyone agrees that ESEA immersed schools and state departments in the proposal-writing and project management business. Under the 1974 Amendments to the act, administrators, teachers, parents, and community representatives came into direct contact with the intricacies of federal funding.

During the decade following passage of ESEA, educators and political scientists have directed attention to the impact of programs first authorized by legislation of the Great Society and War on Poverty period. Misapprehensions that governed the programs' inception and the flaws present in implementation, when coupled with continued racial tension, recurring fiscal crises, a declining school-age population, declining levels of literacy and the concomitant reemerging emphasis on the teaching of basics, and a new questioning of the value of higher education for all children, created a new set of funding dynamics. The social, political, and economic climate of the late 1970s differed significantly from that of the Kennedy and Johnson years; questions of cost-effectiveness and management criteria replaced debate over the need to reorder social

---

*Samuel Halperin, "ESEA: Decennial Views of the Revolution; I, The Positive Side." *Phi Delta Kappan* (November 1975): 147. Reprinted with permission.

†Public Law 89-10, The Elementary and Secondary Education Act, originally comprised five separate titles: Title I, "Better Schooling for Educationally Deprived Children"; Title II, "School Library Resources, Textbooks and Other Instructional Materials"; Title III, "Supplementary Educational Centers and Services"; Title IV, "Educational Research and Training"; and Title V, "Strengthening State Departments of Education."

goals. Expectations were lowered and operational definitions of outcomes were demanded. Educational reforms and social service programs were no longer perceived as tools that could, or should, bring about massive social change.

Despite the change in expectations of federally and foundation-supported programs, new approaches were introduced during the 1960s to cope with the nation's social needs. These approaches will continue to be reflected in the goals and operations of schools, social service agencies, and community organizations in future decades:

> Despite its difficulties, the antipoverty program introduced new techniques for coping with neglected problems such as neighborhood oriented health and legal services, preschool education, cooperative business enterprises, paraprofessional jobs and training programs that screen the hardest cases in, not out. It created, through establishment of local community action agencies, new self-help institutions in the slums, enabling the poor to exert leverage on governments at all levels.[7]*

Federal, state, and foundation support in the form of grants and contracts no longer represents an opportunity open to a privileged few within an organizational position that permits transactions with sponsors. New crises and changing political administrations will certainly affect the priorities and substance of future legislation and foundation programs. Nevertheless, the principle of support for educational and social service programs has been firmly established. The proposal is the means local or state education agencies, institutions of higher education, private nonprofit corporations, and community agencies use to seek necessary funding. Levels of funding may fluctuate, priorities may change, legislation will be amended and criteria for funding will vary, but the proposal will remain the basic instrument for making the decision whether or not to fund a wide range of programs.

THE PROPOSAL AND THE FUNDING SYSTEM

Despite the centrality of the proposal in securing funding, the conditions governing the form and substance of the proposed activities are set by events that occurred before the participation of the parties involved. Examination of a proposal or a contract apart from the events that preceded its writing will not reveal factors that can contribute to the success of the proposal or the funded program. The writing of a proposal is only one link in a chain of events leading up to the funding and initiation of a project.

The social and political environment of the nation, as reflected in the legislative or foundation priorities and guidelines providing authorization and

---

*© 1974 by The New York Times Company. Reprinted by permission.

appropriation for a program, initially defines the problem to be addressed. In turn, the agencies in charge of administering programs, consistent with the intent of the authorizing bodies, are responsible for developing criteria that govern how institutions seeking support may respond. These criteria, which represent the agency definition of the problem or needs, are reflected in the guidelines accompanying the solicitation of proposals. The respondents—universities, school departments, human service agencies—develop their own definitions of the needs. The governmental units that shape the legislation, the agencies that shape the guidelines, and the responding institutions deal simultaneously with two sets of needs: (1) needs endemic to the functioning of the institution and (2) needs related to the generic problem under consideration.

Funding agency criteria for evaluation are not necessarily consonant with the criteria to which an institution must conform in order to bring about institutional reform or educational change. The statement of services offered may not necessarily be consonant with the ability of the submitting institution.

The basic assumption underlying the presentation of the funding process in the following pages is that the possession of proposal writing skills, without an understanding of the events that precede the request for a proposal or without an understanding of the institutional constraints to successful implementation, only enables one to write a proposal appropriate to a single set of specifications. Such skills do not necessarily have any bearing on the success or failure of the project. The proposal must serve simultaneously as a request for aid, a statement of institutional capability, a commitment to program development or service delivery, and finally, a contract for services.

The school, university, or social agency proposal writer may be responsible for program conceptual design, program activity development, project implementation, and management. And he or she may ultimately be held responsible for the success or failure of the project. Without understanding the interdependency of events leading to funding or the multitude of variables affecting day-to-day program operation in a fluid sociopolitical environment, the proposal writer and/or project manager is assured limited success or professional disaster.

The following information will help individuals responsible for developing and implementing externally funded projects to: (1) analyze the environment that precipitates a proposal request; (2) develop planning and management strategies to increase the odds of successful project implementation; (3) translate project development strategies to appropriate proposal documents; and (4) reconcile the project as delineated in the proposal with management, programmatic, and evaluation needs precipitated by day-to-day operation. The information provides a predictable general framework for people hoping to use external funding to improve the delivery of social or educational services. It must be recognized, however, that the difficulty of bringing order to the funding process is not unlike that noted by Seymour Sarason in commenting on the difficulties inherent in analyzing the operations of schools:

8 The Dynamics of Funding

> The situation is not unlike that of an individual who, having become aware for the first time that there are billions of stars in the heavens, sets for himself the problem of understanding their relationship. He becomes aware that his 'subjects' move; that he cannot always be in a position to see them; that even when they are available to him he is faced with the limitation that a single brain has limits as to what and how much it can see and record; that he will have to develop indirect criteria for the presence or absence of things; that he is faced not only with the task of constructing conceptions of what is, but literally reconstructing what was or might have been the past, and even predicting the future history.[8]

The ultimate success of a proposal and ensuing project depends on their ability to meet simultaneously the divergent needs of the target population, the political needs of the authorizing body, the programmatic and political needs of the administering agencies, and the political and programmatic needs of the submitting institutions. Project development and implementation may be thought of as a system of conceptually independent but phenomenologically interdependent sets of events. As such, one way of examining the process is to consider project development and execution as sets of discrete events, with each set contributing to the functioning of the whole—the funding system. The objective here is to examine interactions within and between the various sets of events in order to comprehend the dynamics of the funding system. The initial task is to identify the sets of events, examine the nature of their interactions, and order the interactions unique to each set.

Unlike Sarason's astronomer, the proposal writer has at least the means to identify major galaxies within his or her universe. The following schematic identifies the major galaxies that constitute the funding system universe, charts the movements of the galaxies that constitute the conceptually independent sets of events, and assesses their interrelationships.

CHARACTERISTICS OF THE FUNDING SYSTEM

Figure 1.1 traces the evolution of any funding program and identifies the variables that contribute to the form of the proposal request; it also identifies the points of stress in the system. A discussion of the major characteristics of the individual sets of events or units follows.

Initial Precipitating Events

The nation is always confronted with a multitude of social or economic needs. These needs or problems constitute the inevitable discrepancy between "what is" and "what should be" that occurs in any social order. These needs

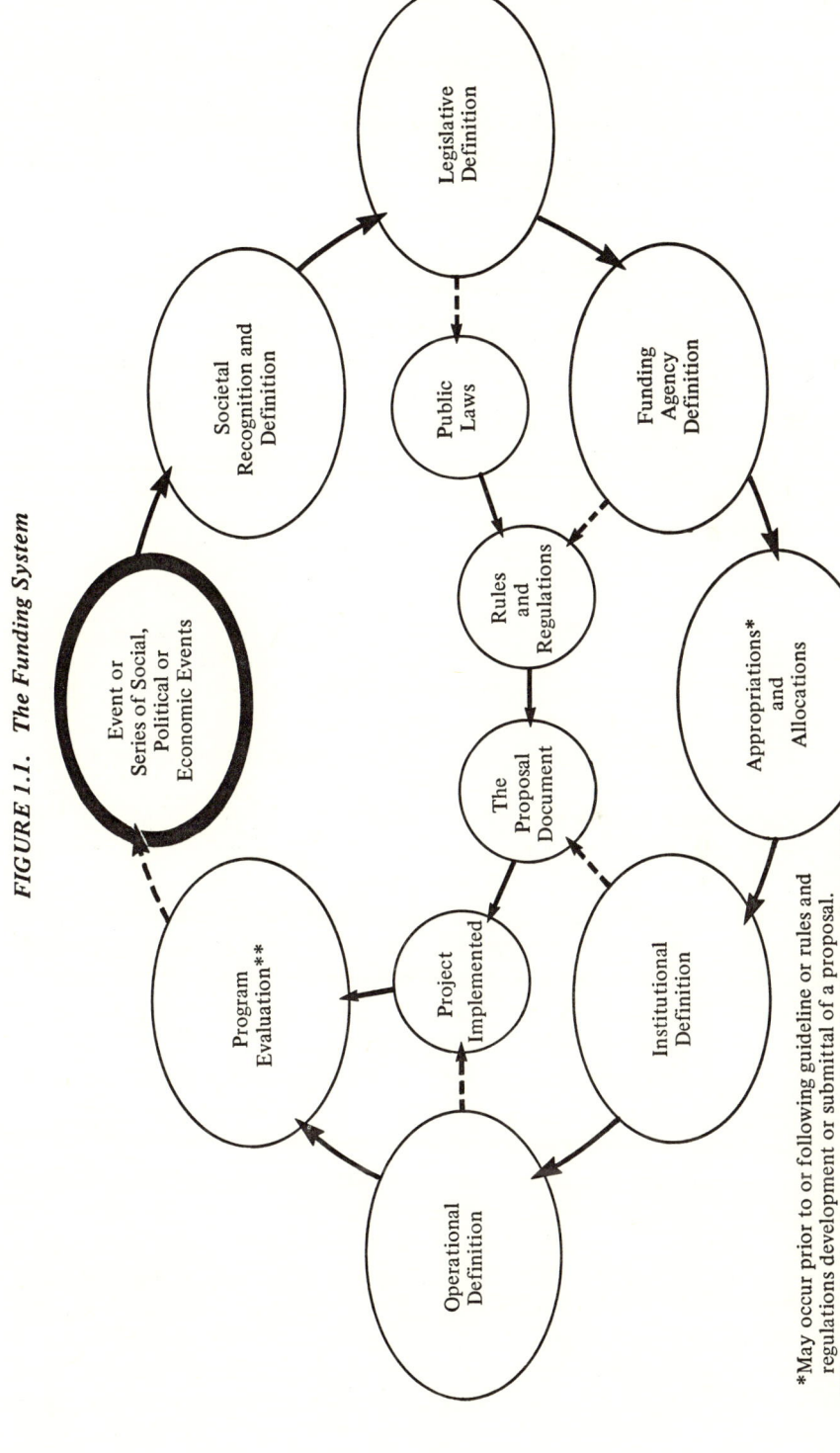

FIGURE 1.1. *The Funding System*

*May occur prior to or following guideline or rules and regulations development or submittal of a proposal.
**Program Evaluation represents the collective assessment of individual projects and constitutes one possible variable contributing to societal recognition and definition.

become relevant to organizational units or individuals participating in the funding system only when external events call public attention to problems. Problems such as national manpower skills, unemployment, literacy, or race relations generally become part of the national consciousness only when they are elevated to near crisis status; the problem is then "discovered" within the context of a specific challenge.

Societal Recognition and Definition

Once a problem becomes part of the national consciousness, persons who want to address the problem attempt to define it and identify the strategies most appropriate to alleviate it. At this stage of development, the problem definition will differ from group to group and from institution to institution, as will the suggested means to address the problem.

Legislative Definition

Once events coalesce into a societally recognized problem, the form of redress most relevant to the funding system is federal and state legislation. When legislative definition of the problem begins, the individual attempting to secure funds for a project can trace, if not predict, elements of the legislative process relevant to proposal development and submittal.

The legislative problem definition is a negotiated definition. On the one hand, it is an individual legislator's response to information provided by a constituency and persons or groups in a position to influence his decisions; on the other hand, it represents what is possible, given the positions of other representatives and parties who influence the legislative decision-making process. As such, the legislative definition may differ substantially from the definition formed by earlier events. Regardless of the definition, however, the problem takes on immediate significance for submitting institutions only when considered against the level of appropriations. The level of appropriations is one indicator of the problem's priority, as assigned by the authorizing body.

Agency Definition

For government-authorized proposal solicitations, the problem definition relevant for the submitting institution or individual is that provided by the government office or funding agency responsible for the program's administration. The funding agency's definition conveyed ultimately in the published guidelines or rules and regulations, reflects both the legislation's intent and the views of the program officers in the funding agency. The funding agency's freedom to define the problem and identify appropriate strategies may differ from program to program and from agency to agency. The greater the degree of freedom or discretionary authority granted the funding agency, the greater the opportunity for differences between the problem definitions of the authorizing and administering units in the funding system.

Institutional Definition

The institutional definition of the problem appears in the proposal document submitted by the potential grantee to the funding agency. The limits of problem definition are always set by the funding agency; submitting institutions, which have their own priorities and perceptions, interpret the definition of the problem by establishing program strategies. The institutional definition, like that provided by any other organizational unit participating in the funding process, is also a negotiated statement. The needs of units within the submitting institution and the varying perceptions of individuals or groups within the institution preclude a single undifferentiated definition of the problem, regardless of the proposal specifications.

Operational Definition

Should funding be secured, the organizational constraints that govern the proposal submittal and project implementation processes always create some discrepancy between the activities and outcomes identified in the proposal and what actually occurs. Slippage from paper to program also results from insufficient knowledge of the factors contributing to the problem and of the negotiation of differing perceptions of the problem and strategies. Implementation of the project tests the feasibility and appropriateness of the specified approach, both on those to be served and others in the institution who will be affected by the program's outcome. The outcomes of these several negotiations and the accommodations to immediate program and organizational needs, combined with the needs of other individual projects, provide the data to assess a program's overall success in addressing a problem; this assessment, in turn, influences the future status of the program and subsequent definitions of the problem.

Collective Assessment

The lifespan of individual programs is affected by the political climate and the cumulative effectiveness of sponsored projects. Unfortunately, variations among projects sponsored by a program are often as great as variations between programs. This obstacle to linking programs directly to outcomes is compounded by political and social variables, unrelated to a specific program's effects, that influence the value accorded programs by authorizing bodies. Consequently, the assessment of projects sponsored by any legislation must be considered as only one of many variables or events that shape future definitions of the problem. The collective assessments of individual projects, together with evolving social and political needs, will determine the future of any program and the magnitude of funding.

ASSUMPTIONS GOVERNING RESPONSE TO THE SYSTEM

Four major assumptions are basic to an appropriate response to the funding system and guide the analysis of the dynamics of funding:

1. Events leading to the implementation of an externally funded project may be ordered as phenomenological units with characteristics unique to that unit but also important to other units.
2. The individual units may be ordered sequentially against a time line with a high degree of predictability, both in the ordering of events and the time constraints unique to each event.
3. Conflict between units in the system, among individuals in the units, and in the shaping of characteristics of individual units is common.
4. Proposal development and project operation are ultimately the products of conflict resolution between and/or within the units.

ELEMENTS SHAPING PROJECT DEVELOPMENT

Using these four assumptions as a starting point, we can place the elements that shape a project in three categories.

1. *Problem definition in the public sphere:* all events that lead to legislative and agency definitions of the problem, as reflected in proposal guidelines
2. *Institutional definition:* all events that lead to the development and submittal of a proposal by a submitting institution
3. *Operational definition and program renewal:* all events that shape the day-to-day operation of the program, the impact of the program on personnel and institutions, and the likelihood of program or project continuity.

Each event within these categories is influenced by the diverse needs and expectations of the groups that shape the outcomes at each stage of the process. Each outcome represents varying resolution of stress endemic to each unit. For the purposes of identifying and analyzing the individual units, and the way they interact to define the funding process, the boundaries are set by the participating groups, by the norms governing behavior among the different populations, and by the nature of the task. In the following discussion, these boundaries mark the demarcation points between the conceptually independent, but phenomenologically interdependent, events observable in the funding process. Table 1.1 highlights the participating groups and the points of stress with which any project developer and director should be familiar. Each set of events may be divided into smaller units of behavior that, when studied independently, may contribute to the understanding of any given event.

No single work can provide a definitive guide to understanding each of the events contributing to the dynamics of funding. This book places proposal writing and project operation within a sufficiently broad perspective to identify factors that will affect the success of any proposal and/or project. Analysis of the events occurring before the proposal request should enable the reader to develop strategies, taking into account factors central to the development and implementation of externally funded programs that are not immediately apparent when responding to a particular set of guidelines. The primary focus of this book is on the cluster of events contributing to agency, institution, and operational definition setting, and the impact of these events on the proposal writer and/or project manager.

CONFLICT AND THE FUNDING SYSTEM

The schematic outlined previously in Figure 1.1 omits one factor crucial to understanding the dynamics of funding—the nature of the interaction between the elements. Like many schematics, it fails to convey the dynamics that transform the static to the fluid and give the phenomenom its very identity. Analysis of educational and social legislation and of related program funding reveals one common characteristic: despite the widely varying program goals, the great variation in funding guidelines, and the manner in which funds are disbursed, a majority of externally funded programs are designed to modify the delivery of educational or social services. By definition, the infusion of funds to modify delivery of services creates dissonance in the receiving institution. The level of dissonance or conflict corresponds to the magnitude of change and the degree to which the program redefines established roles and institutional expectations. The greater the call for change, the greater the likelihood of conflict.

Given this characteristic, a framework for analyzing the dynamics of funding presents itself: change or reform represents "a natural product of the power conflicts and compromises that are inherent in social organizations."[9] Within this conceptual framework of conflict, the identification and analysis of factors within and among the organizational structures helps the proposal writer and project director to order and understand the variables that create the funding environment. The information gained may be processed through one of several change or social system models, enabling the developer to identify,

TABLE 1.1. Project Development Event and Characteristic Overview

Event	Participating Groups	Stress Points
I. Societal or generic identification of problem	General electorate Identifiable constituents Organized interest groups	Different perceptions of problem
II. Legislative definition of problem	Identifiable constituents Political pressure groups Influential elected officials	Differing access to legislative decision-making process
III. Agency definition of problem	Appointed officials Program officers Agency staff Representatives of professional organizations	Differing needs of participating agencies and individuals
IV. Institutional definition A. Identification of proposal developers	Higher education and/or corporate staff LEA staff Community groups Other affected institutions including funding agency*	Problems stemming from need for leadership/representation of participating groups
B. Development of Proposal	Drawn from above	Lack of common expectations and sanctions applicable to participating groups
C. Submittal of proposal to funding agency	Submitting institution(s)	Problems arising from interinstitutional and client accountability demands
V. Operational definition of problem A. Notification of award and announcement of starting date	Funding agency/submitting institution	Program structure and expectations of funding agency, submitting institution, and clients
B. Negotiation of operating budget	Funding agency (program and contract offices)	Program resources/program staffing expectations
C. Selection of staff and participants	Representatives drawn from IV-A or IV-B	Political/programmatic demands
D. Implementation of management and evaluation system	Project director Receiving institution	Expectations of funding agency, submitting institution, staff, and personnel

*informal inputs

TABLE 1.1. (cont.)

Event	Participating Groups	Stress Points

VI. Program renewal
  A. Adaptation
  B. Assimilation
  C. Rejection
	A function of II, III, IV, and V	Differing fiscal and political pressures placed on authorizing units, funding agency, and sponsoring institution(s) not directly related to project activities

analyze, and respond to variables that contribute to project success. As long as any given model is not taken as dogma, and as long as it is recognized that, given the lack of previous systematic examination of the funding process, conceptual closure is premature, application of a model enables the developer to bring some order to the often chaotic world of funding.

Talcott Parsons's concept of the "social system"[10] is a point of departure for understanding the events endemic to funding and managing a project successfully. The application of Parsons's model to educational systems has already received considerable attention in writings that focus on school and social service administration. By applying basic features of the social system concept to events endemic to funding and project management, order, if not predictability, can be brought to the often apparently irrational set of events leading to the proposal request. Understand, however, that deficiencies in any given model and the unique characteristics of specific events preclude a perfect application of the model and suggest the desirability of its continual revision.

As suggested previously, any social system involves two classes of phenomena that are conceptually independent but phenomenologically interdependent: institutions, with specified expectations and roles to fulfill the goals of the system (the nomothetic dimension), and individuals inhabiting the system, with certain personalities and need-dispositions (the ideographic dimension), whose observed interactions comprise the social or group behavior of the system. If we assume, for purposes of this discussion, that the proposal writer or project manager is a faculty member of an educational institution, then this individual is expected to carry out the role of faculty member and conform to the institution's expectations. That individual's success as a member of the institution (that is, retention, promotion, tenure, and salary) will be related directly to the degree to which institutional expectations are met. Simultaneously, our hypothetical educational project developer has need dispositions and a personality that are not determined by the institution.

Individual and institutional expectations of behavior, qualifications, and standards of performance are generally more consonant and less likely to be questioned in quieter periods of history. The nomothetic or normative dimensions of the system in such periods are stable and can be identified more predictably.

However, some conflict always exists between the expectations emanating from the formal roles established by an institution and the need dispositions of individuals within the institution. The possibility for conflict increases dramatically when the institution and/or individuals confront a rapidly changing environment that demands modifications in behavior. The history of educational and human service institutions is filled with evolving demands, such as community participation, new or revised job definitions, changed appointment procedures, new student assignment procedures, and revised admittance standards. Very often, the terms of a grant create the environment for changes. Conflict between the ideographic and nomothetic dimensions of the system, however, is essential: in the resolution of conflict an institution adjusts and retains its contemporaneity.

All systems have imperative functions that must be carried out in designated, established ways. Institutions relevant to the funding system—the legislative and executive branches of government, program offices, and educational or social organizations seeking funding—assume responsibility for carrying out these functions.

For all institutions, "role" becomes the most important analytic unit and represents the dynamic aspects of the individual's position within the institution. For any institution to function effectively, members' roles must be sufficiently complementary for the institution to realize the expectations held of it.

The preceding characteristics of social systems are particularly relevant for the proposal writer or project manager. Projects often systematically inject conflict into the system by placing project staff in new roles that carry new expectations. Even in stable times and in static institutions, the person in a single role is required to conform simultaneously to a number of inconsistant expectations. The faculty member is always responsible to several reference groups, each defining expectations for the same role. For example, boards of trustees or school boards, deans or principals, department chairpersons, faculty peers, and students all serve as reference groups with legitimate expectations of a faculty member that are seldom consonant. The system can only function when the expectations of reference groups are sufficiently complementary to permit members of the institution to direct their energies primarily to the delivery of instructional services.

The potential project developer should recognize that as the project calls for more changes in the institution's traditional expectations and introduces new reference points (such as the funding agency, cooperating institutions, and outside participants), the potential for conflict increases. Faculty members serving as directors of federally funded programs providing minority groups access to universities and professions in which they are not widely represented, teachers directing "open campus" programs, or community agency directors of Head Start programs have often been unsuccessful in conforming simultaneously to the legitimate but mutually exclusive expectations of the several reference groups.

Role conflict also arises from contradictions inherent in the two or more roles an individual occupies at the same time. The expectations held of the developer as project manager or director may differ from those as faculty member, teacher, or social worker. Fortunately, the potential for direct and open conflict can be reduced by a knowledgeable director who can "manipulate the system." There are degrees of manipulation, however, that the director cannot exceed without precipitating major conflict or having the program be co-opted by the host institution.

In the two types of role conflict mentioned, there is a purity of role definition among and between reference groups not often present in day-to-day functioning of employees in any institutional setting. If the project director could unequivocally define expectations of different reference groups over extended periods of time and could predict corresponding behavior, the term "social engineer" would take on new meaning. The project director could, with some degree of certainty, by assessing the various constraints, develop a formula to create exactly the degree of consonance necessary to realize desired ends. However, the dynamic nature of institutions and their relationships to constituents precludes such a development.

The range of expectations held by program officers, program staff, and affected institutional representatives may be great. The receptivity of individuals to specific types of activity cannot be treated solely as a function of the reference group to which they belong. In examining the functioning of any unit in the funding system, individual differences within common reference groups may be crucial in determining receptivity to the effort. When such differences exist, the relationships of individuals to the unit power structure become central to the future status of the program. Regardless of the roles and status of members in any institution, during periods of great change little more than gross generalizations apply to a single reference group. Those few generalizations that can be made today with some degree of assurance may not have been true a decade ago and may not be true a decade hence.

The recognition of conflicting need dispositions and expectations between different reference groups is critical to understanding the dynamics of funding and to implementing successful projects. Many a "successful" proposal writer or project manager has endured a year of constant confrontation within and between different reference groups simply because, in designing the program, the writer or director presumed to identify their needs and expectations.

Application of the social system concept to the funding system generates two working hypotheses or premises that will guide the following analysis of the funding system and identification of strategies for securing grants and implementing of projects.

Premise 1:
The needs and expectations of individuals responsible for initiating legislation, of individuals and agencies responsible for setting program guidelines, of individuals and institutions responsible for administering funded projects, and of the population to be served by the

project are sufficiently dissonant to work against the success of externally funded projects.

Premise 2:

The different organizational units participating in the funding process (the executive and legislative branches of government, the funding agency program office, the submitting institution, and the population to be served by the project) tend to function as closed systems; their organizational behaviors inhibit the development of functional systems that provide the complementarity of unit roles and expectations prerequisite to successful proposal development and project operations.

AN APPROACH TO CONFLICT RESOLUTION

If project development and implementation are thought of as a series of discrete but related events culminating in funding and program implementation, then one can examine these events separately, identify the specific points of conflict, and develop an overall strategy for proceeding. Any strategy developed following this approach must consider the conflicts between and within organizational units participating in the funding process, as well as the conflicts inherent in the creation of new programs. The strategy followed in this book facilitates this approach by initially isolating individual sets of events and identifying units of behavior amenable to systematic analysis.

An institution's response to the proposal request generally activates the change process. Since the proposal sets new or different program and fiscal guidelines, it serves as a new or revised statement of institutional policy. Both the proposed policies to govern the project and the proposed activities can cause stress within the institution. The identification of stress points and the strategies for resolution are basic to developing an effective proposal. The difficulty in developing strategies to carry out these proposal tasks effectively is aggravated by the fact that proposal submittal is seldom a logical extension of long-range planning efforts by submitting institutions. Mann's analysis of a 1973-74 Rand Corporation study of U.S. Office of Education-supported "change agent" programs confirms this observation:

> Most school districts store their needs in a bottomless pit. When outside money appears, the district fishes around the pit until it finds a need that matches the announced purposes of the soft money. That need is then elevated to the status of a priority in order to demonstrate the district's commitment, and not incidentally in order to capture the bucks.[11]*

---

*Dale Mann, "The Politics of Training Teachers in Schools," *Teachers College Record* 77 (February 1976): 324.

The operations identified in Table 1.2 constitute an institutional definition of the problem and represent the tasks and stress points that, in one form or another, must be dealt with in all proposal development efforts. Failure to recognize these points of stress inevitably affects the quality of proposals, the success in securing funding, and ultimately the ability of a funded program to conform to the proposal expectations. It should be stressed that the institutional definition represents only one of a series of conceptually independent events that must be considered within a larger framework. The following operations and tasks, when completed, culminate in a proposal suitable for submittal.

TABLE 1.2. Institutional Definition: Operations and Tasks

Operation	Points of Stress
A. Organizing for Development	
Task 1. Identification of parties to develop the proposal	Different groups affected by the proposed program have varying perceptions of the nature of the problem and the appropriateness of the strategies to be developed.
	Individuals with the necessary status to bring about change in a given institution may have the least to gain by altering institutional or programmatic structure.
	Maximum participation in the development of the program by affected parties may be inconsistent with time constraints for writing the proposal.
	The need of an individual providing inputs for development of the proposal may not be consonant with those of the population purportedly represented.
Task 2. Determination of institutional receptivity to the proposed program	Institutional needs of the funding agency, submitting institution, and affected agencies may differ significantly.
	Offices or organizational units within the institution may have significantly different needs and priorities. Benefits for some may be liabilities for others.
	Institutional assessment of program objectives and potential impact on the institution may be based on perceptions of past programs believed similar to one being developed.

TABLE 1.2. (cont.)

Operation	Points of Stress
	Institutional receptivity to the program may be based largely on "third party" perceptions of the program.
Task 3. Development of strategies for securing proposal approval	Institutional approval requirements may not coincide with approval requirements set by the guidelines for submittal.
	Announcement and deadline dates often preclude appropriate treatment of programmatic or fiscal features that have implications for institutional policies.
B. Developing the Proposal Document	
Task 1. Background and/or problem statement	The funding agency's tastes and requirements regarding style and substance may not be compatible with those of the proposal writer.
	Appropriate balance must be developed between the institutional need for assistance to initiate new program directions and evidence of past commitment and institutional capability as reflected in prior allocations and activities.
Task 2. Needs assessment or related research (may be included under B-1, depending on guidelines provided)	Precise documentation of submitting institution's previous failure to address educational needs may be threatening to individuals within the institution.
	Institutions' retrieval systems are usually inadequate to meet quantification demands set by proposal review criteria.
Task 3. Program goals or general objectives	Agreement on goals as indicated by the proposal request and participating groups may be more formalistic than realistic.
	Conflict may exist between goals set by proposal request and institutional priorities.
Task 4. Delineation of specific objectives	The odds of funding increase proportionately with specificity of objectives; the odds of conforming to

TABLE 1.2. (cont.)

Operation	Points of Stress
	specifications may decrease proportionately if time constraints preclude careful program planning and assessment.
	Premature precision in defining objectives may limit future program flexibility and preclude other inputs relevant to program operation.
	Premature setting of objectives may preclude identification of additional program outcomes of value.
Task 5. Program activity description	The need for specificity in content, timing of activities, and assignment of personnel must be tested against the degree of involvement of those responsible for carrying out activities in developing the proposal.
	The circumstances shaping the development of the program will be sufficiently changed between proposal submittal and notification of funding to necessitate adjustments when program begins.
	While clarifying the sequencing and relationship of project components, pictorial representations serving as summary statements may be elevated to the level of dogma and oversimplify representation of activities to persons not directly involved.
Task 6. Development of evaluation strategies	Balance must be achieved between the project director's need for information to guide program development and the needs of funding office and affected parties (including project director for third party evaluation to meet accountability demands by a wide range of constituents).
	Project director and funding agency need to maximize impact of successful program components and minimize failures, while retaining integrity of evaluation. A balance between political and educational objectives must be assessed.

TABLE 1.2. (cont.)

Operation	Points of Stress
Task 7. Delineation of faculty and staff roles and program governance structure	Referent points for approving decisions may differ for individuals and groups participating in or affected by the program.
	Needs of varying referent groups and individuals may be significantly different to create continual controversy over program- and staff-related decisions.
	Management demands on director may alter relationship with persons with whom the director has worked in other capacities.
Task 8. Budget development	Institution's fiscal policies and payroll procedures may be inappropriate to meet programmatic and personal needs of staff.
	The political impact of budget decisions on participating institutions and individuals may negatively affect realization of desired educational outcomes.

SUMMARY

The preceding operations and tasks identified as being necessary in developing a proposal should dispel any impression that proposal writing can be undertaken without careful assessment of the factors leading to the request. It is equally clear that the program's success and the director's security depend on an ability to assess fully the implications of program or organizational decisions made in the process of writing the proposal.

Bringing order to the complex process of changing existing programs or institutional structures by introducing new activities is achieved by recognizing that the preceding breakdown of variables is only an initial identification of points of stress encountered in the development of the proposal. There are at least as many variables involved when a societally identified need is transformed into legislation; when the legislative definition is transformed by federal and state program offices to meet their perceived needs; when submitting institutions subsequently fit their needs to the format and priorities set by the funding agency; when accommodations are made in implementing the program to secure institutional receptivity; and, when the success of legislatively authorized programs is evaluated against the current sociopolitical environment to determine their future. One can appreciate how difficult it is to order events to bring about any predictability in the funding process.

The boundaries between sets of events and the relationship of events to one another as presented in the chapter model must be considered relatively fluid. Therefore, the model cannot provide a formula to deal with the variables present when responding to a proposal request. The model does offer a way, however, to identify the institutionally prescribed and individual behaviors that constitute the dynamics of funding.

Unfortunately, the manner in which events unfold often precludes setting firm time lines and identifying all program features. Consequently, there is always difficulty in predicting the impact of any action on subsequent events. In turn, this limits the project developer's ability to adjust strategies sufficiently to fit the constraints of an essentially new definition of the problem. Any plan of action is only as effective as the individual's understanding of the constraints affecting the plan's development and the project's implementation.

ENDNOTES

1. Henry Steele Commager, *Documents of American History*, 8th ed. (New York: Appleton-Century-Crofts, 1968), p. 131.
2. Frank J. Munger and Richard F. Fenno, Jr., *National Politics and Federal Aid to Education* (Syracuse, N.Y.: Syracuse University Press, 1961), p. 17.
3. Daniel P. Moynihan, *Maximum Feasible Misunderstanding: Community Action in the War on Poverty* (New York: The Free Press, 1969), p. 23.
4. Stephen K. Bailey and Edith K. Mosher, *ESEA: The Office of Education Administers a Law* (Syracuse, N.Y.: Syracuse University Press, 1968), p. 23.
5. William Way, "ESEA: Decennial Views of the Revolution; II. The Negative Side," *Phi Delta Kappan* (November 1975): 154.
6. Samuel Halperin, "ESEA: Decennial Views of the Revolution; I. The Positive Side," *Phi Delta Kappan* (November 1975): 147.
7. Mark R. Arnold, "The Good War That Might Have Been," *New York Times Magazine* (29 September 1974): 74.
8. Seymour B. Sarason, *The Culture of the School and the Problem of Change* (Boston: Allyn and Bacon, 1971), pp. 31-32.
9. Ronald G. Corwin, *Reform and Organizational Survival* (New York: John Wiley & Sons, 1973), p. 3.
10. Talcott Parsons, *The Social System* (New York: The Free Press, 1951).
11. Dale Mann, "The Politics of Training Teachers in Schools," *Teachers College Record* 77 (February 1976): 324.

2

The Dynamics of the System

The model of the funding system presented in chapter 1 depicts the proposal document as an institutional response to conditions established by the social climate. These conditions are defined by legislative actions, foundation priorities, and the offices and personnel of the agency responsible for administering the program. In defining societal, agency, or institutional needs, the conflicting perspectives of organizational units or individuals must be mediated to develop guidelines for responding to a given need. The proposal writer and/or project manager must, on the one hand, honor these negotiated needs and, on the other hand, reconcile the submitting institution's needs with personal needs and the needs of the people to be served by the funded project.

This chapter applies the social, legislative, and agency definition elements of the funding system model to the formulation of specific educational programs. The reader will note the points of conflict in the funding system, how conflict is mediated by the system, and the means submitting institutions and individuals use to accommodate the political crosscurrents that affect the submittal of proposals and the implementation of most externally funded projects.

VARIABLES AFFECTING PROGRAM DEFINITION

Apparent in the application of the model to the development of specific programs are the many variables that contribute to the final definition given a social problem or need, the form taken by the legislation authorizing the implementation of programs, and the criteria established by funding agencies to govern the solicitation and review of programs. The complex way these variables interact to define each stage of the funding system prohibits the development of formulas that can predict the precise characteristics of emerging programs. To understand the funding process, you should view each stage as a group of variables that interact to define that stage and affect subsequent stages.

TABLE 2.1. Partial Listing of Variables Affecting Social, Legislative, and Agency Problem Definition

Social Definition Variables	Legislative Definition Variables	Agency Definition Variables
State of the economy	Impact of societally defined problems on representatives	Intent of authorizing legislation
Demographic trends	Efforts of lobbies and vested interest groups	Access of individual program offices and bureaus to authorizing bodies and influential representatives
Voiced concerns of electorate	Influence of executive office initiatives	Relationships between program offices and separate programs
Federal and state court initiatives	Influence of senior or powerful legislators	Influence of chief officers
Supreme court rulings		Success of past efforts and ability to communicate success to authorizing bodies
Symptoms of social crisis		

PROJECT DEVELOPMENT AND THE NATURE OF CHANGE

Analyses of major social and educational programs of the 1960s repeatedly concluded that frayed lines of communication between government offices, educational institutions, human service agencies, and community groups contributed to their failure to address the needs of the poor. Societal and institutional deterrents to change were implanted in the system. Whether one worked from without or within, the data suggested that obstacles to change, except in isolated cases and under certain conditions, only confirmed Machiavelli's prophesy that:

> Nothing is more difficult to carry out, nor more doubtful of success, nor more dangerous to handle, than to initiate a new order for things. For the reformer has enemies in all those who profit by the old order and only lukewarm defenders in all those who would profit by the new order . . . . Thus it arises that on every opportunity for attacking the reformer, his opponents do so with the zeal of partisans, the others only defend him half-heartedly, so that between them he runs great danger.[1]

Change is a complex phenomenon. Its nature cannot be communicated easily to one who has not experienced the forces and counterforces that buffet one who seeks to use an externally funded project as a means to modify institutional behavior. The problem of communicating the nature of the experience is made more difficult by the fact that the forces operating to prevent change are seldom evident. More often, these forces are etched as a thin line weaving crazily through the social fabric. The lines intermingle, cross, and disappear from sight, only to reappear and frustrate just when a sense of victory is felt. The barriers to observing and understanding the dynamics of change as they relate to the funding process are usually formidable.

However, in one case study demonstrating the application of the funding model (that of the federal and state funded efforts of the Boston Public Schools to desegregate with the assistance of local universities and cultural organizations), the obstacles to change are highly visible. An additional advantage of using the desegregation projects in Boston as a case study is the style of Boston political behavior. It is bold, ethnic, and easily detected. The tendency of Boston to play out its politics before the media, combined with the intervention of court orders that precipitated and accelerated events at specified times, provides the investigator with benchmarks seldom available when observing the impact of the social and political behavior of organizations. The acceleration of events and accompanying crystallization of points of conflict help the observer identify factors that are present but not always evident in the dynamics of funding.

The second case study, the development of the Teacher Center Program in the U.S. Office of Education, traces the development of authorizing and appropriations legislation and the factors that contributed to the form and content of regulations governing the solicitation of proposals for that program.

Although there is no relationship between the Teacher Center Program and the desegregation programs, the pervasiveness of social, economic, and political factors in shaping the Teacher Center Program is just as evident. The desegregation programs are highly controversial, politically volatile, heavily funded, visible to constituents, and evolve from court interpretations of the U.S. Constitution. The Teacher Center Program possesses none of these characteristics. Nevertheless, it still reflects national trends and forces. As appropriate, references to events shaping other funding programs will be made to demonstrate the applicability of the observations to a wide range of programs.

SCHOOL DESEGREGATION, TEACHER CENTERING, AND THE FUNDING SYSTEM

The issue of school desegregation is complex and involves all dimensions of the social system identified in the schematic presented earlier. The issue of desegregation has generated debate over issues ranging from the role of black culture and the "value structures" of the black and white communities in America (at the nomothetic or normative dimension of the social system model), to issues of self-image and genetic differences (at the ideographic or personal dimension of the model). Despite the complexity, however, desegregation as carried out in Boston provides an excellent case study for using the model developed in the previous chapter. Specific conditions giving rise to the need for change, and the individuals and groups associated with these conditions, can be identified. The alternate bases for choosing courses of action can be defined with a fair degree of precision.

The Teacher Center Program, which gained formal recognition with the passage of authorizing legislation in 1976, was a response to a less emotional but socially significant set of long-standing problems that were central to school operations. Teachers found little opportunity for professional development relevant to individual school needs once they became full-time staff members; many universities failed to prepare teachers appropriately for the positions they assumed; and the lack of coordination among university, school, and community program development activities reduced the effectiveness of services delivered to youth and parents. Pressing social and economic conditions elevated these problems to a priority sufficient to precipitate legislative action. As in most program development efforts, the differing perceptions of the groups and organizations affected by the legislation generated conflict. Like other programs, its status was clearly affected by the changing political and social climate between 1968 and 1977, when the concept was transformed from an idea originating in the U.S. Office of Education to a program carrying legislative authorization and appropriation.

The following analyses present the major factors that affected the development of these two programs and the responses of submitting institutions. The stages or sets of events that comprise the funding system and give the process definition are sequentially analyzed; the social and legislative problem definition stages are followed by the agency and institutional definition stages.

THE BOSTON RESPONSE TO THE RACIAL IMBALANCE ACT OF 1965 AND EDUCATIONAL AMENDMENTS OF 1974 (CHAPTER 636): AN OVERVIEW

The Commonwealth of Massachusetts's Department of Education, Bureau of Equal Educational Opportunity (BEEO), under the 1974 Amendments to the Racial Imbalance Act of 1965 (Chapter 636), was provided with both the authority and appropriations to solicit proposals from and award grants to local educational agencies and other private or public organizations. These grants would support programs to "improve the quality of education in schools in the process of desegregating and provide support for the development of 'magnet school facilities' and 'magnet school programs' designed to attract pupils from outside the district established for the school on a voluntary basis to reduce racial imbalance or racial isolation."[2]

In June 1975, an opinion issued by Judge W. Arthur Garrity Jr. (*Morgan v. Kerrigan*) "obligated the Boston School Committee under rule of law to eliminate segregation and the effects of discrimination in the public schools."[3] The court order also "solicited the talent, support and assistance of colleges and businesses in developing learning opportunities that will remedy the losses students have already suffered and that will lay a basis for improving the quality of education for the total City."[4] With the handing down of the court order, institutions of higher education and cultural institutions in the Boston metropolitan area were invited by BEEO to submit proposals for projects consistent with the ruling.

DESEGREGATION PROGRAM SOCIETAL AND LEGISLATIVE DEFINITION: THE NATIONAL PERSPECTIVE

Despite pressures from an increasing number of registered black voters and the efforts of civil rights activists, the Civil Rights Act of 1957, passed three years after the Supreme Court's ruling that "separate educational facilities are inherently unequal,"[5] was the first such legislation since 1875. Succeeding court decisions and legislation built on these precedents generated a sophisticated body of constitutional doctrine and federal and state school desegregation laws. The court's ruling in *Brown v. Board of Education of Topeka* declared *de jure* segregation (segregation resulting from the official actions or inaction of government officials) unconstitutional. *De facto* segregation (segregation resulting indirectly from private choice or general population shifts) was not ruled illegal. The distinction between *de jure* and *de facto* segregation and what constitutes official action or inaction contributed to the later controversies in Boston and many other northern cities. The courts became a major factor in the process of change through their power to order school systems to correct the effects of practices deemed actively discriminatory.

During the 1960s, under the leadership of Presidents Kennedy and Johnson, civil rights and poverty legislation channeling federal funds into programs to address inequities caused by racial prejudice and poverty increased the visibility of and the national commitment to these problems. Legislation was complemented by presidential commitment, evidenced by passage of strong Civil Rights Acts in 1964 and 1965 that sustained the momentum set by the national leadership. Discriminatory legal barriers discouraging black and other minority group participation as fully franchised citizens began to fall. Tools to enforce the law were also located: the Civil Rights Act of 1964 provided federal agencies with the power to withhold federal funds from school systems using these funds in a racially discriminatory fashion.

Congress, "in view of the fundamental significance of educational opportunity to many important social issues,"[6] requested that a survey of educational opportunity be carried out by the Office of Education's National Center for

Educational Statistics. The findings of the study complied with the provision of the Civil Rights Act of 1964 calling for a survey on the "lack of availability of equal educational opportunities for individuals by reason of race, religion or national origin in public educational institutions at all levels."[7]

The publicity generated by this study continued to focus public attention on the need to integrate the nation's schools. In addition to documenting the rather bleak picture of segregation of both students and staff in schools throughout the nation, it underlined the centrality of integration to quality education.

In 1967, *Racial Isolation in the Public Schools,* a companion report by the U.S. Commission on Civil Rights, reported that in metropolitan areas, where two-thirds of the black and white populations resided, school segregation was more severe than in the nation as a whole.[8] Against a backdrop of executive advocacy of increased educational opportunity, judicial decisions confirming the legal right of minorities to equal opportunity, professional educators' documentation of the failure of schools to reach the underprivileged or disadvantaged, and the active involvement of many young voters pressuring for change, the perception of segregation and unequal opportunity emerged as a national rather than a regional problem. The earlier disorders in Watts and those in northern ghettoes in the summer of 1967 dispelled any lingering doubts about the magnitude of the problem. The introduction to the 1967 Kerner Commission *Report* placed the problem of desegregation in its full sociopolitical context.

> Our nation is moving toward two societies, one black, one white—separate and unequal.
>
> Reaction to last summer's disorders has quickened the movement and deepened the division. Discrimination and segregation have long permeated much of American life; they now threaten the future of every American.
>
> This deepening racial division is not inevitable. The movement apart can be reversed. Choice is still possible. Our principal task is to define that choice and press for national resolution .... [9]

The Commission found that sixteen years after the Supreme Court had declared that racially segregated schools were inherently unequal, less than one-third of the nation's black children attended integrated schools. Commission recommendations placed primary importance on the development of strategies to eliminate *de facto* segregation. Increased aid to school systems seeking to eliminate *de facto* segregation, whether within the system or in cooperation with neighboring school systems, was seen as one viable strategy.

With the passage of the Emergency School Assistance Program in 1970, Congress began providing financial support to school districts and community groups to facilitate desegregation efforts. With the passage of the Emergency School Aid Act (ESAA) in 1974, major appropriations were voted by Congress to support the wide range of programs authorized by the legislation.

Despite increased public attention to desegregation, in the early 1970s the social climate of the nation changed: the loss of national political leaders instrumental in earlier desegregation efforts was compounded by the loss of energy in segments of the broad political base that had been visible at such events as the marches to Selma, Alabama, and Washington, D.C. Protests against the Vietnam conflict diffused some of the energy that had been directed toward resolving domestic problems. Black solidarity in support of integration broke down, partially as a result of frustrations spawned by lack of progress. Community control and black separatism were perceived by many as the only way blacks could cope with the larger white society that appeared to exclude them systematically from full participation.

Richard Nixon's "southern strategy" in securing the Presidency downplayed the value of desegregation. "Law and order" became a major issue even though the administration casually enforced civil rights legislation. The tone for the 1970s was set in a speech by the President: "Integration will be pursued as a goal insofar as it will achieve an educational purpose and will not disrupt the neighborhood school concept or require considerable additional busing of students."[10] Although appropriations for the several programs authorized by ESAA (with the exception of Title I of the Elementary and Secondary Education Act) still represented the largest single source of federal funding for school and supporting agency programs through 1977, the emphasis shifted. Amendments authorizing special projects and subprograms broadened the scope of the program to meet the needs of several population groups. The development of programs in desegregated systems supplanted the implementation of desegregation plans. Presidential and Senate pronouncements and press coverage of efforts to integrate the nation's schools no longer focused on equality or opportunity; busing was the issue and the neighborhood school became the cause.

DESEGREGATION PROGRAM SOCIETAL AND LEGISLATIVE DEFINITION: THE LOCAL PERSPECTIVE

Although developments in Massachusetts and Boston were generally consistent with the national social and political climate, efforts in Massachusetts were distinguished by legislative passage of the Racial Imbalance Act of 1965. Massachusetts became one of the few states that required school systems to develop desegregation.

In analyzing the response of institutions to funding opportunities provided by the Educational Amendments of 1974, the passage of the Massachusetts Racial Imbalance Act becomes critical. The 1965 act provided the original legislative definition of the problem and the legal authorization for the development of proposals for program support. The act also served as a reference point for rulings and orders of the State Supreme Judicial Court and Federal District Court. It also authorized the establishment of the Bureau of Equal Educational

Opportunity (BEEO) in 1971, which was to serve as both an agent of the state board of education in implementing the legislation and eventually as the program office responsible for the solicitation, review, and monitoring of proposals and project developments authorized by the 1974 Amendments. BEEO provided the agency definition of the problem in its proposal guidelines distributed to the Boston school system and to local universities to facilitate their response to the federal court order issued by Judge W. Arthur Garrity Jr. in the spring of 1975. This order obligated the Boston School Committee and its department, under the rule of law, to eliminate segregation and the effects of discrimination in the public schools and called for "match(ing) colleges and universities with particular high schools, both community and citywide, and with selected other schools and programs, in ways that fit the capabilities and needs of the partners. . ." This matching was designed to "enable participating institutions of higher learning to share in the direction and development of curriculum and instruction under court-sanctioned contract with the School Department."[11]

The history of school desegregation in Boston reveals a pattern of events similar to that in other northern cities: lengthy periods of time elapsed between the first strong pressures for desegregation and implementation of desegregation plans; resistance and delay by educational officials to plans designed to address the problem were evident; appeals to federal and state courts argued that changing demographic profiles, rather than school department action or inaction, created segregated school systems; and courts ultimately ruled that *de jure* segregationist policies and practices were present in violation of the law.

The initial pervasive influence of the state courts on desegregation in Boston, in large part, is attributable to the limitations inherent in the Racial Imbalance Act. The act did not provide specific guidelines for judging the efforts of local educational agencies to reduce racial imbalance, means for state monitoring and supervision were limited, and the power of the state board to compel prompt compliance was virtually nonexistent. The ultimate authority to withhold funds, granted to the State Board of Education, was ineffective, strategically unacceptable, and had uncertain delivery capability.

When the Boston School Committee failed to carry out its own desegregation plan for the 1971-72 academic year, the State Board of Education adopted a major shift in strategy: it dropped its role as technical assistant to the schools and assumed an adversarial role in legal confrontations designed to enforce compliance. The fall of 1971 also marked the entry of the U.S. Department of Health, Education and Welfare into Boston's desegregation controversy. DHEW's Office for Civil Rights informed the Boston School Committee that certain educational programs were being administered in a discriminatory manner in violation of Title VI of the Civil Rights Act of 1964. At this point, the legal machinery of the federal government to enforce federal desegregation legislation converged with and supplemented the Massachusetts Racial Imbalance Act. Boston suddenly was faced with the same interplay of judicial and legislative constraints as many other northern cities with increasingly segregated school systems. The conflicts at the state level mirrored those in the larger national sociopolitical context.

As litigation initiated by the Massachusetts Commission Against Discrimination and the NAACP proceeded slowly but inexorably in federal and state courts, the State Board of Education continued to press the Boston School Committee to adopt a satisfactory desegregation plan.

In June 1973, the State Board of Education ordered implementation of a Short-Term Plan to Reduce Racial Imbalance by September 1974. The plan was contested immediately in the courts by the school committee. In rejecting the appeal, the court noted:

> It is high time that such cooperation [between the State Board of Education and the School Committee] commence, without the delay inherent in further footless resort to the courts.[12]

Although the people of Boston may have realized at this point that desegregation was about to become a reality, the waning influence of the civil rights movement and support for civil rights legislation was also becoming increasingly evident. The political and social sentiments of the public were beginning to shape a political and social environment that no longer accorded high priority to integration as a tool to create equal educational opportunity. Signs of legislative "self-correction" of what some considered to be the "liberal excesses" of the mid-1960s became evident: in May 1974, the Massachusetts General Court (the *legislative* branch of the state government) voted to repeal the Racial Imbalance Act of 1965. The governor vetoed the bill but pressed for amendments that would prohibit the State Board of Education from requiring busing to achieve balance. The amendments, opposed by both the Board and the NAACP, were eventually passed and enacted into law as The Amendments of 1974. The concomitant pronouncement of the apparent demise of the Short-Term Plan, however, was premature.

The NAACP had initiated federal court action in 1972 (*Morgan* v. *Hennigan, supra*) charging the Boston School Committee with intentionally operating a segregated school system in violation of the Constitution of the United States. In June 1974, the Federal District Court issued its ruling on the NAACP suit filed two years earlier. Judge W. Arthur Garrity's findings were notable in that, unlike many earlier court rulings, there was no ambiguity in the conclusions reached and less ambiguity in the actions required by the ruling:

> The rights of the plaintiff class of black students and parents under the Fourteenth Amendment to the Constitution of the United States have been and are being violated by the defendants in their management and operation of the public schools in the City of Boston.... Plaintiffs have proved that the defendants (Boston School Committee) intentionally segregated schools at all levels...[13]

The federal court decision, for all practical purposes, signaled the end of the long legal battle to determine whether or not efforts to desegregate the Boston Public

Schools would proceed. The school committee was ordered to implement the Short-Term Plan in the fall of 1974.

The school committee, working under federal court order to implement a state plan for local children with federal (Emergency School Assistance Act) and state (Chapter 636) funding, now found itself serving as a vehicle for broadcasting and intensifying the frustrations of the antibusing residents of the city; "forced busing" and "neighborhood schools" became issues that exacerbated the tensions between groups that were ethnically, geographically, and economically separated within the City of Boston. Although the court decision specifically addressed the issue of neighborhood schools, the issues of forced busing and neighborhood schools mobilized people who heretofore felt powerless to affect conditions that were making life increasingly difficult.

While the school committee continued to mobilize public resistance to the order, the Bureau of Equal Educational Opportunity, functioning as an arm of the state and instrumental in drawing up the Short-Term (Phase I) Plan, found its previous efforts to integrate the schools vindicated. The State Board of Education and BEEO became adversaries to the school committee, whose members could only find absolution in the plan's failure.

As planning commenced for implementation of Phase I and solicitation by BEEO of proposals to facilitate the implementation, many social and political variables not under the control of the funding or submitting agencies were set in motion. The submission of a long-term desegregation plan (Phase II) in the spring of 1975 extended the dimensions of the conflict. As colleges and universities, individual local schools, cultural organizations, and community advisory boards entered the picture, the broader political conflicts were coupled with conflicts among the new parties, the school department, and BEEO, all responsible for implementation of the plan. The dissonance between the social, legislative, and agency definitions of the problem was exacerbated by the role of the court. Institutions seeking funding under agency-established guidelines sought to reconcile the varying needs and perceptions of the affected parties.

TEACHER CENTERS: SOCIETAL AND LEGISLATIVE DEFINITION

The social and political variables that provide sufficient impetus to create Teacher Center legislation first became visible in the post-Sputnik era. The launching of Sputnik by the Soviet Union in 1957 demonstrated dramatically and publically the need to "do something" about teacher training. National Science Foundation Institutes for Teachers, designed to upgrade instruction and prepare additional teachers in the areas of science, mathematics, and foreign languages, were authorized by the National Defense Education Act of 1958 to respond to the problem. Crises in the nation's cities, and the resulting executive and legislatives initiative during the 1960-65 period, highlighted the depth and range of training needs of inner-city schools; there were neither enough teachers to staff classrooms nor appropriately trained personnel to meet the needs of inner-city youth. Conant communicated the essence of the problem when he contended that the existence of thousands of out-of-school, out-of-work youth constituted "social dynamite."[14]

Passage of the Economic Opportunity Act in 1964 acknowledged the special needs of disadvantaged children and presaged the Elementary and Secondary Education Act (ESEA) passed in 1965. Initiatives supported by this legislation, continued executive advocacy for the development of programs to address the educational and employment needs of the poor, a supportive Congress, and regular media coverage of the enactment of programs all contributed to a climate conducive to continued legislative action.

The Elementary and Secondary Education Act of 1965 (ESEA) helped make the manpower problem visible. In late 1966, Commissioner of Education, Harold Howe II, created a Task Force on Education Manpower. In the same year a National Institute Steering Committee and Task Force evolving from a National Defense Education Act funded project was formed with the assistance of program officers from the influential Division of Educational Personnel Training, United States Office of Education. In 1967, Senate testimony of Commissioner Howe summarized the needs that were to shape the immediate legislative agenda:

> Present training programs are not capable of encouraging either the numbers, kinds, or quality of people needed to staff this Nation's educational programs. . . .the critical need for teachers continues and, according to a nationwide study is more acute than it was a year ago . . . . Legislative authority is fragmented, and too often applications must be fashioned to meet legislative requirements rather than education needs.[15]

The stage had been set for the introduction of the concept of "teacher centering." The Educational Professions Development Act, designed to meet these needs, was passed in June 1967. In 1968, the Bureau of Educational Personnel Development (BEPD) was created within USOE to administer the act. This office initially placed the concept of teacher centers in the federal program development machinery. This initiative was stimulated by recommendations resulting from an earlier NDEA-authorized teacher institute project administered by the American Association of Colleges for Teacher Education. In 1968, the institute's publication, *Teachers for the Real World*,[16] recommended a national network of training complexes, " . . . a close relative and important ancestor of the teacher center."[17] One central theme of the teacher center concept adopted by BEPD to guide the administration of EPDA-authorized programs was "the idea of partnership among colleges, schools and communities in planning, carrying out and evaluating programs for personnel development."[18]

The formulation of BEPD during the year Richard Nixon was elected

President is significant for tracing the development of the teacher center concept within the social, legislative, and agency context. Events that shaped the development of the concept, from its introduction in 1968 to the passage of authorizing legislation in 1976 and establishment of Rules and Regulations in 1977 and 1978, were precipitated in large part by actions of the federal bureaucracy. During President Nixon's first term, it became clear that the thrusts of the previous administration were incompatible with the political philosophy of the new President. Given the fiscal demands of the Vietnam conflict and the public's perception of the limited success of programs sponsored by the Kennedy-Johnson policies, it was time to reassess and bring order to the broad base of categorical programs.

Demographic evidence indicated that the teacher shortage would soon be eliminated. Many influential individuals in DHEW and the increasingly powerful Office of Management and Budget believed that the emerging teacher surplus removed the need for additional federal money for programs such as EPDA, a belief buttressed by taxpayer desire for tax relief.

Nixon administration initiatives in the educational and social service domain were consistent with the new sociopolitical climate. The administration proposed special educational revenue sharing to consolidate most of the large formula elementary and secondary education programs. Most of USOE's leverage for reform would be removed, with decision-making authority increased at the state level of government. The administration also supported the concept of "education renewal," a plan to consolidate many USOE-administered grant programs and provide incentive money to school districts to plan and carry out comprehensive programs. Local school systems (rather than USOE) would establish the criteria for program substance. Teacher centers were to be a major component of the renewal effort.

Unfortunately for the teacher center concept, USOE opted to use existing authorizations to implement the renewal program rather than to draft new legislation for congressional action. The leadership in Congress responded by claiming that USOE had overstepped the bounds of legitimate authority, and language was written into the Education Amendments of 1972 specifically banning USOE from implementing the plan. The dissonance between the legislative and agency definitions of the problem was too great to permit program implementation.

Although it is impossible to treat all the variables that contributed to the failure of the renewal program, one observation is relevant to the model for analyzing the funding process:

> The Secretary and the Commission were systematically insulated from an accurate appraisal of what was happening with Renewal: what was happening in their own offices, in the Congress and in the outside world.[19]

The Commissioner of Education failed to build an adequate base of congressional support, groups representing highly visible needs (e.g., special education and bilingual education) communicated the impression that their dollars would be co-opted by the renewal plan and prevented the teacher center concept from gaining sufficient momentum to be transformed into program or legislation. Despite the fact that a 1972 National Task Force on Educational Reform found great receptivity to the training complex, teacher center part of the plan,[20] this receptivity could not be converted into an identifiable national need calling for congressional action.

Although the teacher center initiative was formally abandoned after the congressional action, it was important that a shadow teacher center division had functioned under the EPDA renewal program. Program staff in USOE remained committed to the renewal and teacher center concept. An informal but visible network of support awaiting more propitious conditions to develop the concept was in place; in 1974, such a set of conditions evolved.

During the early 1970s, the concepts of "open education" and "community schools" channeled the general malaise of parents and educators about the state of the schools. Articles on the British primary school and Charles Silberman's *Crisis in the Classroom* popularized the open education concept; teacher centers were basic to the implementation of such programs. The "open classroom" was introduced into many American schools.

The introduction of the open classroom approach was accompanied by compelling demographic and economic data. Between 1967-68 and 1972-73, while school enrollment was rising little more than 4 percent, operating expenditures rose by 63 percent.[21] A statistical report by the National Center for Education Statistics reported in 1975 that the excess of supply over demand for teachers would increase annually, far into the future.[22] Two needs were recognized: increased in-service continuing education opportunities for experienced teachers and increased program and cost accountability. These two needs were complemented by continued community demands for participation in the decision-making process affecting the development of local educational and human service programs.

Given the changed social and political climate and the presence of USOE officials sympathetic to the teacher center concept, only a catalyst was required to transform the general societal definition of the problem into legislative action and federally sponsored program development.

In 1974, legislative efforts were initiated by the staff of Senator Walter Mondale. Senator Mondale, impressed by reports of the English school system, was convinced that giving teachers a greater voice in designing programs for their continued professional growth was instrumental to the success of such programs. The National Education Association, the American Federation of Teachers, chief state school officers, and the American Association of College Teachers of Education formed a shaky coalition with Mondale's staff and USOE officials to develop legislation that passed Congress as part of the Education Amendments of 1976. This legislation reallocated power for teacher in-service training: centers would be run by policy boards having a majority of teachers.

In a letter to the Commissioner of Education, following passage of the legislation, the National Education Association's Director of Governmental Relations,

Stanley J. McFarland, minced few words. He said the legislation represented "a reject[ion] of the basic principal"[23] that schools of education should be the "locus and agent" for teacher education. "For the first time, teachers will have an opportunity to select the expertise and guidance of qualified persons to assist them . . . rather than be forced, as is presently the case, to leave the classroom and attend an institution of higher education training program which has been developed without regard for the particular problems facing them daily."[24] USOE officers had been just as forceful in their testimony to the House Appropriations Sub-Committee hearings in March 1977.

With the issuance of Proposed Rules for the Teacher Center Program, the negotiation of agency and institutional definitions of the problem focused on defining the relationships between state departments of education, local education agencies, and colleges and universities. The resolution of these issues in the Final Rules and Regulations set the terms for individual responses to the proposal requests transmitted in the *Federal Register* in January 1978.

GENERALIZATIONS APPLICABLE TO OTHER FUNDING SETTINGS

Despite the markedly different sets of events that led to the solicitation of proposals under the state-authorized desegregation program and the federally authorized Teacher Center Program, common points in the social and legislative definition-setting processes affecting the two programs apply to most program development settings:

Events in the social and legislative domain, beyond the control of those responsible for formulating authorizing legislation, were instrumental to the introduction and implementation of the programs.

A cadre of staff committed to program goals and support was present in the organization structures. When social and legislative conditions were propitious, these staff members were able to generate support for the program and identify others in positions to help secure necessary program appropriations.

Differences in funding agency and legislative definitions of the problem created strain and called for continuous negotiation between funding agency officers, legislative representatives, and officers responsible for administering programs addressing similar needs.

The terms for participation set by either the authorizing legislation or the Rules and Regulations established eligibility requirements with implications for allocating power among institutions interested in participating in the programs. In both cases, the allocation of power established by the guidelines or regulations was strongly contested.

The specific actions that brought the programs into existence (in one case a court order, in the other program-specific legislation) represented extensions of concepts previously established as legitimate concerns in legislative or program offices.

The action that finally authorized institutions to submit proposals represented a delayed response to problems recognized years earlier.

Analysis of the evolution of virtually any program, from the point of problem recognition to the request for proposal submittal, will reveal similar patterns of precedent building, advocacy of well-placed staff, and negotiation of conflict between interested parties with resulting delays in program implementation. How these elements interact creates repercussions for the agency and institutional defintions of the problem.

The program definition contained in the proposal submitted by an institution is set by funding agency guidelines in the same manner that the program definition set by the funding agency is drawn from criteria set by authorizing legislation. In formulating legislation, differences among priorities of representatives' constituencies and the national priorities accorded to problems placed on the legislative agenda result in tension. In the formulation of program guidelines by the funding agency, tension results from: differing priorities of offices responsible for administering the program; possible conflicts of interest regarding program scope and appropriations between program offices with common interests; and the different political and organizational needs of the larger structure responsible for administering the program according to legislative intent. In developing the institutional definition of the program presented in the submitted proposals, tension results from the differing needs of the submitting institutions and funding agencies. Difficulties in negotiating agency-institutional needs and expectations are compounded by how proposals are solicited and by the widely varying needs of units within submitting institutions. These obstacles and their implications for institutional definition setting, are apparent in the desegregation submittal and in selected other submittals authorized by federal legislation.

VARIABLES AFFECTING AGENCY AND INSTITUTION DEFINITION SETTING: BOSTON AND CHAPTER 636

Grant solicitation activities of the Massachusetts Bureau of Equal Educational Opportunity to facilitate school desegregation can be divided into two stages: Phase I, during which BEEO sought to facilitate the Short-Term Plan through funding proposals submitted by the Boston Public Schools; and Phase II, during which BEEO solicited the assistance of universities, cultural organizations, and community groups in implementing the court-mandated Phase II desegregation plan and appropriated monies to fund proposals submitted by institutions.

Both phases reveal patterns of conflict among participating parties common to the funding process. Depending on the type of institution (institution of higher education [IHE], local education agency [LEA], or community agency) and the nature of the problem addressed, the stresses present in a specific solicitation and response setting may vary. Regardless of the institutional setting, however, the various forms of conflict in a turbulent setting are easily recognized in a less emotional and less complex proposal solicitation situation.

The Educational Amendments of 1974, Chapter 636, authorized the support of two types of activities: (1) general support or Section I Grants that fell into three categories and (2) Section 8 or Magnet Programs that fell into two categories—Magnet School Facilities Programs and Magnet Educational Programs. The legislation authorized at the outset the expenditure of funds to "improve the quality of education" provided by several different types of institutions. The range of authorized programs and eligible parties established a valuable precedent for BEEO's allocation of funds for university use under the Phase II Desegregation Plan.

The first round of BEEO proposal solicitations identified the following eligible parties and populations to be served under Section I of the legislation:

a. Parents, school staff, and community agencies to serve a single school or district;
b. Area offices, to serve an area or section of the school system;*
c. Central office or system-wide programs.[25]

The central problem of school desegregation that the programs were designed to address was a matter of national debate. The range of persons who stood to gain or lose under Chapter 636 programs, the emotions generated by court-ordered desegregation, the accompanying busing of black and white children, and the nature of politics in Boston, virtually guaranteed that conflicts, generally resolved privately, would be highly visible. The tasks to be resolved in developing the proposals and in implementing Chapter 636 programs, however, were similar to those encountered in any proposal solicitation designed to facilitate change. Even responses to noncontroversial submittals (e.g., reading skill development, the delivery of improved health services, or improved nutrition and care of preschool children) give rise to conflict.

BEEO personnel were convinced that, by authorizing individual teachers to submit proposals, the odds for successful implementation of the program would be increased. Simultaneously, BEEO built constraints into the process for reviewing and rating proposals, thus necessitating both parental and administrative participation in the development of proposed programs:

All proposals developed at the school level must be approved by the school principal(s) and then forwarded to the area superintendent...

---

*Operationally these were to represent districts under the control of area superintendents.

for review and rating. Each proposal developed at the school level must contain a complete narrative description of the process of consultation with parents and parent groups, teachers and other school staff to be affected by the proposed program.[26]

After being cleared at the school and district level, all proposals were to be submitted to the school superintendent's office for approval by the school committee. Approved proposals then were to go to BEEO for submittal to the state board of education for final approval.

At the outset, the conflicting needs of parties responsible for the development of programs and administrative units responsible for the clearance of proposals were significant; organizational impediments to the development, clearance, and submittal of proposals within time limits set by the proposal request were many. With the Phase II court order and the entry of collaborating institutions, media coverage of the conflicts in developing and submitting proposals increased. The stakes in winning or losing increased in proportion to the increase in institutional and agency visibility, as the behavior of participating parties later demonstrated.

The following events do not portray the full range of issues affecting implementation of the Boston Desegregation Plan. Rather, they have been selected to highlight common conflicts in the response of institutions to agency proposal requests.

PHASE I–LOCAL EDUCATION AGENCY RESPONSE TO THE FUNDING AGENCY REQUEST

On November 1, 1974, the Superintendent of Schools was notified by BEEO that the Boston Public Schools would be eligible to receive approximately $3 million to support projects authorized under Chapter 636, Section I of the Acts of 1974. The appropriated monies would become available on January 1, 1975, with the requirement that the allocated monies be expended or encumbered before the close of the fiscal year, June 30, 1975. The state department of education would review and act on proposals at meetings scheduled for December 1974, and January and February 1975.

Thus, an enormous management task was interjected into a school system already experiencing dislocation and conflict. The solicitation of proposals from approximately 2,200 eligible teachers, and the development, review, and administrative clearance by the school department of the several hundred proposals that would eminate from the request were constrained by stringent deadlines. In addition to the submittal deadlines set by BEEO, the Boston school department set its own schedule to clear all proposals initiated at the individual school level, prior to submittal to the state.

On November 4, 1974, a circular was sent to all area superintendents soliciting proposals from teachers and informing them that an organizational unit within the school department, responsible for coordinating and monitoring externally funded programs, would coordinate Chapter 636 activities and help teachers develop proposals. Guidelines and instructions accompanied the information. The due date for submitting teacher proposals to principals or headmasters, to assure city clearance and process by the state board of education at its December meeting, was November 18.* Anticipating the needs of the teachers, the coordinating unit contacted various local universities, requesting faculty assistance in developing proposals at a workshop scheduled for November 14. This initial entry of university faculty as technical assistants represented the first informal involvement of the universities; this involvement was formalized by court order the following spring.

At the proposal development workshop (held four days before the first round submittal deadline), it became apparent that all elements leading to faulty proposal development and project execution were present: teachers were unclear about the source of funding and supporting legislation; the majority were unaware of the guidelines; time constraints limited community group participation in developing proposals; the guidelines, when distributed, called for general and technical information not readily obtainable; and most teachers lacked proposal-writing and project-planning skills required for appropriate document development. Finally, the implementation schedule set by the appropriation legislation severely restricted the nature of project activities that could be planned and completed before the June 30 program termination date.

Proposal review teams, comprised of university faculty and school and community representatives, confirmed the presence of these obstacles late in the month. Few of the submitted proposals conformed to criteria other than those governing format; few directly addressed the problems of facilitating the desegregation of the schools; and even fewer addressed the goal of "quality integrated education," which was the political and educational objective of the funding office. Despite the weakness of the proposals, the availability of funds and the political investment of the funding agency practically guaranteed funding for proposals that adhered to the format of the instruction sheet and called for approved program staff. The ritual of the review process had been carried out: proposals had been solicited and judged against a set of agency-defined criteria; different judgments on proposal requests had been made; fiscal officers had been given the data to negotiate budgets and provide for allocations; and successful applicants were notified of approval.

The Chapter 636 effort was, however, marked by several departures from

---

*All proposals initiated prior to Phase II at the school level had to be signed off by the building principal, the area superintendent responsible for specified schools in a given geographic area of the city, the Council of Area Superintendents (composed of superintendents representing areas of study, such as, special education, reading, and staff training), and ultimately the superintendent of schools. After securing these sign-offs, the proposal could be submitted to the school committee for approval. At this juncture, the process of entering into contracts, with another set of necessary clearances, could commence.

the norm that later heightened the level of conflict between the affected parties: appropriations exceeded the total requests of submitters, and allocated funds had to be spent within six months; the impact on the funding process was considerable.

BEEO, cast in an adversarial relationship with the Boston School Committee, was committed to spend the full allocation in the hope of producing some positive outcomes that would further the case for desegregation. The fiscal and political necessity of spending available funds created, in effect, a noncompetitive bidding system more typical of formula allocations such as Title I of the 1965 Elementary and Secondary Education Act. Unlike Title I, however, the trappings of competitive bidding remained. Proposals that would have failed a competitive review were funded, clearly an exception to the rule.

Given BEEO's diminished status in the eyes of the state legislature (reflected in the watering down of legislation that led to its inception), the task of successful program implementation was further complicated by stipulations in the authorizing legislation regarding the administration of funds:

> The board [state board of education], acting through the commissioner of education and on behalf of the Commonwealth, shall enter into an agreement with such school committee.... the Commonwealth shall provide financial assistance to such city, town or regional district school committee, as provided by this section.[27]

Chapter 636 forced the funding agency to modify its behavior in order to secure proposals from institutions, clearly reversing the normal power relationship between funding agencies and submitting institutions. BEEO, serving as an arm of the state board of education, now had to rely on the behavior of the defendant (The Boston School Committee), earlier found guilty of maintaining a segregated school system, for the success of the program. BEEO was forced to assume a facilitative role, rather than its earlier adversarial role. The Boston School Committee held virtually all the power once proposals were approved. BEEO was held accountable for program success by the state board of education and the state legislature, but had limited ability to affect the program's outcome. The ultimate weapon possessed by funding agencies, the withholding of future funds, could not be employed effectively by BEEO, since such action would signal publically the failure of efforts to desegregate the Boston Public Schools. In a belt-tightening fiscal climate, this would have been tantamount to asking for the dissolution of BEEO.

Finally, implementation of Chapter 636 differed from the normal solicitation, award, and monitoring process in that it lacked precedents and accompanying structures and procedures, usually developed through decades of grant and contract solicitation activities. Offices may lack staff, time lines may be difficult to establish, and appropriations may be uncertain, but the federal bureaucracy, however cumbersome, is designed and staffed to carry out the process. The

Boston Public Schools and BEEO, however, had neither precedent nor sufficiently qualified staff to implement Chapter 636.

As Phase I activities were carried out during the spring of 1975, the lack of rules and precedent to govern participants' behavior had their effect. Additional deadlines for proposal review were set by BEEO for February and March, since the first solicitation had failed to award all of the allocated funds. Despite the decreasing time between award announcements and the fiscal year cutoff for expenditures, programs were mounted as late as two months before the close of the school year. Teachers and administrators were encouraged to start programs in anticipation of funding, rather than to await formal notification. Although awards were forthcoming in virtually all of these cases, delays in compensation resulted in bitterness.

Despite efforts of its small staff to reconcile management needs with those of the school department, BEEO continued to be seen by the school committee as an agent of the federal court. Both the school department and BEEO remained entrapped by the organization constraints of their respective bureaucracies. With these constraints, BEEO found itself unable to expend its full appropriation. The initial round of proposal solicitations and awards had identified points of stress that became clearer with issuance of the *Memorandum of Decision and Remedial Orders* by the United State District Court, District of Massachusetts, on June 5, 1975. This document set forth the conditions for Phase II of the Desegregation Plan and marked the formal entry of universities, cultural organizations, and businesses into its implementation.

PHASE II—VARIABLES AFFECTING UNIVERSITY AND COMMUNITY RESPONSE

The Phase II plan touched virtually every element of educational and community decision making in the Boston schools. In the midst of turbulence created by attempts to realign the educational power structure of the city, twenty-two universities, fourteen cultural agencies, and participating businesses and industries pledged their assistance in carrying out the desegregation plan. They became entwined immediately in the conflicts endemic to the redistribution of power and the establishment of new roles.

Major features of Phase II relevant to the dynamics of funding included: (1) the establishment of a citywide school district; (2) the establishment of community school districts; (3) the pairing of universities, businesses, and cultural agencies with individual magnet schools or with community school districts; (4) the revision of administrative and supervisory organizational structures; and (5) the establishment of a citywide coordinating council and community district advisory councils.

The universities, in responding to BEEO's request for proposals in June 1975, were challenged by the dynamic of decision making among the Boston school committee, Boston school department, administration and staff of individual schools, community advisory boards, and vocal community representatives. They also had to deal with the competing needs and expectations of the state department of education, BEEO, university central administrations, and academic units within the universities. Chapter 636 created a funding setting in which numerous variables appearing at many organization levels, and affecting dozen of institutional units, were prominently and publically displayed during the development and implementation of an externally funded project.

The number and complexity of variables affecting Phase II clearly reveal that the funding system model presented in the preceding chapter, like most models, tends to gloss over complexities with a funding agency or submitting institution(s) that has direct interest in a program's form. Nor does the model differentiate between the needs of these parties and those utlimately served by the program. The one-dimensional treatment of the funding agency and submitting institution precludes consideration of all variables that may be critical to successful proposal development and project implementation. The scope of the program, the number of parties involved in development and implementation, and the potential of the project to affect the status quo, all contribute to the dissonance between the funding agency and various organizational units in the submitting institution. Within submitting institutions, the expectations and needs of chief officers, fiscal officers, project officers, and staff may differ. When collaborative efforts are required and project implementation affects several parties, the different needs and expectations of the groups assure conflict in both developing the proposal and implementing the project. The nature of past relationships between the funding agency, submitting institutions, and those affected by Chapter 636 assured conflict in this setting. The response of community organizations to Phase II projects illustrates some variables that often occur. Proposals calling for the participation of groups that have neither worked together previously nor agreed on the distribution of authority or roles invite conflict.

THE COMMUNITY SETTING

At the time of the BEEO proposal solicitation from collaborating institutions, the question of how to draw parents and community members into the development process was clouded by the court order to establish school racial-ethnic councils, community district advisory councils (CDACs), and a citywide coordinating council (CCC) to advise and monitor school and university efforts. Many of the functions of racial-ethnic councils and "home and school associations," which had existed side-by-side under Phase I, were preempted by these new units.

As of September 1975, elections and appointments of members to the community district advisory council had not taken place; the means for involving community and parent groups were not formalized. A wide range of groups with diverse political and programmatic interests sought to participate in the design and implementation of the initial programs. Although the following

TABLE 2.2. Group Involvement

Community Groups	Characteristics
School Racial-Ethnic Councils	Formed under the Phase I Plan and comprised of parents of students attending individual schools, the councils were designed to serve in an advisory capacity to the administration of individual schools. Newly formed racial-ethnic councils, limited to elected parents of students, were the court-authorized bodies for school-community communications.
Boston Home and School Association	Members of individual school associations had access to the Boston School Department and School Committee power structures. As an organization, they were on record as opposed to the Phase II Plan and stood to lose power under Phase II because of the establishment of alternative community advisory units.
Citywide Education Coalition	Formed in 1974, the coalition continued to function as a body designed to increase parental participation in the educational process. Following the Phase I Plan, the coalition assumed a major role in the desegregation process as a disseminator of information and recruiter of bus monitors and transitional aides. The coalition supported the Phase II Plan and was seen by the Boston Home and School Association as an arm of the mayor's office and thus an adversary to the School Committee.
ROAR (Restore Our Alienated Rights)	ROAR was the most visible and vocal organization opposed to busing. At the time of the court order, the executive board's chairperson was city council member and former school committee chairperson, Louise Day Hicks. School boycotts, organized rallies, and protest marches sponsored by ROAR continued to aggravate racial tension in the city.

groups were not associated formally with the state-authorized program, their actions had an impact on the planning of proposals and implementation of projects.

Many additional community, civic, and service associations were affected by the programmatic scope of the proposals. Some had been actively involved for a considerable time in attempts to improve the quality of education for Boston's minorities. Others offered suggestions and criticism, participating in hearings leading to development of the Phase II Plan.

The broad range of parties potentially affected by university activities, and the limited time available to develop the initial proposal, aggravated conflicting perceptions of program objectives and university motivations. As individual groups sought to play an active role in shaping university proposals, the universities found themselves playing the role of power broker, with access to little power. The individual groups, pending the formulation of the CDACs, had little authority but significant power to affect the reception given university efforts by BEEO and the Boston School Committee. Conflicts within the university organizational structures were complemented by extrauniversity conflict.

Benefits to some parties resulted in losses to others: the legitimization and increased power of the ethnic-racial councils was realized at the expense of the home and school associations. Increased local control of program development was realized through a corresponding reduction in school committee and university faculty control. The potential for direct or indirect university influence on program activities was seen as a threat to the authority of teachers and local administrators.

APPLICATION OF THE MODEL TO A LESS COMPLEX SETTING: HEAD START PROGRAM

The previous examination of the stress within and between agency and institutional units reveals the range of intra- and interinstitutional conflicts that may accompany any major proposal development effort. Fortunately for both the soliciting agency and the responding institution, the full range of possible conflicts seldom surfaces in a single program. As the following profile reveals, however, the possibility of conflict between parties affected by proposed projects is not limited to highly politicized or controversial proposal solicitations.

The Head Start program, established by the Office of Economic Opportunity (OEO) in 1965, has become, through subsequent amendments and increased appropriations, a major experimental demonstration program providing health, educational, nutritional, and social services to economically disadvantaged preschool children, their families, and their communities. Transferred to the Office of Child Development (OCD) in 1969 and placed under the Administration for Children, Youth and Families in 1977, Head Start supports more than 1600 projects each year. Although community action agencies (CAAs) have been the primary sponsors, local school systems and other nonprofit agencies may also serve as sponsors.

The ten regional offices of DHEW responsible for processing grant proposals, providing technical assistance to local grantees, and monitoring grantee operations determine the degree to which the proposed plans of submitting institutions conform to the specifications accompanying each subpart contained in the Rules and Regulations. The regulatory requirements pertaining to Head Start program governance are particularly relevant for examining points of stress between funding agencies and submitting institutions. (See Table 2.3.)

48   The Dynamics of Funding

TABLE 2.3. Head Start Program: Composition and Structure of Program Governance

Chart A

Organization:	Composition
1. Head Start Center Committee	1. Parents whose children are enrolled in that center.
2. Head Start Policy Committee (delegate agency).	2. At least 50% parents of Head Start children presently enrolled in that delegate agency program plus representatives of the community.
3. Head Start Policy Council (grantee)	3. At least 50% parents of Head Start children presently enrolled in that grantee's program plus representatives of the community.

U.S., Department of Health, Education, and Welfare, Office of Human Development, Office of Child Development, Head Start Program, Rules and Regulations, *Federal Register* 40, no. 126, 30 June 1975.

The specifications for the functions of the various policy groups and the allocation of authority provided by the funding agency (Table 2.4) introduce points of stress in both the development and implementation of programs.

Given the range of program services and the governance structure characteristics prescribed by the regulations, it is easy to locate points of stress among those organizational units responsible for implementing Head Start programs.

Stress between the funding agency and the submitting institution most frequently centers around the standards, set by the Rules and Regulations, stipulating both the composition and functions of the policy councils. The authority granted the policy councils, in many cases, has led submitting institutions to withdraw funding applications when it became apparent that the councils' priorities were not consonant with those of the Head Start program performance standards. Conflicts over program priorities have been compounded when the power held by policy councils reduces proportionately the power of previously established governing boards of submitting institutions. The reallocation of decision-making authority has also had immediate impact on the development of proposals and the implementation of programs. Policy councils, standing governing boards, and the funding agency are often at odds over the most appropriate approach in conforming to the standards: one decision-making unit may strongly support a community organization approach to the delivery of social services, whereas another may strongly advocate a traditional casework approach. In such cases, any success in securing funding and implementing the program is, in large part, directly related to the ability of the units to resolve their differences.

TABLE 2.4   Head Start Program: Local Program Governance

A=General responsibility B=Operating responsibility C=Must approve or disapprove D=Must be consulted E=May be consulted		Chart B Delegate agency				Chart C Grantee agency			
Function	Board	Executive director	Head Start policy committee	Head Start director	Board	Executive director	Head Start policy council	Head Start director
I. Planning:									
(a) Identify child development needs in the area to be served (by CAA* if not delegated).		A	B	D	D	A	B	D	D
(b) Establish goals of Head Start program and develop ways to meet them within in HEW guidelines.		A	C	C	B	A	C	C	B
(c) Determine delegate agencies and areas in the community in which Head Start programs will operate.		....	....	....	....	A	D	C	B
(d) Determine location of centers or classes.		A	D	C	B	....	....	....	....
(e) Develop plans to use all available community resources in Head Start.		A	D	C	B	A	D	C	B
(f) Establish criteria for selection of children within applicable laws and HEW guidelines.		....	....	....	....	A	C	C	B
(g) Develop plan for recruitment of children.		A	C	C	B	....	....	....	....
II. General Administration:									
(a) Determine the composition of the appropriate policy group and the method for setting it up (within HEW guidelines).		A	B	C	D	A	B	C	D
(b) Determine what services should be provided to Head Start from the CAA* central office and the neighborhood centers.		....	....	....	....	A	B	C	D
(c) Determine what services should be provided to Head Start from delegate agency.		A	B	C	D	....	....	....	....
(d) Establish a method of hearing and resolving community complaints about the Head Start program.		D	C	A	B	D	C	A	B
(e) Direct the CAA* Head Start staff in day-to-day operations.		....	....	....	....	E	A	E	B
(f) Direct the delegate agency Head Start staff in day-to-day operations.		E	A	E	B	....	....	....	....
(g) Insure that standards for acquiring space, equipment, and supplies are met.		A	D	D	B	A	D	D	B
III. Personnel administration:									
(a) Determine Head Start personnel policies (including establishment of hiring and firing criteria for Head Start staff, career development plans, and employee grievance procedures).									
Grantee agency		....	....	....	....	A	C	C	B
Delegate agency		A	C	C	B	....	....	....	....
(b) Hire and fire Head Start Director of grantee agency.		....	....	....	....	A	B	C	
(c) Hire and fire Head Start staff of grantee agency		....	....	....	....	A E	B A	C C	B
(d) Hire and fire Head Start Director of delegate agency.		A	B	C		....	....	....	....
(e) Hire and fire Head Start staff of delegate agency.		E	A	C	B	....	....	....	....
IV. Grant application process:									
(a) Prepare request for funds and proposed work program.									
Prior to sending to CAA*		A	C	C	B	....	....	....	....
Prior to sending to HEW		....	....	....	....	A	C	C	B
(b) Make major changes in budget and work program while program is in operation.		A	C	C	B	A	C	C	B
(c) Provide information needed for prereview to policy council.		A	D	C	B	....	....	....	....
(d) Provide information needed for prereview to HEW.		....	....	....	....	A	D	C	B
V. Evaluation: Conduct self-evaluation of agency's Head Start program.		A	D	B	D	A	D	B	D

*CAA or general term "grantee"

Definitions as used on charts B and C

A. *General Responsibility.*—The individual or group with legal and fiscal responsibility guides and directs the carrying out of the function described through the person or group given operating responsibility.

B. *Operating Responsibility.*—The individual or group that is directly responsible for carrying out or performing the function, consistent with the general guidance and direction of the individual or group holding general responsibility.

C. *Must Approve or Disapprove.*—The individual or group (other than persons or groups holding general and operating responsibility, A and B above) must approve before the decision is finalizing or action taken. The individual or group must also have been consulted in the decision making process prior to the point of seeking approval.
If they do not approve, the proposal cannot be adopted, or the proposed action taken, until agreement is reached between the disagreeing groups or individuals.

D. *Must be Consulted.*—The individual or group must be called upon before any decision is made or approval is granted to give advice or information but not to make the decision or grant approval.

E. *May be Consulted.*—The individual or group may be called upon for information, advice or recommendations by those individuals or groups having general responsibility or operating responsibility.

U.S., Department of Health, Education, and Welfare, Office of Human Development, Office of Child Development. Head Start Program, Rules and Regulations, *Federal Register* 40, no. 126, 30 June 1975.

A second common point of stress results from variations in program priorities among regional offices and submitting institutions. Given regulations that call for the delivery of educational services, health services, social services, and parent involvement, it is not surprising that priorities regarding types of services differ from region to region, program to program, and year to year.

The program performance standards published by DHEW in 1975 provided criteria to normalize or reduce differentiation between programs and thereby reduce regional variations in the interpretation of regulations. The need for such a document confirmed the existence of differing program priorities. Although the funding agency may use performance standards as a tool to stipulate the appropriate balance between various Head Start program elements, the standards do not assure that the submitting institution's focus will match that balance. Conflicting perceptions of the appropriate balance of program priorities between the funding agency and the submitting institution have been most evident when local education agencies (LEAs) have received awards. LEAs understandably have stressed the importance of the educational components of the program and have experienced difficulty in mounting the health and social service delivery and parent involvement components.

Head Start, like the Boston desegregation case study, reveals points of stress affecting both the programmatic and organizational elements that must be addressed when developing proposals and implementing programs. Differing program and organizational priorities within and between the funding agency, submitting institution officers and staff, and parents and community representatives must all be negotiated before program implementation.

SUMMARY

This chapter has traced the evolution of selected programs from the point in the funding system at which a societal problem receives legislative definition through the points of agency and institutional definition, represented in the request for proposals and the response of potential grantees. Attention has focused on identifying stress-producing elements in the process that are products of the varying needs of those responsible for formulating programs and implementing projects. It has been contended that the many conflicts possible in the funding system are a direct result of the process governing the setting of legislation, the formulation of agency guidelines, and the features of programs outlined in proposals of submitting institutions.

The Boston desegregation case study served primarily to identify the form that conflicts may take; conditions surrounding the BEEO solicitation were such that virtually all the possible conflicts were present and visible. The evolution of the Teacher Center Program from idea to agency-defined program revealed more subtle conflicts, common when the social climate is significantly less volatile. Discussion of the major features of the Head Start program demonstrated the pervasiveness of conflict by identifying selected points of stress in a program with markedly different characteristics from those that influenced the response to state-authorized desegregation proposal requests.

The application of the funding system model to the dynamics of the initial stages of the funding system that are mentioned in this chapter will be complemented by more detailed consideration of specific elements of the process in following chapters. The next chapter considers the factors that determine the legislative and agency definitions of a problem. Any institution submitting a proposal must be able to respond directly to legislative and agency constraints, if it expects to be competitive.

ENDNOTES

1. Niccolo Machiavelli, *The Prince and the Discourses* (New York: Modern Library, 1940), pp. 21-22.
2. Commonwealth of Massachusetts, Chapter 636 of the Acts of 1974 (Amendments to the Racial Imbalance Act of 1965).
3. Morgan v. Kerrigan, Civil Action No. 72-911-G, District of Massachusetts, Memorandum of Decision and Remedial Orders, June 5, 1975.
4. Ibid.
5. Brown v. Board of Education of Topeka, 347 U.S. 483 (1954).
6. U.S., Department of Health, Education, and Welfare, National Center for Educational Statistics, *Equality of Educational Opportunity*, Reported by James Coleman (Washington, D.C.: Government Printing Office, 1966), p.1.
7. Civil Rights Act of 1964, 42 U.S.C. § 601-605.
8. U.S. Commission on Civil Rights, *Racial Isolation in the Public Schools* (Washington, D.C.: Government Printing Office, 1967), p. 12.
9. *Report of the National Advisory Commission on Civil Disorders* (New York: Bantam Books, 1968), p. 13.
10. John Herbes, "Liberal Nixon Aids Yield in School Integration Test," *New York Times* (8 March 1970): sec. 4, p. 1.
11. Draft Report of the Masters in Tallulah Morgan, et al. v. John Kerrigan et al., p. 4.
12. Commonwealth of Massachusetts, Department of Education, Massachusetts Research Center, *Balancing the Public Schools*, Bureau of Educational Information Services, 1974, p. 14.
13. Morgan v. Hennigan, D Mass. 1974, 379 F. Supp. 410.
14. James Conant, "Social Dynamite in Our Large Cities," speech delivered before the Conference on Unemployed Out-of-School Youth in Urban Areas, Washington, D.C., May 24, 1961.
15. Testimony before the Senate Subcommittee on Education of the full Committee on Labor and Public Welfare, June 23, 1967, Mimeo pp. 1-3.

16. B. Othanel Smith, Saul B. Cohen, and Arthur Pearl, *Teachers for the Real World* (Washington, D.C.: American Association of Colleges for Teacher Education, 1969).
17. U.S., Department of Health, Education, and Welfare, Office of Education, *Teacher Centers* "I. A Partial History of the Federal Role in the Development of Teacher Centers," by Allen Schmieder (Washington, D.C.: Government Printing Office, 1977), p. 3.
18. Don Davies, "Reflections on EPDA," *Theory into Practice* 13 (June 1974): 210.
19. Stephen S. Kaagan, "Executive Initiative Yields to Congressional Debate: A Study of Educational Renewal 1971-72" (Ph.D. dissertation, Harvard University, 1973), p. 74.
20. Interview with Allen Schmieder, Program Officer, Teacher Center Program, Washington, D.C., June 16, 1977.
21. W. Vance Grant, "Trends in Public School Systems," *American Education* (August-September 1973): 33.
22. U.S., Department of Health, Education, and Welfare, National Center for Education Statistics, Education Division, *The Condition of Education* (Washington, D.C.: Government Printing Office, 1975), p. 177.
23. Stanley J. McFarland, quoted in "Teacher Center Legislation Signals 'Word to the Wise,' " *Legislative Briefs* (May 1977), p. 4.
24. Ibid., p. 5.
25. Guidelines for Proposal Submittal, distributed to applicants for funding under Chapter 636 of the Acts of 1974, Fall 1974.
26. Ibid.
27. Chapter 636 of the Acts of 1974.

3

The Proposal Request: From Authorization to Solicitation

Although many social and political considerations influence the formulation of a program, any application for federal funding must respond directly to the Rules and Regulations governing the administration of the program. The agency's program definition contained in the Rules and Regulations is the negotiated product of legislative intent, agency or program office priorities, and the influence of organized groups affected by the program. Whether they are formal Rules and Regulations of federal funding agencies or less formal guidelines of state agencies or foundations, these problem definitions and recommended strategies for resolution are the single most important source of information for designing a successful proposal document. A federal program officer's recommendation corroborates this observation: "If there is one piece of advice I can give to proposal writers, it is to secure the legislation authorizing funding, the guidelines for proposal review contained in the Rules and Regulations, and if possible the review forms provided to reviewers to evaluate the submitted proposal."[1]

This chapter focuses on events that shape the agency definition of the problem. Those elements that transform authorizing legislation into program Rules and Regulations will be highlighted; those elements that lead to the shaping of legislation will also be discussed. Just as a score serves as the backdrop for any musical production, so the authorizing legislation provides the score from which agency definitions evolve.

The legislative definition of the problem, represented in legal statutes, provides both the ways (authorized activities) and means (appropriations) to approach all federally and state-supported research, development, or training projects. This work omits a full analysis of events leading to the legislative problem definition. Instead, it focuses on elements of the funding system that directly affect proposal development and operation of the funded program.

Since legislation is basic to the dynamics of funding, however, this chapter provides an overview of the steps leading to the passage of legislation so that the reader can appreciate the many forces that bear directly on the priorities of any program and on the widely varying lifespans of programs. Formal and informal legislative constraints that directly affect program development, proposal solicitation, and proposal review and approval are discussed. Constraints that affect funding agency allocations and the functioning of the office (agency) responsible for administering a program are also considered. In the administration of any given program, unfortunately, the precise point at which legislatively imposed constraints become secondary to those established by the funding agency is difficult to determine. Legislative actions have the disconcerting tendency to re-emerge as primary constraints on programmatic features, just when it appears that program operation is under the full control of the funding agency; plans of both the agency and submitting institution must then be set aside or changed, pending resolution of the legislative concerns.

In assisting different types of institutions in developing proposals for submittal to a wide range of federally authorized programs, this author has encountered numerous uncertainties. The variables affecting the formation of Rules and Regulations and the request for proposals can be identified with some degree of precision; the difficulty rests in determining the timing and precise interaction of the different variables that shape the environment to which one must respond. The agency and institution staff's ability to explain what has happened often exceeds the ability to predict what will happen.

Regardless of the uncertainties of prediction, the odds for successful planning increase if you identify the variables, which contribute ultimately to the formulation of the proposal guidelines, and secure sufficient data to hypothesize about the outcomes of the interaction of variables that shape the program features and determine submittal timing. Therefore, the evolution of proposal requests must be considered against the legislative background. By understanding the dynamics of legislation development and the rules that govern the federal aid process, institutions will be able to develop strategies to accommodate the uncertainties. Submitting institutions will also be able to identify and address factors common to all federal, state, local, and even foundation proposal efforts. Furthermore, a clear understanding of the legislative and rule-setting process allows the proposal planner to influence or adjust to the variables that shape the future funding environment.

PROBLEM DEFINITION: FROM LEGISLATION TO RULES AND REGULATIONS PUBLICATION

All proposal requests issued by federal or state agencies originate from the passage of legislation authorizing the allocation of funds to meet the intent of the legislation. Thus, the precise nature of the request for proposals transmitted to potential applicants is a product of the social and political forces that shape any legislation: the political philosophy and legislative agenda of the executive branch of government; the pressures exerted by constituents of individual legislators; the power and influence of committees, lobbies, and vested interest groups; the priorities of influential agency offices; and the differential power and authority of individuals who may gain or lose as a result of the legislation. The complexity of the process is explicable in terms of the authority fragmented within the government and the many private and public interests exerting influence on the legislative decision-making process.

These countless variables seem to defy the efforts of an institution seeking federal funding to analyze funding prospects systematically and develop appropriate strategies. Fortunately, well-defined legislative and administrative procedures have been developed by both the federal government and most state governments to deal with the countervailing pressures. Interested parties can monitor the processing of any piece of legislation and, on occasion, directly or indirectly influence the shaping of the legislation itself. It is imperative that anyone seriously interested in securing federal aid develop an understanding of the legislative and administrative procedures that govern the formulation and implementation of legislation, as well as those procedures that transform legislation into Rules and Regulations.

THE LEGISLATIVE BIRTH OF A PROGRAM

At least two distinct major influences contribute to the birth of a program: (1) the disposition and priorities of the executive and legislative branches of the federal or state government and (2) the disposition and priorities of the major agencies that administer the programs. The relative power of the branches of government and the agencies responsible for areas affecting the general welfare of the nation (that is, education, health, welfare, labor, manpower, human service, and housing) will vary, both as a function of the power of individuals directing agency units and the political, social, and economic state of the nation at any time. The initiative for introducing legislation, although technically residing with the legislative branch, may be generated by any of the government branches or agencies. The birth of a program may be depicted as a drama in six acts:

ACT I: THE IDEA
SCENE 1—THE COMMISSIONER HAS A NOTION
SCENE 2—DATA IS GATHERED
SCENE 3—THE ISSUE PAPER IS WRITTEN
SCENE 4—DISCUSSIONS WITH THE BUREAUS
SCENE 5—RESOLUTION: A NEW POLICY EMERGES

ACT II: FRIENDLY DISCUSSIONS
SCENE 1—TALKS WITH THE DEPARTMENT
SCENE 2—CONVERSATIONS WITH OMB
SCENE 3—WRITING SPECIFICATIONS
SCENE 4—REACHING AGREEMENT

56 The Dynamics of Funding

ACT III: WRITING LEGISLATION
SCENE 1–THE BUREAUS AGREE
SCENE 2–THE CONGRESSIONAL PICTURE EMERGES
SCENE 3–TALKS WITH THE OFFICE OF THE GENERAL
    COUNSEL
SCENE 4–DEPARTMENT CONCURRENCE
SCENE 5–OFFICE OF MANAGEMENT AND BUDGET

ACT IV: CONGRESS ACTS
SCENE 1–THE HEARINGS
SCENE 2–THE COMMITTEE REPORT
SCENE 3–THE BILL PASSES
SCENE 4–THE OTHER HOUSE HAS HEARINGS
SCENE 5–THE OTHER COMMITTEE REPORT
SCENE 6–THE OTHER HOUSE PASSES A DIFFERENT BILL
SCENE 7–THE CONFERENCE REPORT
SCENE 8–AT LAST, A BILL
SCENE 9–THE PRESIDENT SIGNS THE ACT

ACT V: THE OFFICE OF EDUCATION GEARS UP
SCENE 1–THE PLANNING TASK FORCE
SCENE 2–CHANGES
SCENE 3–THE PROGRAM TAKES SHAPE
SCENE 4–THE DEPARTMENT AND OMB CONCUR

ACT VI: GETTING STARTED
SCENE 1–THE FIVE-YEAR PLAN
SCENE 2–THE BUDGET JUSTIFICATION
SCENE 3–OMB HEARINGS
SCENE 4–THE PRESIDENT'S BUDGET
SCENE 5–CONGRESSIONAL ACTION
SCENE 6–WRITING RULES AND REGULATIONS
SCENE 7–COMMENTS ON RULES AND REGULATIONS
SCENE 8–AWARDING GRANTS
SCENE 9–EVALUATIONS[2]

The above script outline falls short only in that the first two acts suggest that the commissioner of an agency and program officers play far greater roles in initiating programs than analysis of past programs would suggest. The influence of the executive and judicial branches of government, special interest organizations (and their lobbyists) and influential senators, representatives, and respected spokespersons may initiate program development activities. The feasibility of alternative scenes in earlier acts of the program birth drama will become apparent in the following narrative. Although the following information on legislative procedure may be familiar to most readers, its relationship to the proposal solicitation process places the events in a sufficiently different perspective to warrant inclusion.

The formal act of program conception is the introduction of a bill by individual legislators or, on occasion, by joint sponsorship of members of both branches of the legislature. The Executive Office, however, in consultation with appropriate commissioners and their staff, may initiate a program, such as in the case of the Elementary and Secondary Education Act of 1965. Initiative may also be provided by commissioners and their offices who interest the executive branch in a particular program. Such was the case when former Commissioner of Education, Sid Marland, and former Secretary of Health, Education, and Welfare, Elliott Richardson, succeeded in inserting the concept of career education into Richard Nixon's 1972 State of the Union address. Their success lead to legislation authorizing expenditures for programs in this area. Similarly, former Commissioner of Education, James E. Allen's phrase "right to read" caught the attention of legislators at a conference report, and monies were authorized under the "exemplary program" provision of the Cooperative Research Act of 1964 to support reading programs. The Right to Read Office, established under this authorization, subsequently secured sufficient legislative interest to lead to the Reading Improvement Act, carried as Title VII of the Education Amendments of 1974 (PL 93-380).

The role of major interest groups, lobbies, and professional associations in introducing and shaping legislation is also significant. The National Association of State Boards of Education, the Council of Chief State Officers, the American Association of School Adminstrators, the National School Boards Association, the National Education Association, the American Federation of Teachers, the Committee for Full Funding of Educational Programs, and countless other lobbies press strongly for legislation to support their constituents.

Individual members of Congress often initiate legislation in response to the pressures of constituent groups that have a wide range of clearly demarcated educational needs (e.g., bilingual and ethinic groups, federal employees, and urban or rural underemployed). In addition to the personal political benefits that accrue from advocating constituent interests, legislators may gain sufficient support from districts and their representatives to pass a relevant bill.

The interaction of these various forces ultimately produces legislation that directs the policies affecting delivery of educational and human services at the national, state, and local level. Legislation and authorized programs represent the negotiated products of personal and political forces, as well as the social and educational values predominant at any time. For the fund raiser, the introduction of legislation is, unfortunately, only the first step leading to the proposal request.

Following formal introduction, federal bills are referred to committee. In the House, most proposed education-related legislation is forwarded to the House Labor and Education Committee, which assigns it to one of two subcommittees on education. In the Senate, bills are forwarded to the Labor and Public Welfare Committee, which assigns then to the Subcommittee on Education. At this point in the legislative process, the legitimate pressure of concerned and affected parties begin to reshape the problem definition that provided the initial incentive for the legislation. Public hearings and private negotiations of committee members are guided by two not necessarily compatible goals: (1) to draft a piece of legislation that will best serve those in need, in a manner consistent with the national interest, or the needs of specific constituent groups and (2) to formulate legislation that is sufficiently acceptable to a majority of committee members to secure passage.

As part of the committees' accommodation process, bills reported "out of committee" for House or Senate consideration often contain elements of other new legislation dealing with similar problems. Although this consolidation process may broaden the scope of a bill and integrate related program thrusts, it can also complicate passage of the bill. The most extreme example is the attachment of highly controversial amendments that are virtually unrelated to program goals. The attachment of controversial abortion amendments to the 1978 HEW-Labor appropriation bill, and the ensuing delays, was one well-publicized example.

Unfortunately, the reporting out of a bill or the passage of a bill by the House and Senate seldom indicates the timeline for the bill's enactment as law and the subsequent solicitation of proposals. The House and Senate rarely pass identical versions of a bill just out of committee. The Education Amendments of 1976, extending the Elementary and Secondary Education Act of 1965, is a case in point. The House version of the bill, passed in March 1976, differed substantially from the Senate version passed in May 1976. To reconcile the differences, the bills were sent back to a conference committee. Once the necessary compromises were negotiated and the bill reported out with conference committee approval, both branches of Congress voted again before sending the bill to the President for signature. Had the bill been changed by either branch, it would have returned once again to the conference committee. The conference committee review process takes the programmatic substance of the legislation farther from the initiating party and introduces an additional stage of negotiation designed to reduce dissonance between the two versions of the bill. This dissonance may be totally unrelated to solving the problem that initiated the bill's introduction.

The implications of the legislative development process are depressing for long-term institutional planning. Legislation can be lost forever in committee; the timing of reporting out and final congressional action is unpredictable; and the importance of executive, legislative, and lobbying influences cannot be overestimated.

The final step in the passage of legislation is the President's signature. Failure to sign, either through a veto or pocket veto, returns the bill to Congress; a two-thirds majority of both Houses is necessary to override the veto, or the legislation is redrafted to meet presidential objections. If legislation is redrafted, the committees must again seek consensus and consent.

Presidential signature provides closure to the first of two critical legislative steps leading to program implementation—the authorization for funding. Authorization establishes and describes the purposes of federal funding and generally sets a dollar ceiling on the annual outlay. Authorization *does not* obligate Congress to allocate a penny for program implementation. To channel money to local educational agencies, colleges and universities, and human service agencies, separate but related executive and legislative machinery must be set in motion. In keeping with the Constitution's dictate that "no money shall be drawn from the Treasury but in consequence of appropriation made by law," all program money must come from an appropriation bill.

At this point, "dollar politics" come into play. The funding director must recognize the difference between *authorization* and *appropriation*. The level of appropriation, rather than the authorizing legislation, is the key variable in determining ultimately the number of projects to be funded and the level of funding available. The funding ceiling identified in authorizing legislation is seldom a reliable indicator of monies available for program support. The Committee for Full Funding of Education Programs has noted that if all legislation on the books were funded to the authorized limit, federal spending on education would at least triple.[3] The important distinction between authorization and appropriation legislation has been obscured by federal and state agencies that solicit proposals after passage of authorizing legislation but before passage of accompanying appropriation bills. The presence of Rules and Regulations and the request for a proposal do not always indicate that monies are available to fund the proposal, and do not always indicate the *level* of appropriations available.

THE APPROPRIATION-SETTING PROCESS

The appropriations process differs in several respects from the authorization process. Appropriation legislation originates in the House after the President submits a proposed budget for the fiscal year. All appropriation and tax bills are reviewed by the powerful Ways and Means and Appropriations Committees and their subcommittees, which in turn submit recommendations for the House to act on and forward to the Senate (where a similar process occurs). The deliberations of these committees often expose representatives' conflicting needs. Just as sponsorship and subsequent enactment of an education statute is often a platform plank for a House or Senate Education Committee member seeking re-election, drawing the line on public expenditures is an equivalent plank for an Appropriations Committee member. The relationship between expenditures for social and educational program support and increased taxes to provide the revenue for such programs does not go unnoticed, particularly in an inflationary economy.

The formulation and passage of appropriation legislation is subject to organizational machinery that often functions indifferently to the aims of the authorizing legislation. Congress is aware, however, of the detrimental effect its rules and procedures have on the implementation of programs. For example, three different federal laws enacted during calendar year 1974 influence the way the congressional budget and appropriations cycle mesh with the traditional school and university planning and fiscal operation cycle: (1) Public Law 93-269

60   The Dynamics of Funding

permits LEAs to carry over unspent federal funds; (2) Public Law 93-344 changes the federal budget cycle and fiscal year; and (3) Public Law 93-380 calls for implementation of an earlier law permitting advance funding of education programs.

Legislation affecting the federal budget cycle and fiscal year and legislation calling for advance funding of federal education programs is important to managers of externally funded programs. More significantly the Congressional Budget Act (PL 93-344) establishes a firm schedule for the authorization and appropriations process. The former legislative process often saw the fiscal year end on June 30, with appropriation legislation to support several agencies and programs for the new fiscal year still pending. To support affected agencies, Congress normally passed a continuing resolution permitting continued operations for a three-month period, at a spending level commensurate with the past fiscal year's appropriation. Consequently, the educational planner was forced to prepare for the implementation of federally sponsored programs having no knowledge of the level of funding available and no indication when such knowledge would be forthcoming. The Congressional Budget Act should at least regularize this process, calling as it does for budget ceilings as well as September deadlines for any reconciliation bill or resolution.

Assuming that the prescribed budget and appropriation schedules are adhered to, the cost of predictability in the appropriation-setting calendar appears to be rather high for colleges and public school systems. The administration submits its budget to Congress in January, with the new fiscal year deadline for congressional approval changed to September 30. Although Congress can now deliberate within a more meaningful time space, education programs remain inextricably linked to the academic year. If appropriation action is not concluded until the end of September, the problems of late funding may be compounded; the new fiscal year is more out of synchronization with the academic year than the old.

Some relief may be found in PL 93-380, which "declares it to be the policy of the United States to implement immediately and continually Section 411 of the General Education Provisions Act, relating to advance funding for education programs."[4] "Advance" or forward funding (the appropriation of funds to programs a year before the money is spent) is designed to release educational institutions from the previous uncertainties under which they functioned. It allows program planners and project directors to predict program support from one year to the next. The constant monitoring of programs eligible for forward-funding under the provisions of this act will provide some degree of predictability about future funding possibilities.

In this initial look at the legislative process affecting regulation setting and proposal solicitation, two executive-initiated actions with funding implications must be considered—impoundment and rescission. During the Nixon administration, executive power to direct the Office of Management and Budget to *impound* (not expend) appropriated funds thwarted congressional overrides of the presidential veto. Subsequent court decisions have ruled that such discretionary action exceeds executive authority, and funding officers need no longer consider this variable. However, the executive branch still has considerable power to affect the timing of grant and contract awards by disrupting the appropriation schedule. Rather than directing OMB to impound funds, the President may request Congress, through the proper appropriation committees, to *rescind* appropriations legislation. Rescission, unlike impoundment, permits Congress to respond to the executive action. Congress may approve the rescission request, thereby watering down or rendering inoperable previous legislation; or, by taking no action for forty-five days of continuous session, Congress may disapprove the request, in effect ordering OMB to release the funds. The current congressional procedure for not approving rescission requests is equivalent to a forty-five day impoundment, after which the accompanying appropriation legislation is enacted. The effect of executive intervention on the time schedule for the solicitation of proposals and notification of awards is illustrated clearly by attempts of the Right to Read Program to generate proposal request, discussed later in this chapter.

Clearly defined legislative and executive procedures and established time lines accompanying the program authorization and appropriation process allow one to trace events at the begining of a program. Although the process has been justifiably referred to as an "obstacle course on Capitol Hill,"[5] the obstacles are generally visible and surmountable. Amid this legislative process, the agency responsible for administering programs must communicate its needs and requirements to institutions that want to implement the programs.

AGENCY DEFINITION OF THE PROBLEM

Legislation authorizes government agencies to issue proposal requests. The precise nature and form of the actual request, however, is the result of extended negotiations and complex administrative procedures and organizational requirements of the agencies ultimately responsible for program administration. The regulations and policies affecting any submittal in most cases fall within the public or private domain. Those in the public domain are recorded routinely and may be secured by interested parties; those in the private domain often may only be obtained by identifying informal channels of "inside" information.

At the federal level, the public agency definition of the problem is communicated officially through the *Federal Register* to institutions seeking funding. Rules and Regulations published in the *Federal Register* constitute legally binding criteria for proposal eligibility and program content; institutions applying for federal grants must base their proposals on these criteria. At the state level, the agency definition generally is transmitted by less formal and precise information accompanying proposal solicitations, unless specifically authorized and regulated by federal guidelines. The same applies to foundation problem definitions. The implications for the submitter of the difference between federal government definitions and state government and private foundation definitions will be discussed at greater length when discussing the analysis of the proposal request.

THE REGULATION-SETTING PROCESS

The variables that shape the Rules and Regulations are as complex as those that shape authorizing legislation. Unfortunately, they are not always as predictable or visible.

All federal agencies are subject to requirements of the Administrative Procedures Act (APA) and the General Education Provisions Act (GEPA), an overlay on the statutory framework of APA. These acts, and their most recent amendments, provide a director of federal funding the necessary information to assess the progress of developing programs and to estimate the release dates of Rules and Regulations and the following request for proposals. Dealing with administrative procedures governing federal grants-in-aid, these acts reflect evolving public concerns. As revised by the Education Amendments of 1974, GEPA requires public participation in the development of rules and publication in the *Federal Register* of all "substantive rules of general applicability."[6] Each procedural requirement is a response to past criticisms of the management of grant-in-aid programs. The latest amendments attempt to reconcile funding agency or program office objectives with the process of awarding grants-in-aid. Unfortunately, conflict between these objectives and the process is built into the system.

> The harmonization of the rulemaking and grant process involves the accommodation of two conflicting pressures. The grant process requires that a rule be established as early as possible in the year of appropriation so that the agency can invite prospective grantees for a program at a stage that gives them enough time to prepare applications, the application reviewers enough time to review them, and the grant officers enough time to negotiate proper grants with successful applicants. As noted above, the rule-making process involves elements that tend to defer the production of a final rule, including the need for legal review, program analysis, public participation, and delayed effectiveness incident to congressional review.[7]*

The 1974 Amendments, also require the Commissioner of Education to file a schedule for regulations and guidelines with the House Committee on

---

*Theodore Sky, "Rulemaking and the Federal Grant Process," *Virginia Law Review* 62 (October 1976): 1033. Reprinted with permission.

Education and Labor and the Senate Committee on Labor and Public Welfare, within 60 days of a law's enactment. The regulations must then be promulgated within 180 days, or both committees must approve any deviations from the schedule deadlines. Whether or not the continually evolving procedures are enforceable, and whether or not the programmatic objectives of the changes can be realized, the implications for those tracking funding opportunities are clear: a funding environment previously governed by few formal rules and regulations has been replaced by one in which rules and regulations govern virtually every move of the funding agency and the respondent. Certainly, the government bureaucracy will continue to make accommodations between program needs and administrative procedures. The only way to chart these accommodations and develop appropriate funding strategies is for submitting institutions to monitor closely the most recent rule-making procedures adopted by program offices.

The translation of legislation into Rules and Regulations governing proposal submittal is shaped by two sets of events: (1) events occurring within and between the organizational units of the funding agency and related government offices and (2) events occurring in the public domain. The former events are primarily private, with resulting changes in regulations reflecting the internal accommodations of affected units; the latter events are primarily public, with changes in regulations reflecting accommodations to external groups and individuals. An understanding of both internal (private) and external (public) events is essential to effective planning.

REGULATION SETTING: EVENTS IN THE PUBLIC DOMAIN

For all programs administered by the Office of Education, upon passage of authorizing legislation, the Commissioner of Education must file a schedule within sixty days with the appropriate congressional committees for the setting of Rules and Regulations. As of August 1976, the schedule must include dates for: (1) the notification of Intent for Proposed Rule Making, (2) the notification of Proposed Rules and Regulations, and (3) the notification of Final Rules and Regulations. Consistent with the APA requirement "that each agency publish in the *Federal Register,* . . . substantive rules of general applicability . . . and statements of general policy or interpretations of general applicability formulated and adopted by the agency,"[8] evolving program specifications and opportunities for response can be identified.

Acting Secretary Matthew's directive, in August 1976, to publish the Intent for Proposed Rule Making represented an extension of earlier steps by the U.S. Office of Education to meet criticism that interested public and private groups and agencies were systematically excluded from participating in the formulation of program guidelines contained in the Rules and Regulations. The decision of the U.S. Office of Education to solicit public comment, by holding regional and local conferences before the formulation of Proposed Rules and Regulations, was designed to meet head-on the criticism that these rules, as previously developed and distributed, called for comments by affected parties after the agenda for program development was set and opportunities for change were minimal. The impact of this procedure remains to be seen. Implementation of this directive, however, involves an additional step in the formulation of Rules and Regulations and aggravates an already severe problem in the proposal solicitation process—the amount of time consumed between program authorization and program implementation. The remaining question is whether value of increased participation by interested parties in developing Rules and Regulations offsets the cost and delays created by an additional step in the regulation-setting process. Regardless, the required notices of intent and public hearings provide the potential applicant with earlier notice of pending opportunities and signal issues basic to program implementation.

Publication of Proposed Rules and Regulations in the *Federal Register*, which formerly provided the potential applicant with the first reading of program guidelines governing proposal requests, now follows the announcement of Intent. Since 1970, this solicitation of public comments by federal offices has become increasingly formalized.* The importance of such comments is often reflected in the differences between the Proposed and Final Rules and Regulations governing the administration of programs.

Ironically, Proposed Rules and Regulations, which have served historically as the guiding document for the submittal of proposals, have often been changed after the closing date for submittal of proposals. While Proposed Regulations ostensibly enable affected parties to determine Final Rules and Regulations, the practice of calling for proposal submittal on the basis of Proposed Regulations has often precluded realization of this objective.

Assuming no major changes between Proposed and Final Rules, the primary value of Final Rules to a submitting institution may be their impact on future planning: they provide the single most important source of program information for continuing programs. When complemented by the latest amendments and current agency priorities, they provide the submitter with sufficient information to identify funding priorities—assuming appropriations are available.

The process of rule setting may also affect the implementation of funded projects. Congress, in an effort to monitor regulation setting more closely, included stipulations in the 1974 Amendments to GEPA that Final Rules related to programs in the Office of Education (and certain other programs) be transmitted to both houses of Congress, concurrent with their publication in the *Federal Register*. A rule may not take effect for forty-five days or, in the case of adjournment, for a staggered period fixed by the statute. If during that period Congress, by concurrent resolution, finds the rule inconsistent with its

---

*Before 1970, the Federal Administrative Procedure Act expressly exempted rules pertaining to federal grants from the APA provisions requiring federal agencies to invite public comment on them before they became final (5 USC P 553[b]). In October 1970, however, HEW ceased to honor this exemption and encouraged public participation in rule making by inviting comments on the Proposed Rules and Regulations, published in the *Federal Register*.

governing act, the rule may not take effect. The 1974 Amendments, in addition to limiting the freedom of program offices to define programs consistent with their perceptions and goals, establish conditions that may disrupt agency and institution plans for program implementation at the last minute.

The interplay between the forces that set the legislative and agency definitions of a problem can be appreciated by examining the events leading to the publication of Rules and Regulations and the solicitation of proposals by the Right to Read Office. Relevant excerpts from the legislation and the Rules and Regulations, examined in the course of the analysis, will familiarize the reader with the style and substance of documents that transmit legislative and agency problem definitions.

Figure 3.1 plots the administrative steps accompanying the birth of any program, as traced in public documents, and provides interested parties the means to develop strategies for response.

Figure 3.1. Regulation Development: The Public Domain

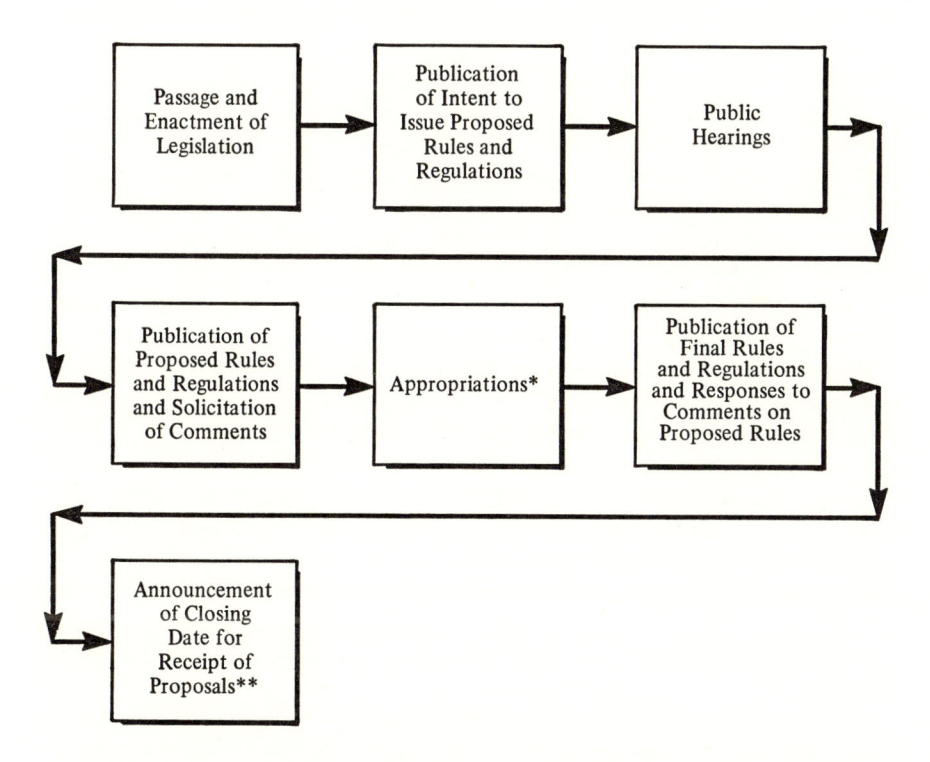

```
┌─────────────┐   ┌─────────────┐   ┌─────────────┐
│ Passage and │   │ Publication │   │             │
│ Enactment of│──▶│ of Intent to│──▶│   Public    │──┐
│ Legislation │   │Issue Proposed│  │  Hearings   │  │
│             │   │   Rules and │   │             │  │
│             │   │ Regulations │   │             │  │
└─────────────┘   └─────────────┘   └─────────────┘  │
┌────────────────────────────────────────────────────┘
│
│ ┌─────────────┐   ┌─────────────┐   ┌─────────────┐
│ │Publication of│  │             │   │Publication of│
│ │Proposed Rules│  │             │   │ Final Rules │
└▶│and Regulations│▶│Appropriations*│▶│and Regulations│──┐
  │and Solicitation│ │             │   │and Responses to│ │
  │  of Comments │   │             │   │  Comments on │  │
  │             │   │             │   │Proposed Rules│  │
  └─────────────┘   └─────────────┘   └─────────────┘   │
┌─────────────────────────────────────────────────────┘
│ ┌─────────────┐
│ │Announcement │
│ │  of Closing │
└▶│   Date for  │
  │  Receipt of │
  │ Proposals** │
  └─────────────┘
```

*Appropriations legislation may be enacted any time following passage of authorization legislation. Appropriations do not necessarily follow the publication of Final Rules and Regulations and the publication of Final Rules and Regulations does not always signal appropriations for a program.

**Announcement of closing date for receipt of proposals may occur prior to setting of Final Rules and Regulations.

Right to Read—From Legislation to Regulation and Solicitation

The Right to Read Program differs somewhat from the norm since its initial authorization was derived from Rules and Regulations governing programs sponsored by the now repealed Cooperative Research Act of 1964. That legislation authorized the USOE "to carry out surveys, mount dissemination projects, and develop exemplary programs in the national interest."[9] During the 1972 hearings on this legislation, congressional subcommittees were impressed by Commissioner of Education Allen's case for the need to improve the reading ability of American youth. Allen particularly emphasized the needs of the "disadvantaged" and, in the course of his presentation, referred to "the right to read" as a right of American citizens. The phrase took hold, the need was recognized, and an initial appropriation of $12 million was authorized under the Cooperative Research Act to carry out exemplary reading programs. Commissioner Allen's remarks and the testimony given at the hearings also prompted Senator Thomas Eagleton of Missouri to develop and introduce legislation specifically addressing the reading problem.

The Right to Read Program, as defined by the U.S. Office of Education, under the authorization umbrella provided by the Cooperative Research Act, encouraged three types of activity: (1) the development of demonstration projects as models for new and improved reading programs in school-based settings; (2) the development of community based projects allowing parents and community residents to participate in formulating and operating reading programs in nonschool settings; and (3) the provision of technical assistance to state educational agencies in coordinating their training efforts and in developing and administering training programs for reading staff.

Between 1972 and 1974, the interaction between USOE executives, program officers and staff, professional associations, practitioners in the field, and interested legislators generated decisions that continued to define the program. The specific program dimensions were generally established by initiatives of the funding agency or program office. The program, from birth through the initial years of development, was a child of the Right to Read Office.[10]

It was not until after the signing of the National Reading Improvement Act in August 1977, which incorporated the Right to Read Program under Title VII of the Educational Amendments of 1974, that the development of the program was shaped by the influences and "rites of passage" that affect the birth and development of all programs passing through the stages of formulation, legislative regulation setting, proposal solicitation, proposal review, and negotiation of award.

Within three weeks of President Ford's signing of Public Law 93-380 (the Educational Amendments of 1974), a task force of Right to Read Office staff was assigned by the office director to draw up regulations to govern the program. After several revisions and consultation with various government offices responsible for assisting in development of the Rules and Regulations, the Proposed Rules were printed in the *Federal Register* on December 4, 1975.

Like all Proposed Rules, they presented the government's citation of the authorizing legislation, the intent of the program, the types of activities authorized and parties eligible to submit, the criteria governing proposal development, and other government regulations and provisions applicable to proposal submittal and the fiscal and program management of a funded project. Comments and recommendations were also invited. The scope of the information contained in the Proposed Rules and the scope of the activities and discrete programs authorized under Title VII of the Educational Amendments of 1974 (titled the National Reading Improvement Program) are reflected in the program Index, Table 3.1.

TABLE 3.1. *Index to Right to Read Proposed Rules and Regulations*

Part 162–National Reading Improvement Program

Subpart A–General	Subpart D–Special Emphasis Projects
Sec.	Sec.
162.1 Scope and purposes.	162.35 Scope and purpose.
162.2 Definitions.	162.36 Definitions.
162.3–162.9 [Reserved]	162.37 Eligibility; number of applications.
Subpart B–Reading Improvement Projects	162.38 Nature of projects.
	162.39 Review and certification by State educational agencies.
162.10 Scope and purpose.	
162.11 Eligible applicants; nature of projects.	162.40 Application requirements.
	162.41 Evaluation criteria.
162.12 Application requirements.	162.42 District-wide project award.
162.13 Review of applications by State educational agencies and State advisory councils.	162.43 [Reserved]
	162.44 Duration of projects.
	162.45 Size of awards; allowable costs.
162.14 Evaluation criteria.	
162.15 Equitable geographic distribution.	162.46–162.49 [Reserved]
	Subpart E–Reading Academy Program
162.16 [Reserved]	
162.17 Duration of projects.	162.50 Scope and purpose.
162.18 Size of awards; allowable costs.	162.51 Definitions.
	162.52 Application requirements.
162.19–162.24 [Reserved]	162.53 Evaluation criteria.
Subpart C–State Heading Improvement Programs	162.54 Allowable costs.
	162.55 Project duration.
	Appendix A–Part B of title VII of Pub. L. 93–380.
162.25 Scope and purpose.	
162.26 Allotments; reallotments.	Appendix B–Manual Guidelines for the Reading Academy Program.
162.27 Standard of excellence.	
162.28 [Reserved]	
162.29 Judicial review.	Authority: Title VII of Pub. L. 93–380 (20 U.S.C. 1901–1982).
162.30–162.34 [Reserved]	

(*Federal Regulations*, pp. 56679–80, December 4, 1975.)

Although all subparts are covered simultaneously under the Proposed Rules, for purposes of analysis and the planning of submittal strategies they may be considered as discrete programs. The scope and purpose, the eligibility of applicants, the participants in the review process, the magnitude and allocation of the appropriations, and the criteria for proposal review differed from program to program.

The Proposed Rules provided the first public opportunity for potential submitters to test the fit between agency and submitting institution definitions of the problem and authorized strategies to address the problem. Legislation and the notification of intent to issue Rules and Regulations provide earlier opportunities to assess the feasibility of responding, but the detailed Proposed Rules allow institutions to determine the desirability and feasibility of developing and submitting a proposal. Excerpts from Subpart A (Scope and Purposes of Program) and Subpart B (Reading Improvement Projects) confirm this observation.

TABLE 3.2. Excerpts from Right to Read Proposed Rules and Regulations

Subpart A—General

§ 162.1 Scope and purposes.

(a) *Scope.* This part applies to projects assisted with funds appropriated pursuant to the National Reading Improvement Program, title VII of Pub. L. 93-380.

(b) *Purposes.* The purposes of the programs carried out pursuant to this part are, through grants and contracts to State and local educational agencies and other non-profit organizations, to:

(1) Provide financial assistant to encourage State and local educational agencies to undertake projects to strengthen reading instructional programs in elementary grades;

(2) Provide financial assistance for the development and enhancement of necessary skills of instructional and other educational staff for reading programs;

(3) Develop a means by which measurable objectives for reading programs can be established and progress toward these objectives assessed;

(4) Develop the capacity of preelementary school children for reading;

(5) Establish and improve preelementary school programs in language arts and reading; and

(6) Provide financial assistance to promote literacy among youths and adults.

(c) *Other pertinent regulations.* Awards under this part are subject to applicable provisions contained in Subchapter A of this chapter (relating to fiscal, administrative, property management, and other matters, 45 CFR Parts 100, 100a, 100b).

(20 U.S.C. 1901)

§ 162.2 Definitions.

As used in this part:

"Act" means title VII of the Education Amendments of 1974, Pub. L. 93-380.

TABLE 3.2. (cont.)

"Elementary school" means a day or residential school which provides elementary education, as determined under State law.

"Commissioner" means the U.S. Commissoner of Education.

"Innovative" means a program element which is new and different to participants in project activities.

"Institution of higher education" means an institution of higher education in any State as defined under the Higher Education Act of 1965, as amended. (20 U.S.C. 1141)

"Local education agency" means a public board of education or other public authority legally constituted within a State for either administrative control or direction of, or to perform a service function for, public elementary or secondary schools in a city, county, township, school district, or other political subdivision of a State, or a combination of school districts or counties recognized in a State as an administrative agency for its public elementary or secondary schools. The term also includes any other public institution or agency having administrative control and direction of a public elementary or secondary school.

"Non-profit educational or child care institution" means any public or private non-profit organization which sponsors a regular, on-going educational or child care program for preschool age children.

"Reading deficiencies" means that reading achievement is less than that which would normally be expected for children of comparable ages or comparable grades of school; for children in grades 2–8 this would mean one or more years below grade level in reading.

"Project" means those activities of a granteee or contractor which the Commissioner determines to be eligible for Federal financial assistance.

"Reading-related activities" means any activities directly or indirectly connected with skills and/or behaviors in the area of reading; for example, listening, speaking, writing activities, reading games, discussing illustrations, classifying and categorizing, and developing auditory and visual perceptual skills . . . .

(20 U.S.C. 1901 and 1921)

§ 162.3–162.9 [Reserved]

Subpart B—Reading Improvement Projects

§ 162.10 Scope and purpose.

(a) *Scope.* This subpart applies to projects assisted with funds appropriated to carry out part A, section 705 of title VII of Pub. L. 93–380;

(20 U.S.C. 1921)

(b) *Purpose.* The purpose of the program carried out pursuant to this subpart is, through grants to eligible recipients, to support:

(1) Projects to strengthen reading instructional programs in elementary school(s) having large numbers or a high percentage of children with reading deficiencies; and

(2) Projects to establish and improve programs in language arts and reading in preelementary school(s), in areas where there are large numbers or a high

TABLE 3.2. (cont.)

percentage of elementary school children with reading deficiencies, to develop the capacity of preelementary school children for reading.

(20 U.S.C. 1921(a))

§ 162.11 Eligible applicants; nature of projects.

(a) *Eligible applicants.* (1) As stated in section 705 of the Act, local educational agencies, State educational agencies, or both, may apply for elementary school projects described in paragraph (b) (1) (i) of this section and the preelementary school projects described in paragraph (b) (1) (ii) of this section. In addition, non-profit educational or child care institutions may apply for the preelementary school projects;

(2) Though multiple applications may be sumitted by a single applicant. In no case will more than one grant for an elementary school project and one grant for a preelementary school project be awarded to the same applicant;

(b) *Nature of projects.* (1) Two types of grants will be awarded pursuant to this subpart;

(i) Projects to carry out in elementary school(s) having large numbers or a high percentage of children with reading deficiencies, programs involving the use of innovative methods, systems, materials, or other elements which show promise of overcoming the reading deficiencies; and

(ii) Projects to carry out in kindergarten(s), nursery school(s), child care institution(s), or other preschool institutions(s) (in areas where elementary schools having large numbers or a high percentage of children with reading deficiencies are located), programs involving the use of innovative methods, systems, materials, or other elements which show promise of developing the capacity for reading of preelementary school children who might otherwise develop reading deficiencies: . . . .

(20 U.S.C. 1921(a), (b), and (c); 1221c(b) (1), 1232c(b) (1))

§ 162.12 Application requirements.

The Commissioner will award a grant to a State educational agency, local educational agency, or other eligible applicant under this subpart only upon an application submitted to the Commissioner which meets the following requirements:

(a) *Project objectives.* The application must set forth:

(1) Specific and measurable objectives related to overcoming reading deficiencies of children in the project school(s) including (only with respect to elementary school projects described in § 162.11 (b) (1) (i) plans and strategies for having the children in project schools reading at the appropriate grade level at the end of grade three;

(2) A proposed time frame for accomplishing these objectives; and

(3) An evaluation component providing for the collection, verification, and analysis of data to measure the extent the objectives are accomplished by the project;

(20 U.S.C. 1921(a), (b), (c) (2))

TABLE 3.2. (cont.)

(b) *Project school(s).* (1) The application must identify the school(s) and the class(es) to be served by the project and provide information on how the school(s) and class(es) were selected for the project, the numbers and percentages of children in the project school(s) with reading deficiencies, and the nature of reading deficiencies of those children, including (only with respect to elementary school projects described in § 162.11 (b) (1) (i) documentation that appropriate measures have already been taken by the applicant to analyze the reasons why elementary school children are not reading at the appropriate grade levels and the results of those measures;

(2) The application must provide demographic information on children in the school(s) to be served by the project, including information on the socio-economic, racial, ethnic, language and cultural composition of the school(s); and

(3) The application must:

(i) Provide information on existing reading programs and activities in the project school(s), including information on the resources and methods used to teach reading or reading-related activities to children and the extent of effectiveness of those resources and methods; and

(ii) Explain how the proposed project will improve or expand upon the existing reading activities and programs, including a description of innovative methods, systems, materials, or other elements which will be used in the project to overcome reading deficiencies;

(20 U.S.C. 1921(a), (b), (c) (1))

(c) *Program requirements.* The Commissioner will award a grant under this subpart only upon an application submitted to the Commissioner which meets the requirements in paragraphs (a) and (b) of this section, as applicable, and which sets forth a reading program which includes the following elements, as applicable:

(1) *All applications.* All applications under this subpart must;

(i) (A) Document that there has been participation in the planning and development of the program described in the application by parents of children to be served by the program, the policy-making board of the applicant, and leaders of the cultural and educational resources of the area to be served, including representatives of such organizations as institutions of higher education, non-profit private schools, public and private non-profit agencies such as libraries, museums, educational radio and television organizations, and other cultural and educational resource agencies of the community.

(B) Include a description of procedures which have been used to provide the public at large in the area or areas proposed to be served by the project with an opportunity to have input in the planning of the program described in the application (such as through public notice and hearings); and

(C) Provide for the continuing participation of groups and representatives described under paragraph (c) (1) (i) (A) of this section in the development and implementation of the program described in the application;

(ii) Set forth a reading program which provides for:

(A) Diagnostic testing designed to identify children with reading deficiencies,

---

TABLE 3.2. (cont.)

including the identification of conditions which, without appropriate other treatment, can be expected to impede or prevent children from learning to read;

(B) Planning and establishing comprehensive reading programs in project schools;

(C) Preservice training programs for project teaching personnel, including teacher aides and other ancillary educational personnel within the project schools, and inservice training and development programs, where feasible, designed to enable these personnel to improve their ability to teach students to read;

(D) Participation of the school faculty, the policy-making board of the applicant, members of the school administration, parents, and students in reading-related activities which stimulate an interest in reading and are conducive to the improvement of reading skills;....

(2) *Elementary school projects.* (i) Applications under this subpart for elementary school programs under § 162.11(b) (1) (i) must set forth a reading program which, in addition to meeting the requirements in paragraph (c) (1) of this section, provides:

(A) Reading instruction focused upon elementary school children whose reading achievement is less than that normally expected for children of comparable ages or in comparable grades of school, but also instruction which provides for every child in classes involved in the project;

(B) Periodic testing for elementary school children on a sufficiently frequent basis to measure accurately reading achievement;

(C) Participation on an equitable basis by children enrolled in non-profit private elementary schools in the area to be served (after consultation with the appropriate private school officials) to an extent consistent with the number of such children whose educational needs are of the kind the program is intended to meet.

(ii) Applicants must also: (A) Indicate the number of children enrolled in nonpublic schools who are expected to participate in each program and the manner of their expected participation; and

(B) Document that there has been participation in the planning and development of the program described in the application by officials representing non-profit private elementary schools in the area to be served with children whose educational needs are of the kind which the program is intended to meet, and provide for what kind of continuing participation by those officials there will be in the development and implementation of the program;

(3) *Preelementary school projects.* Applications for preelementary school programs under § 162.11(b) (1) (ii) must set forth a reading program which, in addition to meeting the requirements in paragraph (c) (1) of this section provides:

(i) A test of reading proficiency at the conclusion, minimally of the first-grade programs into which the preelementary school program is integrated for children who had previously participated in the preelementary school program;

(ii) Assessment, evaluation, and collection of information on individual children by teachers during each year of the preelementary program to be made

TABLE 3.2. *(cont.)*

available for teachers in the subsequent year, in order that continuity for the individual child be maintained; and

(iii) Appropriate coordination with the reading programs of the educational agencies or institutions where the preelementary school children will be next in attendance, including any necessary arrangements by the applicant with those educational agencies or institutions for meeting the requirements relating to testing and test results described in paragraph (c) (3) (i) of this section and paragraph (c) (1) (ii) (E) of this section; and

(d) *Other information.* Applications may include other appropriate information to respond to criteria in § 162.14.

(20 U.S.C. 1921(b))

§ 162.13 Review of applications by State educational agencies and State advisory councils.

(a) The Commissioner will not approve an application submitted under this subpart unless the State educational agency has: . . . .
individual children, including activities to meet the special reading needs of children from diverse cultural and linguistic backgrounds;

(D) Work constructively and positively, on a group and individual basis, with children, parents, and other educational personnel;

(E) Effectively utilize a variety of approaches to the teaching of reading, including sequenced instruction, integration of reading instruction into other subject matter areas, flexible grouping of students based on student interest, needs, and abilities, and individualized instruction; and

(F) Plan and manage overall reading programs, including aspects such as problem-solving techniques, needs assessment and planning instruments, record-keeping, the identification and use of program resources, and program evaluation;

(4) Involvement in the project of school faculty, parents, the policy-making board of the applicant, and leaders of educational and cultural resources of the area to be served (15 points) as measured by such factors as whether:

(i) Two way communication is fostered between the project schools and appropriate groups outside the school;

(ii) Practical involvement of parents and board members in carrying out project activities is permitted; and

(iii) The project staff provides evaluative information to parents and board members;

(5) Periodic achievement testing (5 points), as measured by such factors as whether:

(i) Testing will be done with the children at appropriate times and frequencies;

(ii) The project staff delineates before the testing what the tests are intended to measure, how the test results are going to be used, and the audiences for whom the test results are intended;

(iii) The same level of the same test is used for both pre- and post-testing of children: . . . .

TABLE 3.2. (cont.)

(iv) Project staff will carefully administer and score the tests according to the procedures outlined by test publishers;

(v) There is a clear rationale why the test measures will be criterion-referenced, norm-referenced, or informal; and

(vi) Project staff will scrutinize carefully whether the causes for observed gains are due to the treatment or other factors;

(6) Appropriate use of bilingual education methods and techniques (5 points) as measured by such factors as whether:

(i) There will be increased use of culturally relevant resources appropriate to the children in project school(s);

(ii) Students will be provided a knowledge of the history and culture associated with their languages;

(iii) Students will develop listening, speaking, reading, writing, and other academic skills in two languages;...

(7) Collection and assessment of information on the reading needs of individual children to be made available for teachers in the subsequent year, including that information yielded by periodic testing (5 points), as measured by such factors as whether the assessment is designed to:

(i) Aim at factual information rather than mere opinion:

(ii) Include information on both cognitive and affective factors related to reading; and

(iii) Be done with uniform data collection instruments that can be used as a part of the school's total evaluation design;

(20 U.S.C. 1921(b))

(8) Publication of the test results on achievement by grade level and, where appropriate, by school, without identification of achievement of individual children (5 points), as measured by such factors as whether publication and interpretation of test results is done in a way to:

(i) Protect the children;

(ii) Be understandable to the people who receive the results;

(iii) Present pre-test and post-test results with adequate explanation of the correlations;

(c) *Additional criteria for preelementary school projects.* The Commissioner will evaluate applications for preelementary school projects on the basis of the criteria set forth in paragraphs (a) and (b) of this section, according to the indicated weights, and the following criteria, weighted as indicated:

(1) The extent the project goals are commensurate with the appropriate developmental stages for the children to be served (10 points);

(2) The extent the project assesses the needs of preschool children by employing reliable and field-tested tools which can diagnose, screen, and predict potential readiness for reading (10 points);

(3) The extent qualified teachers use multi-teaching strategies and varied materials and resources in providing reading readiness experience (5 points);

(4) The extent the project takes into account the various modalities for learning (5 points); and

Table 3.2. (cont.)

(5) The extent provision is made for parent education in child management (5 points).

(20 U.S.C. 1921(b))

§ 162.15 Equitable geographic distribution.

(a) In approving applications under this subpart the Commissioner will, to the maximum extent feasible, assure an equitable distribution of funds throughout the United States and among urban and rural areas. In assuring an equitable distribution of funds throughout the United States, the Commissioner will consider: . . .

§ 162.16 [Reserved]

§ 162.17 Duration of projects.

(a) Individual grant awards under this subpart shall be for a period of up to one year, subject to the possibility that continuation grants may be made to support a project for a second year in accordance with the provisions of this section:

(b) Grant awards to support the second year of a project already funded under this subpart may be made, subject to the availability of funds and to the following provisions:

(1) Continuation applications will not be competitive with applications for new grant awards, but will be competitive with other applications for continuation awards; and

(2) Applications for continuation awards will be reviewed to determine: . . .

(20 U.S.C. 1921)

§ 162.18 Size of awards; allowable costs.

(a) Although there will be no formula for establishing any limits to the amount of assistance provided under this subpart, it is suggested that applicants base their total dollar request under this subpart on the product of $15 multiplied by the number of elementary school children to be served within the project school(s);

(b) It is expected that most awards under this subpart will range between $15,000 and $125,000 for elementary school projects and between $5,000 and $25,000 for preelementary school projects with most of the awards made at the lower halves of these ranges. Nothing in this section shall be construed to limit the size of any particular grant award under this subpart; . . .

The substance and style of the Proposed Rules are the result of events within the various agencies responsible for their formulation. These events will be addressed later in the chapter. It is important to note, however, that the Proposed Rules are the preliminary statement of legally binding policies and procedures; not surprisingly, they read more like an insurance policy than an invitation to consider participating in the development of a program.

76 The Dynamics of Funding

The publication of the Proposed Rules was followed by the Notice of Closing Date for Receipt of Applications, published on December 16, in the *Federal Register*. Separate due dates for Reading Academy (Subpart E) Special Emphasis (Subpart D), and Reading Improvement Program (Subpart B) applications were established, reinforcing the independence of the different types of programs.

The deadlines established by this notice created a situation common to the proposal submittal process. The closing dates for receipt of applications preceded the issuance of Final Rules and Regulations, necessitating proposal submittal before possible changes, resulting from submitted comments, that might affect the nature of program activities and the subsequent review of the proposals. Simultaneously, the time available for program planning and proposal development (between the announcement of the closing date and the due date itself) exceeded the thirty-five-day period required by law between announcement of the closing date in the *Federal Register* and receipt of proposals at the regional or Washington receipt points. The cumulative effect was to elevate the Proposed Rules to the status of Final Rules for purposes of proposal planning and development.

A final set of public events that shaped the Right to Read Program and the solicitation of proposals illustrates the interdependency of program offices and the legislative and executive branches of government. The potential of this interdependency to disrupt the planning machinery of submitting institutions and program offices should never be underestimated.

During the last week of the first session of Congress ending on December 19, new reading legislation, designed to broaden the Office of Education's options in administering the Reading Improvement Act programs, was rushed through Congress and submitted to the President for signature. Congress had only appropriated $17 million for implementation of the program and the National Reading Improvement Act provisions required the Office of Education to spend the first $30 million of each year's reading appropriation on direct grants to school-based reading programs. The appropriation provisions of the act thus created a situation in which the State Leadership Training and National Impact programs, funded previously under the defunct Cooperative Research Act, would have to be terminated. In addition, the appropriation stipulations would have had dire consequences for authorized Reading Academy programs that were not school based but for which proposals had already been solicited.

It is not necessary to detail the amendments to the appropriation legislation finally incorporated into the law. It is important to note, however, that these amendments resulted in reallocation of monies among the several programs, and led the Right to Read Office to issue a supplementary request for Reading Academy proposals.

The follow-up requests opened the competition to institutions that had not submitted proposals before the earlier closing date, changed the time lines for reviewing proposals and implementing programs, and reduced allocations to other programs. Private nonprofit institutions, working collaboratively with local educational agencies, were given thirty-five days to submit proposals. At this point, the public proposal solicitation process came to a close. Final Regulations were finally published in the *Federal Register* on May 26, 1976, and funding announcements were made later that summer.

The events influencing the Right to Read Program are particularly informative for the legislative and agency definition stages of the funding process. The origin of the program under the Cooperative Research Act illustrates the interplay of forces within and between government agencies and the legislative branch that contributes to program formulation before legislation. Although external events generally provide the major impetus for most legislatively initiated program thrusts, the ability of federal agencies to initiate programs is demonstrated by this case.

REGULATION SETTING: EVENTS IN THE PRIVATE DOMAIN

The functioning of any large government bureaucracy cannot be understood or appreciated by examining only the public pronouncements of the organization or the visible decision-making process. Just as interactions between individuals and organizational structures (e.g., community agencies, schools, and universities) shape both individual and institutional behavior, the interaction of persons and structures within government offices shapes agency and program office outputs.

A significant number of decisions made in the name of institutions are formed by individuals in the privacy provided by organizational structures. These individuals shape, and are shaped by, the environment of the institution; information shared with the public is shaped by the same environment. Thus, the nature of the decisions and the way they are communicated may not be understood by those outside this environment. Behaviors of government employees may seem illogical and absurd to persons unfamiliar with governmental organizational machinery. Examination of institutional constraints and their impact on individuals responsible for developing programs and shaping proposal requests hopefully will make the process understandable within the governmental context.

Many institutions first secure information from a government funding agency in the Notice of Intent to Publish Proposed Rules or at conferences related to the publication of the Rules. These events, however, generally represent the end of a complex and lengthy procedure in which individuals in organizational units within the government agencies participate. Many inconsistencies in the proposal solicitation process and much of the complexity of the program development process is attributable directly to organizational requirements and institutional norms that govern the processes:

78 The Dynamics of Funding

1. Program requests must conform to the intent of the authorizing legislation, and project scope must be consistent with the level of appropriation.
2. Program criteria in the Rules and Regulations must reflect objectives of program officers responsible for implementing and administering the program.
3. Program features must acknowledge the priorities of the current administration.
4. Rules and Regulations constitute a legally binding document stipulating legally prescribed procedures and policies, and must be consistent with the authority provided by the legislation.

The features of any program reflected in the criteria for proposal review are thus a product of political, legal, and fiscal requirements of individual government offices; in addition, they constitute an implicit statement of educational policy developed by the program office responsible for its administration. The organizational machinery established to develop and process proposal requests provides for input from the several organizational units that set these requirements.

The Office of Regulations in Washington, D.C., is the hub of the regulation-setting machinery responsible for developing proposal requests. Within that office, chart-lined walls record the status of all legislatively approved programs in the regulation-setting process. Checkpoints on the charts, indicating the precise location of all programs, reveal the complex path a piece of legislation must travel on its way to final regulation setting. The major offices and their organizational units that participate in formulating programs are identified in Figure 3.2. These units, and the variables influencing their behavior that are not systematically communicated to the public, make up the private decision-making domain.

The importance of individual offices and the nature of their involvement in building regulations varies from one piece of legislation to another, and from one administration to another. Their roles also may be influenced by the political, programmatic, or personal dispositions or power of the chief administrators of any organizational unit. Certain functions of the various offices remain constant, however, and are critical to understanding the dynamics of issuing proposal requests. Let us examine the role of these offices in the context of the Right to Read regulation-setting process.

FUNCTIONS OF THE PROGRAM OFFICE

Without exception, the program office or bureau is first to translate the authorizing legislation into functional programs. Its power is that of the agenda

TREASURE HUNT
$70,000

Trulyowenfree.net

CAN YOU CRACK MY PICTURE PUZZLE CODE, AND BE THE FIRST TO FIND MY HIDDEN PIRATE TREASURE HOARD?

(I really doubt it...)

FIGURE 3.2. *Rules and Regulations Setting: The Private Domain*

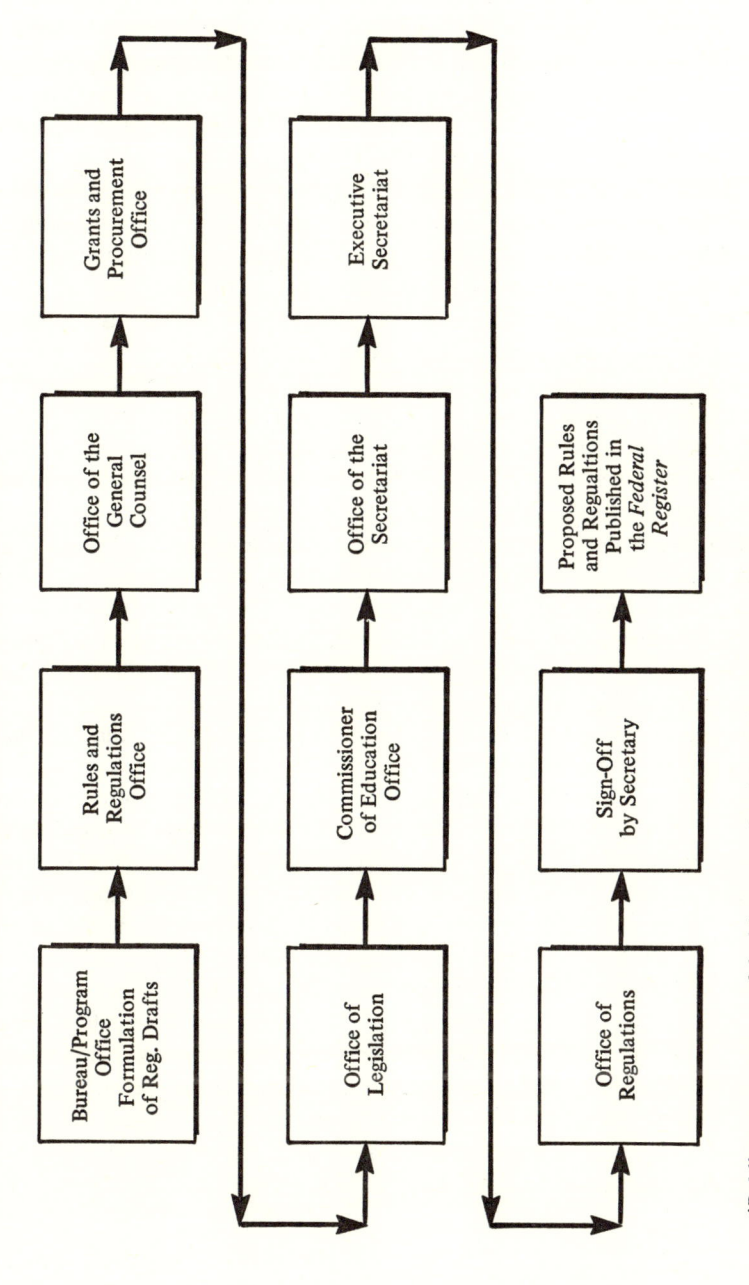

*Public announcement of decisions negotiated in both public and private domains.

setter and program moderator combined. Its role, if carried out effectively, leaves an indelible mark on program priorities; program criteria contained in the Rules and Regulations; the way institutional recommendations are handled; the way the program is implemented; and, ultimately, the program's success in securing future appropriations and surmounting obstacles created by changing congressional moods. Strong program offices, with influential directors and large staffs, can affect considerably any future legislation crucial to their continuation and growth.

In the case of the Right to Read Office, the first item of business was to identify program elements that would address needs identified in the congressional hearings that led to authorizing legislation. As in any organization, formal and informal staff discussions played a major role in shaping the draft documents that contributed eventually to policy statements. In this case, however, criteria for program development were explicit in the legislation; the staff was limited in developing major program features and setting priorities. Discussions focused more on program characteristics and the relative priorities of, and relationships between, the several authorized programs.

This is not always the case. In programs covering broadly defined problems and/or in programs authorized by loosely worded legislation, the latitude given program offices to define a program may be considerably greater. In such cases, conflicts between director and staff and among staff can become major power struggles; the resolution of the conflict is then reflected in the program's characteristics. Moreover, such conflicts may extend beyond the program office and draw other affected offices and legislative units into the fray. Such conflicts occurred often in the formulation of many Great Society programs, in which the wording of authorizing legislation was significantly more general and thus open to widely varying interpretations.*

Regardless of the level of conflict, however, initial discussions in the program office are central to the functioning of the funding system. The program office's problem definition represents an accommodation between the perception of the problem derived from office organizational and programmatic needs and the problem definition implicit in the legislative authorization. The precise nature of the accommodations is reflected in the Rules and Regulations that set the parameters for program implementation.

Initial discussions of the Right to Read task force and resulting draft papers raised questions for other organizational units responsible for regulation setting. The lawyer assigned to Right to Read by the General Counsel's office was requested to review questions of legislative intent. Counsel's answers came from analysis of conference reports of the congressional subcommittee responsible for reporting out the authorizing legislation. Thus, the actions of program office

---

*Discussion of the development of the Teacher Center Program in the preceding chapter alluded to this problem. The ill-fated Teacher Renewal Program, authorized by the Education Professions Development Act of 1965 that first introduced the concept into the U.S. Office of Education machinery, was accompanied by such conflict.

staff were shaped, from the outset, by legal definitions of legislative intent. The program office's role in shaping Rules and Regulations can be sensed by referring to Table 3.3. These excerpts detail initial activities of the task force in drawing up program regulations, before submitting the regulations to other offices for review.

TABLE 3.3. LOG: Part A, Title VII Regulation Development

1974	Sept. 11	Task Force assigned to Title VII Regulations by director
	Sept. 12	Part A assigned to program officer
	Sept. 17	First draft distributed by officer to Right to Read staff for input
	Sept. 18	Meeting with General Counsel; advice to program office that Part A so detailed that it should only require minimal regulations, perhaps just criteria.
	Oct. 9	Advice earlier sought from outside panel of experts received
	Oct. 10	Revised Part A regulations distributed to Right to Read staff
	Oct. 17	Request for written comments on Part A from all staff members from program officer
	Oct. 26	General Counsel indicates that Part A Regulations, as written, do not adequately address several issues
	Oct. 27	Program officers send to Right to Read staff 17 issues/questions about Part A
	Dec. 9	Rep from Office of the General Counsel indicates that Part A Regulations need to be expanded
	Dec. 12	Program officer prepares 13 issues/questions for General Counsel
	Dec. 17	Program officer sends 2nd draft of Regulations to General Counsel and asks staff for comments
	Dec. 23	Office of Grants and Contracts responds in writing to some issues raised by program office; meeting with General Counsel
1975	Jan. 13	Written response to OGC by program officer
	Jan. 17	Program officer gives third draft to Right to Read staff for input
	Jan. 20	During meeting with Sec'y. Weinberger's staff, Right to Read staff asked to respond to issues raised by program officer
	Feb. 14	Program officer sends another draft of regs. to Right to Read staff for review
	Feb. 26	Sen. Eagleton sends letter to Dr. Bell (Commissioner of Education) asking about the role of SEAs in Part A
	Mar. 14	Meeting of Right to Read staff members who wish to comment on the latest draft of the regs.

82   The Dynamics of Funding

Table 3.3. (cont.)

1975	Mar. 14	Revised fourth draft sent to General Counsel after input from Right to Read staff
	June	Large number of letters received from SEAs asking about their eligibility under Part A and amount of money to be granted them under this part of program
	June 30	Right to Read receives General Counsel's revision of the fourth draft submitted on March 14
	Dec. 4	Proposed Regulations printed in the *Federal Register*
	Dec. 16	Closing date of March 16, 1976, published in *Federal Register*
1976	Jan. 5	Deadline for receipt of public comments on Proposed Regulations
	May 26	Final Regulations published in *Federal Register*
	Late August	Announcement of grant awards under Title VII
	Late Sept.	Formal notification of grant awards received by successful submitters

The program finally received definition in the form of Proposed Rules and Regulations in December 1975. In the interim, program policies, content, and procedures were negotiated among and between program office staff, the General Counsel's Office and the Office of Grants and Contracts, chief officers in the U.S. Office of Education, and interested legislators and professionals. Most negotiations took place in the private domain; the decisions represented primarily the reconciliation of functional needs of individuals and organizational units within the government bureaucracy. Some of the functions of the units the program office must deal with continually in the private domain of decision making are treated briefly.

Functions of the Office of the General Counsel and the Office of Rules and Regulations

The office of the General Counsel assists both in developing and reviewing program regulations. The relative importance of the aid varies, depending on the nature of the legislation and the size and capabilities of staff in a program office. Although program office staff are assigned to writing the regulations, understaffed offices occasionally rely on attorneys assigned by the General Counsel to perform this task. The function of the Counsel's office, however, is generally to provide technical assistance in developing regulations. The assigned attorney is responsible for submitting regulations to the Office of Rules and Regulations in a form appropriate for review and rapid clearance. The Office of Rules and Regulations, in addition to its clearinghouse function, may edit the format of regulation drafts during the review process. The form of proposed regulations is thus determined by the Office of the General Counsel and the Office of Rules and Regulations, as well as the program office.

The impact of the General Counsel's Office on the Rules and Regulations is clearly reflected in the form and substance of the document. Attorneys' rulings on legislative intent and the regulations' conformity to this intent directly affect program policy. Rulings determine the eligibility of parties to participate in the program, the nature of clearances required at the state and local level, and the procedures to be followed by the program office in soliciting proposals. Counsel's authority extends, moreover, beyond determining the fit between legislative intent and program office guidelines. As mentioned earlier, all USOE rule-making and administrative functions are governed by the statutory framework established by the Administrative Procedures Act and General Education Provisions Act. General Counsel ruling on conformity to the regulations in these acts bear directly on the timing of request, the dissemination of information about pending rules, and the announcement of awards.

The response of many proposal writers, initially confronting Rules and Regulations in the *Federal Register,* is like that of a law student initially confronting a legal brief. Rules and Regulations governing the submittal of proposals are legally binding statements of policies and procedures, expressed in the vocabulary of the legal profession. As such, they must be analyzed and responded to with some degree of legal acumen.

Functions of the Grants and Procurement Office and the Office of Legislation

After review of the aforementioned offices, but before submission to the Commissioner of Education for review, the Proposed Rules must be cleared by the Grants and Procurement Office and the Office of Legislation. In many ways, this clearance process formalizes steps taken when the Rules were developed. The Office of Grants and Procurement, whose decisions take on greater importance when proposals are reviewed for funding and monies are allocated, is responsible for checking the Rules against the content of the General Education Provisions Act and any allocation specifications in the legislation.

The Office of Legislation, which links the Office of Education with Congress, is responsible for checking the evolving Rules against the intent of the legislation. Generally, there is constant interaction between the program office and Congress throughout the rule- and regulation-setting process. In the case of the Right to Read rule making, Senator Eagleton took great interest in the role of state education agencies. As a cosponsor of the authorizing legislation, he had a vested interest in the fit between the legislation's intent and the regulations' sensitivity to the concerns of those responsible for the bill's inception. This step in the process is particularly important; in effect, it serves as ratification of a negotiated contract between the bill's sponsors and their constituents and the program office responsible for its development. Like any negotiated agreement, events occurring during negotiations can change the environment and render earlier perceptions and agreements inoperable. For this reason, interaction between program offices and Congress tends to become an ongoing part of the rule-making process. What normally constitutes a *pro forma* approval can be transformed into a critical review juncture, should program officer initiatives be greater than those associated with the intent of the legislation. Significant changes in the composition of Congress, between passage of the authorizing legislation and the submittal of Rules to The Office of Legislation for clearance, can affect congressional support drastically.

Functions of the Office of the Commissioner of Education and the Executive Secretariat

With the forwarding of the Rules to the Commissioner of Education and the Office of the Secretary and the Executive Secretariat, the formal announcement of the program is imminent. The Commissioner of Education, representing the executive branch, assesses the pending Rules from the perspective of the administration's policy requests and directives, and tests their compatibility with the administration's goals. The authorizing legislation is already on the books and previous clearances have verified the regulations' conformity to legislative intent and to legal and legislative constraints. Thus, the Commissioner's role mainly is to advise executive staff or others in a position to initiate amendments linked to appropriations, should appropriations not be set. Or, the Commissioner may recommend changes that necessitate returning the Rules for redrafting to offices that previously gave clearance. The situation is rather like landing on "Chance" in the game of *Monopoly* and receiving directions to "go back four spaces, do not pass go."

Assuming no such directive, the Proposed Rules are referred back to the Secretary of Education's office for review by the Executive Secretariat, a body comprised of USOE assistant secretaries representing legislation, administration, management, and planning, as well as the Comptroller and affected bureau of program chiefs. If the representatives concur that the management and programmatic components are clearly specified, the documents are forwarded to the Office of the Secretary for sign-off for publication as Proposed Rules in the *Federal Register*.

TIME LINES GOVERNING DECISION MAKING

The DHEW clearance process, as distinct from the Regulation development process, calls for Regulation sign-offs by the Office of Civil Rights, the Comptroller's Office, and the Office of Human Development, in addition to the offices previously identified. Thus, the potential for delay in the communication of Rules and Regulations to the public is considerable. A request by the Office of Civil Rights for a provision on sex discrimination, or a request by the Office of Human Development for provisions assuring the protection of human subjects, could necessitate additional meetings and the incorporation of such provisions into the regulations.

In the case of the Office of Education, the Commissioner of Education is required to report a schedule for promulgation of Rules and Regulations to the appropriate congressional committees within 60 days after passage of legislation. The law carries provisions requiring proposed regulation setting 180 days after submittal of the schedule. This schedule, however, with the approval of the committees, may be amended to provide additional time.

Given a legal framework of 240 days (with provisions for extension) for the creation of Rules and Regulations, and given the range of perspectives and needs of individuals and organizational units participating in the process, the outsider can appreciate the impact of the internal workings of the federal bureaucracy. This impact is felt on both the form of Rules and Regulations ultimately communicated to the public and on the timing of the release of information.

THE PUBLIC-PRIVATE INTERFACE

Although the public and private domains of decision making have been treated separately in order to illustrate the factors shaping the development of proposal requests, any analysis of funding opportunities must consider both domains simultaneously. The interaction between the public and private decision-making processes at several points in the organizational structure must be recognized. The agency soliciting proposals has its own needs and interests, some of which are public knowledge whereas others are private. Different units within the soliciting agency have their own needs that are influenced by their functions.

There is evidence to suggest that public acts initiated by the federal government will assume increasing importance in shaping proposal requests in the future (that is, notification of intent to publish Proposed Rules, establishment of specified timelines for budget setting, advance notice of proposal due dates, and increased use of public meetings to solicit comments of interested parties). However, precedent and the magnitude of formal and informal bureaucratic structures that shape institutional behavior suggest that private decisions within funding agencies will remain critical to the funding process. This private influence is felt in the decision making of both state governments and private foundations. Program guidelines and submittal procedures accompanying state and foundation proposal invitations generally reflect the negotiations of units and individuals within these institutions regarding program priorities, selection criteria, and solicitation procedures. Although priorities set by state boards, commissions, or agencies must conform to authorization and appropriation legislation, the negotiation of priorities often occurs without communication to interested publics. Most state offices have no formal procedures to disseminate information to the public equivalent to those procedures accompanying the federal regulation-setting process. In such settings, the influence of informal structures on the program development and proposal solicitation processes is increased.

The importance of tracing events in the private domain for one attempting to understand the funding process is related directly to the amount and quality of formal communication between the funding agency and the interested publics. In the case of foundations, annual reports and occasional newsletters provide the only predictable formal communication to potential proposal developers. General statements of priorities, the identification of programs funded in the past, and the indication of foundation fiscal health provide insufficient information for effective responses. Decisions made and priorities set by individuals within foundations are so influential that access to the private domain becomes central to understanding and responding appropriately to the decision-making process of these funding organizations.

SUMMARY

One might conclude, understandably, that the development of the Right to Read regulations, which essentially legitimized an ongoing program, was sufficiently unique to preclude generalizations regarding the funding process. Within the federal bureaucracy, however, specific occurrances between authorization and the request for proposals always vary. The nature of the legislation, the characteristics of a program office, and the priorities of the current administration preclude the identification of "typical" actions. The factors shaping any proposal request, however, remain surprisingly constant: amendments to procedural or program legislation, directives of Commissioners or Secretaries, priorities of program officers, and the relative influence of individuals and organizations within and without the bureaucracy always condition the development of a particular program. If the factors relevant to a program can be identified, and their interactions determined, the applicant can respond effectively.

The generation of any proposal request is precipitated when a duly authorized body recognizes and responds to a societal need. This need is given funding definition by the passage of legislation or the establishment of foundation policies. The definition is then refined or modified to conform to the organizational constraints and program priorities and policies that govern the agency responsible for administering the program. The way a proposal request is developed, the form and substance of the request, the way the request is communicated to potential applicants, and the way funding decisions are made reflect accommodations to stress points in the system responsible for its development.

This chapter focused primarily on the impact that the conflicting needs and perceptions of individuals and organizational units responsible for authorizing programs and of those responsible for administering federal programs have on the development of policies and regulations that ultimately shape the programs. Those features of the system that are communicated routinely to the outsider, thus falling in the public domain, were distinguished from those that can only be identified by securing access to individuals who function in the private domain.

Although attention focused primarily on federal decision making, the variations that occur in state or foundation program setting have been cited. Specific procedures and policies that govern nonfederal program development efforts may differ markedly from those at the federal level. However, the program to which an institution or individual responds is still the product of the negotiation of varying institutional and personal needs. It is important to acquire a knowledge of the negotiated items and the characteristics and functions of the organizational units that create the conditions that shape the proposal response.

The proposal request encountered by the submitting institution represents a statement of a problem as defined by the needs and perceptions of those responsible for issuing the request. The proposal writer, in responding to the request, must remember that it is the needs and perceptions of those issuing the request that must be given primary attention.

The difficulty of reconciling the needs of those to be served with the services or strategies offered in the proposal narrative is compounded by the needs and perceptions of the submitting party. Authorizing legislation represents the legislative definition of the problem; Rules and Regulations and the conditions setting the parameters of the program represent the agency definition of the problem; the proposal represents the institutional definition of the problem.

The way a proposal is developed by a submitting institution is just as complex and significant as legislation development or regulation formulation. The institutional problem definition seeks to accommodate the divergent program and organizational aims of individuals and units within the submitting institution to those of the funding agency and those of persons served by the project. Such an accommodation must conform to funding agency requirements but be acceptable in substance and style of presentation to others in the submitting institution. Chapter 4 discusses the variables affecting the institutional definition of the problem.

ENDNOTES

1. Conversation with Lou Simonini, program officer, Region 1, Equal Education Opportunity Program Office, February 1978.
2. U.S., Department of Health, Education, and Welfare, Office of Education, Office of Planning, Budgeting, and Evaluation, Internal Briefing Paper, 1975.
3. Harry L. Summerfield, *Power and Process: The Formulation and Limits of Federal Educational Policy* (Berkeley, Calif.: McCutchan Publishing Corp., 1974), pp. 288-91.
4. P.L. 93-380, Sec. 412.
5. Robert Bendiner, *Obstacle Course on Capitol Hill* (New York: McGraw-Hill, 1964).

88 The Dynamics of Funding

6. Theodore Sky, "Rulemaking and the Federal Grant Process in the United States Office of Education," *Virginia Law Review* 62 (October 1976): 1019.
7. Ibid., p. 1033.
8. 5 U.S.C., (United States Congress) Sec. 552 (1970).
9. Interview with Tom Keys, Program Officer, Right to Read Program, Washington, D.C., Winter 1976.
10. Ibid.

4

The Proposal Document: A Political and Programmatic Statement

Within the framework of the funding system, the proposal document presents the institutional definition of the problem, linking the agency problem definition with the proposed funded activities to be carried out by the submitting institution. The proposal communciates both an institutional statement of intent and specifications that will govern implementation of the project. The various constraints shaping the agency and submitting institution's perceptions of the most appropriate way to address a problem, however, are generally different enough to create dissonance between the agency and institutional and operational stages of the funding system. Thus, the proposal serves as a negotiated statement of program priorities, proposed activities, and resource allocations for all parties with a vested interest in its development.

Proposal writing may be regarded as an exercise in conflict management or resolution that has three major objectives: (1) the writing and submittal of a document meeting the criteria necessary to secure funding; (2) the development of a program design and management structures appropriate to achieving specified objectives; and (3) the development and initiation of strategies that increase the institution's ability to meet previously identified needs and/or to bring about institutional change. This chapter will focus on these objectives.

Educational and human service agencies increasingly regard external funding as a means to supplement operating budgets. Consequently, a wide range of books, articles, newletters, and monographs on proposal writing have appeared within the past few years. Although many of them are excellent, they tend to treat proposal writing as a discrete event, calling for the application of specific technical skills separable from events preceding and following preparation of the proposal. This approach fails to take into account the goal of the proposal: the establishment of a vehicle to implement either an educational or human service program or research study to meet an institutionally defined need. If proposal development is perceived as an opportunity to secure resources to improve the delivery of services or the development of a product, rather than as simply a means to offset current operating costs, the technical writing approach seriously limits realization of the goal. The proposal developer must consider the objectives and constraints that transcend the writing of the document itself.

Fortunately, the proposal writer has access to the case histories of others who underestimated the professional and personal ramifications of developing a poorly conceived proposal or managing a seriously flawed project. The lessons to be learned from examining funded proposals are important to the individual responsible for developing a proposal and implementing a project. Unless considered within the larger political context, proposal development can be potentially disastrous, both professionally and personally. With this caveat, we turn to consideration of the characteristics of the proposal document.

THE NATURE OF THE DOCUMENT

The proposal for funding is the submitting institution's statement of services to be performed, under specified conditions, over a given period of time for a specified amount of money. The statement of services, whether it be the carrying out of research, provision of training, or delivery of assistance to a specified population, is predicated on the submitting institution's analysis of the needs to be met and the submitter's judgment as to what is possible, given the time and funding available.

Much of the difficulty proposal writers encounter in securing project support stems from their failure to address a major characteristic of the funding system before writing the proposal: the range of interests of writers and submitting institutions and the priorities of funding agencies are sufficiently diverse to require a conscious effort to reconcile them. The proposal must represent a problem and accompanying strategies in a form appropriate to the needs of potential funding agencies; it must conform in style and substance to criteria established by the agency from which support is sought.

Once the proposal is submitted, the applicant's accommodation to the funding agency guidelines and the organizational or political constraints imposed by the institution and other participants is no longer debatable—the project's scope has been set.

In the same manner in which any producer of a proposal for a play or film assesses the tastes and size of the potential market before deciding to mount a production, those responsible for determining the feasibility of securing funding must take equivalent steps in planning and writing the proposal document. The application of the preceding analogy should be clear: To write a "major work" for an audience only willing to support one-act comedies is dysfunctional. The converse also holds true: writing a one-act comedy for an audience looking for a sequel to *Death of a Salesman* is equally dysfunctional. Unfortunately, the proposal writer, unlike the playwright, does not have the opportunity to salvage an "artistic success" through the recognition of the quality of the work, even if box-office success is not realized. The proposal, unlike its theatrical counterpart, can only provide the writer with recognition through its ability to secure funds and guide successful project operation. The proposal, by definition, cannot become an end in itself.

The following generalizations should guide any approach to the development and submittal of proposals for the funding of projects:

1. Although the idea for the proposed program and the need to be addressed may derive from personal interests of the writer or institution, determination of the scope of the problem, the strategies to address the problem, and the form of the proposal cannot take final shape until a decision is made about funding sources.
2. On identification of potential funding sources, proposal development must reflect priorities of the funding agency and proposals must conform to agency formats. Those to be served by the project only influence the funding decision indirectly.
3. The appropriateness of the project's scope, the magnitude of the proposed changes, and the uniqueness of the project or controversiality of the hypothesized outcomes can be intelligently determined only after analyzing the agency's past funding practices, the statutes or policies authorizing the program, and the characteristics of the agency responsible for the program's administration.
4. In addition to identifying the funding agency's priorities, the writer must identify and address the criteria that meet the needs of both the submitting institution and the population to be served.

Treating these generalizations as guidelines, the first step for the proposal writer is to identify the characteristics of the proposal and proposal submittal process in order to apply effectively the technical skills treated in the following two chapters.

THE STRUCTURE OF THE PROPOSAL

Proposal writing has a history sufficient to permit the identification of norms to guide the document developer. Proposal writing adheres to certain structural principles that govern virtually all writing projects. The writer should approach the design of the proposal recognizing that sound program conceptualization is the basis of the document. The following treatment of the proposal components and their relationships will provide the writer with an understanding of the structural characteristics of the proposal necessary to reflect the needs of both the institution and the funding agency.

Initially, the proposal writer must address systematically several program and organization issues, the resolution of which generates the terms that will govern the project's operation. In the same manner that the larger funding process may be conceived of as a series of interrelated events, the proposal document may be analyzed as a series of discrete tasks, all of which are interrelated.

The proposal document is the product of three clusters of tasks: (1) data gathering, analysis, and assessment; (2) formulation and development; and (3) management and program assessment. For each of these clusters, corresponding writing tasks representing components of the proposal document may be identified (see Table 4.1).

The Identification of the task clusters and the corresponding proposal components omits one critical analytic task confronting the proposal writer: the analysis of the balance between funding agency priorities and the needs and capabilities of the submitting institution. Although this analysis is generally incorporated into the document once the decision to compete for funding has been made, too many institutions and individuals pay less attention to this decision than to other tasks involved in the proposal development. The response of institutional officers and program developers to an opportunity to submit a proposal is more often a reflex response than a considered decision. The decision to respond to a funding opportunity must be based on careful analysis of all available information that might affect both the program's operation and the odds for securing funding.

The impact of this initial analysis on the quality of the proposal document

Table 4.1. Development Tasks and Corresponding Proposal Components

Task Cluster	Corresponding Proposal Components
Data gathering, analysis, and assessment	Background or introduction
	Statement of the problem and/or hypotheses**
	Needs assessment*/related literature** or justification for the study**
Formulation and development	Goals or major objectives/or hypotheses**
	Specific objectives/subhypotheses**
	Program activities/research procedures**
	Program summary
Management and program assessment	Program evaluation*
	Program governance, personnel role description
	Budget

*Demonstration, training, or service delivery proposals only
**Research as opposed to training or service delivery proposals

is considerable. The appropriateness of the problem statement, the quality of the data supporting the need for the project, the comprehensiveness of the problem approach, and the demonstrated commitment of the submitting institution to the program is affected immediately and directly by the careful determination of the consonance between agency and institution needs and capabilities. Program support by decision-making officers and staff in the submitting institution and the receiving agency depends, in large part, on the perceived fit between institutional need, capability, program commitment and agency objectives. Any document that results from a forced fit between divergent needs or that fails to articulate the needs and abilities of the submitting institution and receiving agency generally will suffer in the review process.

Since individual proposal components are shaped by the characteristics of those preceding and following, the relationships between the components may be ordered to provide a structure that governs virtually all proposal development efforts. An understanding of the structural elements of the proposal allows the writer to design a response appropriate to a wide range of settings and content areas. Because the content and organization prerequisite to the proposal encompass a limited range of knowledge and are applied to the development of a single specified product, it is possible to diagram a representation of the proposal's structure.

Identifying the relationship of the structural elements makes it possible to identify a "mode of inquiry," that, in turn, provides a means to identify the steps or process that enable the developer to respond to a proposal request with the same level of confidence that a social or natural scientist might bring to a given research task.

Figure 4.1 serves two immediate purposes. It provides a framework for examining the characteristics of the individual proposal components and the interrelationship between the components; it also serves as a referent point for generating a mode of inquiry that characterizes proposal development.

The diagram shows that the definition of the problem that the proposal addresses (2) is both a function of the fit between funding agency priorities (1a) and institutional needs and capabilities (1b) and a function of conclusions drawn from data analysis that qualitatively and quantitatively document and define the problem (3) sufficiently to enable the developer to identify the goals or major objectives (4) for the project. The specific objectives (5) are derived from selected needs that the program seeks to address directly (3). Analysis of proposal development efforts reveals that the identification of specific needs may also follow institutional objective setting. Needs identified in this manner confirm the institution's perception of the problem.

Whether one formulates objectives by analyzing a pool of needs, or generates needs to support general objectives suggested by the funding agency's definition of the problem, specific objectives should always be the converse of the needs. The synthesis of related specific objectives that address a common area of need forms the major objectives or goals (4) of the project. The project evaluation design (8) derives its identity from the specific objectives (5).

Figure 4.1. The Structure of the Proposal

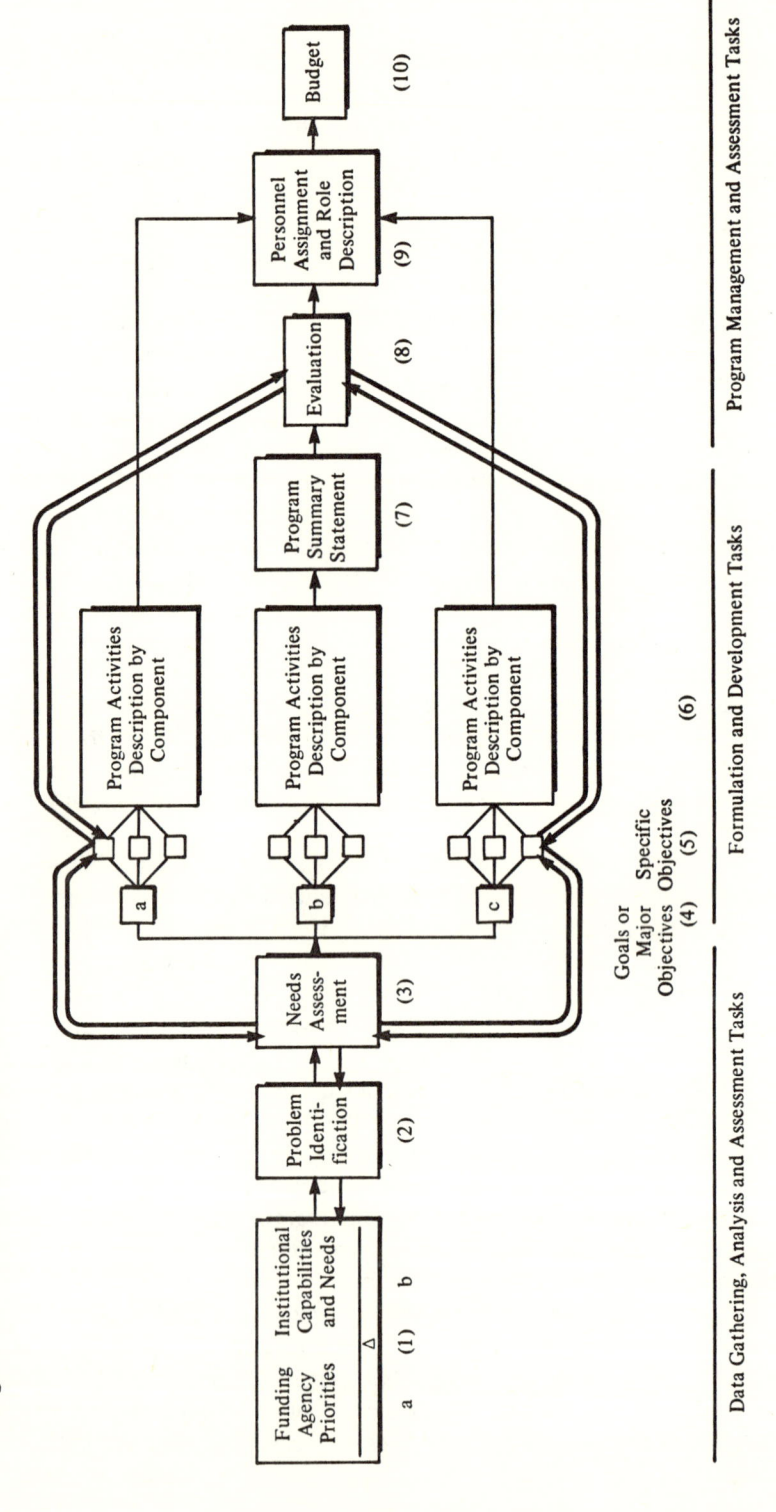

Objectives, representing a standard of performance measured by outcomes, should serve as criteria for measuring a project's ultimate success or failure.

The program activities (6) represent proposed intervention strategies to realize the objectives as measured by the evaluation criteria. Activities are linked to clusters of related objectives (4a, b, c) to enable the developer to differentiate program management and evaluation strategies for programs with multiple major objectives and activities. For example, goals of a program may include training, material development, and delivery of services to a specified population. The strategies applied to each of these major goals will differ significantly; success in achieving each goal may also differ significantly. Finally, personnel assignment (9) is a direct function of the nature and range of proposed activities. The personnel assignments and tasks to be carried out in turn provide the information necessary to generate the budget (10).

DATA GATHERING, ANALYSIS, AND ASSESSMENT TASKS

The proposal structure requires the completion of corresponding tasks that yield the information necessary to develop components of the proposal document. Analysis of the nature of these tasks suggest the feasibility of ordering them around *types* of activity common to most problem-solving ventures.

The initial tasks confronting the proposal planner are data gathering, analysis, and assessment tasks. These tasks have programmatic and political dimensions and should be treated as such. The nature of the available data and the conclusions derived from analysis contribute to the conceptualization of the problem and to the submitting institution's perception of the value of the program. As mentioned earlier, analysis of the balance between agency and institutional priorities is not directly reflected in the proposal document. However, this analysis is so basic to successful funding and implementation of the program that it should be the first task undertaken by the potential submitter. If carefully performed, it provides the basis for deciding whether the gains from submitting and receiving funding exceed what might be lost from not submitting, or submitting and not receiving funding.

The risk assumed by the potential applicant who fails to assess agency/institution compatability, and whose proposal fails to secure funding, is limited generally to the loss of time and effort expended—unless the individual's position or the continuation of a program depend on the securing of funding. The loss, however, that can result from securing funding for a project constructed on a faulty fit between the needs, capabilities, and expectations of the submitting institution and the receiving agency may be far more significant. Since the proposal, by definition, represents an institutional statement of services to be provided under specified conditions, the failure to conform to those specifications once funding is secured can have both a short- and long-term impact on the submitting institution, project staff, those served by the program, and ultimately the funding agency. A program built on erroneous assumptions regarding institutional commitment and capability, or on conflicting perceptions of organizational units or affected groups regarding desirable outcomes and appropriate activities, jeopardizes the status of the director, the institution, and all others involved. The repercussions from the loss of status can extend far beyond the day-to-day functioning of the program and associated individuals.

Analysis of the agency-institution relationship, as set by the conditions of a particular funding opportunity, identifies the preconditions necessary for proposal development. Once the program parameters are established by these conditions, the remaining data gathering, analysis, and assessment tasks contribute directly to the form and content of the document.

The institutional definition of the problem reflected in the program document is shaped by several variables: (1) the writer's and institution's selection of those elements of a large social or scientific problem that they wish to address; (2) the writer's and institution's choice of strategies to address the problem; and (3) the writer's and institution's operational definition of what is possible, reflected in the criteria for evaluating the program's success. The outcomes of completing these tasks are reflected in the proposal narrative.

The potential impact on funded projects of the way the data gathering, analysis, and assessment tasks are carried out and are delineated in the initial components of the proposal is great. As in any planned problem-solving activity, the appropriateness of the strategies selected to address the problem depends on both the reliability and validity of the data providing the information base for planning. The data and the accompanying analyses contained in the initial components of the proposal not only set the parameters for the statement of objectives and program activities or research procedures that follow, they also suggest management strategies and set the expectations of persons with a vested interest in the project's outcome.

The program developer must recognize that program conceptualization is implicit in the analysis and assessment tasks. The strategy for defining the problem and assessing the needs therefore will ultimately affect the choice of objectives, the strategies to realize these objectives, and the criteria for determining the success or failure of the project. In responding to a funding opportunity, the developer is confronted immediately with decisions requiring both professional and value judgments as to what needs are addressable, given the constraints of the governing funding agency.

Conceptualizing both problem and program appropriately is difficult, particularly when projects address issues tied to social policy questions or when the variables defy isolation and subsequent treatment. This difficulty is compounded by the fact that the needs cited in the proposal document may be drawn from individual, institutional, or agency perceptions of service or learning deficits that are not the most appropriate for treatment. Although the proposed project may focus on needs determined by a disinterested analysis of a specific problem, and may accurately reflect the state of knowledge in a given area, the chances are that any statement of needs implies judgment of past behavior or desired future directions. Thus, this statement may represent a value judgment of a group's or institution's current functioning, and such value judgments are often threatening.

Given the power of needs assessments to affect perceptions of the past effectiveness of the submitting institution, decisions as to what needs data to provide the proposal writer, what needs data to place in the proposal, or what interpretations of the data are acceptable statements of need can serve both as political and programmatic statements. The political implications of such decisions can be appreciated if one considers, for example, the potential impact on the administration of a school system of a proposal documenting that 90 percent of the eighth grade students read three grade levels below the national norm.

The deficits identified in the needs assessment that are considered addressable set the objectives, which in turn become the criteria for program evaluation. The failure to secure adequate or reliable information, or an inappropriate analysis of data relevant to the operational definition of the problem and the institution's commitment and capabilities, can contribute to a major discrepancy between anticipated and actual project outcomes. An inappropriate assessment of the relationship between the identified needs and the objectives and strategies set for the project can lead to a seriously flawed program design and result in institutional resistance at the point of program implementation.

The initial planning for project development represents, both politically and programatically, a critical point in the development of the proposal. Politically, data gathering, analysis, and assessment tasks have direct impact on the reception of the proposal by the funding agency, the various organizational units in the submitting institution, and any other individuals or groups affected by the program. The initial proposal components—the background or introduction, the statement of the problem, and the needs assessment—set the stage for the statements of objectives and proposed objectives, implicitly establishing the criteria for evaluation. These components also serve as statements of institutional priorities. These initial tasks structure the future development of the program and signal possible revised allocations of personnel and money. Both programmatic and political variables are thereby set in motion.

FORMULATION AND DEVELOPMENT TASKS

The centrality of data gathering, analysis, and assessment tasks to proposal development is evident in the fact that formulation and development tasks are generated from data obtained in the earlier analyses. The statements of goals, specific objectives, and program activities are outcomes of carrying out formulation and development tasks. The proposal writer's primary constraints at this stage of proposal development are programmatic rather than political and are set by the knowledge relevant to designing the program.

The formulation and development tasks are not devoid of conflict; differences in this stage of program development, however, generally center on the appropriateness of the proposed activities and the priorities accorded the objectives. It should be noted, however, that if more than one institution or party with markedly different perceptions of the nature of the problem is involved in the proposal development, the odds of programmatic issues becoming political ones increase substantially.

The structural link between the formulation and development tasks and the analysis and assessment tasks is evident in the statement of goals and objectives. Major objectives represent clusters of specific objectives that, if realized, define the project's success. The specific objectives are the converse of the needs identified earlier and are derived directly from the institutional definition of the problem, represented in the needs assessment or analysis of past research findings.

Because the setting of goals or objectives is central to the identification of program activities and to the writing of the proposal document, the writer must approach these tasks with an awareness of the problems inherent in any program formulation and development effort. These problems can be exacerbated by the constraints imposed by the dynamics of the funding process, discussed in earlier chapters.

As a result of past program failures, an inflationary economy, and the demands for accountability by authorizing bodies, funding agencies are becoming increasingly concerned with supporting projects that will be demonstrably successful. Soundness of program conceptualization and the appropriateness of program design are the basis of successful program development. Thus, the construction of a model of the important operational components of the program that specifies the expected linkages between program components and outcomes is valuable for the program developer. This causal model should specify how the interactions between the things the program is attempting to change, the prerequisites to program operation that remain constant throughout the program, and the activities designed to bring about the stated changes result in stated outcomes or objectives. If a program is developed against such a causal model, the director's task, once funding is secured, primarily is to assure that the funded program (or activities) occurs on schedule and in the manner proposed.

Unfortunately, however, the nature of the proposal development process and the complexity of many social or educational problems mitigates against the realization of such causal models. A researcher who has evaluated many federally sponsored programs, describes the problem succinctly:

> Instead of following a linear development process from: (a) a theory which specifies that (b) certain program components (c) will regularly lead to certain expected outcomes, the program components probably developed first. The outcomes claimed for the program usually followed temporarily the development of the actual program components, and the outcomes claimed may not accurately reflect what operationally goes on in the program or what one could logically or empirically expect as an outcome. The rhetoric about

the program, or a set of theoretical conceptions about it, is most often the last to occur, as the explanatory and public relations brochures are made up.[1]

The commentator's evaluation of the deficiencies of program development does not consider the numerous factors working against conceptually sound program development that occur before the development and submittal of the proposal. These factors include: the development of a program in response to guidelines that superficially reflect a submitter's area of expertise; the development of programs without systematic and incremental study of the specified problem area; the development of programs within time lines that preclude design considerations; participating groups' conflicting perceptions of the problem to be addressed and the most desirable strategies; and, the need to negotiate a wide range of inter- and intrainstitutional political considerations that are extraneous to program design but that affect program implementation.

Given the magnitude of the conceptualization problem and the likelihood of program design flaws, which are present under the best of development circumstances, the proposal writer or program planner must achieve the best possible fit between the design and the strategies for delivering services. Such a fit is realized best by consciously treating the development activities as an integrated set of tasks. The goal is to establish consistency between and among the formulation and development tasks, the analysis and assessment tasks that precede them, and the evaluation and management tasks that follow.

If the writer has confidence in the accuracy and analysis of the data documenting the program need and the submitting institution's commitment, the formulation and development cluster of tasks can be treated as specifications for activities to be carried out. If these activities are compatible with what is known about the problem they will generate specified outcomes under specified conditions. The program developer must act on hypotheses, convinced that the planned activities will confirm the hypotheses.

Operationally, the writer makes the following statement in identifying objectives and planning activities: if x (the planned activity) occurs, then y (the specific objective) will be realized. Under the circumstances surrounding proposal submittal, the proposal writer must often make intuitive leaps in which the available knowledge does not always justify the claim that x activity will result in y outcome. Given the inevitability of such "leaps of faith," it is imperative that the risk not be compounded by stating x and y in ambiguous or misleading terms. To prevent any misunderstanding or confusion on the part of the reviewer, a writer must state specifically what will occur, under what condition it will occur, and what are the anticipated outcomes. The statements of objectives and activities, as laid out in the proposal, thus provide the operational definition of the causal model. If one regards activities as treatments (in the research sense of the term) the importance of specifying conditions, procedures, and anticipated or desired outcomes becomes evident. The relationship between activities or treatments and objectives and goals is diagrammed in Figure 4.2.

Figure 4.2. Goal-Objective-Activity Relationship

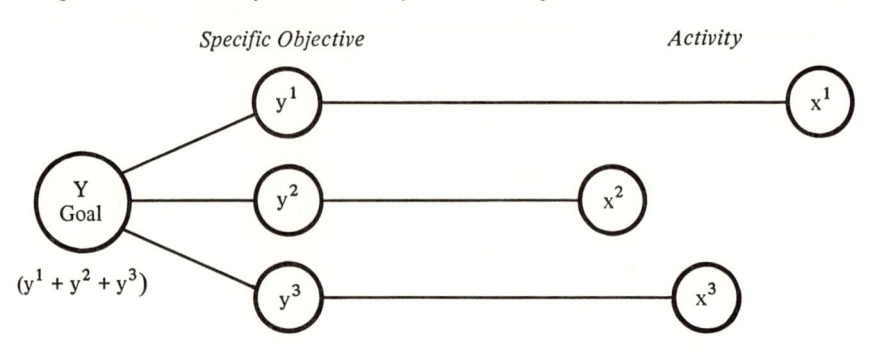

```
         Specific Objective                  Activity
                 y¹ ───────────────────────── x¹
   Y
  Goal           y² ──────────── x²
(y¹+y²+y³)
                 y³ ──────────── x³
```

If x^1 occurs, then y^1 will be the outcome
If x^2 occurs, then y^2 will be the outcome
If x^3 occurs, then y^3 will be the outcome
If $(y^1 + y^2 + y^3)$ is realized, then Y will be achieved

Explanation of Terms
x = activities
y = specific objectives
Y = goal or general objective

Although the precision of clinical research almost always eludes the curriculum or training developer and the provider of social services, program designers must still attempt to isolate and control variables and identify relationships between them.

Given the complexity of many social and education problems, the number of activities proposed and the length of the proposal document often obscure a reviewer's recognition of a writer's attempt to present the activities as series of treatments, under specified conditions and establish time lines, with resultant specified outcomes. A writer's inability to demonstrate effectively the interconnections between various activities may also frustrate a reviewer's assessment of the appropriateness of the proposed program. Fortunately, the proposal writer can take advantage of a program summary, which appears in most proposal solicitations, to overcome this particular documentation problem.

Rather than view the program summary as a modified abstract or recapitulation, the writer should treat this component both as an opportunity to test the validity of the proposed program and as a marketing tool. The milestone chart, a technique drawn from the area of operations research and often applied to business management is applicable. This chart provides a graphic representation of steps to be followed, tne timing of their occurrence, and their relationship to one another in order to develop a product or deliver a service according to specifications. The development of the proposal summary as a milestone chart or bar graph* accommodates both the planning and selling needs of the proposal writer. It also answers the questions of persons who may have a vested interest in the proposal's submittal and review, but have neither the time nor inclination to read the entire document.

MANAGEMENT AND ASSESSMENT TASKS

Over the past several years, funding agencies have paid increased attention to management and assessment tasks associated with funded programs. This attention evolved partially from the failure of some projects to meet expectations during the past decade, partially from the changing social and economic climate, and partially from the increased refinement of the proposal development process. The proposal writer can deal with these accountability concerns in the proposal statements of program evaluation,** project governance, and budget.

Program Evaluation Tasks

Although program evaluation tasks are conceptually discrete from program development tasks, the evaluation component of the proposal is related directly to the development process. Many proposal efforts fail to recognize this relationship and treat program evaluation as an afterthought to the development of the proposal. Although the centrality of evaluation to program implementation and proposed review is being emphasized, the evaluation component may still only amount to a statement of loosely defined criteria and strategies for submitting a final report.

Evaluation components treated as afterthoughts render the proposed program vulnerable in several respects: the rating accorded the proposal suffers; the criteria for assessing effectiveness passes, by default, from the director to the evaluator; the director loses the systematic opportunity to secure information basic to making necessary program adjustments; and future funding and program adoption may be jeopardized. Sound evaluation is an asset to proposal funding, project operation, and continuation of program activities. Considered within this context, evaluation assumes major significance for proposal development and program implementation.

Consistent with the conceptualization of the proposal as a series of interrelated components, evaluation design is shaped initially by the needs assessment,

---

*For procedures for developing proposal summary milestone charts or bar graphs, see chapters 5 and 6.

**Evaluation components generally are not relevant to basic or applied research projects. In the typical research proposal, evaluation is built into the research design or treated as part of the project management presentation.

given its form by the constellation of the general objectives, and indelibly set by the clusters of the specific objectives, which ideally should provide an operational definition of proposed outcomes. The evaluation design's service to the program director is thus directly related to the careful development of these earlier components.

As mentioned earlier, program activities should be developed using a hypothesis-setting approach. Thus, the appropriateness of the evaluation strategies to determine success or failure depend on both the nature of the objectives and the precision with which they were developed. Projects to "improve reading skills" or "identify health needs," as opposed to projects to "increase reading scores by two grade levels on a designated standardized test for a specified reading program" or "identify specified nutritional deficiencies of a specified population undergoing a specified clinical regimen," call for markedly different evaluation procedures. The project to "improve reading skills" fails to define the outcome specifically, thus leaving both the definition and determination of success up to a third party. Although determination of success is a legitimate function of the evaluator, the openendedness of the objective gives the evaluator too much freedom to define program success. The project to "identify specified nutritional deficiencies of a specified population undergoing a specified clinical regimen" provides a definition enabling the evaluator to apply quantitative measures to determine whether the outcomes have been accomplished.

The difference between success in terms of a proposed objective, and success, in terms of value, is important to note. The realization of specific project objectives does not necessarily indicate that the project is of value to the administering institution or that the project significantly affects the problem it is designed to address. The determination of value is ultimately a function of institutional perceptions of priorities and the characteristics of the problem. As such, it is an issue that must be dealt with in the initial stages of program conceptualization.

In developing the evaluation design, the writer must develop strategies to compare performance against standards identified earlier in the proposal. These standards can be used by the developer, rather than by the evaluator or others who may be affected by the program, to measure performance and ultimately define the project's success.

This approach to evaluation design should provide: (1) the identification of criteria to measure performance; (2) the methods and procedures to collect the data on performance; (3) the scheduling of such methods and procedures, including data collection; and (4) the way the data will be used and/or reported.

In designing evaluation strategies, recognize that at least three decision-making audiences, in addition to the funding agency, can use the resulting information: the sponsoring institution, the persons administering the project, and the population affected by project implementation. Moreover, evaluation data inform project administrators of needed program adjustments and provide information to those persons who can influence continuation or termination of the project. Finally, evaluation data can influence the sponsoring institution's receptivity to organizational or policy changes suggested by the project's operation.

Given the audiences for and potential uses of evaluation information, the proposal writer must develop strategies that provide: (1) information to measure the fit between performance and specified standards, at specified dates from project inception through completion; (2) organizational structures to incorporate this information in future project planning; and (3) the most appropriate means through which data, relevant to future program status, can be communicated to interested parties.

The final evaluation product (final report) is important to both the receiving agency and the submitting institution in determining the future status of the program. Consequently, the development of the evaluation component should consider the form of the final report and the way it will address the needs of both the submitting institution and the funding agency. The final report must also demonstrate the relationship between success or failure in realizing the specific project objectives and the project's broader goals. The evaluation design must convince reviewers that the information secured will permit judgments of success or project progress based on clearly communicated standards. Then, the director need only to make certain that responsibility for the collection, analysis, and reporting of the data, in a form suitable for transmission, is firmly fixed and appropriately carried out.

Project Governance Tasks

While an effective evaluation design can provide sufficient information to permit personnel or program adjustments, it does not generally specify *who* makes these decisions. Projects usually bring individuals and/or organizations together in new working relationships. Therefore, the need for clearly defined roles with the accompanying delegation of authority assumes both political and programmatic significance. Staff on newly initiated projects often are confused about others' expectations of them and uncertain to whom they are accountable. Project directors often become mediators between members of the permanent structure, of which they are a part, and the temporary structures established through external funding.

Conflict is inherent in directing any project to bring about change, and pressure is always associated with the reallocation of authority within a structure initiating a new program. Therefore, it is unfortunate that most proposal solicitations do not require much more than a table of organization and a definition of roles as evidence that management tasks have been given proper consideration.

In revising or creating new organizational structures, the proposal writer or program planner must consider those conflicts endemic in creating any new organizational structure, as well as those related to the particular program. Ostensibly, these factors can be treated in organizational charts and personnel job descriptions. However, the range of questions that arise at one time or another in project management demonstrates the danger of being seduced by the apparent order of charts. Some of these questions are:

1. How does the governance structure of the project relate to the governance structure of the sponsoring institution? What are the implications of this relationship for project staffing and day-to-day operations?
2. What are the provisions for mediating disputes between the director and staff? The director and participants? The director and the sponsoring institution?
3. What are the provisions for mediating differences between participating institutions or groups, if more than one is involved in project operations?
4. How are decisions to hire made? Who participates in decision making? Do responsibilities to personnel assumed by the sponsoring institution extend beyond project-related assignments?
5. What are the expectations of persons holding project positions? For what tasks are they responsible? What products are they expected to produce? What time must they formally commit to the tasks?
6. What provisions have been made for meeting program and fiscal evaluation requirements of the funding agency? Who, in addition to the director, is responsible for communicating with the funding agency?
7. What are the provisions for reassigning roles or terminating personnel?
8. What are the provisions for communicating information to interested parties? For receiving and processing information from interested or affected parties?

The preceding questions, which hardly exhaust the possibilities, make it clear that the pro forma organizational chart and job descriptions, often added as afterthoughts to the proposal document, deserve greater consideration. Ultimately, it is the project staff's ability to perform according to specifications, and the project director's ability to align activities with the operations of the sponsoring institution, that determine both the short- and long-term success of the project. The extent to which the assignment of resources and the allocation of power are negotiated before project implementation determines the level of the effort the project director can devote to the development and implementation of the funded program.

Budget Development Tasks

That component of the proposal that most developers are least prepared to deal with is the budget. Budget development, in its narrowest sense, is the design of a plan to allocate and distribute fiscal resources, over a specified period of time according to a pre-established schedule. Fiscal officers and accountants are generally considered to have the skills for such tasks. The allocation of costs, however, establishes the scope of the project, sets program priorities, and determines conditions for staff employment. Therefore, policies and strategies governing expenditure are vitally important to program and fiscal officers representing both the funding agent and the submitting institution. Budget development, consequently, must be an integral part of program management.

In designing the budget component, consider: (1) the precise allocation of monies, including the relative distribution of funds for project personnel (salaries and wages), for project operations other than regular personnel (other direct costs), and for the direct delivery of services to the parties served (stipend costs or per capita expenditure for individuals served by the project); and (2) policies governing the allocation of monies, including guidelines set by the funding agency, established policies of the submitting institution that determine permissiable expenditure, level of salaries, and nonrecoverable costs associated with project operation. The latter set of factors is primarily political in nature, the former programmatic.

If the proposal developer treats the budget as a program management task, the identification of the relationship between program specifications set earlier and those set by individual budget entries can be simplified greatly. Salaries and wages, for example, reflect the level of expertise, amount of time, and number of persons needed to realize the proposed objectives. However, the actual dollar amount assigned to individual budget entries, being set by both institutional precedent and the personnel market, is determined by both political and program variables.

If the performance of specific activities was linked earlier to the realization of specified sets of objectives, and if these objectives can be linked to specific personnel assignments including administrative salaries, the developer can effectively justify the budget. Equally important, the developer can adjust personnel assignments and/or proposed project outcomes before project initiation, if the full level of requested funding is not awarded.

Although salaries and wages represent the major expenditure in most projects, other direct costs, such as, consultants, communications, travel, supplies, equipment, and stipends are instrumental in determining a project's ability to realize the stated objectives. The greater the percentage of the total budget allocated to other direct costs, the greater the potential for inadequate budget planning to disrupt the day-to-day operation and ultimate success of the project. Projects calling for numerous participants, the purchase of large quantities of materials, the delivery of services over a wide geographic area, a wide range of activities, or the establishment of new offices often are handicapped by unrealistic cost assessments. This dilemma results directly from the funding process. The program developer may find the establishment of unit prices for budget items designated as other direct costs perplexing and may complete this budget task by pulling numbers out of a hat. Also, since budget formulation depends on earlier program decisions, it is often framed under time pressures set by the due date for receipt of proposals. Often, there is simply not enough time left to determine other direct costs carefully or to secure the necessary technical assistance.

The previous notation of the technical and systemic factors contributing to difficulties in budget setting provides a logical transition to discussion of the political elements of the budget setting process.

Budget development, by differentially allocating resources to individuals and organizational units is, by definition, political. When more than one institution or different units in a single institution that have not worked together previously collaborate to develop a proposal, the relative allocation of monies to each inevitably becomes an issue. If, in such situations, the relative distribution of funds is not placed on the formal proposal development agenda, the writer or director can expect it to appear at the least opportune moment. Institutions, or units within institutions, often link the allocation of dollars with the allocation of turf and turf is guarded jealously by individuals and institutions. In approaching budget development, it is essential that the roles and responsibilities of participants from the several institutions or units be prescribed before discussing the equating of costs to operations. Negotiations that focus on how services best can be provided, rather than on who get the dollars, will proceed more smoothly. Once program features and accompanying personnel needs are fixed by participating parties, costs can be addressed within the context of professional equity. Remaining political and fiscal negotiations can then be restricted to specific program items. The failure to separate program and political fiscal issues may lead to debate regarding institutional motivations in seeking funding, just as the proposal document goes to print.

Although less volatile, institutional policies also may inject political variables into the budget formulation process. One guideline in budget development must be adhered to without exception: know the fiscal policies and guidelines of the receiving agency and the submitting institution. As obvious as this guideline seems, its inclusion is justified by the number of persons who, failing to adhere to this guideline, have found themselves with completed proposals that the submitting institution will not submit or the funding agency cannot fund.

Institutional policies may intrude in the budget development process at the following points: (1) the determination of pay rates and fringe benefits for staff or managerial positions, (2) the identification of policies governing the allocation of time to the assignments; (3) the identification of both institutional and funding agency policies governing allowable rates for the calculation of indirect costs, and the calculation and feasibility of cost sharing by the submitting institution; and (4) the identification and calculation of indirect costs to be incorporated in the funding request.

The failure to identify relevant policies and negotiate items that do not conform to institutional policies before proposal submittal, and certainly before final budget negotiation, can lead to understaffing and undersupplying. Moreover, the director may become involved in extended negotiations with the institution's fiscal offices; in such situations, implementation must await the outcome of inhouse negotiations. It is also important to note that the failure to prenegotiate institutional policies can lead to a situation in which the intent and ability of the institution receiving the award may later be seriously questioned by project participants not familiar with the fiscal working of the institution.

Firm policies generally govern institutional calculations of indirect costs (those costs attributable to the operation of externally funded projects that are not allowable costs in proposal budgets, e.g., heat, electricity, space, and administration of institutional research efforts). Indirect cost rates are not generally negotiable by a project director within an institution. Local education agencies are prohibited from charging indirect costs on some solicitations, but permitted such charges on others. Indirect costs generally represent a fixed cost that can dramatically affect the total funding request (rates may range from over 100 percent of salaries and wages to 8 percent of the total costs). Being unfamiliar with the policies governing the institution's indirect cost rate before delineating project activities will hinder the early setting of a target figure for the proposal or the allocation of monies for individual sets of activities. Similarly, institutional policies governing the calculation of fringe benefits (institutional share of social security, medical and retirement benefits, etc.) must be ascertained, since they can have a significant impact on the total budget request. In addition to the impact on budget total, the failure to conform to institutional policies pertaining to indirect costs and fringe benefit calculation virtually guarantees that the responsible institutional fiscal officer will refuse to authorize proposal submittal.

In some cases, funding agency policies are not consonant with those of submitting institutions. Since conformity to funding agency policies ultimately determines the fundability of a proposal, the writer or director may be caught in the middle when an attractive funding source prohibits full recovery of indirect costs or fringe benefits, or stipulates some cost sharing. The proposal initiator, in such cases, often has to negotiate between program and fiscal officers within his or her own institution.

Cost policies vary from agency to agency and even from program to program. Therefore, the proposal developer must be familiar with the fiscal constraints set by the funding agency before developing the budget, and even before developing the proposal. The developer must consider the fiscal policies of the funding agency and submitting institution, along with the other program constraints, to determine the feasibility and desirability of responding to a specified proposal solicitation.

PROPOSAL WRITING: PROCESS AS CONTENT

Discussion of the tasks required to develop the proposal and the accompanying political and structural characteristics of the individual components has provided information that permits the developer to consider needs central to the successful implementation of the project simultaneously with qualities central to the successful development of the proposal document. Those characteristics of the proposal common to virtually all development efforts have also been discussed. Having identified a structure to order the components of the proposal, it is now possible to identify a process for addressing the structural features.

If one accepts the task of proposal writing as a series of discrete but related operations common to all responses, regardless of the nature or scope of the problem, the writer then has to structure and order the operations to produce a document that adheres to agency criteria. The challenge presented, in many respects, is like that presented in filing Federal Internal Revenue income tax forms: There is a body of law and precedent reflecting the policy of the authorizing body; there are regulations established by the recipient governing the approach to the task; and there are instructions which, when followed, enable the applicant to produce a document conforming to established criteria with accompanying dollar stipulations. For the proposal writer, the program legislation or the priorities of the foundation's board of trustees reflect the policies of the authorizing body. The Rules and Regulations or program officer guidelines for proposal development constitute the instructions for document development. The missing element in the preceding income tax analogy for the proposal writer is the explicit instructions that will lead to the "right" outcome.

Two generalizations regarding the submittal of the proposal may be inferred from the income tax analogy: (1) any proposal development response to a federal or state agency request, without reference to the Rules and Regulations or guidelines established by the agency, does not have much chance for approval and (2) the developer's ability to identify the relevant data and conform to the explicit instructions available from proposal application kits and funding agency personnel significantly increases the odds of successful proposal reception. The earlier discussion of the relationship between the funding agency's needs and the submitting institution's objectives in developing a proposal dealt with the implications of the first generalization for the proposal writer. The following discussion offers a process for dealing with the implications of the second generalization.

The author's experience in working with persons interested in developing proposal writing skills, regardless of their professional or academic background, has uncovered a basic teaching dilemma. This dilemma, the general-specific conflict, influenced the decision to treat proposal writing as a process with clearly identifiable definitional characteristics.

Prospective submitters legitimately want guidelines appropriate to a wide range of agencies; they also want prototypical proposals. Since funding agencies generally request documents tailored to their particular program specifications, any "how-to" formula leads to overreliance on the characteristics of the ideal proposal. This often leaves students with the impression that the proposal document conforms to a single set of criteria. This impression is shaken, however, by proposal requests that do not conform to the prototype. On the other hand, when the task is approached by "walking through" a specific proposal solicitation and by producing a document that responds directly to a specific set of guidelines, the document often is accorded the status of a prototype. This prototype may, however, be seriously flawed when judged against the criteria of the model proposal. Of greater concern is the fact that such a tailored proposal is of little value in responding to an opportunity governed by another agency's guidelines. This general-specific conflict can be addressed partly by recognizing its existence and adjusting writing effort appropriately. Of greater value, however, is the development of a strategy that directly confronts the problem. One such strategy is to treat proposal writing as a set of processes common to all responses. When considered collectively, these processes provide the means to identify the appropriate content and style of presentation for different audiences.

A STRATEGY FOR LINKING PROCESS AND CONTENT

The feasibility of approaching proposal writing as a process with a specified set of characteristics is suggested by the "structure of the discipline" approach to curriculum development that received much attention during the early 1960s. The proposition that "intellectual activity anywhere is the same, whether at the frontier of knowledge or in the third-grade classroom,"[2] led to the conclusion that "any subject can be taught effectively in some intellectual form to any child at any stage of development."[3] The suggested strategy for curriculum developers was "to redefine the particular subject in the light of the best knowledge available, to identify its central and organizing principles, and to select and arrange applications and illustrations of those principles in an orderly sequence appropriate to the capacity of children of various ages...."[4]

This strategy required scholars to identify "modes of inquiry" basic to their disciplines and the critical skills and their relationships that one would have to master to be considered a biologist or a historiographer. These modes of inquiry constituted the "structure" of knowledge in the disciplines. It was postulated that if one could identify and master the processes necessary to carry out inquiry in a given discipline, then differences between the novice and the mature scholar would be based on levels of sophistication, not on approach.

This emphasis on modes of inquiry led to the development of a sequence of steps representing "the inquiry process." One social studies curriculum project, supported by a USOE grant, identified the following steps as constituting a mode of inquiry:

1. Recognizing a problem from data
2. Formulating hypotheses
    a. Asking analytical questions
    b. Stating hypotheses
    c. Remaining aware of the tentative nature of hypotheses
3. Recognizing the logical implications of hypotheses

4. Gathering data
   a. Deciding what data will be needed
   b. Selecting or rejecting sources
5. Analyzing, evaluating and interpreting data
   a. Selecting relevant data
   b. Evaluating sources
      1. Determining the frame of reference of an author
      2. Determining the accuracy of statements of fact
6. Evaluating the hypotheses in light of the data
   a. Modifying the hypotheses, if necessary
      1. Rejecting a logical implication unsupported by data
      2. Restating the hypothesis
   b. Stating a generalization[5]

The preceding structure should orient the reader to the conceptual basis underlying the following approach to proposal writing. The terms guiding this discussion, namely, *structure, process,* and *content,* and their relationship to proposal writing, are derived from curriculum development principles.

In considering the writing of the proposal document, certain assumptions derived from the preceding discussion shape the approach:

1. The funding process, distinct from the writing of a proposal, is governed by identifiable and related central and organizing principles. These principles, in one form or another, are identifiable in every set of proposal solicitations and responses.
2. The organizing principles governing the solicitation-response activities, in turn, enable the identification of critical skills and their relationships that, when mastered, constitute the "structure of knowledge" defining the funding process.
3. The writing of the proposal, one element in the funding process, applies the principles to a specified set of tasks common to all responses. These tasks may, however, be modified by constraints set by the funding agency for a specific response. The relationships of sets of tasks to one another, for example, needs assessment, objective setting, and proposed activities, are constant and together comprise the structure of the proposal.
4. The proposal structure provides the means to identify and order applications of the principles governing the tasks present in all responses. The proposal structure shapes the processes that collectively constitute the content of the response.

Following Fenton's identification and ordering of steps in a social studies mode of inquiry, a similar ordering central to proposal writing appears in Table 4.2. The steps constituting the inquiry process in the area of proposal writing may be delineated with a high degree of precision. The relationship between

The Proposal Document: A Political and Programmatic Statement 111

TABLE 4.2. *Steps Constituting Proposal Development Mode of Inquiry*

I. Recognizing a fundable problem from data
   A. Collecting and evaluating data from the funding agency
   B. Collecting and evaluating data from the submitting institution
      1. Organizational
      2. Programmatic
II. Recognizing a generic or social problem from data
   A. Collecting data
   B. Evaluating data
   C. Defining the problem
III. Formulating hypotheses and identifying assumptions to govern program development
IV. Assessing consonance of institutional and agency definitions of problem (Analyzing the relationship between I and II)
V. Testing assumptions regarding proposal development plans and strategies against constraints set by funding agency and submitting institution
VI. Conceptualizing the program
VII. Identifying and evaluating alternative program objectives
   A. Identifying objectives which will address the problem
   B. Analyzing the possibility of realizing the objectives in light of findings derived from carrying out steps IV and V
   C. Selecting most appropriate objectives suggested by conclusions drawn from the immediately preceding step (VIIB)
   D. Stating the objectives in performance terms
VIII. Identifying and evaluating alternative program intervention strategies
   A. Identifying activities which directly address objectives
   B. Identifying criteria and methods for determining the degree to which activities were carried out as planned
IX. Assessing alternative evaluation designs and selecting design most appropriate to proposed project
   A. Identifying strategies and confirming criteria to determine whether objectives were realized at criteria levels set
   B. Identifying means by which data derived from carrying out steps immediately preceding may be used to support program development efforts
X. Identifying resources prerequisite to program operation
   A. Analyzing personnel and logistical support necessary for carrying out activities identified
   B. Developing a cost estimate for support of project activities, including costs not directly attributable to operation of the specific program in question (indirect costs and cost sharing)
   C. Testing criteria for determining costs for program operation against criteria set by funding agency
   D. Revise costs as appropriate in light of fit between IX and XA
XI. Stating problem, intervention and evolution strategies, and resources prerequisite to program operation in a document conforming to constraint criteria (form and content) of submitting institution and receiving agency

---

process and outcome, carried as an entry in a proposal document, is easily discerned.

Experience in working with teachers and human service agency personnel has convinced this writer that once an individual understands the structural relationship between proposal components, and masters the skills necessary to carry out the specific tasks consistent with the proposal structure, that person will be able to respond effectively to a wide range of proposal requests. The proposal writer who masters the following steps, which constitute the mode of inquiry generic to proposal development, can identify and master the skills necessary for a proficient program developer.

The first five steps identified in Table 4.2 call for activities that may be classified as data gathering, analysis, and assessment steps. As schematically represented in Figure 4.1, the completion of these steps brings the writer to the statement of objectives, which prepares the groundwork for development of the program. Steps VI, VII, and VIII call primarily for formulation and development activities. Here the program developer must make decisions, based on knowledge relating to the problem, about the specific strategies to be used to realize specific objectives. Issues central to program conceptualization and the appropriateness of strategies must be resolved at this point. Steps IX and X are assessment and management tasks. Step XI represents a synthesis of earlier steps in the form of a written document designed to secure funding from the appropriate agency. The reception given the document by the affected parties is the major criterion for measuring the mastery of skills within the mode of inquiry labeled proposal development.

SUMMARY

The proposal is a statement of institutional commitment to a specified plan of action and calls for new or revised allocations of resources. In addition, it represents a negotiated statement of funding agency and submitting institution strategies relevant to addressing a specific set of needs. As such, it is both a programmatic and political statement; attention has been directed to the implications of both for the development and submittal of the document.

This chapter has identified the structure of the proposal, the nature of the tasks prerequisite for addressing the structural requirements, and the relationship of the tasks to the writing of the components of the proposal document. The proposal document has been treated as a product reflecting the writer's mastery of a mode of inquiry, which is generalizable to any proposal solicitation response. The steps identified as consistent with the mode of inquiry are derived from the structure of the proposal document in which each component is inextricably a part of the whole. The characteristics of individual components are shaped by the preceding and following components. The structure, in addition to identifying the steps that collectively represent the mode of inquiry, relates the steps directly to the writing of the document.

Mastery of the skills inherent in carrying out the steps that constitute the mode of inquiry, coupled with an understanding of the dynamics of the funding process, should provide both the knowledge and technical skills necessary to develop a suitable proposal. The application of concepts discussed in this chapter to the actual development and writing of the proposal document is covered in the following two chapters. The identification of development strategies and the corresponding technical skills now becomes the central task.

ENDNOTES

1. Thomas Johnson, "Causal Modeling in Educational and Social Program Evaluation," paper presented at a meeting of American Educational Research Association, Washington, D.C., April 1975 (Bethesda, Md.: ERIC Document Reproduction Service, ED 1108 603, 1975), p. 4.
2. Jerome Bruner, *The Process of Education* (Cambridge, Mass.: Harvard University Press, 1960), p. 114.
3. Ibid., p. 32.
4. John Dixon, "Conference Report: The Dartmouth Seminar," *Harvard Educational Review* 39 (Spring 1969): 368.
5. Edwin Fenton, *Developing a New Curriculum: A Rationale for the Holt Social Studies Curriculum* (New York: Holt, Rinehart & Winston, 1967), p. 6.

5

The Response to the Proposal Request

Throughout this work, the concept of structure has been emphasized as basic to understanding and mastering the dynamics of funding. The concept is not difficult to comprehend if one recognizes that it deals with the parts of an object and how they are interrelated. Then the value of its application to both funding in general and proposal writing in particular becomes apparent.

Earlier chapters proposed a structure for examining funding in its sociopolitical context. The preceding chapter narrowed the focus to the proposal structure itself. The implications of these structural characteristics for responding to funding opportunities and the application of the concepts already discussed to identifying strategies for developing a fundable proposal are the subjects of this chapter. The choice of approach resulted from analysis of literally hundreds of proposal development efforts that failed for reasons totally unrelated to the quality of the program or proposed research. In general, the failure to carry out data gathering, analysis, and assessment tasks before writing the proposal, and the failure to determine the feasibility of submittal in a given situation, were the causes of funding denials. Therefore, special attention to those variables that come into play before the writing of the document and that ultimately affect the reception given any proposal is justified. The specific elements of the proposal development process that are presented include: (1) the analysis of the proposal request and (2) strategies for proposal development and submittal.

This chapter provides the proposal writer with strategies to assess systematically the feasibility and desirability of submitting a proposal in response to a given funding opportunity. The particular strategies represent applications of approaches derived from the areas of operations research and management.

There are undoubtedly approaches that can be drawn from other fields that are equally appropriate for examining the feasibility of submittal and determining strategies for proposal development. By supplementing knowledge of the structure and process of proposal development with approaches drawn from other areas of inquiry and materials drawn from previous funding solicitations and responses, the proposal developer will be prepared to respond effectively to a wide range of funding opportunities.

As discussed in the last chapter, proposal writing cannot be effective unless the needs and constraints of the submitting institution are tested against the needs and constraints of the funding agency. Ideally, the problem addressed by the proposal should reflect a perfect fit between the needs and priorities of both parties. The identification and negotiation of any discrepancies between their needs and priorities represent the first steps in any response to a funding opportunity. Once these steps have been completed, the writer can produce the document with the assurance that the proposed project is compatible with the submitting institution's interests, addresses funding agency priorities, and conforms to technical criteria and operating policies of both organizations.

ANALYSIS OF THE PROPOSAL REQUEST

Although authorizing legislation, foundation by-laws, and the guidelines provided by offices or individuals responsible for administering programs establish the initial conditions to which the developer must respond, proposal writers often fail to analyze carefully the specific guidelines or priorities of the funding agency. Development of the proposal, without prior analysis of the nature of the request or funding agency priorities, is like developing a game plan for a team sport without identifying the sport or learning the rules. Fortunately, by carrying out some relatively simple tasks before "playing the game," the embarrassment of misreading an invitation can be avoided. Such tasks should include the following steps and strategies.

1. Data Collection Tasks

a. Secure from appropriate education and human service agency offices copies of the laws and amendments governing the state or federal funding programs to which you may be applying;* or

b. Secure from one of the regional foundation clearinghouses or from foundations themselves all possible information pertaining to programs,

---

*For those wishing to take the initiative in identifying funding sources, rather than simply responding to information passed down from state department or federal offices, *The Catalogue of Federal Domestic Assistance (CFDA)*, published by the U.S. Printing Office, provides information on federal domestic programs. The information includes who is eligible, how to apply, and what the submittal deadlines were for the previous year. See Appendix A for additional information.

funding priorities, past projects funded, eligibility of funding, and so forth.*

c. Request from appropriate offices or individuals the guidelines or Rules and Regulations for programs in which you are interested. These will be more specific than the basic laws and will define eligibility, application submittal procedures, and submittal deadlines, and will often provide funding limits.**

2. Data Analysis Tasks

The primary objective in analyzing funding agency data is to determine whether the constraints affecting the submitting institution are consonant with those established by the funding agency. The analysis process commences with the relatively simple task of determining the eligibility of the interested institution; it becomes increasingly refined as decisions focus on the fit between the priorities and programs of the funding agency and the priorities and capabilities of the submitting institution. There is great potential for variation in the complexity of analysis since the scope, complexity, and intent of authorizing legislation and regulations, the range of appropriation levels, and the organizational characteristics of receiving and submitting parties may differ significantly with each solicitation. A decision-making model is needed to identify and order the specific actions required to make an appropriate response under a wide range of circumstances. *Relevance* or *decision-tree analysis* is one such model.

Quantitative relevance or decision-tree analysis is particularly useful for analyzing proposal requests, identifying the submitting institution's alternatives, and identifying the most appropriate strategy for securing funding. This particular analytical approach classifies information relevant to a response in a way that enables the respondent to identify and evaluate systematically the alternative solutions to the problem inherent in the request. Relevance or decision-tree analysis assumes that distinct levels of complexity can be identified in the analysis of a problem. By identifying successive levels of complexity within a system, one can move from general to increasingly specific and finer components

---

*Those wishing to identify foundation sources of funding are directed to *The Foundation Directory*, which lists over 2,500 private U.S. foundations and community trusts. Annual reports of foundations or personal communications with foundation program officers will provide helpful information for determining the feasibility of submittal. Whether government or private sources of support are sought, the value of informal, individually secured information pertaining to all elements of the funding system cannot be overestimated. See Appendix B for additional information on locating foundation funding sources.

**The Federal Register (FR)* is the single most important source of information about federal programs. *FR* is published daily and contains all Proposed and Final Rules and Regulations governing the submittal of proposals to federal agencies. Information provided includes citations of authorizing legislation, criteria for funding, and the definition of eligibility to submit. Although there is no state equivalent of *FR*, many state education and human service offices have carefully developed criteria governing the submittal of proposals and agendas of problem areas to be addressed. See Appendices A, C, and D for additional information on locating federal sources of funding.

118 *The Dynamics of Funding*

of information analysis, in the same manner that a botanist classifying plants moves from general to increasingly refined levels of classification (that is, from phylum to class to sub-class, and so forth).[1] At each step of the information analysis process, the individual must identify, from the available information, the alternative solutions, assign numerical values to them, and then proceed to the next level of decision making, incorporating earlier decisions into the data evaluation. By assigning numerical weights to each of the alternatives, represented as branches, choices can be presented in quantitative terms.

APPLICATION OF THE DECISION-TREE ANALYSIS APPROACH

The implementation of this strategy and its relevance to the needs of an institution preparing to respond to proposal guidelines or Rules and Regulations is illustrated in the following application to two sets of request guidelines: (1) a Program Announcement from the Massachusetts Department of Education, Bureau of Adult Services, and (2) Rules and Regulations governing a more complex request for "Special Projects and Teacher Training in Adult Education," issued by the U.S. Office of Education, Division of Adult Education. The selected examples encompass the full range of complexity that can confront an individual developing a response to a funding opportunity. The specific skills necessary to respond appropriately to either request would support any informed response, regardless of the program goals of the sponsoring agency or the nature of the authorized activities.

Program Announcement, Massachusetts Department of Education

In the beginning of October, 1975, as authorized by the Adult Education Act, P.L. 91-230, as amended under P.L. 93-380, the Massachusetts Department of Education circulated the following announcement to institutions and agencies eligible for funding.

October 1, 1975

ANNOUNCEMENT

The Massachusetts Department of Education, Bureau of Adult Services, has designated funds under Title III of the Adult Education Act for Special Projects and Teacher Training. Adult Basic Education Proposal Applications are being requested from local educational agencies, public and private organizations, Institutions of Higher Education under the Special Projects 309 (1) and Teacher Training 309 (2) Grants, Categories. The Adult Education Act P.L. 91-230, as amended under P.L. 93-380, is designated to address the following educational priorities identified by the department:

I. Collection, analysis, and retrieval of data for Adult Education Programs.
II. Bilingual Models for Adult Education.
III. Programs for Native Americans in their adjustment to the rapid changes of their environment.
IV. Adult Education Programs for institutionalized persons.

Under 309 (2) Teacher Training Funds:

V. Degree-granting programs for professional adult educators.
VI. Collection and dissemination of adult education resource material.

All proposals eligible for review for FY 1976 funds are to be submitted in quadruplicate .... no later than October 31, 1975. All proposals will be reviewed and decisions rendered within 30 days by a selected panel of reviewers.[2]

The decision-tree analysis of clusters of alternatives present within these guidelines provides a structure for making decisions necessary to determine both the feasibility of submittal and the priorities to be addressed in the submitting institution's proposal.

Step I: Identification of Alternative Types of Authorized Activity. From an analysis of the announcement, alternative legislatively authorized programs may be identified and depicted schematically, as in Figure 5.1. At this point in the analysis, decisions can be made regarding institutional eligibility and the characteristics of authorized programs.

Step II: Identification of Characteristics of Alternative Authorized Programs. From an analysis of the announcement, the characteristics of programs

FIGURE 5.1. *Legislatively Authorized Programs*

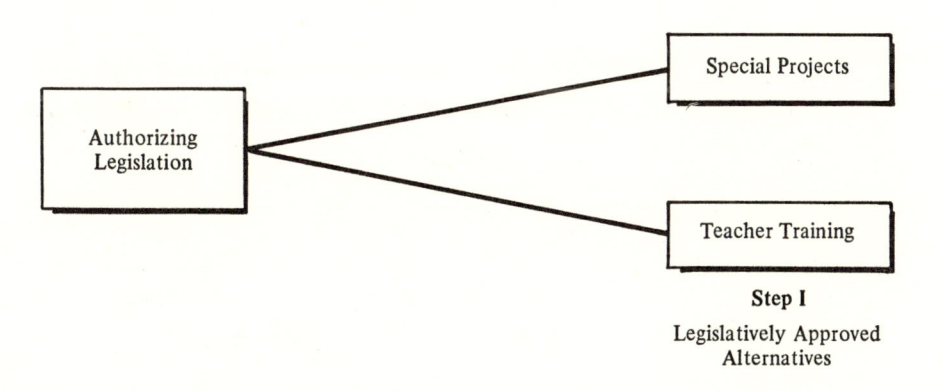

Authorizing Legislation → Special Projects
Authorizing Legislation → Teacher Training

Step I
Legislatively Approved Alternatives

120   *The Dynamics of Funding*

FIGURE 5.2. Characteristics of Programs under Alternate Routes.

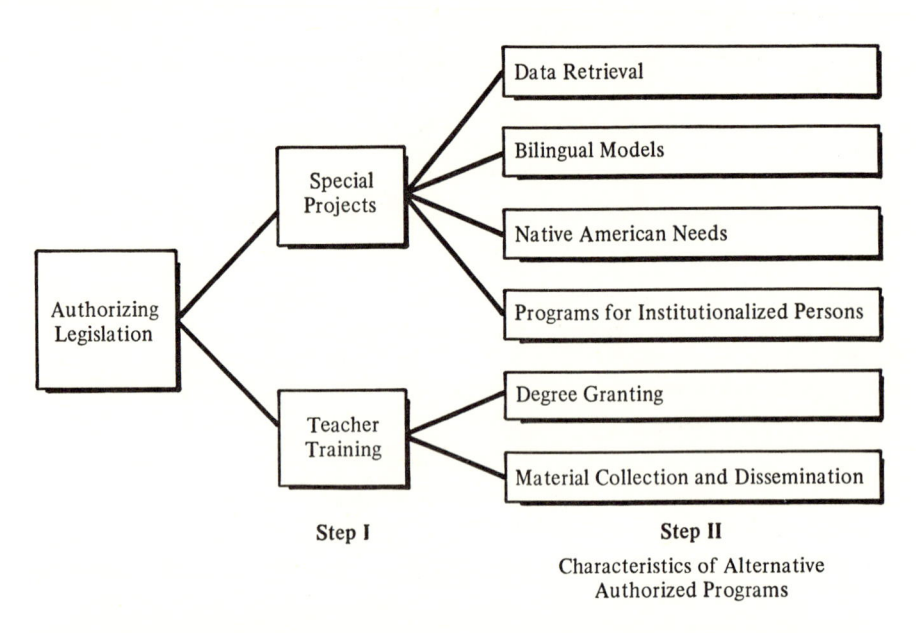

```
                              ┌─ Data Retrieval
                              │
                   Special ───┼─ Bilingual Models
                   Projects   │
                              ├─ Native American Needs
                              │
Authorizing ──┤               └─ Programs for Institutionalized Persons
Legislation   │
                              ┌─ Degree Granting
                   Teacher ───┤
                   Training   └─ Material Collection and Dissemination

    Step I                         Step II
                             Characteristics of Alternative
                                 Authorized Programs
```

requested under the alternative funding routes may be identified. At this point, the potential submitter is provided with six project alternatives clustered under two types of programs. Analysis of these alternatives allows the identification of: (1) funding agency constraint criteria that establish the conditions to which the proposal document must respond and (2) institutional constraint criteria that determine the program's suitability for the submitting institution. The relationship between the conditions set by the request (agency constraint criteria) and the needs and priorities of the submitting institution (institutional constraint criteria) determine both the feasibility and desirability of submitting to the proposal request.

The particular sequence in which the two steps designed to assess the relationship between the agency and institutional constraint criteria are carried out is less important than the fact that they are carried out. Ideally, analysis would start with an identification of institutional constraints and match these against the constraints set by a particular funding opportunity. In practice, however, the constraints of a particular funding request generally are matched against the institutional constraints.

Step III: Quantification of Agency Constraint Criteria. By closely reading the announcement and/or related materials, the constraint criteria to be met in developing proposals appropriate to the characteristics of each alternative authorized program can be determined. For demonstration purposes, this analysis is limited to one program, Bilingual Model for Adult Education.

Agency Constraints–Bilingual Models. As the announcement does not provide specific agency criteria for the Bilingual Models program, the analysis must incorporate data drawn from other sources, if a rational (and fundable) plan for proposal development is to be achieved. Although priorities in the authorizing legislation identify some of the constraints, a more accurate analysis of agency constraints, in such cases, may be achieved through discussion with agency program officers. Such discussions, in conjunction with a review of the legislation, identified the following agency constraints. The proposed program must:

1. Provide basic communication skills development for several ethnic groups for whom English is not the dominant language:
2. Develop mechanisms to link training programs to the employment skills needs of the population served;
3. Develop strategies for employer involvement in program operation;
4. Develop organizational mechanisms to increase opportunities for participant employment; and
5. Identify means to continue training and job placement functions when external funding is no longer available.

Analysis of the preceding agency constraints for program development allow the submitting institution to estimate its capability to conform to the conditions set by the funding request. The probability of meeting the constraints can be expressed as a percentage, with 100 percent representing the ability of the submitting institution to conform fully to the funding agency's expectations. For purposes of demonstration, assume that the probability in this case is 80 percent. In this particular solicitation, the agency constraints indirectly address the issue of institutional eligibility for submittal: institutions of higher education, although not explicitly ineligible under this program, are practically disqualified due to the level of training and employment-related services to be provided. In most proposal requests, eligibility is addressed explicitly and represents a go/no-go constraint that must be addressed before developing the proposal.

Institutional Constraints–Bilingual Models. Agency constraints indicate the feasibility rather than the desirability of submittal. A potential submitter can determine the desirability of submitting by using the same general procedures used to determine the agency constraint criteria. In carrying out this step, however, attention focuses on: (1) the needs of the affected parties (clients) and (2) the priorities and needs of the submitting institution.

The institution considering developing a proposal in response to the sample announcement would have to identify the needs of the parties who would, in effect, be their clients, should the program be developed. Once these needs have been identified, consonance between these needs and characteristics of alternative authorized programs can be assigned to each program.

Assume that the needs of the potential clients have been defined as follows:

Needs of Bilingual Adults in Metropolitan Area

1. All organizations responsible for administering adult education community programs, in areas serving adult populations whose dominant language is other than English, have indicated a desire to implement a range of adult bilingual offerings in communication skills development designed to increase opportunities for vocational mobility and career advancement.
2. A survey of the 260 bilingual adults currently served by these agencies has indicated that 80 percent of the population currently unemployed would be anxious to participate in a program designed to increase skills and improve employment opportunities.
3. Seventy-five percent of the respondents indicated a desire for increased awareness of employment opportunities.
4. Eighty percent of the respondents indicated a desire for activities designed to assist them in identifying their job-related aptitudes.
5. Sixty percent of the respondents indicated a desire to increase language and writing skills in both their native language and English.

More data and greater specificity are necessary in a formal needs assessment. The preceding information, however, is sufficient to make judgments about the type of program the community might seek and the receptivity of clients to a training program that satisfied their interests. Based on this hypothetical list of needs, a scale can be developed and a value or weight assigned to each of the four programs authorized under Special Projects. This value or weight represents the extent to which the program is consonant with community needs. In the Bilingual Models case, the fit between the funding agency constraints (authorized activities and program criteria) and one set of institutional constraints (needs or goals of program participants) might be calculated as in Table 5.1.

Under the agency constraints for the Adult Education program announcement, any organization that identified and could serve the preceding population needs, could consider submitting under the Bilingual Models program. The authorized program does not permit, at least explicitly, on-the-job training or apprenticeships directly tied to employment in a specified field. Therefore, legitimate concern about the current funding channel's ability to meet the expressed community needs (that is, to provide participants with specific skills that can be translated into immediate employment) is reflected in the weighting accorded item 2. The overall score of forty-six out of a possible fifty points, however, indicates sufficient consonance between request constraints and community needs to justify serious consideration of a proposal response.

Although sufficient fit between the agency constraints and the needs of clients of the proposed project is absolutely essential for a proposal to receive

TABLE 5.1. *Consonance of Agency–Client Constraints*

Bilingual Models Program

(1) Increase job mobility for those currently employed

    1 2 3 4 5 6 7 8 <u>9</u> 10*

(2) Develop employable skills for jobless adults

    1 2 3 4 5 6 <u>7</u> 8 9 10

(3) Develop an understanding of the current job market

    1 2 3 4 5 6 7 8 9 <u>10</u>

(4) Help an individual to identify job-related aptitudes

    1 2 3 4 5 6 7 8 9 <u>10</u>

(5) Develop general skills that may not be job related but that meet general needs

    1 2 3 4 5 6 7 8 9 <u>10</u>

                              TOTAL SCORE FOR FUNDING ROUTE <u>46</u>

                                             TOTAL POSSIBLE SCORE <u>50</u>

*A score of 10 indicates that the specific client needs will be directly addressed by the funding route under analysis.

serious consideration, the fit between the submitting institution's needs or priorities and the agency constraints is equally essential to project success. Unfortunately, any disparity in this fit may be hidden by institutions or individuals who tend to define a problem in terms acceptable to the funding agency, in order to secure funding. If the discrepancy between the needs of the agency, the affected parties, and the submitting institution is too great, neither the most creative proposal writing nor the most dedicated project management can prevent the proposal's rejection at the review stage or offset the funded project's inability to realize the proposed objectives. To prevent such occurrences, proposal developers can use the same tasks that led to the assessment of agency/client constraints. This assessment of institutional constraints, however, focuses on the complimentarity of the programmatic and organizational goals of the submitting institution and the funding agency constraints. Appropriate goals for an institution submitting under the Bilingual Models program are reflected in Table 5.2.

Obviously, any organization guided by the goals in Table 5.2 in developing its programs would find an almost perfect fit between agency constraints and those governing its own operations. The Adult Services program announcement seems to have been designed with this particular organization's needs in

124   The Dynamics of Funding

TABLE 5.2. *Goals of Institution "X"*

---

(1) To increase the ability to deliver a wide range of educational services to a large bilingual population

   1 2 3 4 5 6 7 8 9 <u>10</u>

(2) To develop bilingual programs designed to provide communication skill training to adults for whom English is a second language

   1 2 3 4 5 6 7 8 9 <u>10</u>

(3) To develop a supportive service relationship with industries designed to link basic skills development training with industry training

   1 2 3 4 5 6 7 8 9 <u>10</u>

(4) To develop a supportive service program designed to assist individuals in matching their abilities with area employment needs

   1 2 3 4 5 6 7 8 9 <u>10</u>

(5) To develop mechanisms for linking institution's training and service activities with other institutions and agencies providing services to adult bilingual populations

   1 2 3 4 5 6 7 8 9 <u>10</u>

TOTAL SCORE FOR FUNDING ROUTE <u>50</u>

---

mind. Moreover, this organization would probably be ill-advised to pursue any of the alternative funding routes delineated in the program announcement.

Assuming that the analytic steps were applied to each program identified in the request, a relatively objective and carefully considered approach to determine the feasibility of responding would be achieved (see Figure 5.3).

Rules and Regulations, U.S. Office of Education

If the concept and process in the preceding approach are understood, the respondent can safely simplify the process and carry out the analytic tasks by omitting the quantification steps. As long as the principles governing the decision-tree analysis are adhered to, the submitter may use the approach to assess systematically the feasibility and desirability of submitting even under the most complicated proposal guidelines. One simplified variation of the approach and its application to a complicated set of Rules and Regulations follows:

1. List the alternative programs authorized by the specific request.
2. List the parties (for example, local educational agencies or institutions of higher education) eligible to submit proposals.

FIGURE 5.3. Decision Tree for Bureau of Adult Services Announcement

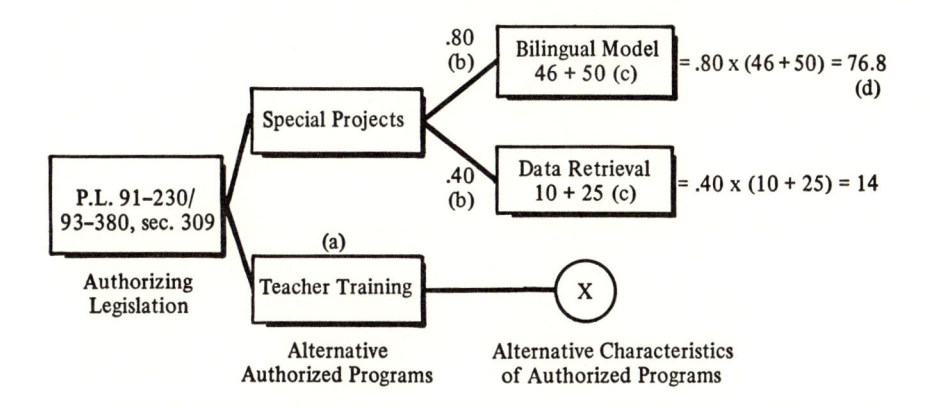

```
                                   .80     ┌─────────────────┐
                                   (b)  ╱  │ Bilingual Model │  = .80 x (46 + 50) = 76.8
                              ┌──────────┐ │   46 + 50 (c)   │                    (d)
                              │ Special  │ └─────────────────┘
                              │ Projects │
                              └──────────┘ ┌─────────────────┐
                                   .40  ╲  │  Data Retrieval │  = .40 x (10 + 25) = 14
┌──────────────┐                   (b)     │   10 + 25 (c)   │
│  P.L. 91-230/│                           └─────────────────┘
│ 93-380, sec. 309│
└──────────────┘      (a)
                              ┌──────────────┐
 Authorizing                  │Teacher Training│──────────( X )
 Legislation                  └──────────────┘

                              Alternative          Alternative Characteristics
                          Authorized Programs       of Authorized Programs
```

KEY:
a. Rejected as option by submitting institution
b. Represents the fit between submitting institution's capability and requirements or constraints set by funding agency, based on possible value of 100%
c. Represents consonance between agency constraints
   (1) needs of population to be served
   (2) priorities of goals of submitting institution
d. Represents total value accorded alternative funding routes

3. On the basis of this information, determine the institution's eligibility to submit. If the request authorizes several programs, determine eligibility for each.
4. Identify the major objectives and characteristics of each program (if provided).
5. From those programs for which the institution is eligible, develop a strategy for quantifying the constraints that need to be considered in determining the feasibility and desirability of seeking funding.

The application of the above steps to analysis of the Reading Improvement Projects, as authorized by the National Reading Improvement Act Rules and Regulations, yields enough information to enable a local school system to decide about the best approach to the request. Table 5.3 identifies the way to use agency-developed materials to assess constraints governing the submittal of proposals. Relevant excerpts from the *Federal Register* announcement appear in Figure 5.4.

After narrowing the choices to one or two funding routes, under a particular set of Rules and Regulations, an analysis of the program constraints accompanying these routes allows the LEA to begin planning the writing of the proposal document. Details drawn from the Rules and Regulations regarding program characteristics, organizational and technical requirements, and the parties to be addressed provide agency constraints to which the proposal must respond. Figure 5.5 identifies the specific agency constraints affecting proposal development for a Reading Improvement Program.

An assessment of institutional capability and receptivity to the program, when set against agency constraints, will determine both the feasibility and (*text continues p. 142.*)

TABLE 5.3. *National Reading Improvement Program Subpart B—Reading Improvement Projects*

Alternate Programs Authorized	Eligible Applicants	Major Objectives and Characteristics
Elementary School Projects (Ref.: Subpart B, 162.10 [b][1])	LEAs, SEAs (Ref.: 162.11[a])	For elementary schools having large numbers or a high percentage of children with reading deficiencies or programs involving the use of innovative methods, systems, materials, or other elements that show promise of overcoming reading deficiencies. (Ref.: 162.11[b][1][i])
Preelementary School Projects (Ref.: Subpart B, 162.10 [b][2])	LEAs, SEAs and nonprofit educational or child care institutions (Ref.: 162.11 [a])	For kindergarten(s), nursery school(s), child care institution(s), (in areas where elementary schools having large numbers or a high percentage of children with reading deficiencies are located), programs involving the use of innovative methods, systems, materials, or other elements that show promise of developing the capacity for reading in preelementary school children who might otherwise develop reading deficiencies. (Ref.: 162.11[b][1][ii])
State Reading Improvement Projects (Ref.: Subpart C, 162.25[a])	SEAs	N/A
Special Emphasis Projects (Ref.: Subpart D, 162.37)	LEAs	The teaching of reading by reading specialists or reading teachers to all children in the first and second grades of an elementary school and to those children in grades three through six who have reading problems. (Ref.: 162.38[a][1])

TABLE 5.3. (cont.)

Alternate Programs Authorized	Eligible Applicants	Major Objectives and Characteristics
		An intensive vocational reading program for elementary school children found to be reading below the approximate grade level or who are experiencing problems in learning to read (Ref.: 162.38)
Reading Academy program (Ref.: Subpart E, 162.50)	SEAs, LEAs, IHEs, and nonprofit organizations	N/A
State Leadership & Training Projects (Ref.: Subpart 162.60)	SEAs	N/A

References indicate subparts and sections in the Rules and Regulations providing the information central to identifying programs, eligibility, and major objectives of the individual programs authorized. N/A notations evolve from noneligibility of LEA applications for specific programs, making further analysis of constraints affecting these programs unnecessary for the submitting LEA. N/A citations would differ markedly for an IHE or nonprofit organization.

FIGURE 5.4. Rules and Regulations

Subpart A—General

Sec.
162.1 Scope and purposes.
162.2 Definitions.
162.3–162.9 [Reserved]

Subpart B—Reading Improvement Projects

162.10 Scope and purpose.
162.11 Eligible applicants; nature of projects.
162.12 Application requirements.
162.13 Review of applications by State educational agencies and State advisory councils.
162.14 Evaluation criteria.
162.15 Equitable geographic distribution.
162.16 [Reserved]
162.17 Duration of projects.
162.18 Size of awards; allowable costs.
162.19–162.24 [Reserved]

FIGURE 5.4. (cont.)

Subpart C—State Reading Improvement Programs

162.25 Scope and purpose.
162.26 Allotments; reallotments.
162.27 Standard of excellence.
162.28 [Reserved]
162.29 Judicial review.
162.30-162.34 [Reserved]

Subpart D—Special Emphasis Project

Sec.
162.35 Scope and purpose.
162.36 Definitions.
162.37 Eligibility; number of applications.
162.38 Nature of projects.
162.39 Review and certification by State educational agencies.
162.40 Application requirements.
162.41 Evaluation criteria.
162.42 District-wide project award.
162.43 [Reserved]
162.44 Duration of projects.
162.45 Size of awards; allowable costs.
162.46-162.49 [Reserved]

Subpart E—Reading Program

162.50 Scope and purpose.
162.51 Definitions.
162.52 Application requirements.
162.53 Evaluation criteria.
162.54 Allowable costs.
162.55 Project duration.

Subpart F—State Leadership and Training Projects

162.60 Scope and purpose.
162.61 Nature of projects; funding requirements.
162.62 Evaluation criteria.
162.63 Project duration.
162.64 Allowable costs.

APPENDIX A—Part B of title VII of Pub. L. 93-380.

APPENDIX B—Manual of Guidelines for the Reading Academy Program.

AUTHORITY: Title VII of Pub. L. 93-380, as amended by Pub. L. 94-194 (20 U.S.C. 1901-1982).

Subpart A—General

§ 162.1 Scope and purposes.

(a) *Scope.* This part applies to projects assisted with funds appropriated pursuant to the National Reading Improvement Program, title VII of Pub. L. 93-380, as amended by Pub. L. 94-194;

FIGURE 5.4. *(cont.)*

(b) *Purposes.* The purposes of the programs carried out pursuant to this part are, through grants and contracts to State and local educational agencies and other non-profit organiations, to:

(1) Provide financial assistance to encourage State and local educational agencies to undertake projects to strengthen reading instructional programs in elementary grades;

(2) Provide financial assistance for the development and enhancement of necessary skills of instructional and other educational staff for reading programs:

(3) Develop a means by which measurable objectives for reading programs can be established and progress toward these objectives assessed;

(4) Develop the capacity of preelementary school children for reading:

(5) Establish and improve preelementary school programs in language arts and reading; and

(6) Provide financial assistance to promote literacy among youths and adults.

(c) *Other pertinent regulations.* Awards under this part are subject to applicable provisions contained in Sub-chapter A of this chapter (relating to fiscal, administrative, property management, and other matters, 45 CFR Parts 100, 100a, 100b).

(20 U.S.C. 1901)

§ 162.2 Definitions.
As used in this part:
"Act" means title VII of the Education Amendments of 1974, Pub. L. 93-380, as amended by Pub. L. 94-194.
"Appropriate" when applied to "grade level" means commensurate with the individual student's age and ability.
"Elementary school" means a day or residential school which provides elementary education, as determined under State law.
"Bilingual education" means instruction designed for children of limited English-speaking ability including instruction:

(a) In and study of English and, to the extent necessary to allow a child to progress effectively through the educational system, the native language of the children of limited English-speaking ability; and

(b) Which is given with appreciation for the cultural heritage of such children.
"Commissioner" means the U.S. Commissioner of Education.
"Innovative" means a program element which is new and different to participants in project activities.
"Institution of higher education" means an institution of higher education in any State as defined under the Higher Education Act of 1965, as amended.

(20 U.S.C. 1141)

"Limited English-speaking ability," when used with reference to an individual, means an individual who:

(a)(1) Was not born in the United States or whose native language is a language other than English; or

(2) Comes from an environment where a language other than English is dominant; and

FIGURE 5.4. (cont.)

(b) As a result of paragraph (a)(1) or (2) above, has difficulty speaking and understanding instruction in the English language.

"Local education agency" means a public board of education or other public authority legally constituted within a State for either administrative control or direction of, or to perform a service function for, public elementary or secondary schools in a city, county, township, school district, or other political subdivision of a State, or a combination of school districts or counties recognized in a State as an administrative agency for its public elementary or secondary schools. The term also includes any other public institution or agency having administrative control and direction of a public elementary or secondary school.

"Non-profit educational or child care institution" means any public or private non-profit organization which sponsors a regular, on-going educational or child care program for preschool age children.

"Reading deficiencies" means that reading achievement is less than that which would normally be expected for children of comparable ages or comparable grades of school; for children in grades 2-8 this would mean one or more years below appropriate grade level in reading an estimated by standardized tests and/or informal testing.

"High percentage," when applied to "of children with reading deficiencies," means 50 percent or more of the students in grades 2 through 8 in project schools or project classes are reading one or more years below appropriate grade level.

"Project" means those activities of a grantee or contractor which the Commissioner determines to be eligible for Federal financial assistance.

"Reading-related activities" means any activities directly or indirectly connected with skills and/or behaviors in the area of reading; for example, listening, speaking, writing activities, reading games, discussing illustrations, classifying and categorizing, and developing auditory and visual perceptual skills.

(20 U.S.C. 1901 and 1921)

"State" means, except as used in Subpart C, the several States of the Union, the Commonwealth of Puerto Rico, the District of Columbia, Guam, American Samoa, the Virgin Island, and the Trust Territory of the Pacific Islands. As used in Supbart C, "State" means the several States of the Union, the District of Columbia, and the Commonwealth of Puerto Rico.

(20 U.S.C. 1942(a)(2))

'State educational agency" means the State board of education or other agency or officer primarily responsible for the State supervision of public elementary and secondary schools or, if there is no such office or agency, an officer or agency designated by the Governor or by State law.

(20 U.S.C. 1901 and 1921)

§ 162.3-162.9 [Reserved]

Federal Register 41, no. 103, 26 May 1976, 214-21472

FIGURE 5.5. *Rules and Regulations*

Subpart B—Reading Improvement Projects

§ 162.10 Scope and purpose.

(a) *Scope.* This subpart applies to projects assisted with funds appropriated to carry out part A, section 705 of title VII of Pub. L. 93–380, as amended by Pub. L. 94–194;

(20 U.S.C. 1921)

(b) *Purpose.* The purpose of the program carried out pursuant to this subpart is, through grants to eligible recipients, to support:

* (1) Projects to strengthen reading instructional programs in elementary school(s) having large numbers or a high percentage of children with reading deficiencies; and

* (2) Projects to establish and improve programs in language arts and reading in preelementary school(s), in areas where there are large numbers or a high percentage of elementary school children with reading deficiencies, and to develop the capacity of preelementary school children for reading.

(20 U.S.C. 1921(a))

* § 162.11 Eligible applicants; nature of projects.

(a) *Eligible applicants.* (1) As stated in section 705 of the Act, local educational agencies, State educational agencies, or both, may apply for elementary school projects described in paragraph (b)(1)(i) of this section and for preelementary school projects described in paragraph (b)(1)(ii) of this section. In addition non-profit educational or child care institutions may apply for the preelementary school projects;

(2) Though multiple applications may be submitted by a single applicant, in no case will more than one grant for an elementary school project and one grant for a preelementary school project be awarded to the same applicant;

* (b) *Nature of projects.* (1) Two types of grants will be awarded pursuant to this subpart:

* (i) Projects to carry out in elementary school(s) having large numbers or a high percentage of children with reading deficiencies, programs involving the use of innovative methods, systems, materials, or other elements which show promise of overcoming the reading deficiencies; and

* (ii) Projects to carry out in kindergarten(s), nursery school(s), child care institution(s), or other preschool institution(s) (in areas where elementary schools having large numbers or a high percentage of children with reading deficiencies are located), programs involving the use of innovative methods, systems, materials, or other elements which show promise of developing the capacity for reading of preelementary school children who might otherwise develop reading deficiencies;

* (2)(i) Applications for elementary school projects under paragraph (b)(1)(i) of this section which propose to carry out reading activities in elementary schools for children above the kindergarten level may involve children in any

---

*Represent choices that determine applicability of succeeding program submittal requirements.

FIGURE 5.5. (cont.)

or all grades within the elementary schools, including children at the kindergarten level;
* (ii) Applications which do not propose to carry out activities for children above the kindergarten level shall be reviewed as preelementary school projects;
* (3) Projects assisted pursuant to this subpart must be designed to establish, to expand, or to improve the reading programs in one or more specific and identified elementary or preelementary schools.

(20 U.S.C. 1921(a), S. Rep. No. 763, 93d Cong. 2d Sess. 125 (1974))

* (4)(i) Reading program activities and services assisted under the project must be directly administered by, or under the supervision of, the grantee;
* (ii) Grantees may not use any Federal funds awarded pursuant to this subpart to award subgrants to other entities or persons;
* (iii) Grantees may, with Federal funds awarded pursuant to this subpart, enter into contracts with other entities or persons to secure services which will assist them in carrying out a portion of the program sctivities, as provided in § 100a.-30 of this chapter, subject to the conditions set forth in § 100a.30 of this chapter which prohibit transfer of responsibility (or conduit arrangements) by the grantee and require a statement of intention to enter into a service contract in the approved application or an approved amendment thereto; and
* (iv) In accordance with paragraphs (b)(4)(i) and (ii) of this section, State educational agencies may receive grants under the subpart only if they will directly administer or supervise reading programs to be assisted by the project in cases where the State educational agency:

(A) Is directly responsible for operating an elementary or preelementary school;

(B) Applies jointly with a local educational agency or other eligible applicant responsible for administering an elementary or preelementary school, pursuant to E100a.19 of this chapter (General Provisions Regulations for Office of Education programs; 45 CFR 100a.19); or

(C) Under arrangements with a local educational agency or other eligible applicant, assumes responsibility for reading activities to be assisted by the project in schools administered by the loal educational agency or other eligible applicant.

(20 U.S.C. 1921(a), (b), and (c); 1221c(b)(1), 1232(b)(1))

§ 162.12 Application requirements.

The Commissioner will award a grant to a State educational agency, local educational agency, or other eligible applicant under this subpart only upon an application submitted to the Commissioner which meets the following requirements:

* (a) *Project objectives.* The application must set forth:

(1) Specific and measurable objectives related to overcoming reading deficiencies of children in the project school(s) including (only with respect to elementary school projects described in § 162.11(b)(1)(i) a plan for having

*Represent choices that determine applicability of succeeding program submittal requirements.

FIGURE 5.5. *(cont.)*

---

the children in project schools reading at the appropriate grade level at the end of grade three;

(2) A proposed time frame for accomplishing these objectives; and

(3) An evaluation component providing for the collection, verification, and analysis of data to measure the extent to which the objectives are accomplished by the project;

(20 U.S.C. 1921(a), (b), (c)(2))

* (b) *Project school(s).* (1) The application must identify the school(s) and the class(es) to be served by the project and provide information on how the school(s) and class(es) were selected for the project, the numbers and percentages of children in the project school(s) with reading deficiencies, and the nature of reading deficiencies of those children, including (only with respect to elementary school projects described in §162.11(b)(1)(i)) documentation that appropriate measures have already been taken by the applicant to analyze the reasons why elementary school children are not reading at the appropriate grade levels:

(2) The application must provide demographic information on children in the school(s) to be served by the project, including information on the socio-economic, racial, ethnic, language and cultural composition of the school(s); and

(3) The application must:

(i) Provide information on existing reading programs and activities in the project school(s), including information on the resources and methods used to teach reading or reading-related activities to children and the extent of effectiveness of those resources and methods; and

(ii) Explain how the proposed project will improve or expand upon the existing reading activities and programs, including a description of innovative methods, systems, materials, or other elements which will be used in the project to overcome reading deficiencies;

(20 U.S.C. 1921(a), (b), (c) (1))

* (c) *Program requirements.* The Commissioner will award a grant under this subpart only upon an application submitted to the Commissioner which meets the requirements in paragraphs (a) and (b) of this section, as applicable, and which sets forth a reading program which includes the following elements, as applicable:

* (1) *All applications.* All applications under this subpart must:

* (i)(A) Document that there has been participation in the planning and development of the program described in the application by (1) parents of children to be served by the program, (2) the policymaking board of the applicant, and (3) leaders of the cultural and educational resources of the area to be served including representatives of such organizations as institutions of higher education, non-profit schools, public and private non-profit agencies such as libraries, museums, educational radio and television organizations, and other cultural and educational resource agencies of the community, subject to the possibility

*Represent choices that determine applicability of succeeding program submittal requirements.

FIGURE 5.5. (cont.)

that, if the applicant believes it to be impracticable for reasons such as the small size of the project for the project to meet the requirement under this subdivision (3), the application must document to the Commissioner's satisfaction the reasons why the requirement is impracticable, and the Commissioner may then waive the requirement;

* (B) Include a description of procedures which have been used to provide the public at large in the area or areas proposed to be served by the project with an opportunity to have input in the planning of the program described in the application (such as through public notice and hearings); and

* (C) Provide for the continuing participation of groups and representatives described under paragraph (c)(1)(3)(A) of this section in the development and implementation of the program described in the application;

* (ii) Set forth a reading program which provides for:

* (A) Diagnostic testing designed to identify children with reading deficiencies, including the identification of conditions which, without appropriate other treatment, can be expected to impede or prevent children from learning to read:

* (B) Planning and establishing comprehensive reading programs in project schools;

* (C) Preservice training programs for project teaching personnel, including teacher aides and other ancillary educational personnel, within the project schools, and inservice training and development programs, where feasible, designed to enable these personnel to improve their ability to teach students to read, subject to the possibility that, if the applicant believes it to be impracticable for reasons such as the small size of the project for the project to meet this requirement, the application must document to the Commissioner's satisfaction the reasons why the requirement is impracticable, and the Commissioner may then waive the requirement;

* (D) Participation of the school faculty, the policy-making board of the applicant, members of the school, administration, parents, and students in reading-related activities which stimulate an interest in reading and are conducive to the improvement of reading skills;

* (E) With respect to tests of reading achievement administered pursuant to paragraph (c)(2)(i)(B) of this section:

(1) Publication of test results on reading achievement by grade level and, where appropriate, by school, without identification of individual children; and

(2) The availability of test results on reading achievement on an individual basis to parents and guardians of any child tested;

* (F) Use of bilingual education methods and techniques consistent with the number of elementary school age children (or of preelementary school age children with respect to preelementary school projects under §162.11(b)(1)(ii)) in the area served by a reading program who are of limited English-speaking ability; and

* (G) Dissemination of information on the results of the program and of the means used to achieve the results to State educational agencies, local educational agencies, other educational agencies and institutions, and the Commissioner;

*Represent choices that determine applicability of succeeding program submittal requirements.

FIGURE 5.5. (cont.)

** (2) Elementary school projects. (i) Applications under this subpart for elementary school programs under § 162.11(b)(1)(i) must set forth a reading program which, in addition to meeting the requirements in paragraph (c)(1) of this section, provides:
* (A) Reading instruction focused upon elementary school children whose reading achievement is less than that normally expected for children of comparable ages or in comparable grades of school, but also instruction which provides for every child in classes involved in the project;
* (B) Periodic testing for elementary school children on a sufficiently frequent basis to measure accurately reading achievement;
* (C) Participation on an equitable basis by children enrolled in non-profit private elementary schools in the area to be served (after consultation with the appropriate private school officials) to an extent consistant with the number of such children whose educational needs are of the kind the program is intended to meet.
* (ii) Applications must also: (A) Indicate the number of children enrolled in nonpublic schools who are expected to participate in each program and the manner of their expected participation; and
* (B) Document that there has been participation in the planning and development of the program described in the application by officials representing nonprofit private elementary schools in the area to be served with children whose educational needs are of the kind which the program is intended to meet, and document the kind of continuing participation by those officials there will be in the development and implementation of the program;
** (3) *Preelementary school projects.* Applications for preelementary school programs under § 162.11(b)(1)(ii) must set forth a reading program which, in addition to meeting the requirements in paragraph (c)(1) of this section, provides:
* (i) A test of reading proficiency at the conclusion, minimally, of the first-grade programs into which the preelementary school program is integrated for children who had previously participated in the preelementary school program;
* (ii) Assessment, evaluation, and collection of information on individual children by teachers during each year of the preelementary program to be made available for teachers in the subsequent year, in order that continuity for the individual child be maintained; and
* (iii) Whenever appropriate coordination with the reading programs of the educational agencies or institutions where the preelementary school children will be next in attendance, including any necessary arrangements by the applicant with those educational agencies or institutions for meeting the requirements relating to testing described in paragraph (c)(3)(i) of this section; and

(d) *Other information.* Applications may include other appropriate information to respond to criteria in § 162.14.

(20 U.S.C. 1821(b))

*Represent choices that determine applicability of succeeding program submittal requirements.

**Applicability dependent on earlier choice regarding population for which program is designed.

FIGURE 5.5. (cont.)

§ 162.13 Review of application by State educational agencies and State advisory councils.

(a) The Commissioner will not approve an application submitted under this subpart unless the State educational agency has:

* (1) (i) Established and appointed an advisory council on reading broadly representative of the educational resources and of the general population of the State, including but not limited to persons representative of:
* (A) Public and private non-profit elementary and secondary schools;
* (B) Institutions of higher education;
* (C) Parents of elementary and secondary school children; and
* (D) Areas of professional competence relating to instruction in reading; and
* (ii) Authorized and provided the opportunity to the advisory council to receive and designate priorities among applications for grants under this subpart in that State; and

(2) First approved the application;

(20 U.S.C. 1921(d), (e)(1), S. Rep. No. 1026, 93d Cong. 2d Sess. 198 (1974))

* (b) Applicants other than the State educaitonal agency must provide a copy of their application to the State educational agency of the State in which they are located 15 days prior to the applicant's submission of the application to the Commissioner;
* (c) The Commissioner may establish a cut-off date for approval of applications by the State educational agency. If the Commissioner establishes such a date, failure by the State educational agency to indicate its approval to the Commissioner within the period specified shall be deemed a disapproval of the application by the State educational agency, and the application will not be considered for funding by the Commissioner;
* (d) (1) The State educational agency must inform the Commissioner, in writing, in accordance with any cut-off date established by the Commissioner under paragraph (c) of this section, of these applications within its State which it approves for funding under this subpart;

(20 U.S.C. 1921(e) (1))

* (2) The State educational agency must include in its written submission to the Commissioner;
* (i) Documentation that it has established and appointed an advisory council in accordance with paragraph (2)(1) of this section, including information on the membership of the council, and that the council has been provided with an opportunity to receive and designate priorities among applications for grants under this subpart in that State (including applications by the State educational agency);
* (ii) Information on any priorities designated by the advisory council among applications for grants under this subpart in that State; and
* (e) While there is no mandated limitation on the number of applications which may be approved by the State educational agency, State educational agencies

*Represents choices that determine applicability of succeeding program submittal requirements.

FIGURE 5.5. (cont.)

are strongly urged to approve no more than ten applications and to forward to the Commissioner the rankings and copies of any written reviews of the applications.

(20 U.S.C. 1921(d), (e) (2))

§ 162.14 Evaluation criteria.

Applications for grants under this part which meet all of the application requirements in § 162.12 and which are approved by the appropriate State educational agency will be evaluated by the Commissioner on the basis of the following criteria, weighted according to the indicated points, totaling 105 points for elementary projects and 230 points for preelementary projects, and the provisions of § 162.15 concerning equitable distribution of funds and State maximums:

*** (a) *General criteria.* (1) The need for the proposed activity in the area to be served by the applicant, particularly as it relates to the percentage or numbers of children with reading deficiencies in school(s) to be served by the project (10 points);

(2) Whether the program to be assisted responds to the reading needs it identifies and holds substantial promise of overcoming the reading deficiencies of children in the project schools (10 points);

(3) The adequacy of qualifications and experience of personnel designated to carry out the proposed project (10 points);

(4) The adequacy of facilities and other resources to carry out the project and, in particular, the use staff will make of those facilities in the project (5 points);

(5) Reasonableness of estimated cost in relation to anticipated results (5 points);

(6) Whether the proposed methods, systems, materials, or approaches of the program are sufficiently exemplary to be utilized in other projects or programs for similar educational purposes (5 points);

(7) Sufficiency of size, scope, and duration of the project so as to secure productive results (5 points);

(8) Soundness of the proposed plan of operation, including consideration of the extent to which (15 points):

(i) The objectives of the proposed project are sharply defined, clearly stated, capable of being attained by the proposed procedures, and capable of being measured;

(ii) Provision is made for high quality evaluation the effectiveness of the project and for determining the extent the objectives are accomplished; and

(iii) Provision is made for disseminating the results of the project and for making the resulting materials, techniques, and other inputs available to the general public and specifically to those concerned with the area of education with which the project is itself concerned;

(9) The likelihood that program activities to be carried out under the project will be sustained and expanded by the applicant following the expiration of Federal assistance (5 points), as measured by:

***Proposal review criteria central to the writing of the document. Function and use of criteria to be treated in depth in following chapter.

FIGURE 5.5. (cont.)

(i) Evidence of financial and other commitment of the applicant, including its policymaking board, to the program; and

(ii) The extent the project is designed to build the capacity of the applicant to plan, expand, and improve effective reading programs on the elementary or preelementary school level; and

(10) Extra points will be awarded to projects which provide for reaching a large number of schools (10 points) through:

(i) Their direct involvement in the project schools;

(ii) A statement of commitment by the applicant and reasonable time-tables to implement, after the expiration of Federal assistance under this subpart, innovative methods, systems, materials, or other elements developed in the project in all other schools administered by the applicant; and/or

(iii) Provisions for dissemination of information to other agencies, institutions, and schools concerning innovative methods, systems, materials, or other elements developed in the project, including documentation of the applicant's access to existing networks of potential users; and

(11) The ranking of the application by the State advisory council pursuant to § 162.13 (50 points);

(20 U.S.C. 1921 (a), (b), (c))

(b) *Specific programmatic criteria.* The extent the proposed project is designed to achieve high quality (beyond meeting minimum requirements) for the following specific program elements required by § 162.12(c) to be contained in each program funded under this subpart:

(1) Diagnostic testing to identify school children with reading deficiencies (5 points), as measured by factors such as whether:

(i) Tests will assist teachers and administrators in making decisions within the classroom and school;

(ii) Tests will diagnose the student's strengths and identify areas to be taught;

(iii) Tests will be used which are most specific and which give recommendations for specific treatments in cognitive and affective area;

(iv) Diagnosis will be an ongoing process; and

(v) Tests are valid and reliable, as well as culturally and linguistically fair;

(2) Planning and establishing comprehensive reading programs (10 points), as measured by factors such as whether;

(i) The program focuses on the training of existing staff and would be carried out with existing staff rather than hiring additional staff members with Federal funds;

(ii) The project objectives are derived from and responsive to the findings of the needs assessment and diagnostic testing in the school(s) proposed to be served;

(iii) The reading program is designed to focus on children with reading deficiencies, but also provides reading instruction for every child in classes involved in the project;

(iv) Provision is made for individualized instruction which allows individual children to proceed at their own pace and in appropriate skill sequences;

(20 U.S.C. 1921)

FIGURE 5.5. *(cont.)*

(v) Continuity in teaching methods from grade to grade is attempted within each project school, while at the same time there is flexibility to adjust methods and techniques for individual children based on the results of diagnostic testing;

(S. Rep. No. 163, 93d Cong. 2d Sess. 125 (1974))

(vi) Children are not separated away from the classroom by ability or lack of ability, unless the applicant demonstrates that separation for a portion of the school day for supplementary instruction:

(A) Is essential to the purpose of the program; and

(B) Is essential to the needs of the child because the child's needs cannot totally be met in the regular classroom; and

(vii) Attention is given in the preelementary school program and in the early primary grades to reading readiness activities.

(3) Preservice and inservice training for teaching personnel (15 points), as measured by factor such as whether:

(i) The training to be provided relates to the assessed needs of teaching and ancillary educational personnel and children in project school(s);

(ii) The training will be offered at convenient times and locations;

(iii) Provision is made for classroom application of newly learned competencies and for follow up technical assistance to staff members;

(iv) Provision is made for evaluation of the training; and

(v) Instructional theory and experiences are offered which provided trainees with a capacity to:

(A) Understand the language arts process, children's literature, and reading readiness;

(B) Use diagnostic techniques to identify the reading needs of individual children and to evaluate student progress toward instructional objectives;

(C) Develop and carry out reading programs designed to meet the needs of individual children, including activities to meet the special reading needs of children from diverse cultural and linguistic backgrounds;

(D) Work constructively and positively, on a group and individual basis, with children, parents, and other educational personnel;

(E) Effectively utilize a variety of approaches to the teaching of reading, including sequenced instruction, integration of reading instruction into other subject matter areas, flexible grouping of students based on student interest, needs, and abilities, and individualized instruction; and

(F) Plan and manage overall reading programs, including aspects such as problem-solving techniques, needs assessement and planning instruments, record-keeping, the identification and use of program resources, and program evaluation;

(4) Involvement in the project of school faculty, parents, the policymaking board of the applicant, and leaders of educational and cultural resources of the area to be served (15 points) as measured by such factors as whether;

(i) Two way communication is fostered between the project schools and appropriate groups outside the schools;

(ii) Practical involvement of parents and board members in carrying out project activities is permitted; and

(iii) The project staff provides evaluation information to parents and board members;

FIGURE 5.5. (cont.)

---

(5) Periodic achievement testing (5 points), as measured by such factors as whether:

(i) Testing will be done with the children at appropriate times and frequencies:

(ii) The project staff delineates before the testing what the tests are intended to measure, how the test results are going to be used, and the audiences for whom the test results are intended;

(iii) The same level of the same test is used for both pre- and post-testing of children;

(iv) If commercially prepared tests are used, project staff will carefully administer and score the tests according to the procedures outlined by test publishers;

(v) There is a clear rationale why the test measures will be criterion-referenced, norm-referenced, or informal; and

(vi) Project staff will scrutinize carefully whether the causes for observed gains are due to the treatment or other factors;

(6) Appropriate use of bilingual education methods and techniques (5 points) as measured by such factors as whether:

(i) There will be increased use of culturally relevant resources appropriate to the children in project school(s);

(ii) Students will be provided a knowledge of the history and culture associated with their languages;

(iii) Students will develop listening, speaking, reading, writing, and other academic skills in two languages;

(iv) The project will prevent the separation of children away from the classroom by language or ethnic background in any activity included in the programs, unless the applicant demonstrates that separation for a portion of the school day for specific language/reading activities is essential to the purpose of the program and needs of the child; and

(v) The project will utilize bilingual teaching and administrative staff;

(7) Collection and assessment of information on the reading needs of individual children to be made available for teachers in the subsequent year (5 points), as measured by such factors as whether the assessment is designed to:

(i) Aim at factual information rather than mere opinion;

(ii) Include information on both cognitive and affective factors related to reading; and

(iii) Be done with uniform data collection instruments that can be used as a part of the school's total evaluation design;

(20 U.S.C. 1921(b))

(8) Publication of the test results on achievement by grade level and, where appropriate, by school, without identification of achievement of individual children (5 points), as measured by such factors as whether publication and interpretation of test results is done in a way to:

(i) Protect the children;

(ii) Be understandable to the people who receive the results:

(iii) Present pre-test and post-test results with adequate explanation of the correlations;

FIGURE 5.5. (cont.)

(c) *Additional criteria for preelementary school projects.* The Commissioner will evaluate applications for prelementary school projects on the basis of the criteria set forth in paragraphs (a) and (b) of this section, according to the indicated weights, and the following criteria, weighted as indicated:

(1) The extent the project goals are commensurate with the appropriate developmental stages for the children to be served (10 points);

(2) The extent the project assesses the needs of preschool children by employing reliable and field-tested tools which can diagnose, screen, and predict potential readiness for reading (10 points);

(3) The extent qualified teachers use multi-teaching strategies and varied materials and resources in providing reading readiness experiences (5 points);

(4) The extent the project takes into account the various modalities for learning (5 points); and

(5) The extent provision is made for parent education in child management (5 points).

(20 U.S.C. 1921(b))

*§ 162.15 Equitable geographic distribution.

(a) In approving applications under this subpart the Commissioner will, to the maximum extent feasible, assure an equitable distribution of funds throughout the United States and among urban and rural areas. In assuring an equitable distribution of funds throughout the United States, the Commissioner will consider:

(1) School-age population within a State;
(2) Urban and rural population distribution;
(3) Percentage of children with reading deficiencies;
(4) A widespread geographic distribution of projects;
(5) Ethnic/racial and cultural diversity of population to be served;
(6) Any other pertinent information;
(b) Not more than 12½ percent of the funds expended under this subpart in any fiscal year may be expended in any State in that year.

(20 U.S.C. 1921(g))

§ 162.16 [Reserved]

§ 162.17 Duration of projects.
* (a) Projects may be for up to two years' duration.
* (b) Applications proposing two year projects must be accompanied by an explanation of the need for two year support, an overview of the objectives and activities proposed, and budget estimates to attain these objectives in the proposed second year.
* (c) If the application demonstrates to the Commissioner's satisfaction that two year support is needed to carry out the proposed project, the Commissioner may, in the initial notification of grant award for the project (which shall be for up to a twelve month period) indicate an intention to assist the project for a second year through a continuation grant.

*Represents choices that determine applicability of succeeding program submittal requirements.

FIGURE 5.5. *(cont.)*

---

* (d) Continuation awards may be made to projects described in paragraph (c) of this section, subject to the restriction in paragraph (a) of this section and to the availability of funds.

(e) Applications for continuance awards will be reviewed on a non-competitive basis to determine:

(1) If the award recipient has complied with the award terms and conditions, the Act, and any applicable regulation;

(2) The project's effectiveness to date, or the constructive changes proposed as a result of the ongoing evaluation; and

(3) The extent continuation of Federal assistance would further a multiplier effect through:

(i) Directly involving additional schools and students in the project;

(ii) Provisions for implementing, after the expiration of Federal assistance under this subpart, innovative methods, systems, materials, or other elements developed in the project in all other schools administered by the applicant; and/or

(iii) Provisions for dissemination of information to other agencies, institutions, and schools concerning innovative methods systems, materials, or other elements developed in the project.

(20 U.S.C. 1921)

§ 162.18 Size of awards, allowable costs.

* (a) It is expected that most awards under the subpart will range between $15,000 and $125,000 for elementary school projects and between $5,000 and $25,000 for preelementary school projects with most of the awards made at the lower halves of these ranges, depending on the size of the service area, the number of children to be served, the scope and nature of the project, and relative local costs. Nothing in this section shall be construed to limit the size of any particular grant award under this subpart; and

* (b) Allowable costs under grants awarded under this subpart shall be determined in accordance with the cost principles provided under Subpart G of 45 CFR Part 100a, subject to the restrictions that:

* (1) A maximum of 10 percent of the amount of the grant award may be spent for evaluation purposes; and

* (2) A maximum of 10 percent of the grant award may be spent for the purchase of inexpensive books for distribution on a loan basis to elementary and preelementary school children.

(20 U.S.C. 1921, S. Rep. No. 1026, 93d Cong. 2d Sess. 198 (1974))

§ 162.19–162.24 [Reserved]

---

*Represents choices that determine applicability of succeeding program submittal requirements.

---

desirability of proposal development and submittal. The assessment should also reflect the formal organization and program constraints that will affect the submitting institution's planning. Finally, agency or institutional factors that are not formally communicated or immediately observable, but that will affect planning, must also be assessed. Factors to consider in carrying out the preceding assessments include:

1. *Agency Program Constraints*: Those stipulations in the announcement that identify the needs to be addressed, the population to be served, the characteristics of the program, and the criteria for proposal review.*

2. *Agency Organizational Constraints*: Those stipulations in the announcement that define eligibility of submitting parties, that identify parties to participate in program development, and that govern the level of funding, length of funding, and policies for project administration.

3. *Institutional Program Constraints*: Those policies and practices guiding past program development efforts, past and current program priorities, and the institution's capability to carry out activities identified in the proposal.

4. *Institutional Organizational Constraints*: Those formal policies of the submitting institution that govern the allocation of authority, the assignment of personnel, and the calculation of costs.

5. *Informal Institutional and Agency Constraints*: Those factors that affect (a) the distribution of power within an institution or agency, (b) the relationship between organizational units within an institution or agency, and (c) the relationship between the institution and other parties, including the funding agency.

At this point, the reader legitimately may be concerned that an undue amount of time is spent in analyzing the proposal request. The decision to treat this element of the proposal development process in such detail was based on a desire to emphasize, from the outset, the major impact that agency and institutional constraints have on successful document development and future program implementation. This decision is reinforced by the fact that both state and federal program offices frequently hold conferences before proposal submittal dates to discuss the analysis of the proposal request and the expectations of the receiving office. If institutional representatives attend these meetings with a working knowledge of the institutional and agency constraints on development, they can secure information pertinent to their institution's needs. In addition, they can better estimate the reception to be given the proposal by the funding agency and the receptivity to be granted the program by the submitting institution if funding is secured.

A second factor contributing to the attention given the request analysis is more pragmatic in nature. The frequency of missed opportunities, ineligible submittals, differing institutional and agency needs, and the accompanying frustration that stems from a misunderstanding of the request or a superficial reading of the announcement, is significant. The number of wasted hours and the problems of project directors that result from inadequately assessing the constraints would be decreased significantly if proposal managers and developers carefully assessed the nature of the task before designing the strategy.

---

*The use of funding agency criteria in writing the proposal will be treated in Chapter 6. Since such criteria provide the technical specifications for writing the document, they do not constitute planning elements of the funding process.

PLANNING FOR PROPOSAL DEVELOPMENT

Once a possible source of funding has been identified, through analysis of a proposal request or through discussions with agency staff, and proposal submittal seems feasible, a new set of development and planning tasks confronts the writer.

The development and submittal of a proposal presents a significant management challenge. The challenge is compounded by the time constraints accompanying the process. The management implications can be appreciated by anyone who has faced the following dilemmas: institutional representatives who are unwilling or unavailable to sign document forms in time to meet a submittal due date; required letters of support from cooperating agencies that arrive too late for inclusion with the document; or, most distressingly, an application control center of a funding agency that refuses to accept a proposal because it arrived ten minutes after the stipulated deadline.

Problems will arise if the task of planning for proposal submittal is treated simply as one of writing a narrative. The developer must realize that: several discrete but related tasks must be carried out in transforming an idea to a plan of action; the power of decisions made during proposal writing to affect funded program operations is signficant; and, the quality of the proposal document and the odds of successful program implementation are largely a function of initial planning.

Any plan for proposal development must take into account the many tasks required to create a product conforming to specifications (the proposal), which is delivered to a designated point (the office specified in the agency guidelines) at a designated time (the date and hour beyond which proposals or applications will not be accepted).

Given the important role that time constraints play in virtually all proposal submittals, the initial task is to order and telescope activities, which under ideal circumstances should take several months, into a significantly tighter time frame. The goal is to reconcile, within a limited period of time, the varying expectations and needs of institutional units and individuals, so as to develop a program, secure funding, and create an environment conducive to project success simultaneously. The proposed approach to planning for development and submittal borrows a tool from systems management.

A SYSTEMS MANAGEMENT APPROACH TO PROPOSAL DEVELOPMENT

The concepts of *system, systems management,* and *network analysis,* when originally conceived, described approaches to increase the efficiency of planning for the development and implementation of complex projects that involved the participation of many groups and individuals. Although the concept of network analysis can be traced to the beginning of this century, the application of the approach to project planning and control can be fixed with greater precision. During the late 1950s, DuPont, in an effort to improve the efficiency of refinery renovation projects, collaborated with the Remington Rand Company in developing a project planning system designated CPPS (Critical Path Planning and Scheduling). At approximately the same time, the United States Navy Special Projects Office developed a technique dubbed PERT (Program Evaluation and Review Technique)[3] to guide the development of the Polaris project. PERT's successful application to the development of the nation's defense system, and the influence of strategically located government officials, led to its adaptation for improving the delivery of human service and education programs. Terms derived from or dependent on systems management or network analysis approaches became part of the jargon of educators. PPBS (Program Planning Budgeting System), *discrepancy analysis, inputs* and *outputs, milestone charting,* and *performance objectives* were terms that appeared with increasing frequency in program planning meetings and agency criteria statements for proposal review.

The writer or developer who uses network analysis or systems approaches to develop a proposal document should understand that they represent management techniques. They enable a planner to identify and predict when the tasks involved in developing and submitting a proposal, and later in implementing the project, will occur. Simultaneously, these techniques provide the means to monitor the unfolding of events, to identify needed adjustments, and to schedule the revision of tasks, as deemed necessary.

Three basic phases constitute the process: a planning phase, a scheduling phase, and a control-monitor phase.[4] As in most projects, the planning phase is the most important. At this point, the manager must identify all those steps or activities that constitute the project, the interrelationship of these activities, and the sequence of their completion. Using a systems or network analysis approach, these activities can be represented in diagrammatic form, with arrows indicating the interrelationship between activities and circles identifying the starting point of following or related activities (termed *events*). Since each activity has a beginning and end, time estimates can be set for all activities.

Once all pertinent planning information has been secured and all decisions governing the approach have been made (information termed *inputs*), the scheduling phase begins. At this point, the developer analyzes the information secured during the planning phase in order to make the necessary adjustments to accomplish the project most efficiently within the time constraints. The product is a schedule that guides project implementation (see Figure 5.6). Although the data can be refined by computers to give a range of estimates relevant to scheduling, the degree of refinement provided by such analysis generally is not prerequisite to the goal of proposal submittal.

The control-monitor phase, as the term implies, enables the project developer to adjust the implementation of the plan to accommodate unforeseen circumstances. The failure to receive materials from participating parties, the inability to identify community participants, delays in writing, and unanticipated

146   The Dynamics of Funding

FIGURE 5.6. *Proposal Writing Schedule (Initial Phase)* *

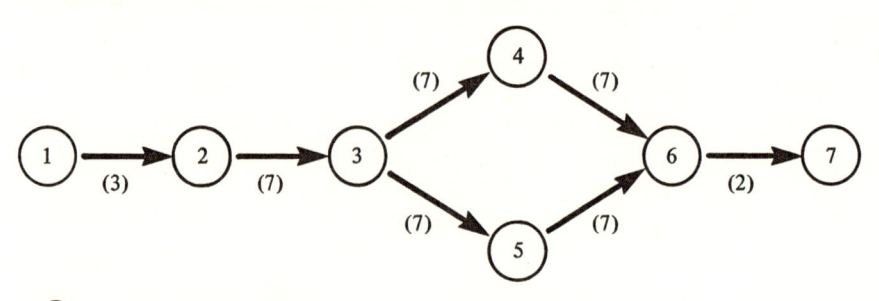

① Announcement received

② Announcement distributed to possible interested parties

③ Comments returned to distributor

④ Community planning committee identified

⑤ Institution committee identified

⑥ Community/institution committee agrees on objectives

⑦ Writer identified

( ) Represent time estimates for completion of tasks

differences between participating groups are some problems that necessitate revisions in plans and the updating of schedules. The developer must update information derived from individual performances in carrying out tasks, making those changes necessary to complete the project on time and constructing a revised diagram or milestone chart.

These strategies for addressing the management tasks inherent in developing a proposal will be applied to a specific set of Rules and Regulations later in this chapter. Before proceeding to the actual application, however, a brief considertion of the approach within the complete context of the problem-solving process will clearly illustrate the applicability of the strategies to the development and implementation of both proposal and program.

The systems model approach to problem solving is a method of analysis in which the planner, once the needs or problem to be addressed have been identified, moves sequentially through an established set of analysis and synthesis tasks. These tasks, in turn, define more precisely the problem and the activities that must be carried out to solve the problem. As defined by a Corrigan Associates' study, *A System Approach for Education*:

> Relevant and practical educational management, then, begins with the determination of educational needs; states feasible and measurable objectives (goals/end products); applies system analysis to

*The proposal writing schedule presented represents only one segment of the proposal planning and development process. Pages 153–159 treat scheduling in greater detail.

determine the "whats" (functions and tasks required to achieve the objectives); then progresses to the selection of feasible and required "hows"; the development and implementation of the "how"; and, finally to the evaluation and revision of the total process.[5]

One model, developed by Corrigan Associates in response to a California legislative mandate that educational institutions establish more efficient management practices, is consistent with the prior guidelines and directly relevant to proposal planning. The system questions and the form and substance of the responses (products of the system process) identified in the SAFE (System Approach for Effectiveness) model, Figure 5.7, places the approach within the broader context of problem solving.

The Corrigan Associates' model is flexible enough to respond to both comprehensive institutional management planning over an extended timespan and the day-to-day planning and decision making that accompanies institutional management. Certain features of the model may not be directly relevant to proposal development. As we apply systems management procedures to the development and submittal of the proposal document, however, the relevance of most of the systems questions and products will be evident.

THE APPLICATION OF THE SYSTEMS APPROACH

The management plan for developing and submitting a proposal that receives the appropriate institutional sign-offs within a designated span of time must consider both the formal and informal institutional and agency constraints identified earlier. The steps suggested by the SAFE model (Figure 5.7), which constitute the proposed planning strategy, may be implemented once the fit between the agency and institutional needs has been analyzed and the appropriateness of submittal has been determined.

Step I. Initial Design and Strategy Development Meeting

The initial analysis of the proposal request should provide an institution with sufficient information to address the system questions: What relevant needs have to be resolved? and What relevant problems have to be solved to resolve the needs? (system analysis step A-1). The nature of the stated priority needs and/or problem statements can then be identified (system output step A-1) and reflected as a system output or product in the proposal. The decision to submit, however, does not necessarily address the questions, What do we intend to achieve? or What is our exact performance commitment for end achievement? (system analysis steps A-2 and A-3). Nor does it provide the developer with priorities, goals, and measurement criteria to define the end product (system analysis outputs or products A-2 through A-4). To answer

FIGURE 5.7. Model of a System Approach for Effectiveness (SAFE)

System Analysis Steps	System Questions Asked
A-1	(A) What are the relevant needs to be resolved? (B) What are relevant problems to be solved to resolve needs?
A-2	What are our intents to achieve
A-3	What is our exact performance commitment for end achievement?
A-4	What are we trying to accomplish — And—How will we know we have arrived successfully?
A-5	What are the hurdles which can stop us?
A-6	How do we neutralize them? What are the major events or "Milestones" to be accomplished to achieve our performance commitment?
A-7	What are subactivities to be accomplished to perform each milestone?
A-8	What are the specific tasks to be accomplished for each subactivity?
A-9	What are the feasible ways and means to perform required tasks & functions?
A-10	Is it feasible to proceed?

System Synthesis Steps

S-1	What are various "ways" for achieving all the whats?
S-2	Who will do what? With what means? How will all whats be scheduled?
S-3	What are the most efficient "ways and means" to perform all the whats?
S-4	What is the best solution plan?
S-5	How do selected methods/means/media work?
S-6	How do we put the solution plan to work?
S-7	How does the plan perform?
S-8	What revisions are required?

© R.E. Corrigan Associates, 1971.

Safe Steps & Tools — System Analysis

- A-1 Assess Needs & Problems
- A-2 Define Goals
- A-3 State Mission Objective
- A-4 Determine Mission Performance Req'ts
- A-5 Determine Mission Constraints
- A-6 Derive Mission Profile
- A-7 Perform Function Analysis — R & C*
- A-8 Perform Task Analysis — R & C*
- A-9 Perform Methods-Means Analysis
- A-10 State Feasibility Go-No Go

System Synthesis

- S-1 Identify Alternate (Feasible Solution Plans)
- S-2 Design Alternate Solution Plans for Implementation
- S-3 Assess Alternate Solution Plans for Costs & Effectiveness Criteria — R & C*
- S-4 Select Most Cost-Effective Plan for Implementation
- S-5 Field Test or Validate Selected Method-Means Combination Where Req'd
- S-6 Implement Solution Plan
- S-7 Evaluate System Performance (Both Process & Product)
- S-8 Revise System for Required Achievement

*Determine new performance requirements and constraints

System Outputs or Products — System Analysis

- A-1 Stated priority needs & problem statements
- A-2 Priority goals derived from needs
- A-3 Priority mission (program) objectives specific to stated goals & needs
- A-4 Measurement criteria defining program or mission output or product
- A-5 Negative forces to be reconciled (program constraints)
- A-6 Gross "Milestones" or events to be achieved in sequence to produce program product or output & reduce constraints
- A-7 Subfunctions to perform each gross milestone
- A-8 Tasks to be performed for each subfunction
- A-9 Alternate method-means which are feasible "ways & means" to perform tasks & functions
- A-10 Final data indicating feasibility to proceed or not

System Synthesis

- S-1 Alternate configurations for "ways & means" to give best results
- S-2 Detailed plans for each alternate: schedule, personnel, times, method-means, costs, budgets evaluation, (PPBES) Mgm't-operation-support req'mt
- S-3 Date comparing alternative plans for costs–efficiency-effectiveness-benefits
- S-4 Optimal implementation plan-and-program descriptive package
- S-5 Performance data indicating prediction of methods-means media (See curriculum)
- S-6 Detailed plans for sensing, correcting, evaluating, communicating for operation-mgm't-products
- S-7 Detailed performance date ± = product achievement,-processes-budgets
- S-8 Recommended changes in system planning-design-implementation

The following model is reprinted from the SAFE P.M.E. Training Manual (Planning-Management-Evaluation) by Dr. Robert E. Corrigan, Corrigan Associates, P.O. Box 5089 Anaheim, CA 92804, copyright 1971.

FIGURE 5.7. **Model of a System Approach for Effectiveness (SAFE)**
Safe Steps & Tools
System Analysis

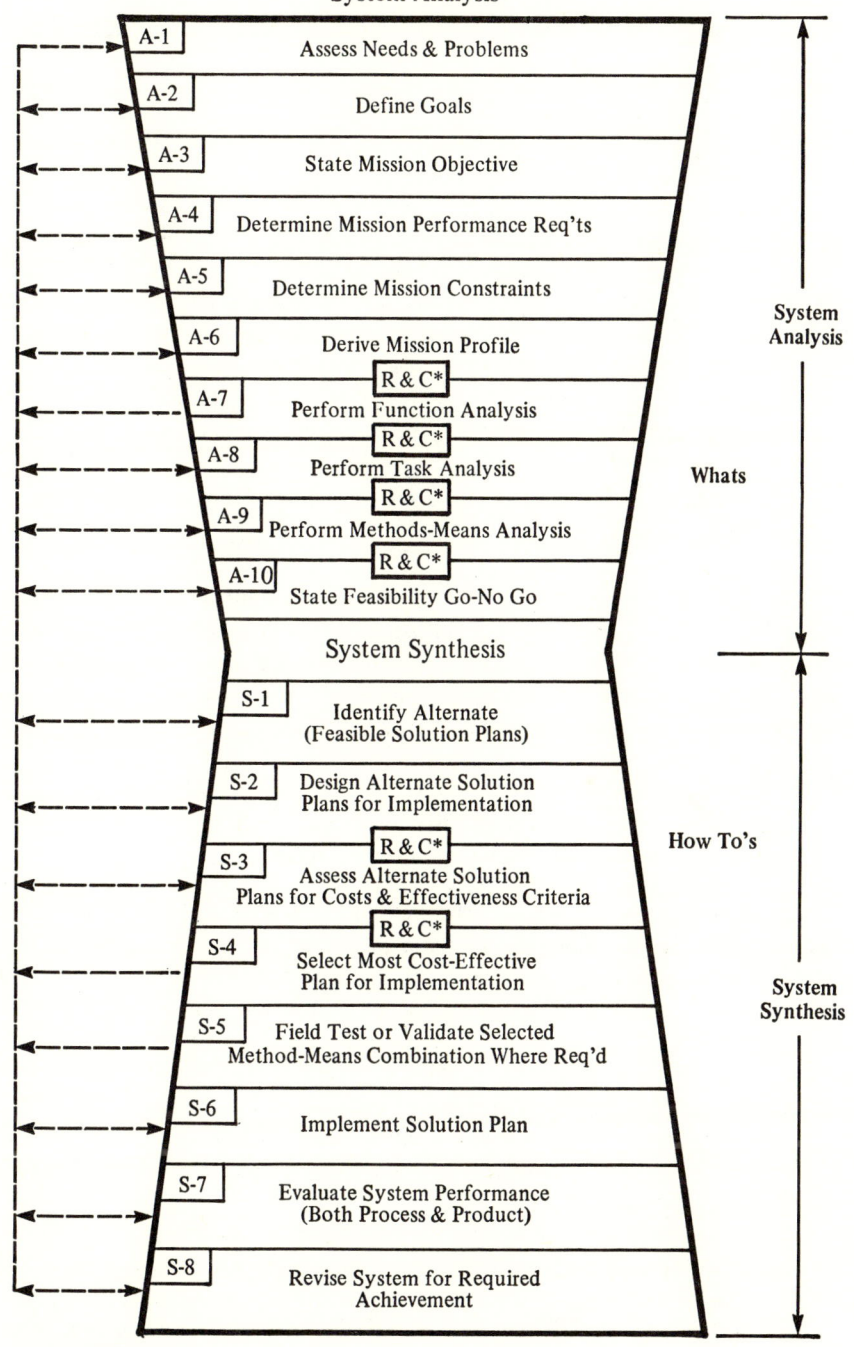

Step	Description	Section
A-1	Assess Needs & Problems	System Analysis / Whats
A-2	Define Goals	
A-3	State Mission Objective	
A-4	Determine Mission Performance Req'ts	
A-5	Determine Mission Constraints	
A-6	Derive Mission Profile	
A-7	Perform Function Analysis [R & C*]	
A-8	Perform Task Analysis [R & C*]	
A-9	Perform Methods-Means Analysis [R & C*]	
A-10	State Feasibility Go-No Go [R & C*]	

System Synthesis

Step	Description	Section
S-1	Identify Alternate (Feasible Solution Plans)	How To's / System Synthesis
S-2	Design Alternate Solution Plans for Implementation	
S-3	Assess Alternate Solution Plans for Costs & Effectiveness Criteria [R & C*]	
S-4	Select Most Cost-Effective Plan for Implementation [R & C*]	
S-5	Field Test or Validate Selected Method-Means Combination Where Req'd	
S-6	Implement Solution Plan	
S-7	Evaluate System Performance (Both Process & Product)	
S-8	Revise System for Required Achievement	

*Determine new performance requirements and constraints

©R.E. Corrigan Associates, 1971.

The following model is reprinted from the SAFE P.M.E. Training Manual (Planning-Management-Evaluation) by Dr. Robert E. Corrigan, Corrigan Associates, P.O. Box 5089 Anaheim, CA 92804, copyright 1971.

these questions, it is necessary to involve those persons directly responsible for the development of the document. Outcomes of this initial meeting should include:

1. Identification of the program goals and the nature of activities to be presented in the proposal document;
2. Identification of the submitting institution representative responsible for developing and submitting the document and other individuals and/or institutions participating in the project;
3. Confirmation of the appropriateness of the decision to submit and the roles and responsibilities of participating organizational units or institutions in developing the document and operating the program;
4. Identification of institutional constraints that could affect program content and the time frame for securing institutional support and appropriate sign-offs;
5. Identification of technical and fiscal support required to develop and submit the document.

At this point, responsibility for proposal development is fixed, initial institutional support is confirmed, and the program and organizational constraints of the institution, which may affect submittal timing, are determined. The individual responsible for managing the submittal can now develop strategies to address both the organizational and program constraints affecting the document's submittal.

Step II. The Identification and Ordering of Proposal Development Activities

To identify and order proposal development activities, the developer must deal with the political and programmatic variables that determine proposal content and affect the ability to deliver the proposal at a designated time. Responses to the system questions: What is our exact performance commitment for end achievement? What are we trying to accomplish and how will we know we have arrived successfully? What are the hurdles that can stop us and how do we neutralize them? and What are the major events or milestones to be accomplished to achieve our performance commitment? (system analysis steps A-2 through A-6) provide the answers necessary to develop and implement the plan for proposal submittal.

In answering these questions, the developer should attend to both the formal and informal organizational constraints that are largely political in nature. The participation of individuals familiar with the institution's organizational environment is essential at this stage of planning. The selection of alternative program priorities, the designation of individuals or offices to participate in the project, the allocation of monies to different units, and the roles proposed for individuals or groups hold major political implications for project development. The axiom, "All in the game win," is central to future project success; the identification of participants, their positions in the organization, and their potential to affect the outcome underlies the planning process. The following strategy therefore is suggested:

1. Identify and list all individuals and organizational units in the submitting institution that may gain or lose status if the proposal is submitted.
2. Identify and list all individuals and groups who, although not involved in the day-to-day operation of the institution, may gain or lose status if the proposal is submitted and the project implemented.
3. Assign a positive or negative weight to each of the identified parties that reflects an estimate of the degree of their gain or loss.

The preceding strategy, applied to the local educational agency of a small-to-moderate-sized town submitting a proposal for an "open-campus program," might generate a table similar to Table 5.4.

The weights assigned in Table 5.4 represent the extent to which individuals or groups, as perceived by those familiar with the institution, stand to gain or lose from project implementation. In this hypothetical setting, the strong negative weighting assigned to the school board would reflect the conservatism of the board and its fear that unsympathetic voters would regard the project negatively and vent their disapproval at election time. In such a setting, the board members might feel they have little to gain and much to lose. The superintendent, who is accountable to the school board but perhaps

TABLE 5.4. *Anticipated Receptitivity of Affected Groups to Proposal and Project*

Affected Individuals/ Groups within Institution	Receptitivity	Affected Individuals/ Groups outside Institution	Receptivity
1. School Board	(−3)	1. Parent Teacher Group	(+3)
2. Superintendent of Schools	(−2)	2. Chamber of Commerce	(−3)
3. Business Manager	(0)	3. Elks Club	(−2)
4. Principal	(+1)	4. YMCA	(+1)
5. Chairman, Social Studies Department	(+2)	5. NEA or AFT Chapter	(+1)

Key: On scale of 0–3, 0 indicates no significant impact, 3 significant impact. (+) indicates anticipated support, (−) indicates anticipated resistance.

philosophically supportive of the program, stands to lose more than he can gain. The planner's challenge is clear: identify the negative forces (those who feel they have more to lose than to gain) and then address their concerns so that they recognize the possible benefits that might accrue if they support the program. Response to the analysis questions previously cited provides the proposal developer with the means to develop proposal content. The synthesis questions and products come into play when determining the substance of the program contained in the proposal.

Once the formal and informal constraints to proposal development and submittal have been identified, the developer can identify and order the major outcomes or "milestones" directly related to proposal development and submittal. Two distinct categories of activity must be addressed—organizational and programmatic. The former category incorporates those constraints established by staffing, resource allocation, and governance stipulations and policies set by the funding agency and submitting institution; the latter incorporates those constraints that evolve from the program content stipulations set by the funding agency and the program priorities of the submitting institution. The following prerequisite activities incorporate the features of systems planning:

1. List the important organizational steps that must be completed to conform to regulations of the funding agency and the submitting institution.

2. List the important program development steps that must be completed to conform to program criteria set by the developer and to criteria for review identified in the program announcement.

3. Place the steps to be completed in a sequential order appropriate to developing and submitting the proposal.

4. Estimate the time needed to complete each step or set of steps.

5. Cluster all tasks having common characteristics and representing discrete sets of activity that were initially ordered separately.

6. Identify activities that may be carried out concurrently.

7. Enter the final deadline for proposal submittal and other fixed dates (school board meetings, advisory board meetings, holidays, etc.), and develop a schedule working back from the deadline. The schedule may be a milestone chart, bar graph, or calendar that identifies the sequence of activities and time allocated for completion.

The preceding sequence of activities, derived from the network analysis or systems management approach discussed earlier, has great value for formal planning for proposal development. To illustrate this value, we have applied

TABLE 5.5a. *Listing of Major Organization Activities—ESAA-LEA Submittal*

Funding Agency Requirements	Time Requirements
1. Advisory committees formed prior to being given proposal for comment and review	(5 days)
2. Advisory committees given opportunity to review and comment on proposals	(15 days)
3. SEA given opportunity to offer recommendation on proposal	(15 days)
4. Notice of public hearing and publication of advisory committee membership	(7 days)
Submitting Institution Requirements	
1. Parties identified to participate in writing of proposal	(3 days)
2. Typing and reproduction of proposal	(5 days)
3. Approval of school officers at building level secured	(3 days)
4. Approval of officers at middle management level in central offices secured—fiscal and programmatic	(3 days)

the sequence to guidelines set by the Emergency School Assistance Act (ESAA).*
(See Tables 5.5[a] and [b].)

The Application of the Approach to ESAA Rules and Regulations

Table 5.5(a) and (b) incorporate data derived from the first four activities prerequisite to the formulation of a submittal plan. An initial clustering of activities around funding agency and institutional organizational constraints, as well as around general program constraints, has also been completed. All funding agency organization contraints are identified in the program Rules and Regulations; time estimates for agency-related activities conform to the agency's recommended time constraints.

The listing of events now can be placed in chronological order to simplify the task of planning for document development.

*ESAA authorizes a wide range of programs, projects, and activities for meeting the "special needs incident to the elimination of minority group segregation and discrimination among students and faculty in elementary and secondary schools; eliminating, reducing or preventing minority group isolation in elementary and secondary schools with substantial proportions of minority group students; and aiding school children in overcoming the educational disadvantages of minority group isolation."[6]

The Rules and Regulations require the planner to take a number of funding agency stipulated, program development constraints into account when planning for proposal writing: advisory committees to review and comment on the proposal must be formed; the state educational agency must have an opportunity to offer recommendations; a public hearing must be held; and student advisory committees must be formed. This particular example is more complex than most; consequently, the time required for development exceeds that required for most submittals. The variation in time for completion revealed in the two following figures demonstrates the impact of alternative management plans for developing and delivering the product.

154   The Dynamics of Funding

TABLE 5.5b. Listing of Program Development Steps— ESAA-LEA Submittal Program

1. Identification of program priorities of the submitting LEA	(5 days)
2. Demographic assessment necessary for confirming eligibility and needs secured	(5 days)
3. Identification of the scope of the program and population to be served	(3 days)
4. Identification of activities drawn from the activities authorized by the legislation that best meet the system's needs (e.g., remedial services, additional professional staff, hiring and training of aides, inservice teacher training, or community activities)	(3 days)
5. Development of a working draft of proposed program activities to share with other directly involved parties	(3 days)
6. Development of a draft proposal incorporating the criteria for assistance identified in the Rules and Regulations	(14 days)
7. Development of a draft in form appropriate for submittal	(5 days)

TABLE 5.6. Listing of Steps for Document Development and Submittal Derived from Tables 5.5a and 5.5b*

1. Parties to write proposal identified
2. Demographic information for confirming eligibility and needs secured
3. Identification of scope of programs and population to be served completed
4. Identification of activities that best meet LEA needs completed
5. Development of working paper completed
6. Advisory committee formed
7. Advisory committee review comments incorporated
8. Development of draft proposal completed
9. SEA comments solicited
10. Notice of public hearing published
11. Public hearings conducted
12. Public hearing & SEA comments addressed in proposal draft
13. Student advisory committees formed
14. Names of SAC members published
15. Names of SAC transmitted to Assistant Secretary
16. Proposal document writing completed
17. Proposed document typed and reproduced

TABLE 5.6. (cont.)

18. Formal approval of building level office secured
19. Approval of middle management officers secured
20. Approval of superintendent of schools secured
21. School committee approval secured
22. Proposal delivered to funding agency stipulated receipt point

*A. Need and Impact Criteria
   1. Need for assistance as indicated by number and percentage
      of minority group children enrolled   (40 points)
   2. Effective net reduction in minority group isolation   (25 points)
   3. Parent and community involvement   (6 points)
B. Educational and Program Criteria
   1. Needs assessment   (10 points)
   2. Statement of objectives   (10 points)
   3. Activities   (15 points)
      a. Project design
      b. Staffing
      c. Delivery of services
      d. Parent or community involvement
   4. Resource management   (7 points)
   5. Evaluation   (5 points)

Each set of criteria identified in the Rules and Regulations provides more detailed specifications relevant to the writing of the proposal. An individual desiring an official statement of these Regulations should consult the *Code of Federal Regulations* 45, part 185 (1974) and the *Federal Register* 40, no. 61, 12 June 1975, 14166–14183.

Sufficient information is now available to identify the tasks that may occur concurrently. The transformation of the data to diagrammatic form serves as a feasibility test of the initial plan. It also may indicate necessary reassessments of time allocations and refinement of the activity clusters.

Taking the proposal due date established by the *Federal Register* as a starting point, the proposed developer works backward to establish a systems network or milestone chart depicting the management schedule. Each of the previously identified activities is assigned an identification number and is placed in sequential order along a time line. Activities occurring concurrently are represented as branches off the central time line. The dates accompanying each event represent the date of anticipated completion and are derived from the time estimates developed previously. The resulting systems network (Figure 5.8) or milestone chart in the form of a modified bar graph (Figure 5.9), generated from data provided in Table 5.6 (which incorporates data from the agency and institutional constraints identified in Table 5.5[a] and [b]), provide alternative management plans for continuous planning, scheduling, and monitoring of the proposal development project. Monitoring of the plan will inevitably identify slippage in the implementation and result in revisions, in order to deliver the proposal at the specified time. Given the nature of the process, the

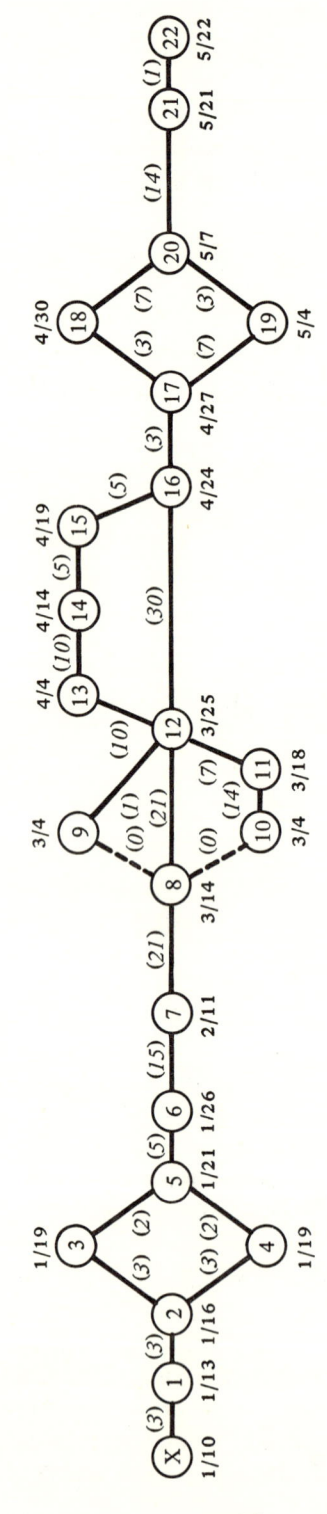

FIGURE 5.8. *Summary Network for Proposal Development Project*

FIGURE 5.9. ESAA–Planning for Submittal Milestone Chart

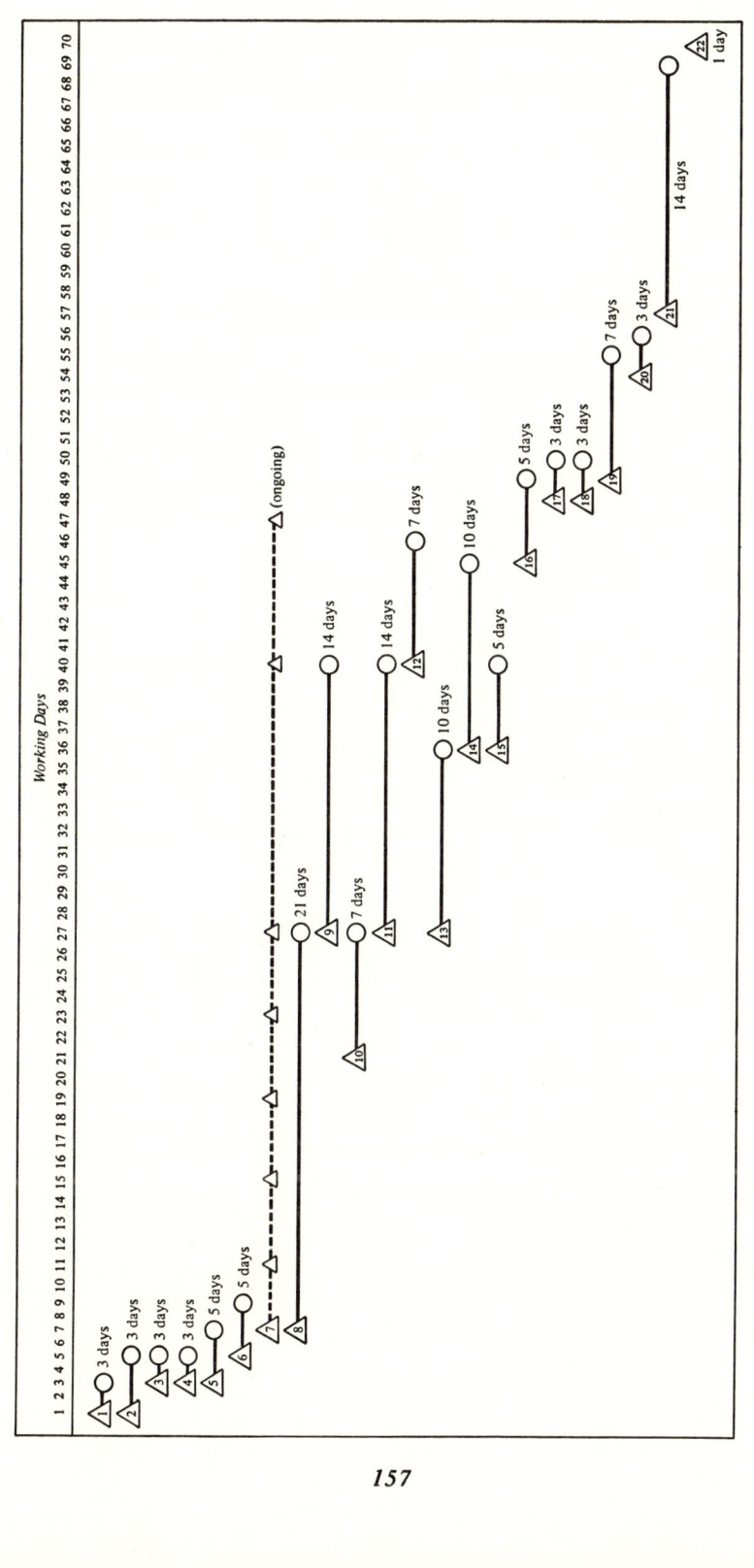

158   The Dynamics of Funding

developer should assume that "anything may go wrong and usually does." An unrevised plan generally indicates a nonutilized plan, which represents a nonplan.

CHARACTERISTICS OF THE PROPOSAL DEVELOPMENT PROCESS: IMPLICATIONS FOR PLANNING

Analysis of the project management plan projected for the ESAA submittal reveals some features of the proposal development process generalizable to other settings (see Table 5.7). The applicability of the generalizations may differ from institution to institution and according to the characteristics of any given set of agency regulations. This applicability, nevertheless, should be tested before any submittal; the implications of the findings should be incorporated into the institution's management plan for submittal.

TABLE 5.7. ESAA Planning Features: Implications for Proposal Development Planning

ESAA Plan Feature	Generalizations to Other Settings
1. Approximately one month elapses between completion of the final proposal by the writers and submittal of the document to the funding agency.	1. The complexity of the sign-off process by any organization has a direct bearing on the time that may be allocated for writing and developing the program. The more parties required for sign-off, the greater the time that must be allocated to institutional and organizational units that meet at specified times (that is, school boards, community boards, citizen advisory groups).
2. By working from the submittal data backward in identifying the time needed for carrying out all the required activities, it is revealed that depending on the plan adopted, from two to four months may be required to complete the mission by a system making a first effort at securing ESAA funding.	2. The writing of the proposal document itself may represent a small fraction of the total time required to carry out all tasks prerequisite to proposal submittal. If funding sources, guidelines, and/or proposal due dates can be identified before the formal distribution of materials, much of the data needed to address institutional constraints can be assessed and acted on before the development of the proposal.
3. Although some planning activities may occur concurrently, meeting the	3. When responsibilities are delegated to other parties, the planner must define roles clearly to assure appropriate monitoring and

TABLE 5.7. (cont.)

ESAA Plan Feature	Generalizations to Other Settings
submittal deadline depends on the timely completion of tasks by parties over whom the submitting party may have little control.	provision of assistance to groups or individuals responsible for specific tasks. In addition, attempts should be made to alter the chronological ordering of activities required for submittal to enable groundwork on the tasks occurring late in the process to be completed earlier. Such things as the development of draft budgets, the testing of institutional receptivity, the collection of appendices, need not await the completion of the proposal narrative.
4. Over a week of time is allocated to data collection and the typing and reproduction of proposal documents.	4. In delegating tasks and identifying personnel and support facilities, consideration must be given to those tasks usually designated as secretarial. An injustice is often done both to the individuals and the term by assuming that these activities will be automatically carried out, or that they may be performed by anyone available. The several sets of activities that contribute to production of the document and its delivery to the appropriate parties are too important to take for granted.
5. The time frames established in the proposal, while providing an overview of the tasks to be completed, do not address the many activities that must be carried out to complete each event.	5. The same planning that is dedicated to the development of the general plan should be dedicated to each of the individual activities, since many are more complex than would appear at first glance. As a corollary, the time frames represent initial "best guesses" and, as such, should be constantly reassessed on the basis of information derived from carrying out these tasks. Some events will occur much more rapidly than anticipated; others may encounter unforeseen obstacles. As information affecting the completion of the proposal within the negotiable time constraints is received, the plan should be updated and adjusted.

SUMMARY

This chapter has identified those constraints that affect the development of the proposal document and has offered corresponding strategies generalizable to a wide range of proposal solicitations. Attention has been directed to those characteristics of the submittal process that have direct and immediate application to document development.

The failure of applicants to analyze the funding agency's needs carefully or to map out the strategies for the development of the document adequately contributes to the failure of most proposals to secure support from either the submitting institution or receiving agency. When proposals receive funding support despite poor or inadequate planning in the early stages of development, crises often occur during the initial months of project operation. For these reasons, the analysis of the proposal request and planning for proposal development require as much consideration as the writing of the document.

The recommended strategies for analysis and planning have been borrowed from the field of management. The relevance or decision-tree analysis approach, which was applied to the analysis of the request, basically calls for the identification of options open to the planner and their selective and systematic elimination until the most appropriate option is determined. The systems or network analysis approach, which was applied to planning for proposal development, represents the identification and ordering of tasks set against a time line. This ordering is designed to yield a product (the proposal document) conforming to specifications (criteria for funding) at a specified time (the proposal due date).

The potential proposal developer is free to take liberties with the specific steps outlined in carrying out the tasks associated with these approaches to problem solving. They may be modified, refined, or simplified to suit any particular solicitation response. The proposal developer, however, does not have the luxury of violating the intent of the strategies provided without seriously reducing the odds of securing funding or successfully operating a funded project.

If the structural characteristics of the proposal and the implications for the design of the document are understood, and if the institutional and agency constraints affecting the development process are identified and addressed, the developer can now consider the technical requirements for writing the document. The following chapter applies the concepts discussed earlier to the writing of the proposal narrative and to the identification of the corresponding technical skills prerequisite for securing approval.

ENDNOTES

1. Joseph Martino, *Technological Forecasting for Decision Making* (New York: American Elsevier Publishing Co., 1972), p. 289.
2. Commonwealth of Massachusetts, Department of Education, Adult Services Program, Program Announcement, October 1, 1975.
3. Howard Simons, "PERT: How to Meet a Deadline," *Think* (May 1962): 13-17.

4. *CPM in Construction: A Manual for General Contractors* (Washington, D.C.: Associated General Contractors of America, 1965), pp. 12-14.
5. R.E. Corrigan Associates, *A System Approach for Education* (Anaheim, Calif.: R.E. Corrigan Associates, 1969), pp. 20-21.
6. U.S., Department of Health, Education, and Welfare, Office of Education, Emergency School Aid Act, Rules and Regulations, *Federal Register* 40, no. 114 (12 June 1975): 14166-83.

6

The Writing of the Proposal Document

An understanding of the funding process and the structural elements of the proposal, without the technical skills prerequisite to writing the document, is of limited value. This chapter bridges the gulf between analysis and application by seeking to provide the reader with the technical skills necessary to develop any proposal. The reader must remember, however, that the format and writing style of any given proposal will vary in response to the differing requirements and tastes of particular agencies and funding sources. The style and format of proposals written for federal agencies, state agencies, and foundations may differ markedly. Style and format may also differ from agency to agency, or as a result of the varying perspectives of program officers within a single agency and the perspectives of readers responsible for reviewing the document.

Given the previous caveats, this chapter identifies those elements that are common to all proposals and that transcend the particular interests of a single funding office. It seeks to provide the reader with the skills and understanding to make those stylistic and structural adjustments necessary to submit competitive proposals to the full range of available funding sources.

THE PROPOSAL FORMAT

The varying criteria set by different funding agencies for the review of proposals make it impossible to develop *the* prototype proposal. There are, however, structural characteristics common to virtually all proposals that permit the writer to transmit program features in a format that can be adjusted later to meet the specific needs of an agency. The following format has the greatest applicability to the widest range of funding opportunities confronting educational and human service agencies.

   I. Abstract
  II. Introduction or Background
 III. Problem Statement or Assessment of Need
  IV. Program Objectives
      A. General
      B. Specific
   V. Program Activities or Methods and Procedures
  VI. Evaluation
 VII. Project Management and Organization
VIII. Budget
  IX. Appendices

Two major variations of the previous prototype must be recognized at the outset: (1) the research proposal, as opposed to training or service delivery proposal, which conforms to requisites of the research community; and (2) the proposal developed in response to a specific format, prescribed by the funding agency in the proposal announcement or in governing Rules and Regulations. The necessary adjustments in the former case can be prescribed; in the latter case, the appropriate adjustments can only be derived from the analysis of specific guidelines or Rules and Regulations. The following format pertains to research proposals.

   I. Abstract
  II. Significance of the Study
 III. Statement of the Problem
  IV. Design of the Study
   V. Review of Related Literature
  VI. Definitions and Limitations
 VII. Time-Activity Program
VIII. Budget
  IX. Bibliography
   X. Appendices[1]

Assuming the ability to design a program appropriate to the problem identified, the submitter can write a proposal draft by adhering to one of the preceding formats. Since the style of the narrative, the allocation of project priorities, and the nature of activities proposed will be determined ultimately by funding agency constraints, the final draft of the proposal should, ideally, await information that identifies the characteristics of these constraints.

The second variation on the initial format is used when the submitter develops a proposal in response to a specific set of Rules and Regulations or criteria for proposal review. In such situations, the format is developed in response to agency data. An analysis of the proposal request provides the information necessary to determine the format and the appropriate characteristics of each component of the proposal. In many respects, such information provided by the funding agency greatly simplifies the task confronting the writer; the writer simply has to "fill in the blanks" with the appropriate information in an appropriate form. Once the Rules and Regulations have been analyzed, technical skills take precedence over conceptual skills. Using information provided by Rules and Regulations for Community Education Programs as contained in the *Federal Register* (see Figure 6.1), we can readily determine the format and content of the proposal to be submitted in response to that particular solicitation. Excerpts from the Rules and Regulations for the programs are followed by a "cut and paste" treatment (Table 6.1) that gives the writer a format to develop the document and sets criteria for the development of each proposal component consistent with the format.

FIGURE 6.1. Federal Register Excerpts: Community Education Program*

§ 160c.17 Criteria for evaluation of applications from local educational agencies and State educational agencies administering community education programs.

(a) *Applicability*. The criteria set forth in the succeeding paragraphs of this section will be utilized in reviewing applications submitted under this subpart by local educational agencies and those applications submitted by State educational agencies which propose to plan, establish, expand, improve, or maintain one or more community education programs which the State educational agency will directly administer, as provided in § 160c.11(a)(1). Total of 210 points).

(b) *General criteria*. (40 points)–(1) *Need for Federal assistance*. The extent to which the applicant documents a need for Federal assistance;

(2) *Plan*. The soundness of the proposed plan of project operation, including consideration of the extent to which:

(i) The objectives of the proposed project are sharply defined (including specific time schedules for their achievement), clearly stated, capable of being measured, and capable of being attained by the proposed objectives;

(ii) Objectives clearly relate to the needs assessed; and

(iii) Costs are reasonable in relation to anticipated results.

(3) *Staff*. The qualifications or appropriateness of staff selected or assigned to the project;

(4) *Training*. Where appropriate, the adequacy of provisions for short-term training;

(5) *Dissemination*. The adequacy of provisions for dissemination of information about the project to potential participants in the community and to other interested agencies, institutions, and individuals;

(6) *Coordination at the applicant level*. The quality of arrangements at the applicant level, with respect to community education generally and, in particular, the carrying out of the project, for coordination by the applicant with other appropriate agencies to the maximum extent possible, and to avoid duplication.

(c) *Overall quality of the project*. (80 points)–The likelihood that the project

FIGURE 6.1. (cont.)

will (1) contribute to the establishment, expansion, or maintenance of one or more community education programs of high quality (beyond meeting minimum requirements) with respect to the elements set forth in § 160c.3(c); (2) develop approaches or results which can be utilized in other programs not directly assisted by the project; (3) develop the capacity of the applicant to plan, establish, expand, improve, and maintain community education programs; and (4) result in the development of exemplary or innovative community education programs (particularly in serving the fundamental community education, health, and other social welfare needs demanding attention) which can serve as models throughout the United States. (Priority will be accorded to applications which focus on achievement of high quality in a limited number of community education programs which can serve as models for the applicant and other agencies to replicate over applications designed to assist a large number of community education programs.)

(20 U.S.C. 1864)

(d) *Relationship to specific community education programs.* (80 points) With respect to each community education program to be assisted by the project:

(1) *School and school board involvement.* The extent to which a public elementary and secondary school and the school board are involved in the project. Examples of factors which could affect this criterion include, but are not limited to: (i) The intensity and quality of involvement by a public elementary or secondary school in the carrying out and administration of the program, as provided in the application; (ii) the extent to which the program will provide for the integration of, and mutual reinforcement between, the participating school's regular instructional program and its community education activities and services; (iii) whether a public elementary or secondary school building will serve as the center for the program and the extent to which community activities and services will be sufficiently concentrated and comprehensive and thereby make maximum use of existing school facilities; and (iv) evidence of commitment by the school board to the support and improvement of the program.

(20 U.S.C. 1864(b), (c), and (d); S. Rept. No. 763, 93rd Cong. 2d Sess. 72-73 (1974))

(2) *Needs and services.* (i) The extent to which the program priorities and the program services and activities respond to identified local needs and target groups and (ii) the extent to which geographic and other constraints to potential participation in the program by members of the community to be served are recognized and resolved.

(3) *Coordination, consultation, and cooperative arrangements.* The adequacy of arrangements to achieve maximum coordination and cooperation among public and private agencies, utilize existing resources, and avoid duplication in the planning for, and provision of services by, the program.

(20 U.S.C. 1864, H.R. Rept. No. 805, 93rd Cong. 2d Sess. 50 (1974))

(4) *Community participation.* The extent of community participation in all aspects of the program, including needs and resources assessment, application

The Writing of the Proposal Document 167

FIGURE 6.1. (cont.)

preparation, and the planning and delivery of activities and services.

(20 U.S.C. 1864, H.R. Rept. No. 805, 93rd Cong. 2d Sess. 51 (1974))

(e) *Distribution of projects.* (10 points)—The extent to which approval of a project will contribute to (1) an equitable geographic distribution of community education programs throughout the United States in both urban and rural areas, and (2) the funding of a wide variety of projects which collectively can demonstrate diverse approaches to effective community education programs and the role which limited Federal resources can play in assisting such programs.

(20 U.S.C. 1864(h))

Federal Register 40, no. 290, 12 December 1975, 57941.

TABLE 6.1. *Proposal Format and Characteristics for Community Education Proposal derived from Rules and Regulations*

(References identify sources of criteria in the Federal Register *program announcement center for setting structure and characteristics on p. 165.)*

	Characteristics
I. Introduction (Ref.: 160c.11(a) cited under 160c.17(a))	Clear statement of problem that proposal seeks to address consistent with the types of assistance authorized by the Rules and Regulations
II. Need for Assistance (Ref.: 160c.17(b)(i))	Documentation of Need (Ref.: 160c. 17(b)(i))
III. Proposal Plan of Operation (Ref.: 160c.17(b)(2)	
A. Program Objectives (Ref.: 160c.16(b)(2)(i) and 160c.17(b)(2)(ii))	Sharply defined (including specific time schedules for their achievement), clearly stated, capable of being measured
	Clearly relate to the needs assessed (Ref.: 160c. 17(3))
B. Program Activities	Must address staff qualifications
	Must delineate provisions for short-term training (Ref.: 160c.17(4))
	Must contribute to establishment, expansion or maintenance of one or more community education programs beyond meeting minimum requirements identified earlier (Ref. 160c17(c)(1))
	Approaches that can be used in other programs

168 The Dynamics of Funding

TABLE 6.1. (cont.)

	Develop capacity of applicant to plan, establish, expand...
	Result in development of exemplary programs which meet fundamental community education, health, and other social welfare needs
	High quality in limited number of agencies rather than general, large-scale assistance.
Relationship to Community Organizations and Community Needs (Ref.: 160c.17(d))	Must delineate School and School Board involvement (1) intensity and quality of involvement (2) integration and reinforcement between regular school program and community education program and services (3) Maximum use of facilities (4) Evidence of commitment by School Board (Ref.: 160c.17(d)(i)-(iv))
	Must respond to identified local needs and identified target groups
	Must identify consultative and cooperative arrangements and avoid duplication
	Must delineate community participation in all aspects of the program
IV. Qualifications of Staff	Identify qualifications
V. Budget	Costs are reasonable in relation to anticipated results—link costs to activities

Analysis of the Community Education Rules and Regulations and the resultant format reveals the tension between the proposal forms earlier cited and the needs of the writer in developing a proposal that responds directly to agency constraints.

Some criteria contained in Rules and Regulations prescribe the format; other criteria are flexible and allow the writer some license in ordering the components. Such license is reflected in the placement of Staff Qualifications in the preceding format. In the Community Education Rules and Regulations, note that three major sets of criteria govern the awarding of points (General Criteria—40 points, Overall Quality of the Project—80 points, and Relationship to Specific Community Education Programs—80 points). A fourth criterion (distribution of projects—10 points) does not relate to the proposal format, but may be important in influencing final funding decisions. As the points are not broken down by project components (e.g., needs assessments, objectives, activities, evaluation), they do not directly set the format. Given the broad categories for ordering point allocation, a knowledge of the basic proposal format allows the writer to order the program components in a way that will secure the number of points essential for a funding recommendation.

The criteria for evaluation contained in the Community Education Rules and Regulations also illustrate the importance of the submitter's familiarity with the complete Rules and Regulations. The desired characteristics of many of the components can often be determined only by referring to statements and conditions in other sections of the Rules that define terms and identify types of assistance available, the nature of activities authorized, and the costs allowable.

Before considering the desired characteristics of individual proposal components, which are pertinent regardless of whether the proposal responds to a set of specific criteria or to relatively open-ended guidelines, the importance of the analysis of the Rules and Regulations to the development of the proposal must be reiterated. In the case of federal grants or contracts, the Rules and Regulations set the scope of the program, identify the activities authorized to address the program goals, determine the eligibility of the submitting parties, and establish the programmatic and technical criteria for evaluating all proposals. When seeking federal funding, the format for the exposition of the program and the characteristics of the individual components of the proposal document must respond to these constraints. In such cases, the options open to the submitter are limited. The possible impact of failing to recognize these constraints is humorously set forth in an imagined letter conceived by a proposal writer who discovered too late that a proposal he had written and submitted had to conform to federal specifications (see Figure 6.2).

CHARACTERISTICS OF INDIVIDUAL COMPONENTS OF THE PROPOSAL

The approach followed in considering the technical qualities of the proposal document is based on the premise that a writer who understands the function of each proposal component will be able to identify the desired characteristics of each component. The writer, therefore, will be able to adjust the style and form of the narrative to accommodate the needs of different funding agencies. In addition to identifying each component's function and desired characteristics, this chapter provides excerpts from funded proposals.* Flaws common to the

---

*The excerpts have been drawn from funded proposals submitted to the offices of Consumer Education, Career Education, Bilingual Education, and the Bureau of Education for the Handicapped and Equal Education Opportunity Programs. Given the range of quality of proposals funded by any given office, the particular selections were identified by program officers as among those receiving the highest ratings of all proposals funded in a particular funding cycle. The differences in style and format generally reflect the varying priorities of the program offices and the type of institution seeking funding. Submittals by local education agencies, institutions of higher education, and private nonprofit and community organizations have been selected purposely for inclusion.

FIGURE 6.2. *An Imaginary Letter to Thomas Jefferson*

July 20, 1776

Mr. Thomas Jefferson
Continental Congress
Independence Hall
Philadelphia, Pa.

Dear Mr. Jefferson:

We have read your "Declaration of Independence" with great interest. Certainly, it represents a considerable undertaking, and many of your statements do merit serious consideration. Unfortunately, the Declaration as a whole fails to meet recently adopted specifications for proposals to the Crown, so we must return the document to you for further refinement. The questions which follow might assist you in your process of revision.

1. In your opening paragraph you use the phrase "the Laws of Nature and Nature's God." What are these laws? In what way are they the criteria on which you base your central arguments? Please document with citations from the recent literature.

2. In the same paragraph you refer to the "opinions of mankind." Whose polling data are you using? Without specific evidence, it seems to us, the "opinions of mankind" are a matter of opinion.

3. You hold certain truths to be "self-evident." Could you please elaborate. If they are as evident as you claim, then it should not be difficult for you to locate the appropriate supporting statistics.

4. "Life, liberty, and the pursuit of happiness" seem to be the goals of your proposal. These are not measurable goals. If you were to say that "among these is the ability to sustain an average life expectancy in six of the 13 colonies of at least 55 years, and to enable all newspapers in the colonies to print news without outside interference, and to raise the average income of the colonists by 10 percent in the next 10 years," these would be measurable goals. Please clarify.

5. You state that "whenever any Form of Government becomes destructive of these ends, it is the Right of the People to alter or abolish it, and to institute a new Government. . . . " Have you weighed this assertion against all the alternatives? Or is it predicated solely on the baser instincts?

6. Your description of the existing situation is quite extensive. Such a long list of grievances should precede the statement of of goals, not follow it.

FIGURE 6.2. *(cont.)*

7. Your strategy for achieving your goal is not developed at all. You state that the colonies "ought to be Free and Independent States," and that they are "Absolved from All Allegiance to the to the British Crown." Who or what must change to achieve this objective? In what way must they change? What resistance must you overcome to achieve the change? What specific steps will you take to overcome the resistance? How long will it take? We have found that a little foresight in these areas helps to prevent careless errors later on.

8. Who among the list of signatories will be responsible for implementing your strategy? Who conceived it? Who provided the theoretical research? Who will constitute the advisory committee? Please submit an organizational chart.

9. You must include an evaluation design. We have been requiring this since Queen Anne's War.

10. What impact will your program have? Your failure to include any assessment of this inspires little confidence in the long-range prospects of your undertaking.

11. Please submit a PERT diagram, an activity chart, and an itemized budget.

We hope that these comments prove useful in revising your "Declaration of Independence."

Best Wishes,

Lord North

Edward Schwartz, "A Letter to Jefferson," *Social Policy* (July/August 1974): 10–11. Reprinted by permission from *Social Policy* published by Social Policy Corporation, New York, New York 10036. Copyright 1974 by Social Policy Corporation.

component under consideration are listed also and a checklist is included so that a submitter can test the technical quality of his or her proposal.

In treating each of the components of the proposal, the writer's task is to secure the maximum number of points possible from reviewers. Although proposals are often reviewed without the use of a numerical rating system,* there is evidence to suggest that numerical ratings are becoming increasingly important. Regardless of the reliability of the ratings assigned to the components, the writer should assume the orientation of a point gatherer or marketing specialist when writing the proposal. By testing components of the developing document against the distribution of points set by the funding agency, or the tastes of the potential funder, the writer can create a self-monitoring system that increases the document's conformity to criteria governing the reviewers' evaluation. Whether or not point allocations figure in the final award decision, the self-monitoring and critical analysis of each proposal component can only improve the quality of the proposal.

ABSTRACT

Function

For funding sources that screen proposals as a first step in the decision-making process, the abstract can provide the basis for:

1. determining whether the submitted proposal is consistent with program priorities of the funding office;
2. determining the eligibility of the submitting institution;
3. assigning the proposal to a specific panel of readers or a specific program office; and
4. determining whether the level of funding requested is consistent with allocation policies of the funding agency.

Characteristics

The abstract or program summary, whether inserted on the forms provided by the funding agency, placed as an introductory page in the proposal, or presented in the form of a letter to a foundation, introduces the submitting institution to the government agency or foundation. In the case of a letter to a foundation, the abstract should be designed to test the foundation's

---

*Foundations, on the whole, have refrained from applying numerical ratings to the review of proposals. It is contended that foundation generally place greater importance on past relations with the proposed directors and the status of the institution and/or individual submitting.

receptivity to the proposed program. Consequently, in such submittals the abstract should be a concise promotional statement. In all cases, the abstract should provide a lucid and concise program summary that identifies the:

1. submitting institution
2. goals of the proposed project
3. scope of the planned activities
4. projected cost of the project.

Given the restrictions placed on the length of the abstract by many funding agencies, and the desirability of a prospectus submitted to foundations not exceeding five pages, the abstract can generally be written most effectively after the proposal has been drafted or the program has been fully conceptualized. Once the program definition is tentatively set, the writer can identify those elements of the project that are central to program operation and consonant with the priorities of the funding agency, within the length limitations set by the funding agency.

Sample Abstract Statements

The following abstracts, included in proposals submitted to the Office of Consumer Education and the Bureau of Education for the Handicapped, contain most of the desired characteristics identified earlier.

FIGURE 6.3. Consumer Education Abstract

The Idaho Conservation League (ICL), a nonprofit statewide citizens organization, is seeking $36,550 to conduct an "Idaho Energy Consumer Action Project" during the period July 1, 1977 through June 30, 1978.

The project's goal is to prepare informed energy consumers to participate in two immediate areas of energy policy making: The Governor's Energy Council and the Idaho Public Utiliities Commission; and to provide information on alternative energy scenarios for Idaho that will stimulate intelligent consumer decision making in the regulated and free energy markets of Idaho.

Because the growth in electrical demand and the type of electrical generation systems developed hold severe social, economic, and environmental consequences for Idaho, electric energy issues and alternatives will be emphasized.

Two "Idaho Public Utilities Institutes" are planned to train at least 160 community leaders (elected and civic) in south, south central, and eastern Idaho. These Institute participants, assisted by project staff, will disseminate the information gained at these sessions to their membership. Local energy consumer committees will insure continuation and follow-up involvement in Public Utilities Commission (PUC) and state agency energy decision making.

Two "Home Renewable Energy Workshops" are also planned as demonstrations of marketplace alternatives to escalating energy costs and dependence. Two hundred constituents of the community leaders from the Institute will

174   The Dynamics of Funding

FIGURE 6.3. (cont.)

directly benefit; an additional number will review the videotape of the workshops. ICL has already received indications that additional home workshops will be conducted at local expense after the need and validity is demonstrated by these two "see" workshops. Local leaders have expressed the desire for these workshops to help activate their constituents on energy policy issues, by building from their constituents's personal experience with energy alternatives.

Follow-up to the Institutes and Workshops will be ongoing, and will include individual community research services, preparation of a slide/tape program on Idaho's energy consumer options, organizing consultation, and preparation of "consumer energy alerts."

Public input to this proposal has been gathered by ICL staff through an extensive series of meetings with community leaders throughout Idaho and particiularly in the target geographical area.

Idaho Energy Consumer Action Project," Proposal submitted to Consumer Education Office, Office of Education, Department of Health, Education, and Welfare, 1976.

FIGURE 6.4. Bureau of Education for the Handicapped Abstract

The Panhandle Child Development Association, Inc. is submitting an Early Childhood Rural Inservice Training Proposal for Idaho and Eastern Washington.

Needs for assistance identified in research data from Idaho and Eastern Washington indicate that services to handicapped preschoolers are being provided by various private, local and state agencies.

State Departments of Education in Idaho and Washington have indicated in support letters the need for quality inservice training and coordination efforts in early childhood education for the handicapped.

Three inservice training delivery models identified in this proposal are:

1. Extended practicum at two model demonstration preschools in Coeur d'Alene, Idaho, and Cheney, Washington, with follow-up consultation.
2. On-site mini workshops with follow-up classroom consultation.
3. Two/three day early education conferences.

Approximately 300 trainees are projected to receive an average of 60 hours of training available for college credit. The cost of this training is approximately $400.00 per trainee if the proposal is funded at the requested amount.

Target trainees for the first year include staff members, parents, and paraprofessionals from agencies currently serving the preschool handicapped.

Target groups to be accelerated in the second and third years of this proposal will emphasize kindergarten teachers serving the mainstreamed handicapped pupil, and public school district school personnel who will be encouraged to initiate programs in early education for the handicapped.

Dissemination activities include development of a project brochure and continued publication of <u>Prime Issue,</u> Early Education News Bulletin.

Panhandle Child Development Association, "Early Childhood Rural Inservice Training Proposal for Idaho and Eastern Washington," submitted to Handicapped Children's Early Education Program Office, Bureau of Education for the Handicapped, Office of Education, Department of Health, Education, and Welfare, 1976.

Common Flaws

The necessary brevity of the abstract can easily lead to the following flaws.

1. The major features of the proposal may simply be extracted from the body of the narrative. Without careful organization and the insertion of appropriate transitional phrases, such statements often provide a clumsy and vague definition of the program.
2. When a proposal request authorizes proposals for more than one program, the statement may fail to indicate the specific program for which the submitter is seeking funding.
3. In training or service delivery projects, the population that the program is intended to serve and the numbers of persons to benefit directly from the program may not be specified clearly.

Abstract Statement Checklist

1. Submitting institution named? _____
2. Program goals identified? _____
3. Proposed activities included? _____
4. Population to benefit identified? _____
5. Number of persons to benefit identified? _____
6. Duration of project specified? _____
7. Project cost included? _____

INTRODUCTION OR BACKGROUND

Function

Although the quality of the introductory statement to the program will seldom result directly in the awarding of points, the introduction can affect the reader's disposition to what follows. By providing a backdrop for the program, it demonstrates to the reader:

1. the credibility and appropriateness of the institution and/or individual(s) submitting the proposal; and
2. the appropriateness of the particular program approach being proposed.

Characteristics

The particular form of the introduction will differ, depending on the nature of the agency from which funding is sought and the degree of latitude allowed by guidelines governing the submittal of the proposal. The introduction, regardless of form, should demonstrate, however, the appropriateness and credibility of the particular institution or individual submitting.

The writer's decision as to what data will demonstrate the credibility of the proposed project must be based on analysis of the funding agency priorities, the authorizing regulations, and if possible the proposal review process. Clearly, a conservative foundation or federal agency will define credibility or appropriateness differently from agencies interested in affecting major social change. With the preceding in mind, the introduction must address the following factors.

1. Institutional Factors
    a. demonstrated prior interest and commitment of the institution or individual to the problem for which funding is being sought
    b. significant past accomplishments of the institution or individual relevant to the intent of the funding agency
    c. particular qualifications of the submitting institution evolving either from the composition of their governing bodies or their relationships with other organizations
    d. past and/or current support relevant to the proposed project received from other funding agencies or organizations that lends status to the submittal.
2. Program Factors
    a. demonstrated past success of the individual and program staff in developing programs that address problems similar to those covered in the proposed project
    b. demonstrated familiarity with related research or involvement with other individuals or institutions with recognized accomplishments
    c. identification of institutionally supported program activities that will complement proposed project activities.

Like the abstract, the introduction should be lucid and concise; jargon should be avoided. Achievements should be documented and written in a straightforward manner. In designing the introduction as a credibility statement, the evidence of credibility must be relevant to the activities for which support is sought.

Sample Introduction Statements

The following examples demonstrate the wide variation in form possible. The Office of Career Education LEA renewal submittal (Figure 6.5.) is succinct. The University submittal (Figure 6.6.) was five pages long; the excerpts illustrate the possible scope of such statements.

FIGURE 6.5. *Office of Career Education Introduction Excerpts*

I. Introduction
   A. Purpose: The Jefferson County School System proposes to continue and refine its comprehensive career education demonstration model which has been replicated for a low income population.
      1. The Project EPIC model has effectively demonstrated the process for replicating a career education program designed specifically to meet the needs for a low income population.
      2. Project EPIC, while refining the K-12 model will go beyond the original model design to be more comprehensive by <u>demonstrating additional activities to include home, family and community</u> in the model for low income student.
      3. Maximum effectiveness requires some additions to the model as well as to continue to provide validation data on a long range basis to <u>document growth in learner outcomes.</u>
      4. Effective demonstration of model, with the additional emphasis on the community and family, will increase the value of further dissemination in other local and national schools and agencies interested in replicating this approach.
   B. Factors affecting the purpose and proposal:
      1. The proposed activities while continuing to demonstrate a K-12 developmental program extend beyond the present to include emphasis on working with the family and the community to provide a full comprehensive program of career education.
      2. The district will provide refinement of the developmental program demonstration. This proposal while including the demonstration will direct its major new activities to the areas of the family and community.

Jefferson County Public Schools, "Educational Preparation for Involvement in Careers" (Continuation Proposal), submitted to Office of Career Education, Office of Education, Department of Health, Education, and Welfare, March 10, 1977.

FIGURE 6.6. *Office of Bilingual Education Introduction Excerpts*

INTRODUCTION

The University component of the proposed project is designed to articulate the direct bilingual service and training needs of the Boston Metropolitan area, Chelsea, and Fall River public schools with the training, service and development capabilities of the Boston University School of Education, College of Liberal Arts, and Metropolitan College.

The timing of the request for this proposal is propitious in that a recently completed needs assessment of the Bilingual Program requested by the Office of the Dean, School of Education, has identified areas in which the School has made significant progress in developing and implementing a bilingual program in addition to identifying areas in need of development both as regard program and staffing and liaison with the Boston, Chelsea, and Fall River Schools, as well as other bilingual programs in the area. These areas will be identified in the History of Program Development to follow.

178 The Dynamics of Funding

FIGURE 6.6. *(cont.)*

Program Development History

The project for which this proposal seeks support has evolved from an initial effort in 1973 between Boston Public Schools and Boston University, School of Education to develop and implement a program for bilingual undergraduate and masters candidates selected, by-in-large, from applicants who have demonstrated through past performance as teacher-aides or teachers in the Boston bilingual public schools a commitment to improving bilingual education in the City of Boston.

Areas of Accomplishment

1. The development and approval of course offerings taught in Portuguese or Spanish and English by the School of Education, College of Liberal Arts and Metropolitan College.
2. The use of already developed and piloted curriculum materials in Spanish for the instruction of college students in the natural sciences.

Areas in Need of Development

1. The development of clearly defined roles and management objectives designed to better articulate local educational agency, University and student activities and expectations.
2. The development of a counseling system for undergraduate trainees with the Counselor Education Department in coordination with the Project Director and LEA directors.

Boston University, "Bilingual Education Teacher Training Project Proposal," submitted to Office of Bilingual Education, Office of Education, Department of Health, Education, and Welfare, May 24, 1976.

Common Flaws

The form and style of the introduction should be determined by the characteristics of the funding agency, the specifications contained in the proposal announcement, and the anticipated orientation of reviewers. The failure to consider the preceding variables represents a general weakness of many submitted proposals. There are, in addition, some specific flaws that occur frequently.

1. The purpose for which funding is sought is not clearly delineated.
2. The exposition of past programs carried out by the submitter and the relevance of the program to the problem being addressed is too lengthy and at times irrelevant to what follows.
3. References to the appropriateness of the submitting institution are not documented and thereby serve only as vague statements of institutional goals barely relevant to the projected activities.

Introduction Statement Checklist

1. Statement designed after analysis of funding and/or funding agency priorities and characteristics? _____
2. Problem that proposed project seeks to address identified? _____
3. Appropriateness of the submitting institution documented? _____
   a. Significant accomplishments? _____
   b. Organization goals? _____
   c. Organization endorsements? _____
4. Appropriateness of program approach documented? _____
   a. Research findings of relevant others cited? _____
   b. Testimonials of relevant others cited? _____
5. Information provided relevant to proposed program? _____
6. Statement concise but informative? _____

PROBLEM STATEMENT AND/OR ASSESSMENT OF NEED

Function

The statement of the problem or needs assessment identifies the shortfall between the current and desired state of knowledge or service delivery that the submitter proposes to address. This component of the proposal:

1. demonstrates the writer's familiarity with the problem to be addressed (thus helping to establish the credibility of the submitter);
2. demonstrates the writer's awareness of funding agency priorities; and
3. determines the objectives and thus strongly influences the activities or procedures that follow in later proposal components.

In selecting and specifically identifying those needs or shortcomings that the project will address, the writer sets his or her own priorities. These priorities, in turn, establish parameters for the program objectives and activities to follow. The definition of the problem or needs assessment is the foundation on which the proposal is structured.

Characteristics

The form of this component of the proposal will vary significantly depending on the type of project. The title of the section will generally reflect whether support is sought for research funds or training and service delivery support. A service or training project will invariably begin with a section entitled "Assessment of Needs" or "Needs Assessment" that identifies specific problems or shortfalls that the project activities will address. This section, unless otherwise specified in the guidelines, should provide data documenting the need for the proposed activities.

In composing this component of the proposal, the writer may choose to provide a general statement of the problem before detailing the specific needs that the project will address. Such a statement should be conceived of as a general needs assessment. Documenting needs beyond the scope of the proposed activities serves some of the same functions as the introduction. Consequently, this entry can preface the needs assessment or be incorporated in the proposal introductory section.

Differences between characteristics of the problem statement or needs assessment that result from the type of program (research/training/service delivery) represent differences in degree rather than in kind. Characteristics common to the problem statement and needs assessment narrative far exceed those unique to one or the other. The problem statement or needs assessment should:

1. be preceded by a succinct statement of purpose that identifies the submitting institution and indicates the type of project (development, training, implementation, research) for which support is sought. (If a statement containing these characteristics is contained in the introduction component, it need not be repeated within this section.)
2. indicate knowledge of the intent of the authorizing legislation and/or priorities of the funding agency, particularly when responding to a specific set of guidelines or Rules and Regulations.
3. identify, in addition to the general need, specific needs that the project will address within the time and funding level constraints set by the guidelines.
4. contain only statements that can be supported by evidence, for example, statistical data, statements from affected or interested groups or clients, citations from professional journals, or references to previous studies.
5. present specific needs in quantifiable terms, for example, 64 percent of the 200 idividuals between the ages of 16 and 18 to be served by the program are performing at 3 years below expected grade level on standardized tests.
6. be sufficiently precise so that identified needs can serve as the basis for identifying specific program objectives or research hypotheses.

Sample Problem and Assessment of Need Statements

Given the many uses of the term *problem* in the development of proposals and the varying use of the term in training, service delivery, and research proposals, the excerpts from funded proposals are supplemented with examples of the use of questions and hypotheses in problem statements drawn from a monograph to aid writers in the development of research proposals.

The following excerpts from the needs assessment included in a community organization's submittal to the Bureau of Education for the Handicapped (Figure 6.7) documents several factors contributing to the need for the proposed project.

FIGURE 6.7. *Bureau of Education for the Handicapped Needs Assessment Excerpts*

1. NEED FOR ASSISTANCE—IDAHO

Idaho is a rural sparsely populated low-tax based state. Data from the State Department of Education and the Office of Child Development indicate a high incidence of handicapped conditions with minimal availability of intervention and prevention programming.

Incidence of Handicapping Conditions—Public Schools

A survey of exceptional children in the public schools in 1968–69 indicated that 26,043 special handicaps were reported. This figure represented the identification of one in every nine children as needing help. (Everyone's Children, State of Idaho Department of Education, 1970)

A 1974 publication, A Study of Exceptional Children in Idaho, State Department of Education, projected the number of exceptional children at 29,367.

Research on Young Children

Three major research studies conducted by the Idaho State Office of Child Development which were summarized by Dr. Howard Schrag in Status of Children in Idaho, 1974, Vol. II., provided the following information:

1. Approximately 2% of 1,000 of the 50,000 families in Idaho with children under six were randomly sampled and interviewed.
    Table 1 from the Status of Young Children in Idaho (Schrag, 1974, p. 158) summarized the types and frequencies of handicapping conditions present in children under six years of age . . . (see table on following page).
2. 3,715 single parents were identified by the 1970 Census Bureau as having children under six years of age. Single parents are suggested as a factor in the provision of adequate emotional environment.
3. Sixty percent of the state's day care facilities provide only some custodial care; 33% provide some education and only 7% have some sort of developmental program.

182   The Dynamics of Funding

FIGURE 6.7. (cont.)

TABLE 1. Types and Frequencies of Handicapping Conditions Present in Children under Six Years of Age

Handicap	State Total	I	II	Regions III	IV	V	VI
Speech	38	8	3	11	3	10	2
Mental Retardation	4	2	—	1	—	1	—
Visual	14	—	3	4	3	1	3
Auditory	9	4	3	2	—	—	—
Seizures	2	—	—	1	—	1	—
Orthodontic	10	4	—	—	1	1	4
Orthopedic	30	3	9	3	4	2	9
Heart	13	4	3	5	2	1	—
Cerebral Palsy	1	—	—	—	—	1	—
Potential Learning Disabilities	11	6	—	1	2	2	—
Cleft Palate	1	—	—	1	—	—	—
Other	30	—	2	5	2	15	6
Total	161	29	24	32	17	35	24
Percent of all children under six years of age		11%	17%	15%	7%	8%	14%	9%

Those recommendations and conclusions from A Study of Exceptional Children in Idaho, 1974, which were relevant to the education of preschool handicapped included the following:

1. "A comprehensive state plan for special education for all exceptional children must be continually implemented . . . to provide a continuum of special education from birth to adulthood."
2. "Coordination of many state and local agencies and institutions must be insured if such a comprehensive service plan is to be achieved."

Two relevant areas of legislative concern identified by A Study of Exceptional Children in Idaho were:

1. "A mechanism should be provided to insure coordination among all state and local agencies responsible for serving exceptional children in Idaho."
2. "Idaho legislative statutes should emphasize the need for programming at early ages, as well as the preference for services with a regular or normal setting."

Panhandle Child Development Association, "Early Childhood Rural Inservice Training Proposal for Idaho and Eastern Washington," submitted to Handicapped Children's Early Education Program Office, Bureau of Education for the Handicapped, Office of Education, Department of Health, Education, and Welfare, 1976.

Figure 6.8, which follows, illustrates a different format used in a proposal, submitted to the Bureau For Equal Educational Opportunity, to support a training institute.

Figure 6.9 illustrates the markedly different qualities of a problem statement in a research proposal. In a research problem statement this component is generally preceded by a discussion of factors justifying the need for the research. This discussion may be carried under the heading of Introduction, Justification for the Study, or Significance of the Study.

Common Flaws

Many of the flaws common to this component of the proposal stem from two major miscalculations on the part of the writer: (1) the problem the proposal addresses is presented in such global terms that any treatment, short of social or political revolution accompanied by a massive infusion of money into a single community, is doomed to failure; and (2) specific needs identified are constructed like a child's Christmas list. "I want" or "I need" is confused with the identification of the discrepancy between the desired and current state of (*text continues p. 185*)

FIGURE 6.8. *Bureau of Equal Educational Opportunity Needs Assessment Excerpts*

Specific Needs Assessment Chart

The Training Institute Project has been developed out of an assessment of the needs described by the participating LEAs. Each LEA, however, differs slightly on the question of emphasis or prioritization of these general needs. To provide a more detailed needs assessments, the . . . University Project Staff Developed a specific needs chart which was used with each LEA to determine:

1. specific project priorities, i.e., using criteria for bias detection, skills in curriculum modification;
2. the number and type of personnel and facilities to be involved;
3. the specific area of school program to be offered, i.e., elementary counseling materials, high school athletic programs.

The following charts detail the specific type and quantity of requested . . . University assistance identified by each LEA.

FIGURE 6.8. (cont.)

Nashua Public Schools
b_x = number of buildings to be involved

LEVEL/AREA	Component: awareness of sex bias	procedure for bias detection & remediation	understand and use criteria for evaluating inst. & curricular material	methods for modifying biased mat. & practices	means for integrating changes into existing curricula	means for integrating changes into existing EEO efforts	skills and materials for training other school personnel
I. Administration							
A. elementary							
1. building personnel			6	6	6		
2. visiting specialists							
B. secondary							
1. building personnel			2	2	2		
2. visiting specialists			8	8	8		
C. system-wide							
1. curriculum coordinators/directors	3	3	3	3	3		
2. program directors esp. voc. ed and pupil services	5	5	5	5	5		
3. project coordinators esp. Title IX and EEO	1	1	1	1	1		
II. Elementary							
A. classroom							
1. curriculum materials							
a. reading and language			6b	6b	6b		
b. science			6b	6b	6b		
c. social studies							
d. physical education							
e. unified arts							
2. classroom (behavior or interaction)	3b	3b	3b	3b	3b		

Boston University, "Institute for Development of Sex-Fair Policies and Practices Proposal," submitted to Equal Education Opportunity Office, Office of Education, Department of Health, Education, and Welfare, January 1977.

FIGURE 6.9. *Illustration of the Use of Questions and Hypotheses in Problem Statements*

Statement of the Problem (single question)
To what extent is a student's social status determined by his parents' status in the community?

Statement of the Problem (general question followed by specific questions)
What is the relationship between educational attainment and unemployment?
Specifically:
What are the levels of educational attainment of United States Unemployment Service registrants in 1977?
What is the relationship between duration of unemployment and educational attainment?
To what extent is placement of unemployed persons in new jobs conditioned by the level of education which they have attained?

Statement of the Problem (general statement followed by questions)
The purpose of this investigation is to determine the relationship between school quality and community size. More specifically, answers to the following questions are sought:
1. Does school quality improve as community population increases?
2. Is there a population range above and below which conditions for achieving school quality are unfavorable?

Statement of the Problem (hypothesis)
There is no difference between the mean score of senior high school boys and the mean score of senior high school girls on a standard mechanical aptitude test.

Statement of the Problem (general statement followed by hypotheses)
The purpose of this investigation is to test the following contentions:
1. That there is a correlation of less than .20 between a test on television repair technique and ratings in actual performance of television repair.
2. That there is a correlation of less than .50 on a television repair technique test as determined by the split halves method.

William B. Castetter and Richard S. Heisler, *Developing and Defending a Dissertation Proposal.* (Philadelphia: Center for Field Studies, Graduate School of Education, University of Pennsylvania, 1977), 16. Reprinted with permission.

---

affairs. Specific needs identified in this manner represent goal statements rather than shortfalls. Identifiable flaws include the following:

1. The narrative reads more like a lengthy social or political essay than a documentation of problems that the activities will address.
2. The problem lacks the precise definition that enables the generation of objectives or hypotheses treatable within fiscal, program, and time constraints set by the funding guidelines.

3. Documentation of the problem is missing or sources of data are unclear or absent.
4. Needs have not been quantified. The specificity necessary to determine whether the distance between the current state and desired state has been decreased by project activities is not provided.
5. Needs are not organized in a way that enables the reader to relate the identified needs with the objectives or hypotheses that follow in the next component of the proposal.
6. Needs identified are presented as value judgments or "I need" statements (e.g., "students need," "community groups need").

Definition of Problem or Needs Assessment Checklist

1. Statement of purpose included (if not contained in previous component)? _____
2. Enables the reader to see immediately the relationship of the problem addressed to funding agency priorities? _____
3. Needs documentated by "hard" data? _____
4. Specific needs to be addressed by proposed project identified? _____ (These needs are population and program specific and should not be generalizable to other settings, unless specifically called for in guidelines.)
5. Stated precisely and, whenever possible, measures the discrepancy between the current and desired state of affairs? _____
6. Stated and organized so that the reader sees the relationship to the objectives that follow? _____

PROGRAM OBJECTIVES

Function

The statement of objectives provides a starting point for the development of activities and establishes the criteria for program evaluation. The ability of objectives to serve these functions is affected greatly by the care given to developing the needs assessment or problem definition. Objectives describe new conditions that will result from addressing the earlier identified needs or deficiencies. They are most effective for activity and evaluation planning when they are identified precisely and concrete specifications are determined for anticipated outcomes. Depending on their use as organizers for the proposal document and presentation of the program, objectives may be identified as general or specific.

General objectives or goal statements:

1. identify the purpose of the program and the major outcomes of the proposed activities; and
2. serve to organize the planned activities when project activities can be broken down into discrete but related components.

Specific objectives:

1. stipulate the individual accomplishments that, when considered collectively, will determine whether the project has realized the proposed general objectives or goals;
2. provide criteria to assist both the developer in identifying appropriate activities and the project manager in assessing the progress of the program;
3. provide criteria against which the project evaluator will develop and implement evaluation strategies; and
4. reflect the conceptualization of the problem, thereby influencing the format of the proposal narrative and the intervention strategies to be selected.

Program Objective Characteristics

One common characteristic should prevail in all statements of general or specific objectives and hypotheses or research questions: the statements should provide the means to make definitive statements of accomplishment (or nonaccomplishment), confirmation, or rejection. Reviews of proposals reveal that writers often ask questions that are unanswerable (or propose objectives whose realization cannot be determined). Examples of these questions or objectives are: "Does a career decision-making program work?" or "Students' attitudes toward schooling will improve." Although the concerns are legitimate, they cannot be dealt with in this form—the criteria for rendering judgement are absent. Objective statements should:

1. describe the condition that will exist if previously assessed needs are addressed as anticipated by the proposed activities;
2. provide the specifications for the anticipated individual accomplishments of the project that, when considered collectively, constitute the goals or general objectives;
3. set the criteria for determining the project's success in identifying earlier needs (criteria may be developed directly from the needs assessment);
4. represent the applicant's selection of desired accomplishments most appropriate to the needs identified earlier (these accomplishments should represent outcomes that the submitting institution feels it can achieve);
5. be stated so that there is no confusion regarding their achievement.

The development of objectives should also be guided by a few technical and definitional considerations. There are two major types of objectives: *performance objectives* represent anticipated changes in a learner's performance as a result of participation in an activity, while *management* objectives represent anticipated changes in an institution's operation as a result of project activities.

Performance and management objectives may be presented as both product and process. *Product objectives* represent the anticipated final outcome of a project activity. *Process* objectives represent intermediate accomplishments necessary to achieve the final or product objectives.

Objectives specific enough to serve as a starting point for the writing of activities and criterion statements for program evaluation should provide the following information:

1. What must be done to demonstrate completion?
2. Who is to do it?
3. Under what conditions must it be done?
4. What criteria will be used to determine if it has been done?

When the achievement of some objectives is contingent on the completion of others, they should be arranged in sequential order. Such ordering of the process objectives facilitates the writing of the activities section of the proposal.

Before examining the prototype objective statements extracted from successful proposals, it will be helpful to "walk through" a hypothetical mission set by the developer. The following general statement of what the developer might wish to accomplish is revised and refined until it evolves into a measurable performance or behavioral objective.

1. *Improve California Education*
   This gross statement must be revised until it is more precise and relates to reducing or eliminating a defined documentable need.
2. *Increase California student mastery of critical skills and knowledge areas and improve self-concept of learners.*
   The planner, by specifying the fundamental critical skill and knowledge areas which might be associated with the way in which a student perceives himself, has further refined the objective.
3. *Measurably improve California in-school mastery in reading and arithmetic and produce an increase in self-concept of learners.*
   The concept of "measurability" has now been introduced; the population ("who") is further defined; and the "what" (reading and arithmetic) has been initially addressed.
4. *Increase California in-school student performance as measured by X valid reading test and Z valid arithmetic test by 10 and 12 percent mean improvements, respectively, and improve learner self-concept as measured by 0 valid instrument within two years.*
   Statement 1 has now been transformed into an acceptable ob-

jective by supplying performance criteria and the basis for evaluation. Further refinement would still be possible: the number or percentage of students for whom an increase would be deemed as being acceptable to the developer and the age or grade-level of students would need to be specified on any proposal of a scale smaller than a statewide intervention suggested in the initial mission statement.[2]*

In writing objectives, the developer must remember that the quantification of objectives is not limited to test-taking situations. Operational definitions of success communicable to interested parties are possible in all human service and education programs.

The writer's task is to transform abstract or general statements of good to specific and concrete examples. Examples of performance and management objectives, presented both as process and product outcomes, identify some of the formats available to the developer.

FIGURE 6.10. *Performance and Management Objective Statements*

Performance/Product:	Given 7 months' participation in an afterschool reading clinic consisting of 40-minute class sessions meeting three times each week, 80 percent of the pupils will show a one month gain in reading achievement for every month of participation, as measured by a standardized reading achievement test.
Performance/Process:	Given the establishment of an after-school reading clinic, pupils enrolled before November 1 will be in attendance 90 percent of the class periods at least 7 months, as indicated by the teacher's class attendance records.
Management/Product:	Given six months' experience using automatic bookkeeping machines, 99.9 percent of the invoices received by the accounting division will be processed within 30 days of being received.
Management/Process:	By the sixth week of the program's operation, six automatic bookkeeping machines capable of processing invoices will be installed in the accounting division, as verified by equipment delivery tickets.

PUTTING IT TOGETHER: A GUIDE TO PROPOSAL DEVELOPMENT. Copyrighted 1975 by the Board of Education of the City of Chicago, Chicago, Illinois. Reprinted by permission.

*Roger A. Kaufman, EDUCATIONAL SYSTEM PLANNING, © 1972, pp. 55-56. Adapted by permission of Prentice-Hall, Inc., Englewood Cliffs, New Jersey.

190   The Dynamics of Funding

Sample Objective Statements

Despite the variations in form, excerpts of objective statements drawn from the Bureau of Education for the Handicapped (Figure 6.11), Career Education (Figure 6.12), and Bilingual Education Title VII (Figure 6.13) proposals contain most of the characteristics cited earlier.

FIGURE 6.11. *Bureau of Education for the Handicapped Objective Excerpts*

PRINCIPAL OBJECTIVE II

By the end of the program year, a fully developed, visible infant/family training model will be functioning.

Subordinate Objective: Program Development

   A. All Procedures and Program elements indicated by this proposal will have been developed, tested, and revised where indicated. Written draft statements of the below will be available.
   1. Program Organization
   2. Staffing—including job descriptions and qualifications
   3. Population Served
   4. Curriculum: Infants
   5. Curriculum: Family, including particular provisions for
      (1) fathering, (2) extended family participation and (3) affective components
   6. Recruitment package

Cantilucian Center for Learning, submitted under Handicapped Children's Early Education Program, Bureau of Education for the Handicapped, Office of Education, Department of Health, Education, and Welfare, Fall, 1976.

FIGURE 6.12. *Office of Career Education Objective Excerpts*

II. Goals and Objectives

   A. Goal #1

   To provide low income children with a career education environment and varied experiences which will enable them to achieve objectives in each of the following:
   1. increase basic academic skills
   2. increase awareness of work values
   3. increase awareness of and knowledge about work
   4. increase and improve self-concept
   5. increase career decision-making skills

   Objective 1.
   After participation in the Career Education Program, the students at each grade level will demonstrate an increase in basic academic skills. Indicators would include evidence of increase in the ability to:

FIGURE 6.12. (cont.)

(a) use numerical computation, concepts and applications skills
(b) use reading and language arts skills
(c) identify education as relevant to life

Instruments used will be:
Gr. 1-8 Stanford Achievement Test
Gr. 9-12 Test of Academic Skills

Program effectiveness in increasing academic skills will be determined by:
Using regression equations and comparing actual performance to predicted performance by grade, across schools. Comparison will also be made with control groups at each grade level.

Objective 2.

After participation in the Career Education Program, the students at each grade level will demonstrate an increase in the awareness of work. Indicators would include:
(a) recognition of work values
(b) positive attitudes toward work

Instruments used will be:
(Grades K-5) Curriculum-embedded criterion-referenced test
(Grades 8-12) Partner in Career Education Secondary test

Program effectiveness in increasing awareness of work values in grades K-5 will be determined by a minimal performance level of 75/65 (that is 75% of youngsters will sucessfully complete 65% of the criteria items on the "Curriculum-Embedded Criterion-Referenced Test").

Data for grades 8-12 will be compared to local base-line data collected in 1976 and to the similar data from Texas schools, also from 1976. Comparison will be made with a control group of grade 10 students (provides operational definition of an earlier goal statement pertaining to increased home-school-community communication).

Specific Objectives

1. After participation in the orientation and training sessions, members of the work community will participate as partners in utilizing the community as a classroom. Indicators would include:
   (a) community-wide survey of resources
   (b) speakers
   (c) student shadowing experiences
   (d) student internships
   (e) teacher internships
   (f) feedback on curriculum
   (g) work experiences
   (h) joint teacher-community projects
   (i) participation in parent-teaching discussion groups

A minimum level of acceptable performance will be:

Community resource book	150 participants
Speakers	600
Shadowing	75
Student internships	200
Teacher internships	200
Curriculum feedback	50
Work experiences	150
Joint projects	30
Parent discussion groups	30 sessions

2. After orientation to and involvement in the Career Education Program during 1977-78, members of the community will provide feedback on the program. Indicators would include:
   (a) parent responses
   (b) community responses
   (c) advisory committee
   (d) student responses

   A minimal level of performance will be 60% of the questionnaires returned with a 2 to 1 ratio of positive-negative responses by May, 1977.
   (copies of survey instrument in the appendix)

3. After orientation and participation in training activities members of the home and families of the pilot schools will demonstrate an increase in knowledge of ways to facilitate their child's career development and to work with the school. Indicators would include:
   (a) participation in training sessions
   (b) knowledge of world of work model, as it is implemented
   (c) knowledge of decision-making process
   (d) knowledge of child's age group
   (e) knowledge of methods of facilitating child's awareness, exploration, and preparation activities/experiences
   (f) knowledge of method for school and family to work together

   Instruments used will be a staff designed pre-post test designed to co-ordinate with training objectives.

   Minimal level of performance will be 75/65.

Jefferson County Public Schools, "Educational Preparation for Involvement in Careers" (Continuation Proposal), submitted to Office of Career Education, Office of Education, Department of Health, Education, and Welfare, March 10, 1977.

FIGURE 6.13. *Bilingual Education Title VII*

INSTRUCTIONAL OBJECTIVES

The following objectives are proposed for the 1976-1977 school year.

Cognitive Area: Oral Language. In an attempt to promote both fluency and high quality of the English/Spanish spoken by students in the bilingual program, the following five objectives are proposed, as measured by the John T. Dailey Language Facility Test:

FIGURE 6.13. (cont.)

Product Objective	Grades	Objective
		English
1	K-1	At least 50% of the A students, 70% of the B students and 90% of the C students will reach or exceed the 50th percentile.
2	2-6	At least 70% of the A and B students and 90% of the C students will reach or exceed the 50th percentile.
		Spanish
3	K-1	At least 80% of the A and B students will maintain, reach or exceed the 50th percentile.
4	2-6	At least 70% of the A and B students will maintain, reach or exceed the 50th percentile.
5	2-6	After three years of SSL instruction, at least 50% of the C students will reach or exceed the 10th percentile

Affective Area: An important aim of the bilingual project is to promote the emotional/social growth of the students in the program. Growth in this area is measured by two project-developed instruments:
1. An affective behavior inventory completed for each child at specified intervals by the biningual teacher.
2. A self-report inventory (Spanish and English forms) administered in the child's dominant language.

Product Objective	Grades	Objective
22	K-6	At least 75% of the bilingual project students will demonstrate positive self-concept, social attitudes and behaviors as reflected in the behavior inventory.
23	3-6	At least 75% bilingual project students will demonstrate a positive self-concept and social attitudes, as measured by the self-report inventory.

Santa Barbara County Schools, "Bilingual Project," submitted to Office of Bilingual Education, Office of Education, Department of Health, Education, and Welfare, 1976.

Common Flaws

In addition to the temptation to overestimate what is possible, two distinct types of flaws contribute to poor ratings for this component: (1) those that reflect structural deficiencies in the proposal and (2) those that reflect technical deficiencies in the wording of the objectives. Examples of the former include the failure of objectives to relate to needs assessment or evaluation design components of the proposal. Examples of the latter include the failure of objectives to define and communicate the outcomes clearly to the reviewer. Objectives that

194   The Dynamics of Funding

are specific but unrelated to the identified needs almost assure proposal rejection and program failure. In such a case, the activities planned to realize the objectives cannot address the need justifying the program. Vague statement of objectives can leave the funding agency guessing about the outcomes, weaken the evaluation design, and precipitate conflict over the program's intent among parties whose support is central to the project's success. In developing the proposal document, the writer should be aware of the following specific flaws noted by the proposal reviewers.

Structural Flaws

1. The statements of objectives are neither directly related to the problem definition nor derived from the assessment of needs presented earlier in the proposal document.
2. The objectives are not relevant to the intent of the funding agency, as provided in the program announcement or the Rules and Regulations governing the solicitation.
3. Individual objective statements are not organized to show their relationship to specific need statements or specific activities identified in preceding or following proposal components.
4. The relationship between general objectives and/or goal statements and specific objectives is not clear.

Technical Flaws

1. Anticipated outcomes are not identified in terms of performance outcomes or product specifications. (What is to be done? Who will do it? Under what conditions is it to be done? What criteria will be used to determine if it has been done?)
2. The proposal fails to differentiate between performance and management objectives, process and product objectives.

Program Objective Checklist

1. Objectives directly related to goals of funding agency? _____
2. Objectives directly related to documented needs? _____
3. Objectives stated in measurable or quantifiable terms clearly communicable to all interest parties? _____
4. Objectives realistic, given institution, agency, and social constraints? _____
5. Objectives organized to enable the reviewer to associate objectives with proposed activities? _____
6. Objectives organized to differentiate between goals and specific outcomes? _____

PROGRAM ACTIVITIES OR METHODS AND PROCEDURES

At this stage of proposal development, the submitting institution has demonstrated the appropriateness of its particular request for support and its knowledge of the problem to be addressed. It has also identified those elements of the problem to be dealt with and what will be accomplished with funding. In identifying the means to realize proposed objectives, the submitting institution seeks to convince the reviewer that planning, development, and management skills match the analytic skills that, ideally, were demonstrated in earlier sections of the proposal. This task, in large part, is a function of the care with which earlier sections of the proposal were developed. The accurate assessment of needs and setting of objectives identifying the particular needs to be addressed, determine appropriate organizational and content parameters for the proposed activities. If projected accomplishments are realistic, are based on documented needs, and are stated in quantifiable terms, then defining and communicating the proposed activities is simplified greatly. If needs are unclear and objectives are open to varying interpretations, the obstacles to effective task completion are almost insurmountable.

The importance of the foundation laid earlier in the document to the exposition of the activities, or methods and procedures, will become increasingly evident as the functions, characteristics and common flaws of this component of the document are discussed.

Functions

The activities or methods and procedures component serves at least three major functions in presenting the case for funding.

1. It provides the funding agency with the performance and management specifications for the project.
2. It sets program and management expectations for submitting institution administrators, project staff, and all other groups affected by the program.
3. It provides an opportunity for the submitter to gain credibility by demonstrating a knowledge of alternative approaches and applications to the selection of activities and strategies that comprise the proposed program.

Characteristics

The preceding functions of the activities component apply to both research and training or service delivery projects. The characteristics of the two types of

196   The Dynamics of Funding

proposals are sufficiently different, however, to justify the identification of two sets of characteristics, one applicable to research proposals (methods or procedures) and one applicable to training or service delivery projects (activities). The following are characteristics of training or service delivery activity statements. Training or service delivery activities should:

1. be organized to enable a reader to relate activities planned with objectives set;
2. provide a reader with the sequence of events and indicate both anticipated starting and completion points for each event or set of events;
3. be sufficiently specific to enable a reader to know who will be doing what at what time, and who and how many will be receiving the benefit of the planned activity at any given time;
4. indicate, whenever possible, anticipated outcomes of specific activities, in the form of product specifications, level of service delivered, or skills attained by participants;
5. indicate the way ongoing evaluation may contribute to adjustment of activities as project proceeds; and
6. include a summary statement, in the form of a milestone chart or bar graph, that depicts the beginning and end for individual activities, the sequence of activities, and the relationship between discrete sets of activities.

Figure 6.14 summarizes the characteristics of the research, as opposed to training or service delivery, proposal. The functions of the component are similar but the format differs significantly.

FIGURE 6.14. *Characteristics of Research Proposal Procedures/Methods Component*

Procedures/Methods
1. Provides specific discussion of design, sampling, analysis and instrumentation
    a. Design Characteristics
        i. Includes discussion and rationale for *how* the study will be undertaken; relates to previous research
        ii. Identifies independent and dependent variables, with specifications of which are to be manipulated, which are to be controlled and which are to be left uncontrolled
        iii. Accounts for all hypotheses identified in objectives
        iv. Identifies sequence of steps for carrying out design
        v. Presents as appropriate, rationale for each design decision
    b. Sampling Characteristics

FIGURE 6.14. (cont.)

      i. Identifies sample size and indicates generalizability to population
      ii. Provides rationale type of sampling
   c. Analysis Characteristics
      i. Indicates methods to be used and how consistent with objectives, design and sampling
      ii. Indicates why particular mode of analysis selected and details how analysis will be carried out
   d. Instrumentation
      i. Describes conceptual and operational measures used in study
      ii. Discusses prior instrumentation; where appropriate discusses reliability and validity of the measures
      iii. Identifies anticipated end-products
         a. Indicates possible outcomes—what conclusions can be drawn when hypotheses have been put to an empirical test?

Ivan Charner, "The Research Proposal as a Component of Counselor Training," *The Counseling Psychologist* 6, no. 1 (April 1976): 72.

The task of incorporating the preceding desired characteristics into the narrative can be facilitated by referring to Figure 6.15. If the writing of this section is approached as both a development and a management task, the initial information necessary to identify and order the activities can be drawn from the earlier statement of objectives or hypotheses. Then, by linking activities or procedures sequentially to proposed outcomes or hypotheses to be tested, the earlier identified management and performance objectives can be transformed into statements of program content.

FIGURE 6.15. A Strategy for Activity Development

1. Identify the major objectives or goal statements and the dates on which you expect the objectives to be realized.

                                                                   | Objective 1 |
                                                                   | June 30, 1978 |

| Objective 2 |
| May 30, 1978 |

2. For each major objective, identify and list in reverse sequential order the specific objectives that must be realized to accomplish the final general objective or goal.

198 The Dynamics of Funding

FIGURE 6.15. (cont.)

Objective 1 Specific Objectives	Objective 2 Specific Objectives
z	z
y	y
x	x
w	w

3. Once objectives have been ordered sequentially, commencing with those to be completed last, identify and place activity or activities planned for the realization of the objective alongside each objective.

General Objective 1: _____

Specific Objectives   Activity*

a. $\underline{\quad z \quad}$ $\Bigg\langle$ $\begin{array}{l} z^1 \underline{} \\ \\ z^2 \underline{} \end{array}$

b. $\underline{\quad y \quad}$ $\Bigg\langle$ $\begin{array}{l} y^1 \underline{} \\ \\ y^2 \underline{} \end{array}$

c. $\underline{\quad x \quad}$ $\Bigg\langle$ $\begin{array}{l} x^1 \underline{} \\ x^2 \underline{} \\ x^3 \underline{} \end{array}$

4. Estimate time necessary to complete each activity and the date the activity should begin and be completed. Transform into a program calendar or milestone chart: [as shown at the top of p. 199]

FIGURE 6.15. *(cont.)*

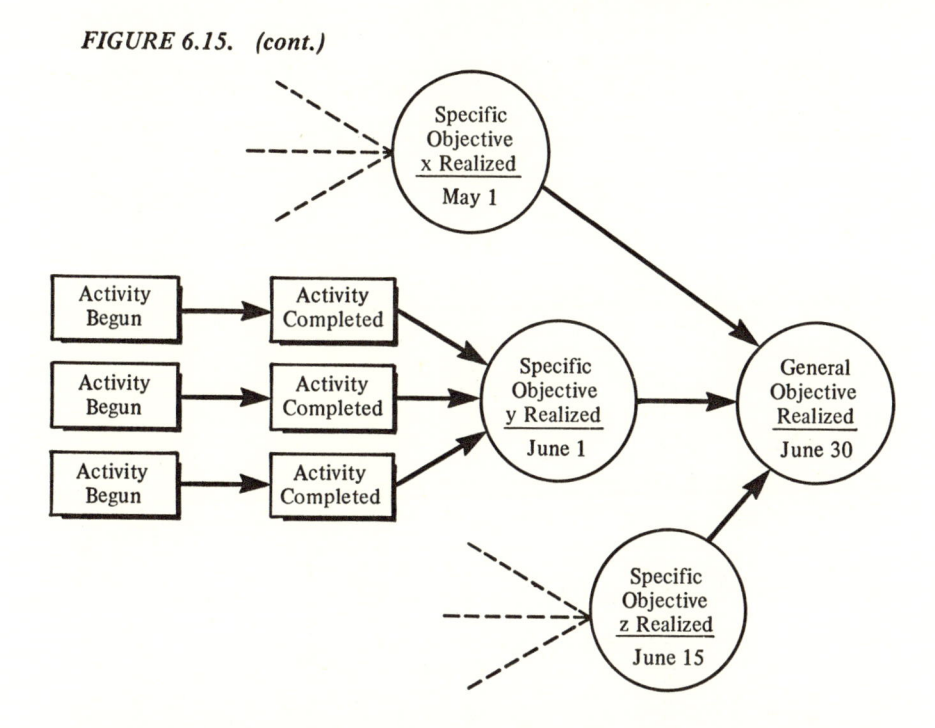

*Activity statements should include what will occur, who will be responsible for carrying them out, who will benefit, and what facilities and materials will be necessary for their completion.

The writer has considerable latitude in the style of presentation chosen for this section of the proposal. Whether the presentation is a calendar of events or carefully worded detailed narrative, however, the organization and time ordering of activities and the relationship between activities and expected results are still required.

Sample Activity Statements

The possible variations in form of this proposal component are illustrated by the following excerpts from a proposal submitted to the Office of Career Education (Figure 6.16), materials contained in a manual for applicants for ESEA Title IV Projects distributed by the Commonwealth of Massachusetts (Figure 6.17), and a proposal submitted to the National Science Foundation (Figure 6.18).

These formats can serve as outlines for the exposition of program activities and the provision of additional detail deemed relevant by the submitter. The style and format, it must be stressed, should reflect the tastes and expectations of the receiving agency.

FIGURE 6.16. Office of Career Education Activity Excerpts

MAJOR ACTIVITIES AND SUBTASKS

Training	Home-Student Discussion Groups	Child Development Process	Decision-Making Process	Career Awareness Exploration and Preparation	Advisory Committee	Volunteers	Strategies for Facilitation Home-student Relationship
• Review training design with the advisory committee • hold monthly training sessions to include: • nature of child decision making skill • awareness of world of work • ways of discussion with students • ways to assist in breaking down sex/race in the work community • evaluate training • provide feedback • refine if necessary	• Form Committee • survey parents-identify topics • survey students-identify topics • implement discussion groups-include counselors • evaluate discussion	• Review Training module • gather materials • implement module • evaluate module • provide feedback • refine if necessary	• Review training module-differentiate elementary, middle, senior high • gather materials • emphasis on process developmental • implement module • evaluate module • refine if necessary	• Implement session on awareness of world of work: 1) 15 clusters 2) job market 3) opportunities for training 4) advancement possibilities 5) related fields within clusters • coordinate knowledge of the world of work with decision-making process • design activities whereby parents can provide awareness for their children • evaluate module • refine if necessary	• Parent group at each school 1) identify needs 2) plan training 3) review evaluation data	• Parent Steering Committee at each school will assist in organizing and implementing a school volunteer program as relates to career education	• Review training module 1) identify ways in which parents and students can explore together 2) facilitate joint design of activities 3) provide training to give parents necessary skills to work with their children

Jefferson County Public Schools, "Educational Preparation for Involvement in Careers" (Continuation Proposal), Submitted to Office of Career Education, Office of Education, Department of Health, Education and Welfare, March 10, 1977.

The Writing of the Proposal Document 201

FIGURE 6.17. *Time–Action–Budget Plan*

Part V.
The following table outlines the complete series of activities, scheduled thoughout the funding calendar, with approximate budget allocation for each stated objective:

Objective # _____ : _____

_____

Estimated Cost _____

Step #	Action Plan	Person Responsible	Time Plan
			J A S O N D J F M A M J J A

Commonwealth of Massachusetts, Department of Education, ESEA, Title IV, Manual for Project Applicants, 1977.

FIGURE 6.18. *Excerpts from National Science Foundation Training Program Proposal*

PROJECT OPERATION

The workshop is designed with two purposes in mind. The first is to provide first hand, hands-on experiences in natural and environmental science that demonstrate the use of the outdoor classroom in all seasons, weather conditions, and times of day. The second is to provide teachers with "handles" to certain areas of natural science content. These areas are carefully selected to increase the chances

FIGURE 6.18. (cont.)

of successful mastery and reduce the feelings of overwhelmed confusion with which many teachers view the outdoor world.
Each camp weekend will follow roughly the following format:

Friday Evening:	Group Meeting 8:00 P.M.
	    Hands-on indoor group activities, Planning, Sharing resources, Assembling equipment, Demonstrations
	Night Activity 10:30 P.M.
	    Star/Moon watch, Track and trap setting, Night hike

Saturday A.M.:	Bird Watching, Track and trap monitoring, 7:00 A.M.; Study Group, 9:00 A.M.
Saturday P.M.:	Group Hike 1:00 P.M. Observation skills increase each weekend Study Group, 3:00 P.M. Ideas evolve from follow-through on hike/group activity to personal focus
Saturday Evening:	Independent Study 8:00 P.M. Show and Tell 9:00 P.M. Night Activity 10:30 P.M.
Sunday A.M.:	Group Hike 9:00 A.M. Independent Study 11:00 A.M.
Sunday P.M.:	Data-Sharing Show and Tell 1:00 P.M. Evaluation and Planning

Each on-campus day will be scheduled as follows:

8:30 – 9:30	Assemble, review resource materials, visit with staff, tend to administrative details.
9:30 – 11:00	Class Session—Introductory Ecology and Intermediate Earth Sciences.
11:00 – 12:30	Class Sessions—Ecology and Introductory Earth Sciences
12:30 – 1:00	Lunch
1:00 – 3:30	Laboratory and workshop activities. These sessions will be organized into topical interest groups in ecology, earth science, field resources and equipment/ materials preparation.

The multi-option activities are sequenced to develop group process; to reveal the resources of the field site, the materials, the literature, and people, and to increase the independence of the participant.
    The second half of each participant's program will focus on the field studies activities, the evaluation of environmental materials, and the development of materials and/or activities for school use. This component will be structured by grade level interests so that where possible, teachers with similar professional responsibilities will be working together.

FIGURE 6.18. (cont.)

The sessions to be conducted on campus will focus on background and preparation for the upcoming session at the camp. Approximately equal time will be devoted to each of the three courses at these all-day Saturday sessions. The Science courses will be lecture-discussions with laboratory activities requiring special equipment available only on the campus. The field studies-science education component will utilize Departmental and University library and resource facilities to select materials for testing at the camp. Some time will be devoted to the preparation of collecting materials, use of field books, keys, etc., and preparing experiments such as water and soil analyses. (See Appendix B for a list of topics in Ecology and Geology.)

The Department of Science and Mathematics Education has developed a resource center which is open to teachers in the late afternoon and evening hours. Under the auspices of this center the Department will sponsor an all day workshop-conference in November 1979 for the Field Studies program. This follow-up conference will focus on exchanging experiences in implementing environmental science activities in the school systems of the participants, and evaluating the effectiveness of these activities. On an informal basis the center will be open and of service to the participants on a continuing basis during and after the grant period.

Boston University, "Four Seasons Field Studies in Science," proposal submitted to National Science Foundation, Scientific Personnel Improvement Branch, February 1978.

Common Flaws

Most of the flaws commonly found in the activities or procedures and methods component of the proposal stem from the writer's failure to understand the function of this section. The statement of proposed activities is a response to a request for management and performance specifications to govern the actions of all parties involved in project implementation. It is not a call for a general exposition of project goals; it is not a statement of general intent; and it is not a statement of an approach to a general problem or the reiteration of the submitter's past efforts to address the problem. Specific symptoms of this failure to understand the function of this section include:

1. little or no display of knowledge of other published or recently completed work;
2. specific plans for conducting activities missing or not linked to objectives;
3. time lines unrealistic or missing, particularly regarding start-up dates and schedule for realization of process objectives;
4. poor organization and/or overly long description (reader is unable to identify what will occur at what time);
5. principles of good design, validity, and reliability of data in surveys, test protocols, and controls for observer's bias not followed (research

proposals), or findings from earlier training or service delivery projects not incorporated into program design; and

6. guidelines not adhered to for presentation of activities and/or types of activity authorized by funding agency.

Activity Statement Checklist

1. Activities authorized by the Rules and Regulations or program announcement? ____
2. Activities delineated and related to objectives? ____
3. Activities presented in logical order with specified start-up and completion times? ____
4. Basis for selection of particular activities concisely documented? ____
5. Clearly communicable overview or summary of activities set against a timetable? ____

PROGRAM EVALUATION

As funding agencies have become increasingly sensitive to demands for accountability, the importance of proposals including strategies for assessing project activities has increased. In the early and mid-1960s, many evaluation sections of proposals were little more than postscripts to the narrative; the submitter made a token gesture to accountability by indicating that a third party would develop and carry out evaluation activities. Within the last decade, however, program management and evaluation has become almost as important as program content. Evaluation design and strategies are now an integral part of the proposal, reflecting on the quality of the program and often figuring significantly in the proposal rating.

Functions

The evaluation design and accompanying implementation strategies serve both programmatic and management functions in the exposition of the proposed program. Specifically, the evaluation component allows the writer to:

1. define anticipated accomplishments and inform interested parties how success will be determined and communicated; and
2. set objectives against a time line for expected accomplishment.

The writer can use the evaluation section to summarize the anticipated activities and outcomes of the proposed project with a high degree of specificity, thereby demonstrating to the reviewer the care and precision with which the proposed program has been developed. The evaluation activities can also serve two critical management functions.

1. Directors and staff can obtain information about project operation that will enable the adjustment of activities necessary to realize project objectives.
2. After project completion, all interested parties will possess information that may assist future program development.

Characteristics

Unfortunately, the evaluation component of the proposal cannot be transformed into a single set of steps that will assure a submitter the maximum numbers of points allocated to this section. The design and strategies can be arrived at only after identifying the types of decisions the evaluation information is designed to inform.

All decisions can be classified as pertaining to *ends* (intended or actual) or to *means* (intended or actual). Ends and means include: (1) intended ends (goals), (2) intended means (planned procedures), (3) actual means (procedures in use), and (4) actual ends (attainments). These categories inform four types of decisions a project director will be called on to make in evaluating the project:

1. planning decisions to determine objectives
2. structuring decisions to design procedures
3. implementing decisions to utilize control and refine procedures
4. recycling decisions to determine project accomplishments.

The nature of decisions a director must make determines the type of project evaluation design. For instance: *context evaluation* serves planning decisions; *input evaluation* serves structuring decisions; *process evaluation* serves implementing decisions; and *product evaluation* serves recycling decisions.

Context evaluation calls for both empirical and conceptual analysis contributing to the development of program objectives. Input evaluation provides information concerning the utilization of resources available to the developer. These two types of evaluation, ideally, should be carried out before document development. Evidence strongly suggests, however, that such systematic evaluation is absent in the designing of projects or, for that matter, in most educational and social programs. Since the evaluation strategy is generally set after a course of action has been decided, the characteristics of the evaluation section are generally drawn from process and product evaluations. The evaluation design should:

1. identify the functions the evaluation is designed to serve (the audiences to be served, the nature of the information);

2. identify (from the objectives) criteria against which the information will be judged;
3. identify the sources of information, the instruments and measures for collecting the information, and a master schedule for information collection;
4. Provide a format for organizing the information and the means for analyzing it;
5. specify the audiences for the evaluation reports, the means of disseminating the information, the schedule for dissemination;
6. define staff responsibilities for carrying out the evaluation and determine the schedule for reporting findings and producing reports.

If it is not possible to include a person with evaluation expertise in developing the proposal, the writer can use a relatively simple approach that incorporates most of the desired characteristics. That is, systematically to identify and list the specific objectives, the activities designed to achieve the specified outcomes, the procedures and standards (or criteria against which data will be assessed) used to collect and analyze the information, and the timetable for the collection and analysis of data. These tasks can be presented in tabular form (Table 6.2) that, when complemented by a minimal narrative, will answer the questions raised by most proposal reviewers.

TABLE 6.2. Categories for Collection and Analysis of Data

Project Outcomes (Objectives)	Activities	Procedures for Data Collection	Standards	Timetable

The writer can meet most of the requirements of the evaluation task if the information provided in the chart is complemented by an identification of means for analyzing any discrepancies that may occur between anticipated outcomes (represented by the specific objectives) and actual outcomes (identified by the analysis of the data); and the means for adjusting program activities or objectives, in light of any discrepancies, are included in the narrative. It must be reiterated that if proposal guidelines call for a major evaluation component, the writer who is unfamiliar with the range of evaluation models should secure consulting help for the development of the design. Despite such help, however, the writer must participate in developing this component. The design must offer strategies to assess systematically the degree to which *the objectives set by the developer* are realized as a result of *the strategies set by the developer*, through *evaluation tasks carried out by the evaluator.*

Before examining some sample evaluation statements, the proposal writer is advised to consider, as appropriate, the implications of recommendations for evaluation strategies as issued by the Bureau of Education for the Handicapped for field-initiated programs.

Criteria for Useful Methodologies.

Methodologies must be designed to yield information that is understandable to policy-makers.
Methodologies should be designed to involve all personnel.
Methodologies should be useful to teachers.
Methodologies should provide answers for parents and school boards.
Methodologies should help states keep track of progress.
Methodologies should provide information useful to the Congress.
New methodologies should build on existing methodologies to insure ease of adoption.[3]

Although these criteria relate to a specific program, they are increasingly applicable to the wide range of programs dependent on the support of several constituent groups served by individual programs.

Sample Evaluation Components

The excerpts from the Office of Career Education proposal illustrate the manner in which a discrepancy evaluation model may serve as the evaluation design.* The excerpts from an evaluation report of an LEA Title VII Program demonstrate the link between objectives and the evaluation design and reporting of findings.

FIGURE 6.19. Career Education Evaluation Excerpts

V. Evaluation Plan
 There are two main components to the evaluation plan for EPIC:
 • process or formulative evaluation
 • product or summative
 The distinction is simple-product evaluation will attempt, using the tools of research design, to assess the degree of congruence between the stated objectives of the project and the actual outcomes. Process evaluation will be used to detect defects or deficiencies in the installation or implementation of the project at each school in order to provide decision-makers with information that will ensure congruence between planned and actual activities.

*Simply stated, discrepancy analysis evaluation calls for the systematic testing of program status against process objectives. Data derived from the testing, which reveals any discrepancy between the anticipated attainments and actual attainments, is then used to adjust goals or activities as appropriate.

FIGURE 6.19. (cont.)

A. The product evaluation plan for students is directly related to the statement of learner outcomes in an earlier section of this proposal. A skeleton of the plan referenced to each outcome area follows:

Student Outcome	Grades Involved	Design	Instrumentation	Data An.
1. Self-awareness	K-3 4-6 7-12	Random sample pre/post test Sept. 77 May 78	SOS level 1-4 SOS level 1-7 C.M.I. Competence Area, A-1	t-test on gains .05 sig. level
2. (a) Academic Skills	1-8 9-12	Population pre/post test May 77-May 78	Stanford A. Test Test of Academic Skills	Regression Analysis
(b) Vocational Skills	4, 8, 12	Random sample pre/post testing Sept. 77-May 78	Texas CEMS that correspond to Obj. III D & E	
3. Work Values	K-5	Population periodic testing following instructional objective	Curriculum embedded criterion-referenced tests	75/65 criterion

B. Process Evaluation

The process evaluation plan for EPIC is comprehensive in scope because an attempt is made to monitor the performance of the six most important role groups in the project:

> students
> teachers
> school staff members
> project staff
> community
> parents

During the development phase of last year's project, basic information about the operation of the project was restricted to quantity—how much? how many? when? etc., and quality was assessed indirectly by sampling people's perceptions.

This year EPIC is building into its operation

> a criterion-referenced set of objectives which will provide an information base for a computerized management information system on students as well as project staff activities.
>
> school profiles will be provided to individual teachers, grades and schools on the accomplishment of project youngsters relative to the set of career education objectives.

Using all of the above techniques, quarterly reports prepared by Research and Evaluation provide the project management with information that ensures a self-correcting system that can achieve its objectives.

FIGURE 6.19. (cont.)

PROCESS EVALUATION ACTIVITIES

Activities included in the Process Evaluation tentatively scheduled for the Career Education Program during the 1976-77 school year are:

(a) Observation (OBS) of Career Education teachers and classroom by members of Process Evaluation staff;
(b) Conducting surveys (QUES) of Career Education teachers (and their principals) and parents of participating children;
(c) Interviewing (INT) Career Education teachers, and students in the Program;
   (Observation and interviews are done on a sample basis, as is the survey of parents.)
(d) "Action Plans" (AP) on which Program staff report their plans for the quarter, are submitted at the beginning of each quarter;
(e) "Accomplishment Reports," (AR) on which Program staff report actual performance during the quarter, are submitted at the middle and end of each quarter, and "Change Request" which explain any change in plans already submitted . . . .

Evaluation Activities

Activity	Population	Date
Action Plan, First Quarter	Staff	9-15
Observation	Classroom Sample Breckinridge, South Park	10-25-29
Questionnaire	Teacher Sample five schools	11-5
Accomplishment Report, First Quarter	Staff	12-1
Action Plan, Second Quarter	Staff	12-3
Observation	Classroom Sample Western, Central Fairdale	1-17-21
Questionnaire	Teacher Sample five schools	1-28
Interview	Teacher Sample Breckinridge, South Park	2-28-3-4
Accomplishment Report	Staff	3-9

Jefferson County Public Schools, "Educational Preparation for Involvement in Careers" (Continuation Proposal), submitted to Office of Career Education, Office of Education, Department of Health, Education, and Welfare, March 10, 1977.

FIGURE 6.20. *Dunkirk Bilingual Program Excerpts*

Component: Instructional
Section: First Grade

Objective	Sample Size (N)	Criterion Type	Statistics	Results Attained	Results Proposed	Status	Summary
1. To demonstrate skill in reading in the dominant language.	ED = 21	% demonstrating one year's growth in English.	N achieving one year's growth in English = 16.	16/21 = 84%	60%	24% above proposed.	Objective attained.
	SD = 6	% demonstrating mastery.*	N achieving a score of 75% or above = 5.	5/6 = 83%	60%	23% above proposed	Objective attained.
2. To demonstrate skill in math.	N = 27	% demonstrating one year's growth.	N achieving one year's growth = 25.	25/27 = 92%	60%	32% above proposed.	Objective attained.
3. To demonstrate ability in a second language.	ED = 21	% demonstrating mastery.	N achieving a score of 80% or above = 16.	16/21 = 84%	60%	24% above proposed.	Objective attained.
	SD = 6	% demonstrating mastery.	N achieving mastery of 70% on BSM = 5.	5/6 = 83%	60%	23% above proposed.	Objective attained.

*Since grade level norms do not exist, the criterion type was modified to a mastery level of 75%.

FIGURE 6.20. (cont.)

Component: Curriculum Development

Objective	Development Status	Dissemination	Objective
1. To develop: a) behavioral objectives and activities for social studies units in Puerto Rican History and Culture in grades 4 and 5.	Identified by Curriculum Specialist.	To be disseminated in Fall, 1977, when there will be a 4th grade class.	Completed as proposed.
b) assessment instruments for each Puerto Rican History and Culture unit.	Developed by Curriculum Specialist.	Distributed to bilingual staff K–3 for field testing.	Completed as proposed.
c) behavioral objectives for units in language arts, math and science in Spanish for 4th and 5th grades which parallel English curriculum	Developed or identified by Curriculum Specialist and School 3 Principal.	To be distributed in Fall, 1977, when there will be a 4th grade class.	Completed as proposed.
d) scope, sequence and activities curriculum for teaching English and Spanish as a second language in 4th and 5th grades.	Developed by Curriculum Specialist	To be distributed in Fall, 1977.	Completed as proposed.

FIGURE 6.20. (cont.)

Component: Parent Involvement
Results Summary

Objective	Number Proposed	Number Conducted	Number Status	Attendance Proposed	Attendance Achieved	Attendance Status
1. To attend parent meetings.	at least 1	5	Objective attained	50%	Average attendance for 5 meetings is 100%	Objective attained
2. To attend academic workshops (Activities a–f).	5	5	Objective attained	50%	80%	Objective attained
3. To attend community, home-service, and cultural workshops (Activities g–l).	5	6	Exceeds proposed	30%	50%	Exceeds proposed
4. To serve as resource persons.	N/A	N/A	N/A	5% volunteering	28%	Exceeds proposed
5. To attend PAB meetings.	N/A	N/A	N/A	N/A	75%	Objective attained
6. To participate in home-school visits.	1 visit to each of 74 families	82 visits made	Exceeds proposed	100% visitation, 1 visit each family	Visited 33% once 13% twice 17% three times 17% four times 20% more than four times	Exceeds proposed
7. To conduct sociolinguistic survey on	40 project parents	40 project parents	Objective attained	40 project parents	20 low S.E.C. 20 middle S.E.C.	Objective attained

Madan Mohan, Evaluation of the Dunkirk Bilingual Program," Title VII, Grant # G007503688 (Fredonia, N.Y.: State University College, 1977).

Evaluation Flaws

If evaluation is defined as "the process of delineating, obtaining, and providing useful information for judging decision alternatives,"[4] most of the observable flaws in submitted proposals result from a failure to interpret this definition literally. Some proposals also fail to recognize that criteria for determining "useful information" should be established by the project objectives. Specifically, the writer should avoid the following flaws:

1. Strategies for gathering data are not specified and time lines for the sequential collection of information are lacking.
2. The type of information to be collected is not specified and criteria for evaluating the information are not adequately defined.
3. The criteria for evaluating the information and decisions are only peripherally related to the proposed objectives.
4. Strategies for the collection of information fail to meet scientific criteria for a valid evaluation (e.g., technical prerequisites for reliability, validity, and objectivity are not taken into consideration).
5. Audiences the evaluation is designed to inform or serve are not identified.

Evaluation Component Checklist

1. Objectives directly addressed by measures chosen to assess outcomes? ____
2. Means for collecting data specified (e.g., interviews, test administration, polling, enumerating incidents, etc.)? ____
3. Time lines for collecting *and* reporting data stipulated? ____
4. Responsibility for collecting, analyzing, and reporting data clearly assigned? ____
5. Criteria for determining the degree to which project has been successful in realizing the objectives, or criteria for conforming or rejecting hypotheses, clearly delineated? ____
6. Format for reporting the evaluation data stated; parties to receive reports identified? ____

PROJECT MANAGEMENT

Project management, in the proposal context, generally defines the terms for staff participation, identifies the decision-making process that will govern project operations, and identifies the way authority will be allocated among institutions and individuals. This component may also provide an overview of project operations, as well as project governance within the preceding context.

214 The Dynamics of Funding

Functions

The project management component serves two sets of functions: (1) those relating to the program exposition and (2) those with implications for project initiation if the proposal is funded.

Specific functions of this management component related to the exposition of the program include:

1. It confirms and operationally defines the relationship between individual groups, and institutional units identified as participating parties in earlier components of the proposal.
2. It provides a means for setting program features against staff assignments, and fixes the responsibilities of parties identified earlier as central to project implementation.
3. It serves as an information base for generating proposed project costs and negotiating final budgets, should project approval be forthcoming.

Functions of the management component related to the initiation of the project (and that demonstrate the submitting institution's ability to manage the project) include:

1. It defines the mechanisms for recruiting personnel and establishes the time lines for personnel selection.
2. It identifies the procedures for making intraprogram decisions pertaining to project operation and staff appointments (and dismissal).
3. It identifies the procedures for making intrainstitutional decisions regarding both project and staff appointments.*
4. It relates staff assignments to prescribed activities set against prescribed time lines.**

Characteristics

Although the management of a project is governed by both the policies and procedures of the submitting institution and the organization and features of the specific program, these policies and procedures are not always consonant. Provisions must be made for articulating institutional and project-specific policies and procedures. Although the specific elements and the amount of de-

---

*Many decisions affecting program operations are beyond the authority of project directors. Specified domains of decision making are jealously guarded by boards of trustees, institutional fiscal and program officers, school boards, etcetera.

**This function is relevant when the component is perceived as a plan of operation. In many cases, the same function can be served by using appropriate charts summarizing the activities component of the proposal.

tail included in this component will vary with the guidelines for a particular submittal, the previously cited functions can be addressed by insuring that the management component:

1. contains an organizational chart and accompanying narrative that specifies the manner in which authority for decision making is distributed.
2. contains an implementation plan, setting the major events or milestones against a time line for initiation and completion. (If a time line is provided in the earlier summary of activities, the implementation plan may simply include a schedule of events drawn from the earlier summary.)
3. delineates clearly the programmatic and administrative responsibilities of all project personnel. To the degree possible, and as relevant, responsibilities should include specifications of outcomes for which individuals will be held accountable.
4. summarizes qualifications of staff relevant to their roles in the proposed project. This presentation should enable the reader to sense the appropriateness of the assignment as well as the qualifications of the individual. (Resumes may be attached as an appendix.)

If the management component narrative incorporates the preceding characteristics, the reviewer and potential director should be able to answer all questions pertaining to project governance, the assignment of staff responsibilities, and the relationship between assignments and tasks to be undertaken.

Given the wide range of expectations held for this component, the format may differ greatly from proposal to proposal. Some of the functions cited may, in certain cases, be treated within the budget component. Regardless of the specific placement of the functions, the writer and/or director must, on the basis of self-interest, be sure that the functions are addressed. The failure to resolve policy issues adequately, to fix responsibility for decision making, and to establish a common set of expectations on the part of all project participants before funding can lead to serious disruptions in project implementation.

PROJECT MANAGEMENT SAMPLES

The Career Education organizational chart is shown in Figure 6.21. In the full narrative it is followed immediately by descriptions of the roles for each of the identified offices and for project staff. The operating plan (Figure 6.22) summarizes activities and fixes staff responsibilities.

The EEO Title IV sex desegregation milestone chart (Figure 6.23) is a variation on the pattern followed in the Career Education Operating Plan. The milestone chart is followed by an organization chart that, in turn, is followed by role definitions for staff.

216 The Dynamics of Funding

FIGURE 6.21. Career Education Management Excerpts

e. ROLES AND ORGANIZATIONAL STRUCTURE
  (1) Organizational Structure

   The proposed project will be implemented under the Department of Instruction.
   The project represents the total curriculum and draws upon the special expertise, contributions and responsibilities of many departments (Elementary, Secondary, Guidance, Vocation Education, Special Education and Evaluation).

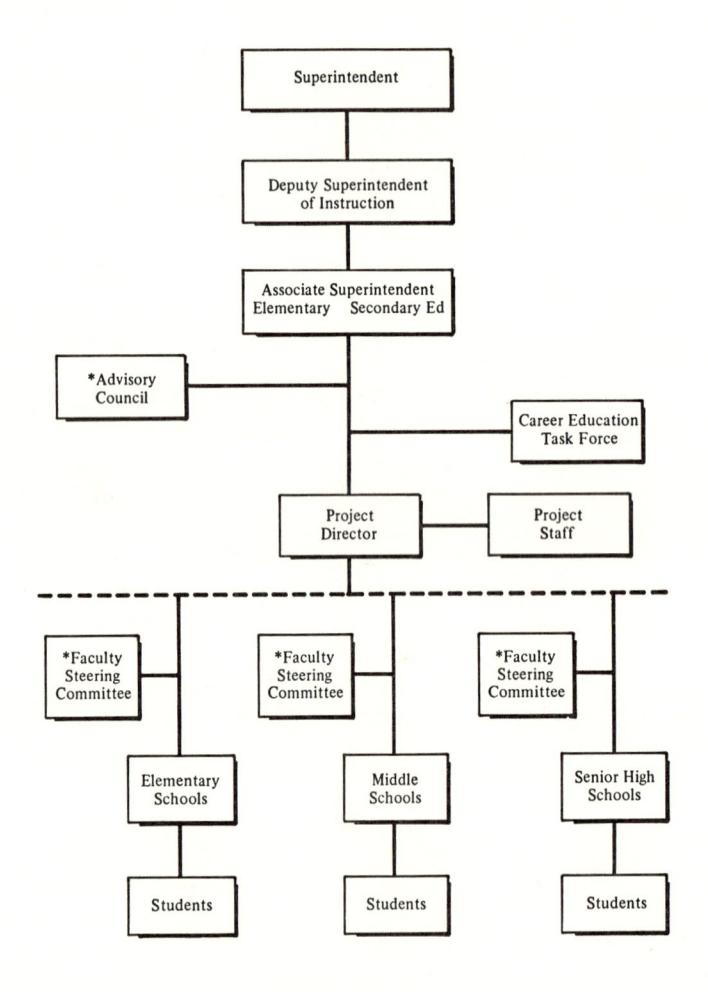

```
                    ┌─────────────────┐
                    │ Superintendent  │
                    └────────┬────────┘
                             │
                    ┌────────┴────────┐
                    │Deputy Superintendent│
                    │   of Instruction │
                    └────────┬────────┘
                             │
                    ┌────────┴─────────┐
                    │Associate Superintendent│
                    │Elementary  Secondary Ed│
                    └────────┬─────────┘
       ┌─────────────┐       │
       │ *Advisory   ├───────┤
       │  Council    │       │
       └─────────────┘       │          ┌─────────────────┐
                             ├──────────┤ Career Education│
                             │          │   Task Force    │
                             │          └─────────────────┘
                    ┌────────┴────────┐  ┌──────────┐
                    │    Project      ├──┤ Project  │
                    │    Director     │  │  Staff   │
                    └────────┬────────┘  └──────────┘
         ┌───────────────────┼───────────────────┐
    ┌────┴─────┐       ┌─────┴────┐       ┌──────┴───┐
    │ *Faculty │       │ *Faculty │       │ *Faculty │
    │ Steering │       │ Steering │       │ Steering │
    │Committee │       │Committee │       │Committee │
    └────┬─────┘       └─────┬────┘       └──────┬───┘
    ┌────┴─────┐       ┌─────┴────┐       ┌──────┴───┐
    │Elementary│       │  Middle  │       │Senior High│
    │ Schools  │       │ Schools  │       │ Schools  │
    └────┬─────┘       └─────┬────┘       └──────┬───┘
    ┌────┴─────┐       ┌─────┴────┐       ┌──────┴───┐
    │ Students │       │ Students │       │ Students │
    └──────────┘       └──────────┘       └──────────┘
```

Jefferson County Public Schools, "Educational Preparation for Involvement in Careers" (Continuation Proposal), submitted to Office of Career Education, Office of Education, Department of Health, Education and Welfare, March 10, 1977.

FIGURE 6.22. *Career Education Operations Plan*

OPERATING PLAN

Goal #3 (2nd phase) To provide the home and family community with the necessary career education knowledge and skills to facilitate their child's career development and to work in partnership with the school to include:

1. participation in training sessions
2. knowledge of world of work
3. knowledge of decision making process
4. knowledge of child
5. knowledge of methods of facilitating child's awareness, exploration and preparation
6. knowledge of methods for school and family to work together

Project Completion Date	Action Steps	Staff Member Responsible	July	Aug	Sept	Oct	Nov	Dec	Jan	Feb	Mar	Apr	May	June
	31100 Form parent groups each school													
3-15-77	31101 Identify parents	D.,H.F.Sp.,P.		△15										
9-20-77	31102 Establish procedures	H.F. Sp.		①1	△20									
9-25-77	31103 Schedule meeting	H.F. Sp.			△25									
	31200 Conduct training sessions													
6-30-77	31201 Review training modules	H.F. Sp.	△30											
8-30-77	31202 Form advance group	H.F. Sp.		△30										
5-30-78	31203 Conduct sessions	"			⑤15							△30		
5-30-78	31204 Evaluate session	"			⑤15							△30		
6-10-78	31205 Provide Feedback	"			⑤15									△10
	31300 Conduct Parent-Community Discussion Groups													
11-30-77	31301 Form Groups	H.F. Sp.				①①20								
12-10-77	31302 Schedule Groups	"					△10							
6-30-77	31303 Conduct groups	"				①①		①①				△30		
5-30-77	31304 Evaluation Groups	"										△30		
6-10-78	31305 Provide Feedback	"												△10

*Phase II—Home-Family-Community   **Major New Activities

Jefferson County Public Schools, "Educational Preparation for Involvement in Careers" (Continuation Proposal), submitted to Office of Career Education, Office of Education, Department of Health, Education and Welfare, March 10, 1977.

FIGURE 6.23. EEO Management Excerpts Milestone Chart

Program Activity	Person(s) Directly Responsible	Pre-funding Activity	Time Projections 1 2 3 4 5 6 7 8 9 10 11 12
To establish a core team of school personnel with the authority and Skills to implement sex-desegregation program	Project staff in conjunction with Title IX Coordinator	◄	
To familiarize core teams with their school district's Title IX Self-Evaluation	Title IX Coordinator	◄	◄ ◄
To develop and conduct a 5 day summer training program for core teams from 3 urban school districts	Project staff, after consultation with Title IX Coordinators		◄
To develop a system-wide plan and appropriate strategies to promote a greater awareness of the components of sex-fair education to a substantial proportion of the school staff	Core teams after consultation with Project staff		◄
To plan and conduct at least 3 one-day on-site workshops per school district to advance goals of equal educational opportunity in specified areas	Project staff in conjunction with core teams		◄ ◄

Source: Boston University, "Institute for Development of Sex-Fair Policies and Practices Proposal," submitted to Equal Education Opportunity Office, Office of Health, Education, and Welfare, January 1977.

FIGURE 6.23. *(cont.)*

Organizational Chart

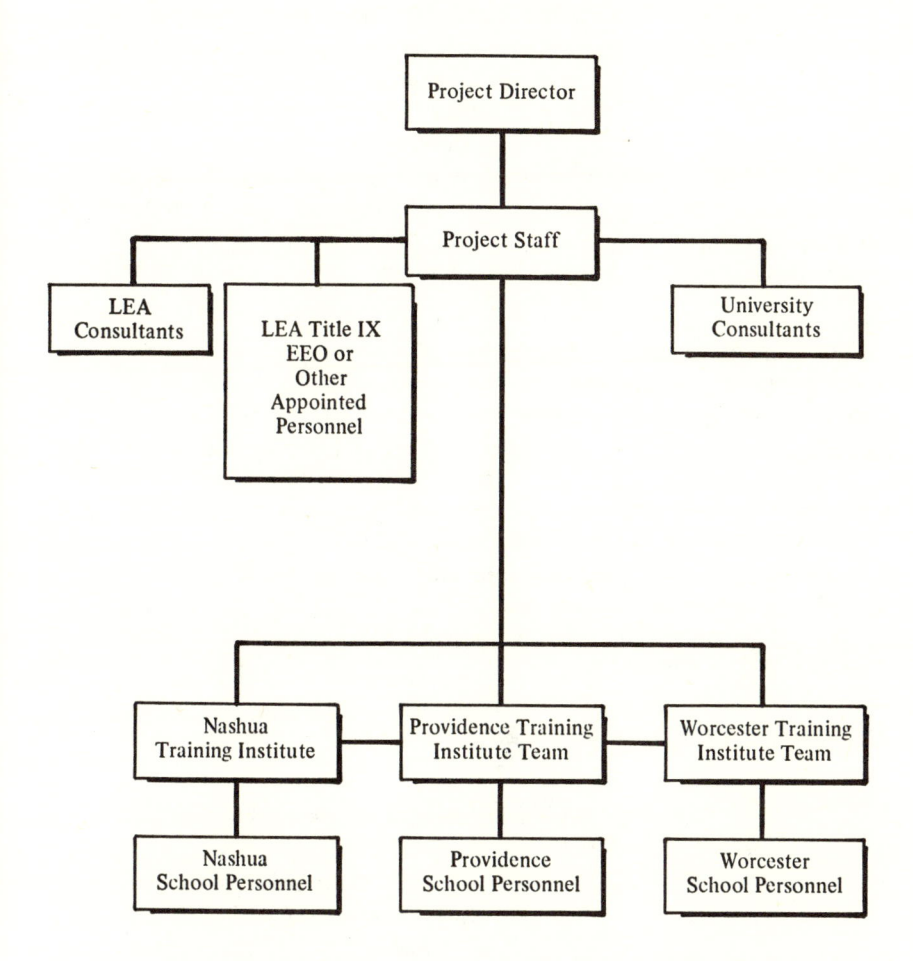

```
                        ┌─────────────────┐
                        │ Project Director │
                        └─────────────────┘
                                 │
                        ┌─────────────────┐
         ┌──────────────│  Project Staff  │──────────────┐
         │         ┌────┴─────────────────┴────┐         │
┌─────────────┐ ┌──────────────┐            │     ┌──────────────┐
│    LEA      │ │ LEA Title IX │            │     │  University  │
│ Consultants │ │   EEO or     │            │     │ Consultants  │
└─────────────┘ │    Other     │            │     └──────────────┘
                │  Appointed   │            │
                │  Personnel   │            │
                └──────────────┘            │
                                 │
         ┌───────────────────────┼───────────────────────┐
┌─────────────────┐    ┌──────────────────┐    ┌──────────────────┐
│     Nashua      │    │ Providence Training │    │ Worcester Training │
│ Training Institute │ │  Institute Team  │    │  Institute Team  │
└─────────────────┘    └──────────────────┘    └──────────────────┘
         │                      │                      │
┌─────────────────┐    ┌──────────────────┐    ┌──────────────────┐
│     Nashua      │    │    Providence    │    │    Worcester     │
│ School Personnel │   │ School Personnel │    │ School Personnel │
└─────────────────┘    └──────────────────┘    └──────────────────┘
```

Each project staff person is responsible for communication with 1 LEA

A. Project Director

The director will be responsible for the overall implementation of every phase of the program: The development and conduct of the summer training institute; the development and conduct of three one-day on-site workshops per school system; the coordination of nine on-site training meetings for core teams and other designated school personnel in each school district; the planning and conducting of two day-long follow-up workshops for core teams; and the planning and facilitation of a day-long dissemination conference for urban school districts.

B. Project Staff . . .

Common Flaws

Flaws common to the management component of the proposal generally stem from two sets of totally unrelated factors: (1) the proposal developer may be unaware and/or disinterested in personnel management and institutional policies and consequently fails to articulate program activities and organizational planning central to successful implementation; and (2) program/organization planning is hindered by the conditions surrounding the development and submittal process. There is often insufficient time to delineate and/or negotiate management procedures and policies relevant to implementation of a proposed project. The following specific flaws common to this component reflect the distance between program content and necessary management structures.

1. Role definitions or job descriptions of staff are not sufficiently delineated for the reviewer to relate responsibilities of individual or associate personnel to program activities presented earlier.
2. Time lines for implementing the project are inconsistent with those set by the funding agency. They are inconsistent with the authorized start-up date and seriously underestimate the number of tasks that must be completed before the program is fully operational.
3. When open or consultant positions are requested, there is neither sufficient definition of these positions nor the criteria for personnel selection to communicate the necessity for these position(s) to those reviewing the proposal.

Management Component Checklist

1. Organizational structure (intrainstitutional and intraproject) affecting project operation presented? ____
2. Responsibilities for decision making clearly identified and directly linked to individuals or offices identified in organizational chart? ____
3. Time line of project's major events presented? ____
4. Role definitions or job descriptions for all major staff positions included? ____

BUDGET

The budget may be defined as an operational statement of the program in monetary terms. The writer's task in developing this proposal component is to translate program activities into dollars. If the writer is unfamiliar with the language of the program developer and the fiscal officer, technical assistance is necessary to assure accurate translations comprehensible to both parties. Budgets that fail to conform to the regulations of both the submitting institution and receiving agency, or fail to identify accurately the costs of carrying out proposed activities, contribute to the rejection of many proposals and the failure of many projects.

Functions

The budget serves both management and program functions. As a statement of management policy:

1. it reflects institutional and program priorities in the ways requested funds are allocated to units and persons within the submitting institutions;
2. it defines responsibility for project decision making within the submitting institution and allocates power among institutions when several are involved in the project; and
3. it may demonstrate the submitting institution's commitment to the program.

As a programmatic statement:

1. it defines events scheduled to occur by translating the activities into dollars;
2. it sets program priorities by allocating dollars among and between program components and personnel; and
3. it establishes base lines for negotiations that will occur if the project is approved. If costs can be linked directly to specific activities, budget negotiations can become almost synonymous with program negotiations.

Characteristics

The budget statement attaches a price tag to goals and proposed activities. Consequently, a detailed plan of project activities and the submitting institution's fiscal policies should serve as the information base for budget development. Any budget built on such an information base is likely to be acceptable to both the submitting institution and the funding agency. Characteristics of a well-developed budget include:

1. Every budget item must be related directly and demonstrably to activities described in the program narrative.

2. Items normally included should be divided into three broad categories.
    a. Direct costs—all those costs directly related to carrying out the activities proposed for a particular project (e.g., personnel, supplies, equipment, travel, communications, consultants, stipends).
    b. Indirect costs (also referred to as overhead)—those costs incurred by the submitting institution, in operating externally funded projects, that are not recoverable from a single project and that are *recognized* and *allowed* by the requesting agency.
    c. Cost sharing—the institution's share of total project cost (may take the form of "in-kind" in which services are redirected or "actual" when this must be allocated).
3. The identification of individual costs within the preceding categories must conform to guidelines of the submitting institution and those set by the funding agency for the specific proposal response.
4. Direct costs for identified salaries and wages should be assignable to specific personnel who, in turn, should be designated to carry out specific activities and/or realize specific objectives.
5. The manner in which specific costs (salary base or unit costs and time periods) have been calculated for each item should be identifiable by all readers.
6. The policies governing the calculation of the budget and its format under a given solicitation should only be set after identifying the guidelines set by the funding agency and the fiscal policies of the submitting institution.

The budget statement is a mechanism through which the submitting institution identifies the costs associated with the particular strategy it has selected to address a problem. The accepted budget imposes mutual obligations on the funding agency, the submitting institution, and project directors. As such, depending on the requirements of the funding agency, it constitutes a formal or informal contract. It should, therefore, be developed and negotiated with the care appropriate to the writing of any promissory note.

Sample Budget Formats

The following examples illustrate the range of format that guides budget development. Accompanying notes define the terms that, regardless of format, are used in most submittals.

FIGURE 6.24. Office of Education Budget Format

SECTION A – Budget Categories

Project Component(s)	Degree Program(s); Non Degree or Certification Program(s); Other Component(s) (For these project components sequentially list the sub-components by title)					
	1.	2.	3.	4.	5.	6. Total
Personnel	$	$	$	$	$	$
Fringe Benefits						
Travel						
Equipment						
Supplies						
Contractual						
Student Financial Assistance						
Consultants						
Other						
Total Direct Charges						
Indirect Charges (8% maximum)						
Total	$	$	$	$	$	$

Section A Explanations

Budget Exhibit II-4

SECTION B – Budget Summary

Project Component(s)	Estimated Unobligated Funds		New or Revised Budget		
	Federal (a)	Non-Federal (b)	Federal (c)	Non-Federal (d)	Total (e)
Degree Program(s)	$	$	$	$	$
Non Degree or Certification Program(s)					
Other Component(s)					
Total	$	$	$	$	$

SECTION C – Budget Estimates of Federal Funds Needed for Balance of the Project

Project Component(s)	Future Funding Periods (Years)			
	First (a)	Second (b)	Third (c)	Total (d)
Degree Program(s)	$	$	$	$
Non Degree or Certification Program(s)				
Other Component(s)				
Total	$	$	$	$

FIGURE 6.25 *National Science Foundation Budget Format Summary*

SUMMARY PROPOSAL BUDGET

ORGANIZATION AND ADDRESS	FOR NSF USE ONLY
	PROPOSAL NO.
PRINCIPAL INVESTIGATOR/PROJECT DIRECTOR	DURATION (MONTHS) PROPOSED / REVISED

		NSF FUNDED MAN MONTHS			FUNDS REQUESTED BY PROPOSER	FUNDS GRANTED BY NSF (IF DIFFERENT)
		CAL.	ACAD	SUMR.		
	A. SENIOR PERSONNEL (LIST BY NAME; SHOW NUMBERS OF PEOPLE IN BRACKETS; SALARY AMOUNTS MAY BE LISTED ON SEPARATE SCHEDULE) GPM 205.1b					
	1. P.I./P.D.				$	$
	2. CO P.I./P.D.				$	$
	3. CO P.I./P.D.				$	$
	4. CO P.I./P.D.				$	$
	5. CO P.I./P.D.				$	$
NSF USE	6. ( ) ──── SUBTOTALS A1 - A5 ──── FACULTY AND OTHER SENIOR ASSOCIATES (ATTACH EXTRA SHEET IF NECESSARY)					
11115					$	$
	7.				$	$
	8.				$	$
	9.				$	$
	10.				$	$
	11.				$	$
11117	12. ( ) ──── SUBTOTALS A7 - A11 ────				$	$
	B. OTHER PERSONNEL (LIST NUMBERS IN BRACKETS)					
11141	1. ( ) POSTDOCTORAL ASSOCIATES				$	$
11149	2. ( ) OTHER PROFESSIONALS				$	$
11150	3. ( ) GRADUATE STUDENTS				$	$
11152	4. ( ) UNDERGRADUATE STUDENTS				$	$
11182	5. ( ) SECRETARIAL - CLERICAL				$	$
11183	6. ( ) TECHNICAL, SHOP, OTHER				$	$
	TOTAL SALARIES AND WAGES (A+B)				$	$

FIGURE 6.25 (cont.)

11200	C. FRINGE BENEFITS (IF CHARGED AS DIRECT COSTS)	$	$
	TOTAL SALARIES, WAGES AND FRINGE BENEFITS (A+B+C)	$	$
	D. EQUIPMENT (LIST ITEMS AND DOLLAR AMOUNTS FOR EACH ITEM)		
23181	TOTAL EQUIPMENT	$	$
	E. MATERIALS AND SUPPLIES	$	$
32630			
42111	F. DOMESTIC TRAVEL	$	$
	G. FOREIGN TRAVEL (LIST DESTINATION AND AMOUNT FOR EACH TRIP; GPM 731)		
42112		$	$

NSF FORM 1030 (10-77) CANCELS NSF FORMS 98, 135, 569 AND 633 EFFECTIVE 10-1-77
PAGE 1 OF 2 PAGES

FIGURE 6.25 (cont.)

		PROPOSAL NO.	
52500	H. PUBLICATION COSTS/PAGE CHARGES	$	
62315	I. COMPUTER (ADPE) SERVICES	$	
	J. CONSULTANT SERVICES (IDENTIFY CONSULTANTS BY NAME AND AMOUNT; GPM 516)		$
	K. PARTICIPANT SUPPORT COSTS, IF ALLOWED BY PROGRAM GUIDE (ITEMIZE) GPM 518		
	1. STIPENDS $		
	2. TRAVEL $		
	3. SUBSISTENCE $		
	4. OTHER - SPECIFY $		
	5. TOTAL PARTICIPANT COSTS (K1 + K2 + K3 + K4)		$
	L. ALL OTHER DIRECT COSTS (List items and dollar amounts. Details of subcontracts, including work statements and budget, should be explained in full in proposal.) $ $ $		$
65001	M. TOTAL OTHER DIRECT COSTS		$
	M. TOTAL DIRECT COSTS (A THROUGH L)	$	
	N. INDIRECT COSTS (Specify rate(s) and base(s) for on/off campus activity. Where both are involved, identify itemized costs included in on/off campus bases in remarks.)		
74100	TOTAL INDIRECT COSTS		$

FIGURE 6.25 (cont.)

			$	$
	O. TOTAL DIRECT AND INDIRECT COSTS (M + N)		$	$
74500	P. LESS RESIDUAL FUNDS (If for further support of current project; GPM 252 and 253)		$	$
75000	Q. AMOUNT OF THIS REQUEST (O MINUS P)		$	$

REMARKS

NOTE: SIGNATURES REQUIRED ONLY FOR REVISED BUDGET (GPM 233). THIS IS REVISION NO. _____

SIGNATURE OF PRINCIPAL INVESTIGATOR/PROJECT DIRECTOR	DATE OF SIGNATURE	TYPED OR PRINTED NAME AND TITLE
SIGNATURE OF AUTHORIZED ORGANIZATIONAL REPRESENTATIVE	DATE OF SIGNATURE	TYPED OR PRINTED NAME AND TITLE

FOR NSF USE ONLY

INDIRECT COST RATE VERIFICATION		PROGRAM OFFICER APPROVAL
Date Checked	Date of Rate Sheet	Signature

Grant Number	Amend No.	Proposal Number	Dur.	Chg.	Institution	Organization	Fund Acct.	Program	Object
						Award Date		Proposed Amount	Prpsd. Dur.

NSF FORM 1030 (10-77)
PAGE 2 OF 2 PAGES

227

228   *The Dynamics of Funding*

Common Flaws

Since program staff, rather than fiscal officers, generally write at least the first draft of the budget, the developer is often subject to two reviews in the development and submittal process—that of fiscal offices of the submitting institution and that of program or contract offices of the funding agency. At both of these review points, budget flaws may jeopardize the securing of funding. The following flaws are identified frequently by both sources.

1. The budget fails to conform to fiscal policies of the submitting institution (e.g., rates for determining pay, fringe benefits, or indirect costs).
2. The budget fails to conform to established guidelines and the recommended format of the receiving agency.
3. The basis for calculating specific costs is either not identified or not clearly communicated.
4. Costs of individual items (personnel or other direct costs) cannot be associated with specified program activities.
5. Costs are not realistic, either in relation to appropriations planned by the funding office or to activities identified by the submitting institution.
6. Computational errors are present.

Budget Submittal Checklist

1. Format conforms to funding agency guidelines (cost sharing, indirect costs, allowable items, etc.)? ____
2. Formulas for calculating pay, fringe benefits, and indirect costs conform to submitting institution's policies? ____
3. Allocations for individual items relate to proposed activities and specific personnel? ____
4. Basis for calculating all nonpersonal costs is identified? ____
5. Dates for project commencement and termination, and schedule for commitment of funds, are included? ____
6. Cost allocations among items are communicable to program as well as fiscal staff? ____
7. Total amount requested is consistent with activities and level of funding identified by the funding agency? ____
8. Budget has been approved by appropriate fiscal officer(s) and contains accurate computations? ____

APPENDICES

The proposal appendix is one of the least understood and most misused sections. The negative impact of inappropriate appendices on the evaluation accorded the total proposal generally does not compare with that of earlier flawed components.* The developer who fails to use appendices appropriately, however, fails to take full advantage of the opportunity to demonstrate to the funding agency the planning that has contributed to proposal development. The appendix provides a rare opportunity for the writer: he or she stands to gain significantly more by developing it well than he or she may lose by developing it poorly.

Functions

The potential contribution of effectively developed appendices can be recognized when one considers that they can:

1. support earlier claims regarding the qualifications and commitment of the submitting institution;
2. demonstrate the level of planning, the degree of participation of affected parties in the development of the proposal, and the commitment of others to the effort; and
3. lend credibility to the submitter by demonstrating familiarity with previous research and/or efforts to address the problem (by providing additional documentation of specific claims made earlier in the proposal).

Characteristics

For an appendix to realize the above functions, it must include the following characteristics.

1. Data and support materials provided in the appendices must be directly relevant to the proposal narrative. References in the narrative should direct the reader to the appropriate appendix.

---

*The exception is the failure to provide support information specifically required by the funding agency (e.g., sign-offs from community groups, letters of support from participating institutions, or resumes of principal investigators).

2. Information should be sufficiently concise to encourage reading of the materials. It should represent a logical extension of earlier points rather than a separate proposal.
3. Only information that cannot be incorporated in the body of the proposal without disrupting the flow of the narrative, thereby distracting the reader from the nature of the project and the need for the program, should be included.
4. Information should provide the reviewer a clearer idea of the nature of anticipated accomplishments and needs contributing to program development than might be possible in the earlier narrative (for example, research or needs assessment data, program planning activities, implementation schedules, prototypes of materials to be developed).
5. Commitments of cooperating institutions, agencies, and community groups should be as specific as possible and address both the major project features and the roles of cooperating parties.
6. Items that may be included in the appendices include:
    a. resumés of principal personnel
    b. descriptions of facilities, complementary programs that will enhance program efforts, and affiliations with other organizations relevant to the proposed activities
    c. program support data, including research abstracts, tables of statistical data, and prototype materials
    d. letters of support or commitment from cooperating or affected agencies.

Not every proposal solicitation calls for appendices. When required, however, the precise format should reflect the preferences of the funding agency. Some funding agencies may discourage or set limits on the number of pages permitted for support materials. Even when restrictions are not set on the form or length of the appendices, the developer should only include items directly relevant to claims made earlier in the proposal. If appendices seem irrelevant to the earlier narrative, the reviewer may not even read them.

Common Flaws

To avoid the mistakes common to the development of appendices, remember that they are, by definition, support materials; appendices must be subordinate to the preceding narrative and must not assume their own identity. Flaws that result from a failure to recognize the proper relationship between the appendices and the program narrative include:

1. Materials provided are not particularly relevant to the proposal narrative.
2. Materials do not provide additional information for assessing the quality of the program, the qualifications of the submitting institution, or the personnel relevant to the proposed activities.

3. Materials are overly general or too lengthy.
4. Materials fail to conform to restrictions set by funding agency.
5. Letters of commitment are lacking or unsigned. (When regulations require such materials, their absence may disqualify the proposal from review.)

Appendix Checklist

1. Appendices referenced in program narrative? _____
2. Materials directly relevant to concerns of funding agency (e.g., qualifications of personnel, institutional commitment, support facilities)? _____
3. Materials indexed to facilitate identification of relevant data? _____
4. Included materials cannot be placed logically within the body of the proposal? _____

SUMMARY

The approach to writing the proposal document has been guided by features of the funding system that have immediate impact on the form and substance of any proposal document. The proposal represents a response to the needs of the agency inviting submittals; the form and substance of any document must address both the program criteria and organizational requirements set by the funding agency.

Within the constraints set by a particular agency, however, elements common to the writing of most proposals can be identified. These elements evolve from the structure of the proposal and enable the submitter to identify, in the absence of explicit guidelines, basic formats to guide program exposition. The proposal writer's task has thus been portrayed as one in which the writer seeks to fit a general format to the specific requirements governing a given submittal.

The writer who recognizes the nature of the task, and understands the function of the proposal components and the characteristics of each component, can draw on the examples and checklists provided in this chapter when responding to an opportunity to secure external funding.

ENDNOTES

1. William B. Castetter and Richard S. Heisler, *Developing and Defending a Dissertation Proposal* (Philadelphia: Center for Field Studies, Graduate School of Education, University of Pennsylvania, 1977), p. 16.
2. Roger A. Kaufman, Educational System Planning (Englewood Cliffs, N.J.: Prentice-Hall, 1974), pp. 55–56.

3. U.S., Department of Health, Education, and Welfare, Office of Education, Bureau of Education for the Handicapped, "Informal Memorandum on Research Questions Related to Evaluation Methodologies to Test the Effectiveness of Programs and Projects for Handicapped Children," September 1977.
4. William J. Gephart, Robert B. Ingle, and Gary Saretsky, *Similarities and Differences in the Research and Evaluation Process* (Bloomington, Ind.: Phi Delta Kappa, 1973), p. 15.

7

From Paper to Program

Despite the heavy investment by foundations and federal and state agencies in developing and implementing educational and social service programs over the past decade and a half, there is virtual total agreement that the social and educational aspirations of both sponsors and developers have significantly exceeded accomplishments. Explanations of why programs have failed to meet expectations are many and varied; perceptions of the factors contributing to underachievement are shaped by the occupational positions, political orientations, and personal experiences of persons who have developed and initiated programs and persons who have been served by those programs.

This chapter analyzes some of those factors that inhibit the successful implementation of externally funded programs, and dispose parties affected by innovative programs to allocate blame or credit. It also seeks to provide the project manager with the understanding and skills necessary to reduce the discrepancy between what is promised in the proposal document and what transpires after notification of funding and initiation of the project. If the reader approaches this analysis recognizing that the announcement of funding can signal the prelude to defeat as easily as victory, the link between the development of the proposal and what is to follow becomes apparent.

Analysis of the funding process reveals two discrete but related elements that directly affect efforts to initiate a successful project: (1) procedural factors, which include the proposal review, budget negotiation, and notification of funding processes and (2) design and institutional factors, which include program plans and staffing specifications identified in the proposal and characteristics of the organizational climate of the submitting institution(s) that directly affect project operations. The impact of procedural elements on project implementation is immediately and easily identifiable; their ultimate, impact on

234   The Dynamics of Funding

success or failure of the project, however, is probably overestimated. Delays in review of the proposal, reallocations of money, and late notification of funding, although detrimental to program start-up, can generally be compensated for by careful planning. Flaws in program conceptualization, personnel assignments, and project organization are more difficult to remedy once a project has begun. Likewise, the organizational climate of the sponsoring institution is not easily modified and will affect project operations from implementation to completion.

The complexity of factors affecting project initiation increases as one moves from the consideration of procedural elements to design and institutional elements; the task of identifying strategies to affect these elements becomes correspondingly complex.

PROCEDURAL FACTORS AFFECTING PROJECT IMPLEMENTATION

Before examining the specific procedural obstacles to successful implementation created by the review and announcement process, it is important to note two sets of factors that affect the recommendations given the proposal and the timing of the formal notification of award. These *may be identified* as proposal-specific factors and program-specific factors. Proposal-specific factors are those prescribed and predictable procedures set by a funding agency that govern the review of any proposal and grant award; program-specific factors are events that affect the operations of the program office responsible for administering projects. Table 7.1 is a partial listing of factors broken down by category, with the proposal-specific factors listed in the order in which they usually affect the process.

TABLE 7.1.   *Prenotification Procedural Factors Affecting Project Implementation*

Program-Specific Factors	*Proposal-Specific Factors*
Modification of level of appropriations	Proposal review by readers
Modification of allocations of money between programs in program offices	Recommendation for funding to program officers
Publication of Final Rules and Regulations (Federal programs)	Decision memorandum to office staff authorizing announcement (informal) of program approval to submitters
	Negotiation of budget with contract officers
	Grant Award Document cut and notification of appropriate Congressmen (for Federal awards only)
	Formal notification of award to submitting party in the form of a Grant Award Document (Federal programs)

A major planning dilemma confronting an institution submitting a proposal, which has major implications for the ultimate implementation of the project, is the difficulty of ascertaining the time frames for the announcement of program recommendations and the formal notification of award. The time span between submittal and notification is generally long, whereas span between notification and implementation is generally short. The inability to predict the timing of events precisely creates organizational and programmatic problems that reduce the chances for smooth project start-up.

Fortunately, analysis of the individual factors that affect the proposal's status during the review and notification process reveals features of the system that can guide the submitter. Identifying and analyzing these features and understanding their impact on the review and announcement enables the establishment of reasonable time estimates for planning of relevant criteria to inform planning decisions at each stage of the review and announcement process. Decisions made prior to formal notification of award may be of sufficient importance to make the difference between project success and failure.

Review of the Proposal

A U.S. Office of Education program officer noted in an interview that the range of variables affecting the review and selection of funded proposals should be sufficiently discouraging to lead the majority of submitters to seek other means of program support. Analysis of the features of the review process and the idiosyncracies of individual program offices, unfortunately, lends some credence to this observation. There are, however, a limited number of possible variations to the process and an almost unlimited number of ways to determine which variations are being used during a particular review. Thus, the process has at its base rational, if not predictable, underpinnings.

Chapter 6 focused on the significance of criteria established by the funding office to the rating accorded a given proposal. Criteria set by the funding agency for the process to be followed in reviewing the proposal also have implications for the plans set by the institution awaiting notification; the particular process followed by an office may directly affect the timing of the announcement and even the relationship between the agency and institution, once the project is in operation.

Review processes generally may be classified as either external or internal. In the former, the proposal is reviewed by consultants rather than office staff; in the latter, staff of the soliciting office, and possibly staff of other program offices in the agency, conduct the review. When the funding office employs an external review process, two approaches are possible: reviewers may gather on specified dates to review all of the proposals submitted under a given solicitation; or the proposals may be distributed to consultants in the field who, on completion of the review, return the proposals to the program office with scores and comments. Determining the precise location of a proposal in the review process is usually easier under the external review approach—the dates for such reviews are generally available from the program offices. Although a proposal's rating generally cannot be communicated at this point, the submitter may be able to determine the anticipated date of announcement and, on occasion, the extent of competition and the reception given the institution's proposal.

Internal or in-house reviews generally do not lend themselves to charting on a time line. The internal review often results from the program office's failure to secure an administrative appropriation to hire outside consultants. Timing of the internal review, therefore, is influenced by the office's work load, staff size, number of proposals submitted, and the differing priorities of individual staff members. Moreover, the review may become so inextricably linked to the politics of a given office that the status of a given proposal may often be ascertained only through informal communications with staff members the submitter has known previously.

One important qualification regarding in-house reviews relates to foundation review processes: although foundations may engage both external and internal reviewers, the process, from program inception to announcement of funding, is generally more predictable than the federal process. Boards of trustees or directors, who ultimately must approve any major grant, meet on specified dates to make specific decisions (unlike the U.S. Congress or state legislatures). Hence, once the foundation has encouraged the submittal of a full as opposed to a preliminary proposal, the submitter usually is able to determine specific dates for the funding announcement and the authorizations for program start-up.

The Funding Decision

Once the proposal review has been completed and evaluation reports have been submitted to program offices, events leading to the announcements of funding are determined largely by organizational protocol and the level of appropriations available to the program office. Events contributing to decision making at this point may be characterized as *political, programmatic,* or *fiscal.* The nature of the interaction between political, programmatic, and fiscal decision making determines the final funding decision and the timing of notification of award. The failure of the submitting party to differentiate between a decision to support a program and a fiscal decision establishing the level of support can have disastrous repercussions. Proposal ratings, program approval, and budget notification are discrete events and must be recognized as such.

Until the program office receives authorization from other units in the funding agency to notify submitters of proposal approval or rejection, the submitting institution can only set informal and tentative plans based on deductions from clues received about the progress of the proposal in the review process. Once the review process is complete, the final decision to support a program and the timing of announcements may still await the resolution of issues not directly related to the proposal's rating.

1. The ability of an office to fund a proposal is determined by the level of appropriations committed to the office at the time of notification. Although an office generally will have established appropriations at the time of the request for proposals, any modification of the level of appropriations to support the authorizing legislation will delay notification of award and affect the level of funding and even the decision to fund.
2. Although allocations among programs in a program office that support more than one type of program generally are set at the time of proposal solicitation, political pressures may result in modifications among programs, delaying the formal announcement of awards and affecting the level of funding.
3. In reviewing the ratings given proposals, the chief program officer has the authority to ask for second readings of proposals that did not originally receive high enough ratings if, in his judgment, these proposals relate to program priorities not adequately addressed in proposals judged technically superior. Subsequent support of these proposals may affect allocations to proposals reviewed earlier.
4. Although proposals submitted to federal offices may be submitted in conformance with Proposed Rules and Regulations, announcement of awards may not be made until Final Rules are approved.
5. Notification to submitters of action on submitted proposals by program officers does not constitute legal notification of award; nor does it establish the fiscal dimensions of the program. Negotiations of budget generally are carried out by contract officers rather than program officers. Formal notification of award clearly cannot occur before the final negotiation of budget.
6. After negotiation of contracts for approved projects, a limited number of additional projects may be funded with monies secured from reducing individual project budgets. This small *second tier* of funding will necessarily follow the original round of announcements.

For purposes of planning, it is important to note that up until formal announcement of proposal approval, the submitting institution is a semipassive but interested observer of the process, unable to act decisively on information received. On initial notification of program approval and request for budget negotiation, however, options requiring action are presented. The submitter now is in a position in which actions taken or not taken directly affect project implementation.

Budget Negotiations

The need to differentiate between program office and contract office approval when preparing implementation strategies exists for both state and federally administered programs. Although the relationship between funding allocations and program implementation is just as important in foundation supported programs, program and budgetary negotiations tend to be more closely related in the foundation review process.

Ultimately, the precise level of funding, the schedule of payments, and authorization of payment for identified personnel and support costs determine the project director's ability to conform to proposal specifications. The potential impact on project implementation of what amounts to a dual program and fiscal approval system for many government sponsored programs depends greatly on the relationships between program and contract offices in an agency. The time available for planning between notification of program approval, negotiation of the budget, receipt of the grant award document or contract, and the project start-up date also has great impact. When the level of funding is negotiated almost immediately after notification of program approval, and project start-up dates quickly follow, the factors contributing to possible slippage from expectations are significantly different from those occurring when the process covers an extended period of time. In the latter case, the submitting institution is provided with options for careful planning; in the former case, the constraints on effective planning are more stringent.

The failure to recognize the impact of the relationship of program and budgetary elements on project implementation, and the failure to plan accordingly, gives rise to a range of problems. Consider the following incidents:

> A local educational agency received notification from the state officer responsible for administering programs authorized by Title IV of the Elementary and Secondary Education Act of 1965 (as modified by the Education Amendments of 1976) that its proposal had been approved for funding. The LEA administrative officer was simultaneously informed that the level of approved funding was $16,000, representing a cut of slightly less than $4,000 from the proposed budget. After telephone consultation with the project director, the LEA officer submitted an agreed upon revision on the appropriate forms to the Title IV Office. The funding level stipulated by the Title IV Office had been obtained quickly by deleting a project component that supported the development of curriculum materials by teacher-aides and teachers. These materials were to be used by aides in individualizing classroom instruction, an objective not accorded a high priority by the submitting LEA.

> A community agency received notification from the Office of Child Development's (OCD) regional office, responsible for administering Head Start programs, that the agency's request for $18,000 above the preceding year's level of funding could not be honored and that $18,000 would have to be removed from the budget. Anxious not to jeopardize the continuity of funding, the project staff proceeded hastily; an $18,000 item to provide lunches, snacks, and paper goods for the Child Nutrition program stood out. Staff immediately concluded that the LEA could assume these costs under

the School Lunch Act and the regional OCD was instructed to delete this item. The LEA would later be contacted to work out arrangements for the deleted program component.

The two preceding incidents represent responses of an LEA and a community agency to two markedly different program authorizations with markedly different patterns for administration and allocation of funds. They do, however, reveal one common phenomenon: adequate program planning in the proposal was undercut by a hasty response to a revised funding level. In responding to the immediate need to adjust the submitted budget to levels stipulated by the funding agency, the submitters, in different ways, established conditions that later would seriously deter the projects from realizing the established goals.

The LEA Title IV proposal developers, who deleted the teacher-aide component without consulting community representatives who had participated in the development of the proposal, confirmed suspicions of community representatives that they were powerless to affect school decision making; aides were only tolerated by the LEA as long as outside monies could be secured; and opportunities for necessary training for regular employment in the system would never be available. Whether these community perceptions of the school's attitude were accurate is of secondary importance. More important, a precipitous budget decision confirmed the suspicions of some and created an environment requiring the project director to spend a significant portion of his time, in the initial months of project operation, mediating among administrators, teachers, and community and parent representatives in an effort to "cool" the conflict. A more carefully considered budget decision would have permitted the director to devote full attention to developing the materials and facilitating the instruction identified in the proposal.

The Head Start grantee, on submittal of the revised budget omitting provisions for the nutrition program, immediately began negotiations with the school department. After a month and a half, the school department concluded that it did not wish to collaborate with the community agency. The agency, which had borne the nutrition costs for one month and had made staffing commitments to implement the educational program, found itself in a situation in which program objectives, governed by the fiscal limits of the revised budget, could only be realized by dismissing staff. Adjustments that could have been made rather easily before program inception now would cause considerable conflict. Personnel action appeals, debate on plans to shorten the duration of the project, conflicts among staff about the wisdom of alternative plans, and the accompanying bad publicity all contributed to a strife-ridden project that fell far short of meeting its educational objectives. By failing to confirm the promise that support for a component of the program would come from another source, the project directors met the budgetary stipulations within the prescribed time but sacrificed the integrity of the program design and set the stage for personnel conflicts that rendered the proposed service undeliverable.

The potential of hasty budgetary decisions to affect program implementation detrimentally is not limited to situations in which funding requests are lowered. Although the project director is not often presented with funds exceeding those requested, the "embarassment of wealth" occurs with sufficient frequency to justify its consideration in planning. If the scope of the project is broadened or personnel needs expanded by increased appropriations, the impact on planning for implementation can be significant.

The preceding incidents illustrate graphically the inextricable relationship between program and fiscal decisions. Understanding this relationship and being aware of the pressure for hasty decisions, the budget negotiator must seek sufficient time, under the deadline set by the negotiating office, to consider, if not resolve, the conflicts created by the incompatibility between procedural needs of the funding office and program needs of the submitting institution. Unfortunately, recognizing the dilemma and identifying strategies to solve it do not always compensate for the constraints on effective implementation created by the time lag between program announcement and budget negotiation, and between budget negotiation and formal announcement of award.

Award Notification

One major caveat should guide all actions of institutional representatives who receive verbal notification of program approval: such notification does not constitute legal announcement of award and does not, therefore, authorize commitments to individuals, groups, or organizations affected by the award. This is true even after the budget has been negotiated and the fiscal parameters of the project have been set. The grantee must await formal notification of award, in the form of a Federal Grant Award Document, a state issued contract, or a letter of notification from a foundation. Otherwise, there is the risk that last minute changes in appropriations, or more commonly, changes in the date on which the grantee is authorized to commence activities, may necessitate major program adjustments before project implementation. Commitments to personnel, organizations, or those to be served by the project, before formal notification, invite fiscal and program difficulties with which the director will have only limited means to deal.

Obvious difficulties resulting from informal and unauthorized commitments, when the project later fails to materialize, need not be treated here since they occur infrequently and generally are made by anxious staff on the basis of informal and unreliable information. Difficulties that evolve from commitments made after receiving notification of funding from a reliable source, and after negotiation of the budget but before receipt of the formal notification setting the terms of the award, are far more common. Given the need to plan for implementation, such commitments are understandable; they can, however, contribute greatly to a project's slippage from expectations. Two incidents illustrate this point:

A university (Institution of Higher Education or IHE in government terms) received notification from a state board of education that a proposal to work with a local education agency in developing a competency-based vocational education curriculum for a regional vocational-technical school had been approved at the budget level stipulated in the proposal. The proposed program called for activities to commence at the beginning of the school year and to continue through the following June 30. On the basis of verbal communication of approval, with the assurance that the contract governing the award was being processed in state budget offices and would be forthcoming shortly, the program commenced.

As required by federal and state regulations, an LEA prepared the fiscal year 1976 Title I plan in the spring of 1975. Working with a preliminary funding estimate, and covered by the "hold-harmless" provision assuring an LEA 85 percent of the funding award of the preceding year, the LEA made commitments to staff in June and commenced planning for the coming school year. When the fiscal year 1976 award was received on August 1, 1976, however, the grant award was substantially more than the 1975 award.

These incidents illustrate quite different sets of circumstances. Both, however, created situations in which the implementation of the project was adversely affected by the need to begin activities or make commitments before receiving the appropriate award document. The contract governing the IHE's activities slowly worked its way through the state bureaucracy; carrying the appropriate sign-offs from the contracting offices, it reached the university in early November. The contract stipulated, however, that activities carried out before the November 1 date of signature were unauthorized and that reimbursement for those activities was not allowable. To cover earlier expenditures, the university had to request a "no-cost extension" to enable them to bill beyond the proposed termination date, thereby recovering funds already expended. Failing to secure approval for this request, the university retracted earlier cost-sharing commitments, leaving the project director with insufficient support to carry out the project as projected in the proposal. Relationships between the dirctor and fiscal officers of the university, and between the university and the LEA, consequently were severely strained, hindering program development efforts.

The LEA responsible for carrying out the Title I project, finding itself with additional funds, rapidly mounted plans to broaden the range of services. Given the haste of planning and the late date of notification, the LEA was unable to deliver services effectively in the additional schools included in the program. It also was unable to hire the personnel necessary to implement the program according to schedule in the new settings. Although this incident, unlike the preceding incident, did not place individual staff members under strain, the result was substantially the same. The project director sought to adjust to the new terms imposed by the funding agency, after the commencement of program activities. Additional time demands, however, and the new conditions governing implementation of the project, precluded realizing project goals that might have been achieved if the final terms had been set before program inception.

Unfortunately, the last two incidents slip into the "no-win" domain of decision making. The project director is in a position in which the timing of announcements establishes almost insurmountable obstacles to effective project implementation.

Up to this point, emphasis has been placed on factors, specific to the review of proposals and the announcement of awards, that adversely affect project implementation. We must now consider the impact of late funding on the operation of federally funded projects. The phenomenon of late funding is so pervasive that it merits special attention. It represents, unfortunately, the logical outcome of the interaction of many variables in the awarding of grants over which the writer or director has little control. It creates a set of conditions that, in one form or another, affects the implementation of a significant proportion of federally funded projects.

LATE FUNDING AND PROJECT IMPLEMENTATION

The administrative machinery that processes the proposal from point of submittal to notification of funding often places the submitter in the position of a mail-order buyer who is notified that, due to unavoidable delays, the winter apparel ordered in season will not be delivered until mid-spring. The product may be sufficiently attractive or functional to justify accepting the late delivery, but the utility of the article will be restricted. Late arrival of goods is generally a symptom of problems in the production and delivery system; late notification of funding is the most common symptom of problems in the program appropriation, proposal review, and notification system. Unfortunately for the submitting institution, late notification of funding presents dilemmas of significantly greater magnitude and complexity than those of a delayed mail-order delivery.

The following summary of a federally appointed HEW Task Force depicts the scope of factors contributing to the problem and summarizes points made in chapter 3.

> The Federal process which results in the authorization, appropriation, and administration of national programs of educational support is an extended and complex process involving cooperation at all levels of government. For example, Congress must carefully consider the substance and content of new programs, and it must determine a suitable level of funding. Federal agencies must develop necessary administrative rules and regulations. States must coordinate the actions of their legislatures with those of their local governments, and local school districts must plan, budget and hire necessary staff.[1]

Congressional concern with the impact of late funding on program operations dates back to at least 1967. However, findings resulting from a U.S. Office of Education (USOE) directive to carry out "a full and complete investigation," authorized by Section 824 of Public Law 93-380 in 1974, will serve as our primary source of information.[2] It is ironic that, during the period of time between the USOE's request for proposals (RFPs) to study the impact of late funding and the implementation of the project, two major changes in the funding process took place: the U.S. Office of Education implemented the concept of forward funding and the federal government changed from a June 30 to a September 30 end date for the fiscal year. The proposal submitted by the institution that received the contract to carry out this study did not address these two major changes in the funding process. Changes that clearly affected the implementation of federally funded projects were not present at the time of the reviewed proposal solicitation. There is a sense of poetic justice in that the project to study the impact of late funding was itself scarred by the phenomenon it sought to study.

The prior comments notwithstanding, the study carried out during the 1975 and 1976 fiscal years is useful for understanding and responding to funding opportunities. The research design guiding the analysis of data, drawn from over 200 local education and state education agencies (SEAs), demonstrates the scope of the impact of late funding on project implementation. Factors identified by the investigation as relevant to the study appear in Table 7.2.

TABLE 7.2. *Factors Relevant to Research Design*

A. *Curriculum and Program Planning and Implementation*
   1. Personnel recruiting
   2. Personnel retention
   3. Purchasing—program supplies and equipment
   4. Delays in program implementation
   5. Program effectiveness (in terms of stated objectives)
   6. Facilities
   7. Coordination with other organizations
B. *Financial Management*
   1. Budget preparation
      Income estimates
      Expenditure estimates
   2. Cash management and flow
   3. Expenditure control
   4. Accounting
   5. Reporting
C. *Community Impact*
   1. Commjnity involvement
   2. Community expectations
D. *Data Collection Requirements*—for grant application or proposal and reporting

U.S., Department of Health, Education, and Welfare, Office of Education, Office of Planning, Budgeting, and Evaluation, *A Study of Late Funding of Elementary and Secondary Education Programs,* prepared by Peat, Marwick, Mitchell & Co., February 1976.

The range of items in Table 7.2 clearly indicates why an institution seeking federal funds cannot assume the stance of a disinterested party when considering the effect of late funding on project implementation. If the director recognizes that each of the items cited are central to both the project's implementation and the submitting institution's day-to-day operation, the need to consider management strategies beyond those of day-to-day operations should be clear.

Although ESEA Title I programs were selected for detailed analysis (Title I programs were funded in virtually every LEA, were the most significant in terms of absolute dollars, and comprised approximately 50 percent of the 1975 appropriation for elementary and secondary education), the researchers felt that the general conclusions would be applicable to almost every other categorical program. This author's survey of programs for human service agencies confirms that most of the general conclusions drawn from the study are applicable to these agencies. Personnel recruitment and retention, and financial management problems resulting from late and/or unpredictable levels of funding, may even be greater for the agency with private nonprofit status than for the local education agency. Schools and universities, unlike many human service agencies and private nonprofit organizations, are not generally in a position in which cash flow problems, although important to the institution, can cause the institution or program to close. There is evidence, however, that with the increasing costs of higher education and the decline in the college age population, cash flow will become increasingly important to the university administrator. The centrality of cash flow to the functioning of these institutions unquestionably will increase their sensitivity to committing to program implementation before receiving notification of award and establishing the terms of payment.

Before considering some of the specific late funding problems identified by LEAs and SEAs participating in the study, a limitation to the generalizability of the findings must be noted. The report's conclusions regarding the impact of late funding on community involvement and expectations are drawn solely from the analysis of LEA responses; they may not reflect accurately the personal experiences of developers who have worked with or for community agencies, collaborating with community groups in the development of projects. The vested personal and organizational interests in project success of such organizations that depend almost totally on external funding for the delivery of services generally far exceed those of school systems or universities.

When small community-based human service agencies find it impossible to define the level of funding or to identify the date of announcement of award, they may not even be able to initiate activities upon late notification. Should acceptance and project implementation still be possible, many of the necessary personnel resources may be unavailable. If implementation is still possible at this juncture, many of the problems identified by the LEAs and SEAs in the Peat *et al.* study will be present. The following incident clearly illustrates the increased vulnerability of institutions or agencies, which lack a predictable fiscal base, to the stress caused by late funding.

An urban community health center had long depended on the city budget to enable it to carry out, on a modest scale, a broad range of counseling, preventive health, and community education programs for youth and young adults in the neighborhood it served. Learning that the city's financial plight would preclude the center receiving an allocation for the coming fiscal year, efforts were made immediately to seek funding by collaborating with a local university with which many of the staff had established strong working relationships. Proposals were developed and submitted to several possible funding sources in early spring, 1976. On September 30, 1976, notification was received from a federal office that the program had been approved. Since the city's fiscal year ended on the preceding June 30, however, staff central to the program's operation had already located other jobs. Moreover, community clients no longer perceived the center as a focus for community activity and the lease on the site had expired. The grant-supported program started, virtually from scratch, at another location. After six months operation, the program had progressed almost to the point of development reached at the former site at the time of proposal submittal.

Community involvement in the start-up of the project was seriously limited due to the late start-up date. Debate over the nature of the relationship to the university, and energies expended in identifying and selecting a new director (the former director had found employment at another agency when funding appeared questionable), contributing to the slippage from expectations. The Peat et al. study's conclusion that "the primary effects of late federal funding appeared to be uncertainty and insecurity"[3] was certainly borne out by the experiences of participants in the above project.

In reviewing the summary of findings of the late funding study, the particular needs of groups and agencies for which the reader may be seeking support should be kept in mind. Then, the examples and findings will provide the prospective submitter with the knowledge necessary to address, if not resolve, the potential difficulties of implementing projects that evolve from late funding. The conclusions of the study are accompanied by examples consistent with the finding for each area analyzed—program planning, financial management, personnel management, and community relations.

Program Planning Conclusions

Finding: Federal funds are received too close to the beginning of classes to allow for orderly and timely program implementation (or are even received after classes start).[4]

Example: An Education of the Handicapped Act program, Part B, was funded in late July for the 1975-76 school year. However, the LEA was not able to hire a coordinator until late August because of late notification. As a result, as of October 1, 1975, program activities were still being planned rather than implemented.

Finding: Late Federal funding hinders LEA efforts to effectively prepare a coordinated curriculum comprised of separate Federal, State and LEA programs.[5]

Example: An LEA has four bilingual programs that receive appropriations from three governmental bodies, awarded by four administrative offices, but directed toward one target population: ESEA Title I supported by the federal government and awarded by the U.S. Office of Education; ESEA Title VII supported by the federal government and awarded by the U.S. Office of Education; and the State Departments of Education and regular programs supported by the state and local education agency. USOE guidelines call for each of the programs to supplement one another but coordination is virtually impossible given the differing dates of announcement and the uncertainty of appropriation levels.

Finding: Grant awards are often received too late in the grant period for effective use during that period.[6]

Example: In May 1975, a SEA received a fourth quarter grant award that resulted in an increase of $700,000 for vocational education. In reacting to prior USOE criticisms about excessive carry-over, the SEA encouraged LEAs to spend at a rapid rate, thereby seriously damaging good planning and program effectiveness.

Finding: The carry-over has almost universally helped the SEAs and LEAs cope with late and uncertain federal funding.[7]

Example: One LEA intentionally budgets for a Title I carry-over of $300,000 each year for salary costs during the first quarter of the subsequent year. To illustrate the need for this approach, as of September 5, 1975, the LEA had not received its Title I award for 1976.*

Financial Management Conclusions

Finding: Without firm knowledge of funding levels, the support requirements for Federal programs cannot be effectively budgeted during the regular budget preparation, review, and approval cycle.[8]

Example: To compensate for uncertain federal funding, one LEA reserved $100,000 of the fiscal 1976 budget as a contingency fund to be used for federal program support. This fund was used to attract and support any federal program awards the LEA had not anticipated that called for matching funds or additional administrative costs.

Finding: Purchasing delays caused by late funding often result in the receipt of program material well after the program has been implemented.[9]

---

*Section 412(b) of the General Education Provisions Act permits funds appropriated for obligation in one fiscal year to be available to the recipient for obligation until the end of the succeeding fiscal year, in specified programs.

Example: Purchase orders for an ESEA program were issued and program funds obligated between October 1974 and March 1975. As of August 31, 1975, some of those orders had not been filled. Those orders had to be cancelled and the de-obligated funds reverted to the Treasury Department.

Finding: Delays in the timely receipt of federal cash often force local education agencies to borrow the cash needed to make Federal program expenditures.[10]

Example: One LEA faces a 60-90 day lag between the submission of the monthly reimbursement request to the SEA (for a federal program) and the receipt of the reimbursement check. As a result, this LEA is forced to float federal program expenditures out of local funds for 120 days.

Personnel Management Conclusions

Finding: Late Federal funding reduces the ability of LEAs to find and hire professional personnel with specialized skills who are relatively scarce in some areas.[11]

Example: One LEA, in a progress report on a Basic Equal Educational Opportunity grant for 1975, reported that counselor aides were recruited and assigned in September and October because of the unavailability of applicants.

Finding: Many Local Education Agencies postpone the hiring of Federal personnel until after the award has been received.[12]

Example: District policy is to notify or hire professional staff by April. Since most federal program awards are received during the summer months, personnel whose employment is contingent on federal funds are notified of employment from two to six months after regular contracts have been issued. The policy has substantial negative effects on personnel morale.

Finding: Local Education Agencies may issue teacher contracts which are contingent upon receipt of the Federal funds.[13]

Example: Each spring, vacancy notices for positions in federal programs that the LEA believes will be funded and vacant are announced. The vacancy notice states that all positions will be filled "subject to funding." Many qualified persons, for obvious reasons, will not apply under those conditions.

Finding: Uncertainties and funding delays in Federal programs hinder the recruiting and retaining of Federal program personnel.[14]

Example: Currently the number of certified teachers within this state far exceeds the available positions. Faced with the prospect of being hired for a federal program in August, without a continuing contract, rather than in March or April, with a continuing contract, many teachers seek new positions that may be less attractive professionally but more secure economically.

Community Relations Conclusions

Finding: Community expectations are frustrated and unfulfilled partly because of late funding.[15]

Example: Parents of Title I children became angry when the LEA limited program spending during the fall (the Title I award was tentative and expenditures were restricted to salaries) and then had surplus funds available in April and May when the final award was received.

The implications of the findings of the Peat et al. study for the operation of university, community, and private nonprofit corporation programs are significant. In some instances, the problems present greater obstacles to community agencies than to public schools; community agencies are not able to float expenses, awaiting the receipt of funding, or to set aside monies to cover program expenses until the precise level of funding is determined. They are not able to recruit qualified personnel in anticipation of funding, nor are they able to hold staff for 60-90 days while waiting for state or federal dollars to meet payroll obligations. For universities, the problem of retaining and recruiting qualified personnnel, whose salaries depend on the receipt of federal or state grants or contracts, may assume greater significance than for LEAs. Most universities are not in a position to attract experienced qualified personnel to assume "soft money"* positions in June and July for the next academic year. Those already holding positions by virtue of earlier funding, like LEA personnel, often view themselves as second-class faculty when contractual commitments are made by the institution several months after commitments to individuals covered by regular budget line items. Whereas problems created by late or uncertain funding may be more severe for universities and social service agencies, program implementation constraints arising from the lack of synchronization between federal and academic fiscal years are not as stringent for agencies whose activities are not developed against academic time boundaries. The short period of time between official notification of the level of funding and the scheduled start-up date in many proposals, however, affects virtually all institutions and agencies seeking federal or state program support.

LEGISLATIVE RESPONSE TO LATE FUNDING PROBLEMS

Unfortunately, major elements of the Peat et. al. recommendations, designed to alleviate the negative impact of late and uncertain levels of funding on elementary and secondary school projects, are not applicable to settings other than public schools. The significance of the findings transcends school operations; recommendations contained in the study do not. Strengthening the hold-harmless provisions permit LEA and SEA planning to proceed with the assurance that a district will receive a specified percentage of the prior year's allocations. These provisions are valuable, however, only when a district is submitting for an ongoing entitlement program, not for a competitive grant or contract.

---

*A term used for funds to support personnel or activities not supported by the regular budget of the institution.

The carry-over provision, which provides a constructive option to the June spending spree, applies only to designated programs. Although the provision has assisted many districts greatly, enabling year-to-year planning by providing a predictable funding base and assuring money to meet costs during the initial months of operation, the provision only applies to continuation programs. Most programs allow institutions to apply no-cost extensions, or to assign unobligated funds in one year's budget to the succeeding year, but these options do not provide predictable, or necessarily desirable, means of adjusting to late start-up dates. Evidence also suggests that as the availability of funds for new awards assumes increasing importance in funding offices, and as states become increasingly conscious of the value of reverting unobligated funds to the state treasury to offset budget deficits, the almost automatic past approvals of no-cost extensions will succumb to more stringent policies.

Perhaps the best method to overcome the negative effects on project implementation of procedures governing announcement of awards is advance or forward funding. Advance funding was seen by Congress as a means to make the funding process more predictable. It provides parties eligible for submittal under designated programs with knowlege of the appropriation level one year in advance. It also addresses problems caused by the differences between the fiscal calendars of the federal government and schools. If the concept of advance or forward funding is expanded to cover a broader array of programs, it has the potential to alleviate many of these procedural problems. Giving the U.S. Office sufficient time to analyze program plans and proposals, and increasing the planning period for submitters, will increase opportunities to develop more effective implementation strategies. The expectation that forward funding will provide a panacea for the procedural elements of program implementation must, however, be resisted. This approach, coupled with the USOE policy implemented in October 1977 that provides a single notice of closing dates for most categorical programs several months in advance of the specified dates for proposal submittals, may solve some of the problems emanating from hasty proposal development. Current policies, however, do not address many of the procedural elements of the process that determine the timing of formal notification of award and the effects of this timing on project start-up. Likewise, a broader application of the advance funding concept will not affect significantly the difficulty of coordinating the planning of LEAs, public and private agencies, colleges and universities, and state offices with the authority to administer both state and federal programs.

DESIGN AND INSTITUTIONAL FACTORS AFFECTING PROJECT IMPLEMENTATION

Although there is sufficient evidence to support the contention that the award and notification process adversely affects the implementation of projects, temptation to place the blame for implementation difficulties solely on the bureaucracies responsible for administration of federal and state programs must be resisted. In the final analysis, project success or failure can be attributed directly to the quality of the design of the program, the skills of the project director, and the way the project is perceived by the host institution. To paraphrase Iago in Shakespeare's Othello: "[Bureaucracy!] Tis a fig. Tis in ourselves that we are thus or thus."[16]

This section focuses on the initial phase of the implementation stage, that period of time in a project's lifespan from receipt of official notification of funding to the carrying out of initial planned program activities. Only those factors contributing to the slippage from expectations that occur in the initial phases of project implementation are discussed.

Many elements that must be considered in the initiation or preimplementation period of a project's life were discussed under planning strategies for proposal development. The possible repercussions of failing to recognize, in the earliest stages of planning, the potential impact of any new program on groups or individuals affected by project implementation underlie the approach advocated for project planning. Unfortunately, full treatment of the range of variables that affect the implementation of projects, and their impact on institutions and social problems alike, is not possible in this work.

A review by Rand researchers of the literature on educational innovation revealed that efforts of the federal government to stimulate change in local school systems has yielded disappointing results; evidence suggested that projects were seldom implemented as planned. The researchers concluded that the apparent failure of many projects to live up to expectations was less a result of inadequate technologies or treatments than a function of the way promising treatments were implemented in the local institutional setting.[17]

The discrepancy between the strategies or activities contained in a proposal, and the strategies actually followed during implementation of the project, represents adaptations to three conditions confronting the director: (1) discrepancy between anticipated conditions for project implementation and those present at the time of project start-up; (2) the testing of the proposed strategies against the realities of the institutional setting; and (3) discrepancies between anticipated and actual outcomes in the initial phase of project operation, which cannot be attributed to sins of omission or commision in program design.

Before elaborating on the preceding conditions, it must be understood that the adaptation or revision of implementation strategies to accommodate the environment at hand, although representing a slippage from original expectations, often presents less risk to realizing project objectives than blind conformity to proposal specifications. The failure to adjust implementation strategies to the constraints of procedural factors discussed earlier, and to the environmental factors present at notification of award, may significantly increase implementation difficulties.

One cannot proceed to implement a project assuming that present conditions are identical to those at the time of proposal submittal. The impact of events that occur between the date of proposal submittal and the date of notification of award is heightened by the fact that an institution's approval of a document and its authorization to implement a program bring markedly different factors into play. The approval of a document often represents only an approval in principle, and is quite different from an approval in practice. The stress created by this difference is often aggravated when project directors fail to recognize the inevitability of discrepancies between proposed strategies and strategies required, or possible, upon notification of award and the accompanying stress. In failing to anticipate discrepancies, directors also fail to assess conditions affecting the implementation of the project and to identify strategies appropriate to the actual state of affairs. There is some reason to believe that many difficulties encountered during project implementation stem from directorial behaviors. This author once observed a director optimistically launch a program, which he noted was proceeding extremely well, with a 50% staffing complement. The community was up-in-arms over his failure to appoint the advisory board promised in the proposal, and the host institution was visibly questioning his motivations. We can equate the director's behavior with that of a creature representing a cross between a lemming and an ostrich (Lemostrich?). Such a creature's behavior would be characterized by placing his head in the sand and periodically backing toward the sea. Assuming that most directors will not act like Lemostriches, however, the task now is to identify specific factors that contribute to the discrepancies between the specifications in the proposal and what occurs during the initial stages of program implementation.

Some of these discrepancies may result directly from a process over which the submitting institution has little control. There are several areas, however, over which the submitter has direct control, that compound the flaws inherent in the system. These flaws (stresses) may be injected into the proposal plan of action both before and after budget negotiation. Before addressing institutional factors, which are less amenable to the director's control, attention focuses on fiscal, personnel, and management factors that the director controls during project development, that have direct bearing on program design and project implementation.

Program Budget Allocation

The adverse effect of "giving away" a personnel position or program element that may be central to a project's success, through hasty or inadequately planned budget negotiation, was discussed earlier. Less conspicuous but equally important is the discovery of oversights in budget development, which were not recognized at the time of negotiation and may only become apparent on implementation. Although often relatively small in terms of dollars, these oversights can disrupt the implementation of the project.

> A community agency failed to include a budget item for the costs assumed by participants enrolling in a continuing education program for unemployed female parents. The failure to recognize the

inadequacy of public transportation and the participants' needs for child supervision, either on site or at home, and the corresponding failure to allocate monies for these needs discouraged many interested parents from enrolling. The number of participants served by the project was thus significantly lower, and the characteristics and needs of the population attending were significantly different than projected in the proposal.

A local school system failed to budget monies for travel costs for field trips that were central to implementation of an innovative curriculum development project. The directors had assumed that buses owned by the school department would be available at no cost to the project. The superintendent and school committee had failed to correct the error prior to proposal submittal. The compromise reached after notification of funding was unsatisfactory to the director and was resented by the school committee, which felt it had been misled at the time of submittal. Thus, the start-up of the program's field component was delayed and the scope of the field activities was reduced significantly.

Staff and Participant Qualifications and Availability

The funded project often allows the submitting institution to supplement current faculty or staff positions, enabling it to deliver services or develop programs that otherwise could not be accomplished. Project success, in such cases, depends heavily on the institution's ability to identify and recruit qualified individuals. When funding is secured to develop and implement training projects that address the needs of specified populations (e.g., bilingual, aged, children with special learning needs, and minority group members), the recruitment and selection of eligible *participants* is just as important as staff recruitment and selection. When recruitment and selection of either new staff or participants constitutes one of the first project implementation tasks, failure to establish appropriate selection criteria and recruitment strategies in the proposal can present a major obstacle to the project's realizations of proposal goals. The types of slippage possible and the potential impact on project implementation are illustrated by the following examples.

A university proposal, designed to provide a training program leading to a B.S. degree for bilingual candidates, stipulated that the director would be recruited from a pool of candidates having the same ethnic background as the project participants. In addition, the director had "to meet the same criteria for selection established for regular faculty appointments." Given the July 1 announcement of funding and the September 1 start-up date, the university opted to appoint a candidate who met the ethnic criteria but not the stipulated academic criteria. Within a month of the project's start-up date, it became clear that the director was not being accorded the status of a faculty member by other members of the faculty; such status was central to the director's responsibility to coordinate development of the program. The resultant difficulties in introducing proposed new courses, altering admission policies, and incorporating project activities in the ongoing program seriously limited program success.

A local education agency received funding for a project to develop program activities for students characterized as "low motivation-normal ability as measured by standardized testing instruments." The proposal also specified that students would be asked to volunteer for the program, with parental consent a prerequisite to participation. The number of volunteers meeting the stated criteria was significantly below that anticipated and enrollment was immediately opened to all volunteers, regardless of academic ability. Demands on faculty increased and the program goals were thus changed. Ultimately, the stated achievement objectives could not be realized, due mainly to the low standardized test scores and achievement patterns of the new population participating in the program.

Institutional Support and Qualifications

Discrepancies between what an institution claims it can accomplish and what, in fact, it can accomplish are built into the proposal development process. Discrepancies between stated priorities and actual priorities are also common. The quest to secure money may, at times, seduce an institution to present statements of qualifications and support that are neither borne out by past experiences or future intentions. The notification of award, in such cases, often amounts to a test of an institution's intent and ability. Failure to recognize the potential for differences between statements and fact, can create possible disillusionment for the director and seriously jeopardize the project's implementation. The following examples demonstrate a few symptoms of such discrepancies to which a director should be alert.

Faculty in a major university were strongly encouraged and subsequently commended by the dean of a school to submit proposals in response to a solicitation for a new program. After notification that one of the proposals had received funding, the proposal developer and project manager was disappointed to receive no further acknowledgement from the dean. Two months after notification, the dean announced at a faculty meeting that, as a result of funding of the proposal that provided staff support and participant stipends for minority candidates, the school would be "confronting new problems because of the nature of the students to be selected to participate in the program." Conflict between the project director, who was responsible for implementing the program for candidates with different backgrounds from the majority of previously enrolled students, and the dean continued throughout the project's duration. This conflict significantly affected the project's ability to realize the proposed objectives.

A community action agency, in cooperation with an urban school system, submitted a proposal for support of storefront learning centers to complement educational experiences provided by local schools. It became evident, shortly after announcement of funding, that the curriculum provided in the storefront settings linked such issues as tenants' and students' rights to the teaching of basic skills. The school department thus found that conformity with program terms set in the proposal placed them in a position in which continued full support of the program jeopardized their relationships with vocal political leaders and the Parent Teachers Association. The principals of the participating schools consequently retracted from the advocacy elements of the program. Conflict between the agency and the school department over this issue continued throughout the duration of the project and ultimately contributed to the discontinuaton of funding, since the funding agency's priorities emphasized community action elements of supported programs.

A local education agency stressed its past efforts to develop programs for children with special learning needs and cited the strong qualifications of staff to carry out a funded program. At the time of notification of award, teachers scheduled to participate in the program had already received other assignments in the system. Efforts to reassign teachers met with strong resistance from parent groups and the project was mounted with new untested personnel, with some of the original teachers serving as consultants. It quickly became apparent that the revised staffing arrangement seriously reduced the institution's delivery capability.

Institution and Community Collaboration

Government agencies and foundations have long supported the concept of collaboration among institutions as a means to increase the impact of projects. In recognizing the need for those served by projects to participate in project development and operation, opportunities for collaboration have been extended to parent and community groups. Many institutions have also recognized the programmatic value of collaboration in securing funding and increasing the delivery capability of a project. The delicate nature of collaborative relations is strained by the inevitable need to assign and balance responsibilities among participating parties and to develop a consensus from varying priorities and needs. This strain is exacerbated by the limited time available for proposal development. The clear allocation of authority and responsibility between institutions and/or groups often cannot be developed before proposal submittal. Consequently, opportunistic motives for collaboration initially may exceed programmatic motivations. After notification of funding, the allocation of authority and the delegation of roles often becomes the major implementation issue. The potential for governance rather than program development issues to take center stage is great.

A university, in collaboration with a community multiservice center and a state department of education, received funding for a project to provide training for parents serving as teacher-aides and to develop curriculum materials for an independent state-sanctioned community school. The proposal failed to specify which party had final responsibility for the content of the parent training program and the nature and form of classroom materials. It also failed to delineate responsibilities of the two codirectors, one representing the university and the other the community. When it became apparent that the university and the agency regarded both the training and curriculum components differently, and when the school principal insisted on demonstrating his authority to approve or disapprove classroom materials, the codirectors found themselves continuously negotiating appropriate governance structures and allocation of power. The failure to define the roles and authority of the codirectors resulted in conflict between them during the entire project, and constant program adjustments to meet the demands of the center, the state, the university, and the school administration.

In collaboration with several school systems, a private, nonprofit organization, possessing a national reputation for developing innovative curriculum materials, received support to train teachers and administrators and develop curriculum materials to be used in local school settings. The teachers and administrators, in many cases, having received the training and taken steps to implement the curriculum in the local sites, soon became aware that their goals and ideas of the program were markedly different from those of the local community, as communicated by the school board. Curriculum implementation and refinement dissolved, and negotiations designed to accommodate the program goals to community demands rapidly became the most time-consuming activity.

These two examples lead to a consideration of characteristics of the institutional environment created by the interaction of new programs, supported by external funding, and time-honored and sanctified programs, which have given the institution its programmatic and organizational identity. Many of the problems that need to be considered when confronting institutions with new working relationships are also present within institutions seeking to alter past behaviors or inject new behaviors into the system.

INSTITUTION ENVIRONMENTAL FACTORS CONTRIBUTING TO PROGRAM SLIPPAGE

There is evidence to support the observation that projects seeking to change existing practices or introduce new practices immediately become "locked in a kind of arm wrestle to change the other before they are changed by the other."[18]

Although this metaphor communicates the institutional dilemma confronting the project director, it is insufficient in two respects: (1) arm wrestling

256 *The Dynamics of Funding*

generally calls for only two players and (2) arm wrestling produces a winner and loser. The pressures, affecting the outcomes of project implementation are not limited—they emanate from several points. In addition, projects seldom clearly identify winners and losers; the nature of the interaction between an institution and a project is such that outcomes cannot be measured by such absolutes. The concept of interaction, however, is central to understanding the characteristics of project implementation. Three types of outcomes resulting from project-institution interaction, as identified by Rand researchers, provide a sound reference point for discussing factors that contribute to the ultimate success or failure of a project:*

1. *Mutual adaptation:* Both the project design and the institutional setting were adjusted to meet the needs of one another.
2. *Nonimplementation:* Neither the project nor the setting was able to adjust to the needs of one another and no change occurred.
3. *Cooptation:* The project adapted to the indifference and/or resistance to the institution by casting off those objectives which called for significant change. Implementation in such cases was essentially *pro forma*: materials might be developed or purchased, services delivered, but no organizational changes, which would be prerequisite to continuation when funding was no longer available, were in evidence.[20]

In analyzing the factors contributing to the project's ability to conform to expectations, the most pervasive factor affecting implementation tended to be the motivations that initially prompted the institution to seek funding. Projects initiated in response to a locally identified need, and accompanied by a commitment to resolve a problem, fared better during implementation than projects that were essentially knee-jerk responses to the availability of funds. Projects reflecting a commitment to problem resolution seemed to be capable of accommodating institutional pressures without a loss of identity. These adjustments, in many cases, constituted slippage from some of the original objectives. Many times, however, they increased the likelihood of bringing about organizational changes and changes in practice, thereby enabling the projects to realize their

---

*The Rand research project sought to answer the following questions: How do school districts select, introduce, implement, incorporate, and spread different kinds of innovations? and How do differences in federal programs, in project characteristics, and in local settings affect how projects are begun, carried out, continued on local funds, and disseminated?

Programs included in the survey of 293 "change agent" projects in 18 states included:

Elementary and Secondary Education Act Title III, Innovative Projects (consolidated in 1976 under Title IV ESEA);

Elementary and Secondary Education Act Title VII, Bilingual Projects Vocational Education Act, 1968 Amendments, Exemplary Programs; and

Right to Read Programs (initially authorized under the Cooperative Research Act).[19]

major goals. Some of the adjustments cited in the Rand study, characterizing projects in which mutual adaptation occurred, suggest alternatives open to the director during a project's lifespan:

> reduction or modification of idealistic project goals
>
> amendment or simplification of project treatment
>
> downward adjustment of behavioral changes in staff or overly optimistic effects of project on students
>
> adjustments to unanticipated changes in standard practices or relationships between staff and administrators.[21]

Clearly, the first three adjustments, seen by the Rand researchers as central to successful implementation, reflect adjustments of the program design to the environment and/or design flaws in the proposed program. The final adjustment represents a response to pressures affecting day-to-day implementation of the project that, although anticipated, cannot be isolated or resolved prior to program implementation.

In day-to-day project operation, the goal of mutual adaptation calls for a management strategy to identify and achieve sufficient consonance between the needs and expectations of the individuals, organizational units, and institutions involved in, or affected by, the project. This consonance enables the delivery of proposed services and the continued operation of the project with institutional support. The complexity of the task becomes apparent by examining the range of interactions that can occur in the implementation of any project (Table 7.3).

Each interaction requires negotiation between the desired, institutionally

TABLE 7.3. *Implementation Interactions and Reference Points*

Individual Roles	Institutional Units and/or Referent Groups
Director ↔	Funding agency
Director ↔	Sponsoring institution
Director ↔	Relevant governing and community buildings
Director ↔	Project staff
Director ↔	Sponsoring institution staff
Director ↔	Participant representatives
Staff ↔	Sponsoring institution administration
Staff ↔	Director
Staff ↔	Peers
Staff ↔	Participants
Participant ↔	Sponsoring institution
Participant ↔	Director
Participant ↔	Staff
Participant ↔	Peers

prescribed behaviors and the personally identified needs and conflicting expectations of legitimate referent groups: therefore, the potential for conflict should be evident. While a certain amount of conflict will always exist in implementation, there are limits beyond which it cannot go if the system still is to function. The degree to which individuals participating in the project (director, staff, participants) perceive their roles and expectations as consistent with those rewarded by the institution greatly influences the project's ability to meet its objectives, assuming the appropriateness of the approach to the problem. The task of the director implementing the project is to manage the inherent conflict creatively and constructively.

Working with the preceding perspective, conclusions drawn from selected studies provide the project manager with criteria for assessing planned implementation procedures and identifying characteristics of the implementation process that render projects particularly vulnerable. Attention is directed initially to a study of projects implemented under Title III of the Elementary and Secondary Education Act of 1965.*

Characteristics identified as being important to later project adoption by school systems included:

> Projects which were expected to change something perceived as negative in a community/school system (racism, a change in the power structure) had more trouble being adopted than those which were less threatening.[22]
>
> The credibility of project planners, in terms of their being representative of and known to the community, was more important than their actual numbers.[23]
>
> School committee and school system endorsement from the beginning was more marked in adopted than non-adopted projects. The support in adopted projects was financial, as well as moral.[24]

Consider the comments of directors of two nonadopted projects that had grandiose objectives and implications for the distribution of decision-making power in the community and the school department. These comments are particularly relevant for those attempting to develop and implement a project that calls for substantive change rather than supplementing on-going activities.

---

*Title III was designed to stimulate and assist in the development of model elementary and secondary school programs through competitive awards to local school districts. In 1975, Title III ESEA was superseded by Title IV ESEA, which consolidated several programs. Under the new Title IV, local school systems may compete for funding under three sections: Part A, which includes a component for one-year programs to enhance implementation of Chapter 622 (Equal Educational Opportunity); Part B, which provides for statewide distribution of federal funds for library and learning resources under a predetermined formula; and Part C, which offers funding on a three-year basis for innovative programs reflecting state board of education priorities.

> If I had to do it over again, I'd recommend a different model in the first year—one that would be decided by a significant number of teachers and administrators in the system. I would have involved more of the official people . . . and gotten more formal school involvement.[25]
>
> If I had to do it over again, I would make early contact with the school committee . . . I would analyze the political forces in the community for sure . . . and implement some strategies to forestall pending crises.[26]

The preceding recommendations are particularly appropriate for initial project planning. Although there are opportunities to make adjustments based on such advice during project implementation, the degree of freedom is limited once operations begin. Some additional findings of the study apply after notification of funding has been received and operations have begun.

> Adopted projects tended to rely more on the process of evaluation—both internal and external—and saw it as a more important component of their program than projects which were not adopted.[27]
>
> Adopted projects tended to change their overall objectives much less frequently than non-adopted projects. Individual strategies or objectives might be revised but program emphasis remained constant.[28]
>
> The changes which adopted projects effected tended to be more observable and tangible than those of non-adopted projects. Descriptions of outcomes were more specific and dealt more with skills or products than with attitudes. Outcomes could be clearly communicated to others.[29]
>
> The main ongoing outside determinant of adoption was not the state department of education, but the community which was served by the project.[30]

Conclusions regarding the qualities of the project director, which research indicates are basic to project success, were elusive. Some clues were, however, identified. Directors of adopted projects tended to be skilled in the project area of study, were more involved than the others in outside professional organizations, and generated more positive and empathetic relationships with their workers while exhibiting strong leadership. Directors of adopted proposals also had more experience in the community and all possessed strong management skills.

The preceding discussion of factors contributing to project adoption supports the notion that the director must continuously and simultaneously negotiate anticipated project outcomes with the sponsoring institution, staff, and participants. Such negotiations demonstrate to participants that appropriate adjustments are being considered to address their expectation of the project.

Full conformity to the terms set by the proposal, at the cost of community and institutional support, clearly places the director in the position of having the project rejected by those groups whose support is central to the day-to-day development of the project. Without such support, success will be little more than ritualistic. Widmer's findings lend support to the observation of the Rand researchers: "A receptive institutional setting is a necessary but not sufficient condition for effective implementation . . . Mutual adaptation which we believe is the key to serious change—requires an effective implementation strategy, one that *takes advantage of institutional support.*"[31] [emphasis added]

Before some generalizations are offered to guide a project's transition from paper to program, a review of factors that contributed to the failure of two projects in quite different settings will provide the reader with a point of reference for understanding the generalizations that follow.

A university-based educational change project, in the late 1960s, sought to change one junior high school in the Bedford-Stuyvesant section of New York City "into a school of unusual merit in the education of disadvantaged children." This project exhibited a number of factors that contribute to the breakdown of projects that involve more than one institution in bringing about changes in organizational relationships.

The project's overall strategy was to affect the total environment by saturating the school with concerned adults (college students, college faculty, staff, and community members). By assigning teachers and the additional manpower to "clusters," which would develop new curriculum materials, teaching strategies, and support services, its aim was to develop a teaching-learning environment significantly more meaningful to both students and the teaching staff. The slippage from expectations was so great within the first few months of operation that the project virtually ceased to function; little remained other than the balance of the almost one-half million dollars granted to the institution.

> By the end of the first semester, 1966, the [project] had almost nothing to show for its efforts. In some Clusters, more than half the regular teachers had stopped coming to weekly Cluster meetings. Minor conflicts over scheduling, classroom assignments, parent permission slips for trips, and so on, grew more frequent. In January, the professor who served as Director of Instruction resigned because there didn't seem to be much time for educational policy or any other planning. One Cluster coordinator resigned and accepted a college teaching position. "I had the feeling," he said, "that we were going nowhere." Another coordinator recalled precisely the day he "gave up." "Emotionally," he said, "I quit in February. It just didn't make any difference if I came in or not." Three project teachers—extra classroom teachers hired and paid by the project—also resigned in January. The project Director of Evaluation recalled that even before the new year, the project was "all but wiped out . . . . For us

as a team the first 4-6 weeks were both the beginning and end of the project."[32]*

What contributed to this disillusioned state of affairs? The analysis provided by MacMillan is consistent with the conceptual framework presented earlier in this work and with the experiences of the author. In looking at the relationship between decision making and the institutional environment as it affected the project in question, the researcher concluded:

> Although the proposal espoused teacher participation in decision making, the first major resolution reached by the staff, the creation of "cluster," was made without the participation of teachers. The effort to involve teachers in decision making was subverted almost before it ever began.
>
> The initial orientation sessions for all faculty and staff left teachers confused about the specific expectations and the anticipated outcomes for the project. The director's open-endedness and ambiguity in responding to teachers' queries left them confused about what decisions would have to be made both regarding their roles and the development of the program.
>
> Many of the responsibilities of the cluster leaders fell under the jurisdiction of department chairmen, who had not been invited to participate in planning sessions. Teachers immediately were placed in a position in which they were responsible to conflicting authorities—the chairmen and the cluster leader. In many cases conflict over power relationships extended to the principal.
>
> Teachers never identified with the process of problem solving which provided the theoretical framework for project program development. In the environment of the particular school innovation in teaching was not rewarded; "control" was.

Failure to link the strategies and program to the organizational environment effectively appears to have been exacerbated by the failure of project leadership.

> The diagnosis of the organizational environment was shallow. The directors did not adequately analyze the pressures on the teachers . . . , "what makes up the system they're in, what their problems are, their investments are, their vested interests . . . how they've already had to conform to the system because they have been there a couple of years."
>
> Project staff failed to establish the links with outside resources promised in the proposal. Failure of the staff to provide resources from other schools of the university (Law, Social Work, Dentistry)

*Reproduced by special permission from *The Journal of Applied Behavioral Science*, Charles B. McMillan, "Organizational Change in Schools: Bedford-Stuyvesant," Volume 11, Number 4, 1975, pp. 437-453, NTL Institute for Applied Behavioral Science.

was as much the fault of the reward structure of the university and the priorities of faculty in these units as of the leadership style of project staff.

Given the position of the project director in the bureaucratic structure in which he assumed major leadership tasks with little authority, voluntary support of others was crucial. When he opted to defy the standard operating procedures which governed the cooperating school's decision making, the project became a series of confrontations over program jurisdiction.[33]

In order that the foregoing analysis not seem too harsh, it must be recognized that the school was an intrinsic part of a much larger bureaucratic structure with firmly established norms governing the behaviors of its members. The major error in attempting to change signficantly its environment and functioning may have been in setting overly ambitious goals. The goals, however, were consistent with the naiveté that characterized many other efforts during the late 1960s to bring about significant change through the implementation of projects.

The final case study vividly depicts the institutional resistance a project developer must be prepared to deal with, even in a seemingly noncontroversial area. It also demonstrates the need to develop implementation strategies that consider characteristics of the particular environment, as individual projects progress from idea to implementation.

An educational research group was formed as an organizational entity after the breakup of a campus school at a small college. One of the major expectations of the college administration was that the group would attract outside funding to the university. From the beginning, the group encountered difficulties.

> The valued activity at the institution was classroom instruction. Since most of the group's functions fell outside this domain, the group became regarded as "illegitimate," despite the full backing of the administration.
>
> The project director opposed the idea that the group's primary responsibility was to secure funding. Some grant proposals were therefore either delayed or vetoed, bringing the group into direct conflict with college administration expectations. The director's resistance to administration directives ultimately led to his domain.*

Stress encountered by the group led to other reactions that had a snowball effect in bringing the ill-fated group ultimately to the point of dissolution.

> The group became more isolated from the campus community; this isolation tended to solidify the group but simultaneously led it to respond in almost a paranoic manner to any criticism.

*Paraphrased with permission from Ronald Hull, "The Degradation of an Education Research Group: A Case Description," *Educational Researcher* (June 1976): 12.

> Sensing their isolation, group members increasingly began to question the effectiveness of the director. In concert with the administration of the institution, the power nucleus of the group initiated steps to encourage the director's resignation.[34]

In analyzing this case, the researcher identifies what he calls "degradation mechanisms," which an institution may use to prevent the success of any effort not fully consistent with its dominant value structures. This concept is particularly helpful in understanding the environmental climate that may affect any new project. With a little imagination, the particular symptoms noted by Hull can be applied to programs with markedly different missions and structural characteristics.

> Staff, who made up the dominant identity of the institution, were permitted to cooperate with the "outside" group in mounting of project, but is was made clear by administration and peers that these activities were judged as secondary to their instructional assignments.
>
> The terms of the appointments given to group members were different than faculty given "regular" appointments. Although they were given faculty status, no clear-cut expectations were provided to enable them to judge whether they were conforming to expectations. Their assignments fell outside the perview of regular rules and policies specified by the university to govern faculty appointments.
>
> The administration increasingly relied on sources outside the group for information that ultimately would affect decision making about the future status of the group.[35]

An added twist to the dilemmas the project group might have faced, had they been truly successful, has implications for any significant "change" project and is suggested by the following observation:

> It is the damnation of out-groups for excessive achievement, however, which gives rise to truly bizarre behavior. For, after a time and often as a matter of self-defense, these out-groups become persuaded that their virtues are really vices. And this provides the final episode in a tragicomedy of inverted values.... Prompted by the practice of moral alchemy, noteworthy achievement is a vice; the achievements must be discounted.[36]

RESPONDING TO THE CONDITIONS OF IMPLEMENTATION

It should be evident at this point that the procedural elements that hinder project implementation are compounded by flaws in the project design and pressure points in the institutional environment. While a definitive identification of flaws and strengths of past efforts generalizable to all implementation effects is impossible, certain generalizations can serve as guidelines for successful implementation.

It is conceptually possible to separate the initiation stage of the project, when ideas are transformed to plans presented in the proposal document, from the implementation stage. Analysis of past projects, however, clearly suggests that the director of implementation cannot disown the pressures originating from the way the proposal was developed and submitted. Whether the project director prepared the proposal is of little importance once notification of funding is received and the project must be implemented. Given the functional relationship between the initiation and implementation stages of project development, elements characteristic of the initiation stage are considered in the following generalizations. For purposes of convenience, the generalization and accompanying recommendations are broken down into three categories—formulation, management, and leadership. Formulation recommendations cover the initiation stage and the first decisions regarding implementation; management recommendations address the initial phase of the implementation stage; and leadership recommendations cover the entire project operation.

Program Formulation: Generalizations and Recommendations

1. Despite the findings that the numbers of persons participating in the planning and development of the proposal does not increase the likelihood of successful implementation,[37] *who participates in the planning seems to be of central importance. Persons holding status in the submitting institution, or in groups whose participation is central to project success, should be included in the proposal development process prior to submittal of the document.*

2. The prior generalization notwithstanding, individuals believed antagonistic toward the proposed project, or who perceive the project as a major threat to their status, may subvert efforts if they are brought into the proposal development prior to conceptualization of the program.[38] *Such individuals should be brought into the process once the goals and basic design have been set. Adjustments to accommodate their interests can then be made without jeopardizing the basic thrust of the project.*

3. The receptivity of the institution to change is a critical determinant of eventual project success or failure. *During the initial stages of proposal development, efforts should be made to assess the flexibility of role expectations held of staff, past efforts to develop staff or improve on the delivery of services, and past history of staff in implementing projects.*

4. The more complex the institution submitting the proposal, and the larger or potentially more controversial the proposal objectives, the greater the likelihood of conflict during implementation.[39] *Projects to bring about major change require, therefore, extended periods of time for planning and careful*

assessments of the organizational climate, the need for the program, and the interests of those affected by the project.

5. Overly ambitious, unclear, or inappropriate objectives given the constraints affecting project operation, often prevent ultimate realization of objectives. Major changes in goals, once the project has commenced, generally contribute to the project's nonimplementation. *Objectives should be concrete and tangible; consultation with individual(s) with demonstrated expertise in the area addressed, about the soundness of design, appropriateness of intervention strategies, and the feasibility of anticipated outcomes should be secured before document submittal.*

6. Lack of planning for unanticipated bureaucratic requirements, space and material needs, assignments of staff, identification of participants, and recruitment of additional personnel contributes to implementation difficulties.[40] *An inventory of organizational and facility needs should be developed prior to implementation.*

After notification of program approval, the tasks to be undertaken constitute a blend of planning and management activities. Since planning at this stage is directed toward implementation rather than conceptualization, the tasks are primarily managerial activities rather than formulation activities.

Management Generalizations and Recommendations

1. Since the project director may not have developed the proposal, the choice of a director can be one of the most important decisions confronting the submitting institution. The institution must recognize that, if the project calls for significant change, bringing in a director from outside the institution may threaten the status of others in the institution. Conversely, appointing an individual who has little status in the eyes of management, staff, and participants presents different problems. *Selection of the director calls for identifying an individual who possesses status, or can achieve it from within the institution, but who is not perceived as a threat by the institution.*

2. When more than one institution is collaborating, an individual's status within a single institution is seldom transferable to other institutions. *In projects that rely on major participant involvement in program planning, or that call for collaboration between institutions, provisions must be made to include representatives of these parties in the selection of a director.*

3. Given the potential for program disruption by budgetary decisions made in response to funding agency constraints, *the senior program officer should be directly involved in any budgetary response to the funding agency.*

4. Given the impact of procedural elements of the funding notification process on the implementation of programs, and the frequency of late funding, the project cleared for implementation may differ in many respects from the project submitted for consideration. *The director should reassess the project activities and concomitant fiscal needs at the time of budget negotiation, rather than awaiting formal notification of award. Together with an internal or*

external evaluation specialist, discrepancies between the organizational and programmatic features existing at submittal and those set by the terms of the negotiated award should be identified before project implementation (and again one month after project start-up).

5. Given the flaws that inevitably occur in planning the document, the time period following the first clue that funding may be forthcoming should be used to correct these flaws. *Before hiring or appointing the first staff members, or taking the first implementation step, the director should consult with representatives of parties with a vested interest in the project, delineate role descriptions of staff, make concrete objectives, and reassess time lines for all project activities.*

6. The assumption that all interested parties within the submitting institution have read the proposal, or are aware of the proposed project, can lead to serious difficulties in the initial implementation stages. *Even prior to notification of funding, the director should share the proposal with those who may later facilitate or impede project implementation; the approach should ascertain everyone's expectations, should funding be secured.*

7. Historically, document reference to community advisory groups or participant review boards has often represented a token statement to satisfy funding agencies and participants. Both funding agencies and community groups are increasing demands that the collaborative relationships be honored in the implementation of the project. *Directors of all collaborative projects must establish both structures and procedures that allow the inputs of all collaborating parties to form an integral part of the project's governance and program development structures.*

8. Once funding has been obtained, some institutions and individuals tend to assume that the task has been completed. This orientation is particularly relevant when the motivation for submittal can be categorized as more opportunistic than problem solving. To reduce the slippage from expectations that may emanate from such an orientation, *the director should establish time lines for the completion of tasks, identify persons responsible for carrying out tasks, and identify how and when periodic assessments of success or nonsuccess will be carried out.*

9. Given the potential for confusion over roles, expectations, and responsibilities of all parties, *the project governance structure must inform participants of precisely the process by which disputes may be resolved and the manner in which all program decisions will be made final.*

10. Externally funded projects do not constitute, by definition, part of an institution's ongoing program. *Means to communicate project activities continuously, to all who may ultimately contribute to the project's continuation, should be incorporated into project operating plans.*

The importance of support for project activities by persons other than those responsible for administering the project should by now be evident. Securing such support is an integral part of the director's responsibility. In the following consideration of project leadership, no attempt is made to analyze the concept of leadership per se, an abbreviated treatment cannot do justice to the extensive work of others in this area. Instead, some observations are offered, drawn from personal experience and the literature, that may be considered comments on the art of directorship and its implications for project development.

The observations are based on the assumption that project directors seek, however modestly, to bring about change and that "changes in a system, when they are reality-oriented, take the form of problem-solving."[41] If the director is a problem solver, the task is one of tuning both structures and process "both to human problems of relationships and morale and to technical problems of meeting the system's task requirements set by its goals...."[42]

Leadership Generalizations and Recommendations

1. Despite conflicting evidence that the effectiveness of a project depends on the planner and director being the same person, or the director being recruited from outside the institution, the author's experience tends to confirm the finding of the Ford Foundation study. It concluded that the most successful projects were those in which the directors were present at time of planning and remained through the implementation, evaluation, and adaptation phase.[43] The immediate implication of this observation for project implementation is that *the person responsible for implementation must enthusiastically support the objectives of the program and the strategies identified, and must communicate this commitment to others.*

2. Related to the preceding is the idea that in order to effect the identified changes, *the director must be in a position to negotiate effectively with those responsible for the traditional mission of the institution and with all parties affected by implementation of the new mission implied in the project.* This task is easier if the director already carries status in the submitting institution.

3. Given the constraints affecting the implementation of any project, adjustments in program generally become essential to project success. *The project director cannot be a doctrinaire or social reformer who is unwilling to adjust the project to the social and institutional realities affecting its implementation.*

4. Related to the preceding, *the director's flexibility must be coupled with skills for securing information on the project's functioning and systematically making adjustments in light of this information.*

5. Although the director's personality appears to be critical to project success, even the most charismatic individual can find it physically impossible to handle all the burdens of project management. *The greater the project's scope and the more ambitious the objectives, the greater the need for the director to delegate and fix responsibility with other staff, as appropriate.* Given this need to delegate responsibility, the "second rung" of leadership assumes great importance in implementing large-scale projects.

6. Because the responsibilities inherent in the directorship of a funded project may be significantly different from those carried out by the individual

in a previous role, *the ability to delegate responsibility generally will be facilitated by a directive rather than nondirective leadership style.*

7. While a charismatic personality is often central to both the development and successful implementation of the project, evidence suggests that such individuals are upwardly mobile. They often fail to develop institutional structures that permit adaptation or continuation of projects once they leave.[44] Without depreciating the value of charisma, *projects that seek to bring about institutional change must place equal emphasis on the development of supporting organizational stuctures and the development of strong personal relationships between project and institutional staff and administration.*

Given the procedural, programmatic, and institutional factors that influence the transition of a project from paper to program, the challenge confronting the planner or manager in any project implementation setting is significant. The challenge is confronted best by identifying implementation strategies not necessarily expressed in the proposal. Such strategies must provide for: establishing priorities among the organizational needs central to implementation in the particular setting; identifying implementation objectives that address needs unique to the specific organization setting; and developing management strategies that directly address these implementation objectives, which when collectively realized will define successful implementation of the project.

ENDNOTES

1. U.S., Department of Health, Education, and Welfare, *Report of the Task Force on Timing of DHEW Appropriations for Educational Programs* (Washington, D.C.: Government Printing Office, 1967).
2. U.S., Department of Health, Education, and Welfare, Office of Education, Office of Planning, Budgeting, and Evaluation, *A Study of Late Funding of Elementary and Secondary Education Programs*, 5 vols., prepared by Peat, Marwick, Mitchell & Co., February 1976.
3. Ibid., 4:35.
4. Ibid., 5:8.
5. Ibid., p. 9.
6. Ibid., p. 11.
7. Ibid., p. 12.
8. Ibid., p. 18.
9. Ibid., p. 21.
10. Ibid., p. 22.
11. Ibid., p. 27.
12. Ibid., p. 28.
13. Ibid., p. 30.
14. Ibid., p. 33.

15. Ibid., p. 38.
16. William Shakespeare, *Othello*, Act I, Sc. iii, line 323.
17. Paul Berman et al., *Federal Programs Supporting Educational Change*, 5 vols. (Santa Monica, Calif.: The Rand Corporation, 1975).
18. Dale Mann, "For the Record," *Teachers College Record* 77 (February 1976): 315.
19. Berman et al., *Federal Programs Supporting Educational Change*.
20. Paul Berman and Milbrey Wallin McLaughlin, *Federal Programs Supporting Educational Change*, vol. 4, *The Findings in Review* (Santa Monica, Calif. The Rand Corporation, 1975), pp. 10-13.
21. Ibid., p. 11.
22. Commonwealth of Massachusetts, Department of Education, *What Makes Innovation Work in Massachusetts*, Jeanne Widmer, publication #3275, 1975, p. 33.
23. Ibid., pp. 33-35.
24. Ibid., p. 35.
25. Ibid.
26. Ibid., p. 36.
27. Ibid., p. 51.
28. Ibid.
29. Ibid., pp. 51-53.
30. Ibid., pp. 77-81.
31. Berman and McLaughlin, *Federal Programs Supporting Educational Change*, 4:21.
32. Charles B. MacMillan, "Organizational Change in Schools: Bedford-Stuyvesant," *The Journal of Applied Behavioral Science* 11 (October 1975): 437-53.
33. Ibid., pp. 439-453.
34. Ronald Hull, "The Degradation of an Education Research Group: A Case Description," *Educational Researcher* 5, no. 6 (June 1976): 12.
35. Ibid.
36. Robert Merton, quoted in R. Hull, p. 12.
37. Widmer, *What Makes Innovation Work in Massachusetts*, p. 27.
38. Ronald G. Corwin, *Reform and Organizational Suvival* (New York: John Wiley & Sons, 1973), p. 122.
39. *A Foundation Goes to School: The Ford Foundation Comprehensive School Program, 1960-1970* (New York: The Ford Foundation, 1972), p. 42.
40. Berman and McLaughlin, *Federal Programs Supporting Educational Change*. 4:95.
41. Robert Chin and Kenneth D. Benne, "General Strategies for Effecting Changes in Human Systems," in Gerald Zaltman, Philip Kotler and Ira

Kaufman, *Creating Social Change* (New York: Holt, Rinehart & Winston, 1972), p. 245.
42. Ibid.
43. *A Foundation Goes to School*, p. 42.
44. John Goodlad and Robert H. Anderson, *The Nongraded Elementary School*, ed. William B. Spauding (New York: Harcourt, Brace & World, 1959), p. 190.

8

Strategies for Responding to the Funding Environment

Previous chapters have asserted that the writing of a proposal to secure a grant or contract is just one element of a complex sociopolitical phenomenon termed the funding process. The framework formulated for understanding the funding process has identified several discrete but interrelated components that, taken together, give definition to the process:

the social or generic definition of the problem
the legislative definition of the problem
the funding agency definition of the problem
the submitting institution definition of the problem
the operational definition of the problem

In addition, each component of the funding process is shaped by the characteristics of the organizational units that develop and administer individual programs and by the needs and expectations of individuals who staff these units. Consequently, the differing needs of the organizational units participating in the process assure the presence of conflict or stress in the system.

One of the challenges confronting institutions seeking to maximize external funding opportunities, and individuals seeking to direct successful projects, is to analyze systematically the interaction between elements of the system and to project the anticipated needs and expectations of individual units comprising the system. Assuming the analysis and projection challenges are met the institution then must provide the support structures and technical assistance prerequisite to an effective response to the current or projected funding environment.

This chapter illustrates the application of concepts, discussed in preceding chapters, to the development of a funding and management approach that accomodates the needs central to analyzing and responding to the funding environment. It begins with an analysis of the variables in the funding system that can affect the environment to which the funding manager must respond.

FORECASTING THE FUNDING ENVIRONMENT

In the same manner that the weather at a single geographical location on any given day represents the interplay of relatively constant global forces, resultant weather systems or fronts, and local topographical features, the funding environment encountered by a given institution, at any given time, represents the interplay of national political, social, and economic forces with those forces unique to the agencies that develop and administer funded programs. One who would seek to forecast future developments in the funding environment must be in a position to identify the equivalents of pressure differentials signaling the development of fronts, locate already established fronts, make estimates of their rates of movement, and identify factors that will influence the weather accompanying the arrival of the front. The ability of any funding officer to develop or maintain programs by securing external funding depends on a knowledge of: the permanent features of the funding environment; the pressures that may lead to the establishment of new funding "fronts" or thrusts; and the evolving current and pending programs that bear watching. Such knowledge makes it possible to predict the results of interaction between the variables and to forecast funding opportunities for a given area.

GENERAL CHARACTERISTICS

> National educational and social policy-making mechanisms provide an inhospitable environment for substantial policy change; the inhospitality stems not as much from an unwillingness to consider new programs, but because the sequential approvals required to move an idea from proposal to program affords many points of access through which organized interests may exert vetoes.[1]

Experience indicates that at the state and federal levels of government, groups with a vested interest in maintaining the status quo have more access to the decision-making process than those actively interested in bringing about change. The funding environment thus is one in which change generally represents an incremental redistribution of resources, over an extended period of time, rather than a massive infusion of money on short notice. The implications are evident: the introduction of legislation calling for major changes, or executive pronouncements on the need for major legislation, do not represent a *fait accompli.*

> Washington is a different kind of company town . . . . It's the only company town in American that makes an intangible product—federal laws and services for the nation.[2]

The pablumlike rhetoric of this promotional statement is actually more revealing than it first appears. Given the nature of the product and the way government machinery works, access to the decision makers or their staff, whether in executive, legislative or individual program offices, is valued highly. "Who you know" assumes functional significance. Information is a by-product and becomes a valuable commodity in the "horse trading" accompanying most major legislative and program office decisions. The functional significance of knowing the right people extends to the outsider seeking support for a project. At the federal level, preliminary information about the status of legislation and accompanying program office priorities allows the program developer and/or proposal writer time to plan extensively thus placing the institution in a strong competitive position when Rules and Regulations or program announcements are distributed formally. Much of the information secured through informal channels will later be distributed formally. The time differential and the difficulty of locating information, however, make personal contacts a functional prerequisite for securing knowledge about program and funding developments.

Such contacts may facilitate the securing of information at the federal level, but they are a necessity for those who seek funding from state governments and foundations. Foundations and state program offices generally have weakly defined structures for the systematic disclosure of relevant information. The open-endedness of many state and foundation proposal requests, the absence of a state equivalent of the *Federal Register*, the ambiguity of foundation annual reports, and the various ways state offices and foundations solicit and review proposals, necessitate direct access to staff and program officers.

> Government programs are characterized by a multiplicity of goals and lack of any conceptual framework to bring order to the host of federal and state authorized educational and social service programs. Both federal and state government actions are the result of their being pressured by events which they are ill-equipped to control.

This characteristics of the funding environment is the most easily understood but the most perplexing for those seeking to forecast future developments. The variables that contribute to the multiplicity of goals and lack of apparent order are easily identified; how they will interact to define particular programs is more elusive. Actions leading to the enactment of programs represent responses of the executive, legislative, or judicial branches to the nation's social, political, and economic climate at a given time. Specific problems that result in governmental action generally represent symptoms of large problems addressed earlier in other forms. Since several organizational units within the bureaucracy can legitimately lay claim to the expertise or appropriations to address the problem, the locating and mapping of programs and their relationships to one another can be a nightmare.

Government machinery is designed to meet the diverse needs of constituent groups through a process of compromise and adjustment. Interests are addressed as they appear; adjustments to meet interests are made as they become necessary. In forecasting future developments, therefore, one must: identify those interests of constituent group(s) or individual representatives that will propel the government into action; distinguish what form the government action will take (executive initiative or directive, legislation, court ruling, reordering of priorities in individual program offices, or administrative directives at the department program or contract office level); and estimate both the time required to transform the pressure to action and the ultimate impact of the action on the total funding environment.

> Within the bureaucratic structures at both the federal and state level reside program officers who by virtue of their long periods of service and commitment to clearly defined program goals are in a strong position to influence the shaping of new programs when the external pressures for the development of such programs are consonant with their interests.[3]

There is a tendency to forget that, within any system with formal mechanisms for the negotiation of interests and the concomitant development of new programs, the informal influence of individuals can be considerable. Within the federal and state bureaucracies, there are civil servants whose knowledge of the system and commitment to specified program goals may become, under the proper environmental conditions, a significant factor in the development of new programs. Although the job titles and organizational placement of these individuals may change from administration to administration, their ability to influence the development of emerging programs should not be underestimated. Although they may not have the power to shape the larger environment, they often can influence the funding environment in particular program areas. Such individuals, consequently, are invaluable information sources for the developer assessing the larger funding environment. Under proper conditions, they can also be particularly helpful in developing strategies to respond to a particular program development.

ORGANIZATIONAL CHARACTERISTICS

The general characteristics of the funding environment evolve from the relatively constant structures and customs governing the working of the relevant organizational units. These structures and customs influence the ways evolving social and economic needs are analyzed and pertinent strategies and products are developed. The implications for assessing the funding environment are clear; consistent with the model that has governed this work's approach to funding, a social or generic problem does not acquire functional significance for the grantsman until it is recognized as worthy of attention by those who provide the funds. Forecasting of future funding environments requires the identification of high priority items already on the agenda of funding agencies (offices authorized to develop programs and commit funds) or items that, given current social, economic, and political trends, are likely to become a concern of organizational units that authorize or administer programs.

Any participant in organizational decision making will acknowledge the power of the person setting the agenda to influence the weight given to any particular item. It must be noted that there are many points in the governmental agenda-setting process at which influential persons or units in the executive, legislative, or judicial branches can assume the power of the agenda setter, introducing new items or indefinitely delaying action on current items. To a lesser extent, the same opportunities for agenda alterations occur in the decision-making machinery of a large foundation.

The first step in forecasting is to identify the organizational units relevant to establishing the funding climate; next, one must identify the items on their agendas that may be relevant to future funding configurations. These items must then be evaluated against the full range of social and political variables that give the funding system definition. In the following application of this approach, efforts are made to provide the funding manager with long-term strategies and the means to keep current on the identifiable trends or critical factors influencing funding priorities.

The format presented identifies by category the organizational units that can affect the funding environment significantly; gives an example of actions taken by these units that affected the funding environment; and identifies the social, political, or economic variables in the total funding system that resulted in that action. The examples represent significant agenda items that have the potential to affect future agenda items, in turn influencing the funding environment in the immediate future. The implications of the environmental variables for proposal writing and strategy development are discussed later in this chapter.

The organizational variables that define the funding enviornment at a particular time may be categorized as: executive-initiated actions, legislative actions, judicial rulings and advocacy group actions, Office of Management and Budget (OMB) regulations, General Accounting Office (GAO) reports, and HEW rule-making procedures. While these variables represent primarily federal organizatinal features, the discussion of each category provides enough information to identify state and foundation correlates.

Executive-Initiated Actions

Examples: Establishment of a Cabinet-Level Department of Education; Proposal for a Basic Skills and Educational Quality Act.

The two examples illustrating executive-initiated actions that have affected the funding environment reveal three major forms such initiatives can take: (1) reorganization and/or development of new administrative structures responsible for program development and administration; (2) appropriation requests contained in the fiscal year budget submitted to Congress by the Administration; and (3) program proposals submitted to Congress. The characteristics of these initiatives may differ significantly. Their affect on the funding environment may only be felt after other government units have authorized the actions identified either explicitly or implicitly in the request of the executive office.

The establishment of a cabinet-level Department of Education has been a formal agenda item since at least 1964, when a Task Force on Government Reorganization appointed by President Johnson made the recommendation. The possibility of the establishment of such an office affecting the funding environment, however, attracted public attention when presidential candidate Carter supported its establishment. "A Department of Education would consolidate the grant programs, job training, early childhood training and many other functions currently scattered throughout the government. The result would be a stronger voice for education at the federal level."[4]

The impetus for the office and the accompanying consolidation of programs gained momentum with the 1978 State of the Union Address:

> The Administration will also work with the Congress for the creation of a separate Cabinet-level Department of Education, and for legislation to replace and reform expiring Federal education acts.
> These legislative proposals will concentrate on:
> — increasing basic literacy;
> —ensuring that students are prepared for jobs;
> —supporting post-secondary education and lifelong learning; and
> —strengthening the partnership between Federal, State, and local governments.[5]

The need to increase basic literacy has been transformed to an executive-initiated action in the form of the proposed Basic Skills and Educational Quality Act. Under this act, the mandate of the National Reading Improvement Act would be broadened to include all the basic skills; submitting agencies would assume responsibility for documenting how they are using federal monies from all other program sources to address basic skill needs. In addition, most programs currently authorized under the earlier Special Projects Act will cease to be funded separately and will have their funding levels set by OE rather than by Congress. The current form of these programs (Career Education, Community Schools, Metric Education, Consumer Education, Arts Education, and Gifted and Talented) will thus be altered significantly. Some will be incorporated within the proposed program and others authorized as separate programs.

Contributing Conditions. Three conclusions of a study commissioned by the American Council on Education directly address the factors leading to the recommendation for a cabinet-level Department of Education: (1) "Relatiomships between the federal government and the educational systems of the nation are now in poor repair."[6] The researchers go on to conclude that Congress and the executive branch have "created detailed program controls without understanding the difficulties of administering them . . . ."[7] The observation seems to be confirmed by the National Education Association and National School Board and American Vocational Association support for such an office. (2) "First-rate leadership to cope with the range of educational issues is virtually impossible under the present Department of Health, Education, and Welfare."[8] The researchers conclude that a Department concerned with health insurance legislation, the administration of Medicaid, Medicare, and Social Security, and a host of civil rights issues, cannot adequately carry out the planning prerequisite to the effective development and implementation of education programs. This problem is aggravated by the conclusion that: (3) "Adequate and balanced consideration of Resource Allocation for education programs is unusually difficult in the present Department of Health, Education, and Welfare, where annual increases for 'uncontrollable' programs exceed the total departmental allocations for education."[9]

In this setting, the legislatively proscribed increases for Social Security, Medicare, and Medicaid are greater than the total education allocation, and the fiscal climate creates enormous pressure to hold back budget increases. The proportion of money allocated to education programs receiving annual appropriations, consequently, is affected significantly and adversely.

Many of the factors contributing to the need for increased efforts in the area of basic skill development were cited earlier in the book. To recapitulate, the alarming persistency of student inability to communicate, calculate, and perform well on standardized tests has fostered the "back-to-basics" sentiment, providing valuable public support for the proposed legislation. This visible public concern is supported by internal Washington political pressures: "The small bunches of authority tucked away in the federal establishment hang like albatrosses around the Commissioner of Education's neck."[10] Besides addressing an issue of public concern, the proposed act, by consolidating the small programs currently authorized under the Special Projects Act, potentially provides administration officials with greater control of the programs over which they preside. Simultaneously, the administration's goal to consolidate and simplify government operations (on paper at least) would be served by passage of the act.

Both of these examples are politically attractive; they honor campaign pronouncements while addressing public concerns regarding the functioning of the federal bureaucracy and the perceived deficiencies in basic skill instruction.

Projected Status. The proposed establishment of a cabinet-level Department of Education has possible major implications for the allocation of authority and fiscal resources. The number of obstacles to implementation, created by the need to negotiate these reallocations, will determine the substance, timing, and impact of this initiative on the funding environment. The projected timing of such efforts is further complicated by the wide range of pressing international and domestic issues, not directly related to education, that confront the Carter administration. Most of the administration's recommendations, regarding which agencies and programs of the executive branch should be included in the proposed Department of Education, parallel those contained in S. 991 introduced by Senator Ribicoff of Connecticut. There is little doubt, however, that areas of difference will generate considerable debate. The timing, consequently, will be greatly affected by the way the different executive and legislative recommendations, and the differing needs of the affected agencies and programs, are resolved. Public hearings and federal intramural negotiations, set against general social and economic pressures confronting the administration, will determine the precise characteristics of changes in the funding environment caused by this executive-initiated action.

The evolution of the proposed Basic Skills and Educational Quality Act will be easier to track. The administration's 1979 budget called for the largest dollar increase in elementary and secondary education programs since 1966, with the largest increases proposed for Title I of the Elementary and Secondary Education Act (ESEA). Although the 1980 fiscal year budget proposed by the President reduces federal education program budget authority requests from the preceding year, regular Title I levels are maintained with supplemental appropriations designed to serve districts having high concentrations of disadvantaged children. These executive actions, although not directly related to the educational quality proposal, signal future administration approaches: categorical programs will address the needs of particular groups, accompanied by increased appropriations, in contrast to the previous administration's efforts to hold the line on expenditures while fostering a block grant approach.

There is little question that the basic skills performance level of American youth will remain a major concern for the public, and that the relationship between basic skill acquisition and student employability will be noted. Given the increasing consciousness of the need to address the relationships between education and work, it is hard to conceive of a change in the nation's political and economic climate sufficient to alter the priorities established in the Basic Skills and related appropriations and program proposals. The evolution of the executive initiatives, regardless of the agencies or departments of auspice or the precise form of initiatives, can be forecasted fairly accurately. Developing information access points, identified earlier in this work, will reveal events occurring in both the private and public domains of decision making.

Legislative Actions

Example: The Youth Employment and Demonstration Projects Act of 1977.

The Youth Employment and Demonstration Projects Act of 1977 added several new programs to a significant piece of existing jobs legislation, the 1973 Comprehensive Employment and Training Act (CETA) administered by the

Department of Labor. Title I of the 1977 Act created a new year-round Young Adult Conservation Corps; Title II added three new programs to the existing Title III of CETA—Youth Incentive Entitlement Pilot Projects, Youth Community Conservation and Improvement Projects, and Youth Employment and Training Programs. All three programs are supervised directly by CETA's existing network of prime sponsors. School districts, community groups, and/or nonprofit agencies may secure federal funds for salaries or stipends to youths receiving training or jobs from participating institutions.

Contributing Conditions. The Employment and Training Administration (ETA) of the Department of Labor does not have firm figures on the number of jobs created by the three programs. The programs were responses however, to a continuing high unemployment rate particularly alarming among youths and blacks. The congressional conference report on the bill regarded the program as a response to the need to explore methods of dealing with the structural employment problems of the nation's youth; the "discovery" of structural unemployment in the economy, however, is hardly a revelation. The signficance is that appropriations for youth employment programs were included in President Carter's Economic Stimulus Appropriations Request and that the act was passed after an election campaign in which employment was a major issue. A longstanding problem may assume greater significance for human service and educational institutions seeking to develop programs as a result of political and economic pressures confronting the nation. Likewise, it is interesting that two of the newly authorized CETA programs provide employment opportunities in fields directly related to energy conservation and preservation of the natural environment.

The changes in the CETA program were proposed ostensibly "in order to reflect the experience gained during the first three years of implementation, clarify existing policies and provide for new approaches to the grant process."[11] There is little question, however, that continued high unemployment, voter support in the 1976 election for the creation of jobs, the continuing spectre of restless unemployed youth, and the linking of the legislation (somewhat tentatively considering the small percentage of funds allocated to community conservation projects) to the energy crisis make the bill read like a compendium of America's troubles.

The architects of the bill strengthened its potential staying power by insuring that "All in the game win." Seventy-five percent of the money goes to prime sponsors according to a formula incorporating the number of persons unemployed, the number of persons residing in areas of substantial unemployment, and the number of low-income families in the sponsor's service area, relative to other prime sponsors in the state. Remaining monies are to be used by: governors in providing state-wide services; local education agencies in collaboration with prime sponsors; and Indians and migrant farm workers in developing special programs. Since local government units are generally prime sponsors, every level of government and several population groups stand to gain from the continued authorization and appropriation to carry out projects under this act.

Given these vested interests and the projected persistence of unemployment problems, CETA or some variation certainly will become a fixed entry in the funding environment.

Projected Status. It is likely that unemployment and energy will continue to represent social problems crystallizing around specific constituent needs. Since these problems probably will not respond significantly to treatment or resolve themselves (unlike the teacher shortage problem), there is little doubt that appropriations under this act will withstand many of the budget cut pressures of the early 1980s. Similarly, other acts addressing employment needs, whether they focus on school and youth, career awareness and mobility, or job training, should find a receptive environment. The level of funding and the number of new programs will be determined by several factors, including: the intensity of the unemployment problem; the ability to control inflationary aspects of these bills; and the ability of program offices and prime sponsors to diffuse the controversy over alleged mismangement of major programs, such as CETA, during the initial years of operation. The CETA program is particularly informative for projecting future funding environments. Like many past educational and social programs, it provides training opportunities to address a larger social problem, with all of the political perils that accompany a program dispensing nearly 12 billion dollars annually to local communities. One evaluator of the program has summed it up as follows: "Five years after its inception, CETA is (a) another welfare program; (b) an exploitive rip off; (c) an effective program that has substantially reduced unemployment; (d) all of the above."[12] The question is not whether CETA will survive in a Proposition 13 climate, but rather what form it will take as legislators respond to evolving social and political economic pressures.

Judicial and Advocacy Group Actions

Example: The Courts and the Handicapped
The role of the courts and advocacy groups in influencing the funding environment is generally associated with their role in influencing legislation to desegregate public schools. What is not generally appreciated is the pervasive judicial influence on the total funding environment through rulings on a wide range of cases. The relationship between court decisions, funding availability, and program development is evident in the growth of programs for the handicapped.

It is difficult to identify another area of program development in which executive initiative, legislative response, advocacy group actions, and related court rulings are consistently harmonious. The relationships are so mutually reinforcing that, when considering the needs of the handicapped child, the proposal developer need only question what form the assistance will take. The relationships between the several sets of variables that influence the funding environment, produce an ideal state seldom approached in other areas of program development. This ideal state, however atypical, is an ideal benchmark for assessing the favorability of the environment for other types of programs.

Contributing Conditions. The impact of court-exerted pressure on the development and enforcement of state and federal legislation is evidenced by the more than forty completed cases since 1971 in which the courts have upheld plaintiff claims to enforce handicapped children's constitutional rights. The responsibility of schools and other organizations to honor handicapped children's constitutional rights derived its major impetus from a 1971 state court decision. Citing constitutional guarantees of due process and equal protection under the law, the Pennsylvania Association for Retarded Children filed suit on behalf of thirteen retarded children arguing that their access to education should equal that of other children. In a consent agreement, the courts found in their favor. In 1972, the federal court in the District of Columbia made a similar ruling,[13] extending the decision to cover the full range of handicapping conditions. The judge ruled that all children have a right to "suitable publicly supported education, regardless of the degree of the child's mental, physical, or emotional disability or impairment."[14]

Concomitant federal support for programs for the handicapped assumed significantly increasing importance for the funding environment with the passage of the Education Amendments of 1974. P.L. 93-380 is particularly noteworthy in that it specifies the due process requirements protecting the rights of handicapped children and requires states to submit plans specifying how they expect to achieve full educational services for handicapped children. The 1975 Education for All Handicapped Children Act, P.L. 94-142, unlike most education laws, carries no expiration date. It thereby assumes the status of a permanent instrument, carries significantly higher authorizations for basic State Grants programs, and establishes, as national policy, the proposition that education must be extended to handicapped persons as a fundamental right.

Court rulings increasingly have been incorporated into state statutes and have contributed to the formulation of federal legislation. It is doubtful, however, that the impact of handicapped legislation or court rulings on the funding environment would have been as significant without the efforts of strong professional associations, such as the Council for Exceptional Children, the activities of organized parents groups and other advocacy groups, and the strong support of national leaders (both President Kennedy and Vice President Humphrey had handicapped children in their families). Nevertheless, court rulings have determined the form of much of the legislation and have directly affected state and federal appropriations to meet the costs associated with full compliance.

Projected Status. It appears that the judiciary's major influence on the future funding environment for education of the handicapped will occur through judgments on issues of compliance. The stipulation in the new Education for All Handicapped Children Act requires schools to educate children in "the least restrictive environment."[15] This probably will be the basis for future rulings that may have major implications for inservice staff development and program development, and could influence the priorities of funding for the handicapped.

Given the many state statutes complementing the federal regulations, and the problems of program implementation associated with law enforcement, states are likely to increase their partnership with the federal government in developing plans and allocating monies to meet the intent of federal and state legislation. As issues of cost become increasingly critical to local governments, the state's role in determining federal allocations will increase. Advocacy groups will continue to play a major role in assuring compliance with current law and in extending full educational opportunities to specific segments of the handicapped populations not fully served at this time (e.g., prekindergarten, bilingual, and the urban poor).

In assessing the future impact of court decisions and advocacy groups on the total funding environment, past events seem to suggest that the courts, in both their precedent-setting and compliance roles, will continue to play an active role. In attempting to forecast the future environment, take particular note of efforts of advocacy groups and pending court cases that address the issues of equity (e.g., equal educational opportunities for women, implementation of desegregation plans, and educational provisions for bilingual students). Advocacy groups continue to call for assistance to private and parochial schools, with cost implications for public schools if private and parochial schools are forced to close. It is likely that the delicate balance of parochial and private schools with public schools will be modified by the courts, affecting both the availability of funds and the eligibility of parties receiving funds.

As a final note, the ability of court rulings or well organized advocacy groups to alter the funding enironment significantly is clearly affected by the state of the economy. States that require "mainstreaming" of children with special learning needs are already beginning to encounter resistance, given the impact of such program costs on tax rates. The issue of financing education primarily through the property tax, and the resulting disparity in educational opportunities, has already been addressed by the courts. The issue will remain a major one in the immediate future; the ultimate resolution can alter the funding relationship between federal, state and local government units. Any change in these relationships will have immediate implications for the development of programs and the securing of support funds.

Office of Management and Budget Actions

Example: Circular A-95—State and Local Review of Proposals
In 1969, the Federal Bureau of the Budget (BOB), since reorganized as the Office of Management and Budget (OMB), issued Circular A-95 that established a procedure for local review of proposals. Applicants were required to follow a prescribed process notifying appropriate state and local agencies before submitting the proposal to the federal funding agency. Originally, the only education programs covered by A-95 related to school construction. Within the past few years, its scope has been extended to include virtually all federal programs having an identifiable impact on state or local community development activities.

Contributing Conditions. The main objective of A-95 is to coordinate program planning and development efforts at the local and regional level, and to reduce conflict, overlap, or even duplication among federally and locally supported programs. As such, the expansion of the regulation's scope hardly resulted from sudden insight into the existence of a new problem. Since OMB is the largest and most bureaucratized arm of the executive branch, and serves budget formulation, legislative review and clearance, and management functions, its sensitivity to the executive and its power to influence and implement executive decisions is evident. OMB is the link between budget and legislative decision making; when major executive branch policies are made, OMB is involved.

The era of expanding federal roles in education and social service programs officially ended in 1968; unofficially it had ended a few years earlier when the government agenda became dominated by Vietnam. During the Nixon administration, which was committed to reducing the waste in federally administered human service and education programs that were generally ineffective, OMB played a major role in implementing administration policies. It often thwarted congressional overrides of presidential vetoes of educational and social spending bills by controlling the flow of funds. The Nixon and Ford administrations were publicly committed to a balanced budget, cost saving, and more effective utilization of services already available. Given the shift from federal to state authority in the setting of priorities and administering of programs, the development of A-95 and its subsequent evolution directly reflects these policy goals: A-95 was designed to decrease waste resulting from inadequate coordination of federally administered programs. It provides an opportunity for governors, mayors, and other state and local officials, operating through A-95 stipulated clearinghouses, to influence federal decisions on projects. Local control and the "defederalization" of programs is thus honored; the status quo is not threatened.

OMB, an agency with its own set of perennial biases, derived from its function of determining the cost effectiveness of any given program, found in A-95 an opportunity to carry out its normal functions and still reflect the particular concerns of a specific administration.

Projected Status. The economic factors that gave birth to the cost-effectiveness priorities of the Nixon and Ford administrations changed little in 1978. Although the Carter campaign touched on the federal government's role in meeting the educational and social needs of the nation, the emphasis placed on reducing the rate of inflation and balancing the budget signaled that cost management would be a major concern. Confrontations between the executive office and Congress in revising the 1978 fiscal budget seem to indicate that the executive office will continue to curb spending. In such a setting, any forecast of the funding environment requires a close watch on regulations set by OMB to govern the management of programs. The role of OMB in the formulation of the budget and in the review and clearance of legislation proposals must also be monitored.

The relative power of OMB under the Carter administration, however, may be significantly reduced by the Congressional Budget Act of 1974. During the

284   The Dynamics of Funding

Nixon administration, Congress attempted to restore some of its power it felt was being usurped by the Executive by creating its own Budget Committee and establishing constraints on its own behavior. The Office of Technological Assessment was established and was responsible to Congress rather than to the President. Congress thus provided itself with a source of expertise and information necessary to develop and defend proposed authorization levels, information it considered more reliable than that provided by the executive office or lobbyists. Simultaneously, it increased opportunities for any member of Congress to offer inputs before a bill reached the floor of the House or Senate, and it set maximum levels for program appropriations within the total congressional appropriation. The committee and accompanying subcommittees thus severly restricted individual legislators from reporting inflated appropriation requests out of committee knowing that the political mileage gained from such requests would not be diminished by later necessary reductions.

In forecasting future environments, the functioning of the Congressional Budget Office, and its relationship to the Executive and OMB, will be a critical variable in determining the status of pending appropriations and the management of established appropriations. If congressional independence can be maintained when the administration and a majority of Congress are of the same party, and if the Congressional Budget Office can effectively guide and monitor congressional decision making regarding funding of education and social service programs, then the actions of this office increasingly will affect projections of the funding environment.

Whatever the eventual distribution of power between OMB and the Congressional Budget Office; whatever the scope of programs affected by Regulation A-95; and whatever regulations to monitor program expenditures are established by OMB, there is little question that project management variables rather than programmatic variables will become increasingly important in setting the environment.

General Accounting Office Reports

Example: "Project Head Start: Achievements and Problems"[16] *and "Man: A Course of Study"*[17]

Much in the same way that OMB performs data gathering, fiscal monitoring, and advisory functions for the executive branch, the General Accounting Office (GAO) carries out information gathering and advisory activities for Congress. Previously examined organizational variables within the funding environment primarily affect the inception of new programs, from the point of general problem identification, through the stages of legislative, agency, and institutional definition, to the point of program operations. GAO is an important variable in determining the funding environment since its authority to assess programs influences both on-going programs and ensuing amendments to the authorizing legislation. GAO assessments represent a critical variable in determining the future of a program and play an important role in linking the on-going to the new in the funding system.

Project Head Start: Achievements and Problems, a GAO report submitted to Congress by the Comptroller General in 1975, assesses Project Head Start, administered at that time by the Office of Child Development (OCD) in the Office of Human Development. The report reviewed the administration of Head Start by OCD and eight grantees and the related administrative activities of the three regional offices responsible for the programs. The review of program activities focused on parent participation, eligibility, recruitment, average daily attendance, and services to the handicapped.

The GAO study of the National Science Foundation curriculum development project, Man: A Course of Study, reviewed the procedures followed by NSF in the selection of curriculum development projects and all aspects of the development process, including the selection of curriculum content. Both the Head Start and NSF evaluations cited deficiencies in program administration and carried remedial recommendations. For purposes of assessing the funding environment, the conditions that produced the reports and their implications for future program development are far more significant than the findings themselves.

Contributing Conditions. The introduction to the Head Start report alludes to the conditions precipitating the study: "Because of Head Start's substantial Federal funding (since 1965 Head Start has delivered services to over 5.3 million children at a cost of approximately $3.16 billion), the need to follow up on previous GAO recommendations, and Congress' continuing interest in this program . . . GAO assessed the program's results and its management. . . ."[18]

The key for projecting the future environment provided by the introduction is found in the reference to "Congress' continuing interest." Head Start's genesis in the now defunct Office of Equal Opportunity legislation, the continued high levels of appropriations, and numerous highly publicized studies failing to show conclusive benefits to the children served are reasons alone for active interest. Congress' continuing interest was also assured by the steadily decreasing numbers of children enrolled between fiscal years 1969 and 1974 and, with the exception of 1970, the continued increase in federal appropriations for the program. The word "interest" assumes greater functional significance for assessing the future environment because the numbers of children and parents served represent a large and vocal constituent group.

The case of the program, Man: A Course of Study, (MACOS) differs dramatically from the Head Start case both in terms of the political vulnerability of the program and the sensitivity of the issues raised. An attack by Congressman John B. Conlan on MACOS during debate on the NSF authorization vividly demonstrates the difference: "Student materials have repeated references in stories about Netsilik cannibalism, adultery, bestiality, female infanticide, wife-swapping, killing old people, and other shocking practices."[19]

Without judging the merits of the charges, public resentment over government sponsorship of such materials did exist. The GAO report was authorized by Congressman Olin Teague, Chairman of the Science and Technology Committee, after the preceding debate that included the introduction and defeat of an amendment requiring NSF to send all research grants to Congress for review.

The significant differences between these two cases demonstrate the importance of assessing the political environment that spawns GAO program investigations.

Projected Status. The impact of GAO actions on individual program development and future funding environments is in large part determined by the interests of its congressional master. In addition, the impact of GAO findings is determined to a great extent by the political vulnerability of a program and the sensitivity of the issues raised by GAO. In the case of Head Start, many variables serve as deterrents to major restructuring or dismantling of the program. The same factors that assure continuing congressional interest (for example, longevity of program, the numbers and nature of population served, past levels of appropriations, and nature of services provided) contribute to the programs's stability. GAO recommendations to the Secretary of HEW, based on the program study, were reflected in the Secretary's directives to the Office of Child Development regarding program administration. These recommendations, in turn, were reflected in administrative and programmatic guidelines provided to individual Head Start programs, which, in turn, serve as additional program review criteria for regional offices.

In contrast, the recommendations of the GAO report and an accompanying report by an independent review group, appointed by the Science and Technology Committee, placed pressures on NSF. These pressures will be reflected in any reluctance of NSF to support future program development regarded as controversial.

A specific program without a built-in political constituency (e.g., lobbies, large constituencies, and organizations with vested interests or broad public appeal) thus may be affected significantly and immediately by GAO reports at the time of appropriation hearings. For programs with outside support, GAO reports represent a "call to arms"; the debate serves as a catalyst to negotiate future programs. Such debates can result in revised legislative and agency definitions of the problem which in turn alter the funding environment. The GAO's agenda and reports thus provide the funding environment analyst with an inventory of issues to address in designing a funding strategy for any program office or problem area in the unenviable position of attracting the "continuing interest" of Congress.

The organizational variables previously discussed (executive initiatives, legislative actions, judicial rulings and advocacy group actions, OMB directives, and GAO findings) all contribute to shaping governmental responses to the social, political, and economic climate. The precise programs and strategies adopted by program offices, whether at the federal or state level, are thus largely determined by the interplay of the permanent organizational units of the bureaucracy responsible for developing and administering government sponsored programs. The relative influence of the three federal branches of government and individual offices within the government bureaucracy may change under various administrations and over time. There are always, however, identifiable loci of power within any governmental structure that are central to the decision-making processes. These loci may be organizational units within the large bureaucracy or individuals in the bureaucracy whose influence exceeds the authority associated with their position. To forecast the funding environment with any reasonable degree of accuracy, one must be able to identify these sources of power and trace their movements.

The preceding analysis focused on organizational units rather than individuals responsible for shaping the funding environment; organizational units generally outlast the individuals who compose them. Nevertheless, one must be able to locate the individuals within the organizational structure who may be labeled "power ascendant." Chairpersons of legislative committees, senior legislators and staff, newly appointed Secretaries and Assistant Secretaries of federal departments, and newly appointed program officers or chiefs are potential major influences on the funding environment. Any assessment of the future funding environment must include identification of these individuals and their priorities. This assessment assumes increased importance during changes of administrations and changes of executive leadership in the private or foundation domain. The accurate analysis of the relationship among organizational units within any organizational structure, and the power relationships among individuals in these units, provides the forecaster with information to refine funding strategies that conform to the needs of those soliciting and granting awards.

THE PROPOSAL DOCUMENT AND THE FUNDING ENVIRONMENT

The preceding discussion focused on the major variables that shape the funding environment and identified some of the social, political and economic conditions that are likely to affect the way these variables are played out in the immediate future. Attention now turns to designing the proposal document so that it reflects the evolving concerns created by the changing environment.

Two not necessarily related types of criteria guide the review of the proposed program: (1) the credentials of the submitting institution of individual and (2) the technical quality of the proposal document. Although both sets of criteria continue to guide the deliberations of funding agencies, evidence suggests that, in the public sphere at least, the technical quality of the proposal lately has assumed increased importance. In addition, the applicant's ability to demonstrate the capacity to develop and implement an effective management system has become almost as important as the ability to design conceptually appropriate program features. These two trends represent a logical response to the evolving funding environment. With the significant increase in appropriations for educational and human service programs during the past decade, and the corresponding increase in applications received by funding agencies, it is no longer possible for reviewers to judge individual applications on the basis of first- or second-hand familiarity with the qualifications of the submitting individual or institution. The "opening up" of the funding process and the sensitivity of both federal and state governments to charges of favoritism has led to a system that, on the surface at least is more objective and hence more open. In such an environment the technical quality of the document assumes increased importance.

Although the proposal submittal process is formally more open, paradoxically the increasing management orientation of funding agencies handicaps many community organizations for whom much legislation is designed; they do not possess the technical expertise prerequisite to competing successfully.

The application of a management and systems perspective to the program development task was initiated during the Kennedy administration by Secretary of Defense McNamara. The social climate of the 1960s, however, was not conducive to its use in the area of social and educational services. During the past decade, several factors have created an environment amenable to the introduction of management systems into the education and human service funding environment: the failure of many projects to realize their goals during the past decade; the increased concern of Congress with program outcomes and the utilization and dissemination of resources and findings; and the increasing sensitivity of executive and legislative branches of government at all levels to cost effectiveness. There is reason to believe that the concern with project management reflected in the management, evaluation, and budget guidelines accompanying the solicitaion of proposals by many program offices—and certainly inherent in the zero-based budget concept that often enters the jargon of federal and state program planners—will remain central to responding effectively to the funding environment.

Given the current and projected state of the funding environment, the following characteristics of the environment must be addressed in the development of the proposal and must be accorded top priority by institutions seeking to develop or maintain a successful track record in securing grant or contract support.

1. The increased cost consciousness of both submitting institutions and funding agencies requires submitting institutions to pay closer attention to budget formulation tasks. Unfortunately, many program developers demonstrate a trained incapacity in the area of fiscal allocations and the determination of cost effectiveness.

    Given the impact of fiscal decisions on both the submitting institution and the reception given the proposal by funding agencies, development strategies must provide opportunities to consider fiscal policies and budget allocations long before the proposal is presented for institutional sign-off. The development of the budget generally has represented the final task in document preparation. Considering the current environment, the failure to incorporate fiscal planning with program planning will invite increasing difficulty for the submitting institution.

2. Despite increased levels of appropriations during the past decade, the projected economic climate and the increased awareness and need for external support indicate an increasingly competitive funding environment. In such a climate, the submitting institution must address the question: How is this proposal different from all other proposals? One strategy that responds to the question is the collaborative submittal; the submittal of proposals by previously formally unaffiliated institutions. As noted earlier, development of successful collaborative proposals requires that the responsibilities of each submitting party be clearly delineated, that accountability systems be agreed on, and that the allocation and administration of funds among the parties be determined clearly before submittal.

One additional caveat is in order: in making fiscal allocation decisions, the submitting institution or primary contractor must determine the subcontractual or compensation options permitted by the guidelines governing the submittal.

3. In response to the increased emphasis on project management plans, the proposal should clearly identify the scope and level of effort needed to carry out individual components of the program. The level of effort should include: the length and percentage of time required for individuals to carry out tasks; the identification of personnel to carry out the specified tasks; and the costs associated with the carrying out of specific tasks. Criteria for assessing the project's progress in realizing the objectives should be stated in operational terms, and should be presented in a form that permits periodic and regular testing against a prescribed time line. Evaluation, in addition to its time honored function for the funding agency, should be treated as a management tool.

4. As a result of the increased emphasis on "objective" evaluation, proposals increasingly are being evaluated in terms of points received. Although it is difficult to regard point allocation and objectivity as synonymous, the task of proposal writing is one of securing the maximum possible number of points. In developing the proposal document, it is therefore imperative that the institution honor the distinction between the document as a narrative exposition of a program, perceived and executed by a program specialist, and the document as a technical report, drawn to specifications set by the funding agency. Provisions for technical rewrites by appropriate staff should be included in planning for the development of the document.

In many respects, the immediate effect of the evolving funding environment on proposal development is to narrow the differences traditionally associated with grant as opposed to contract submittals and project operation. Grant and contract activities are now functionally similar in that performance specifications set against time lines established by the funding agency are central to proposal review and project operation, regardless of the instrument of conveyance.

The grant recipient is not compelled to bill for services upon completion. However, the increasing emphasis on linking costs with activities, delivering services against prescribed time lines, and enforcing periodic program and fiscal reporting procedures established by regulations demands increased accountability in the day-to-day operation of both the grant and contract. The major difference between the grant and contract, as a vehicle of support, was that the former provided support for what the institution wanted to do and the latter provided support for what the agency wanted the institution to do. That distinction is becoming a matter of semantics rather than substance.

Developments in the funding environment during the past decade have left little room in the system for institutions that seek funding only when in the mood. To compete successfully, an institution must develop organizational structures that support individual staff or faculty initiatives essential to the development of fundable proposals. Attention now turns to those features and functions of organizational structures that are central to institutional success in securing grant or contract awards.

THE SUBMITTING INSTITUTION AND THE FUNDING ENVIRONMENT

Many times, this author has been impressed by the inappropriate or inadequate support systems provided to proposal writers and project managers by schools, universities, and human service agencies. Proposals are submitted and projects are run often despite rather than because of the institutional support structures. This observation should not be surprising for these institutions regard the securing of grants as only one of several institutional goals, and proposal writing and project management are often perceived as tasks above and beyond the call of duty. Rather than reflecting on the motivations of most of these institutions, the preceding simply reflects their failure either to recognize or to act on the organizational demands created by the decision to compete for external funding. Those few institutions that are exceptions to the previous generalization fall into two categories: those that, by virtue of past funding success, have established relatively autonomous units, with their own support structures and accompanying reward systems for their staff, within the larger organizational structure; and those that have adopted creatively and selectively some of the organizational features and strategies common to major private consulting firms that treat the securing of grants and contracts as organizational ends.

The ability of any individual to respond effectively to the funding environment is determined largely by the dynamics of the institution of which he or she is a member. Thus, any institution hoping to compete successfully must create an organizational system that responds simultaneously to the needs of its members and to the larger funding environment. The features of such a system are identifiable. The following management system and accompanying functions represent a synthesis of features common to institutions that have competed successfully in securing grants and contracts. This writer's personal experiences also suggest that the institution must be able to carry out the proposed functions and tasks in order to reduce the conflict endemic to the initiation and implementation of externally funded programs and to respond successfully to funding opportunities.

INSTITUTIONAL STRATEGIES FOR RESPONDING TO THE FUNDING ENVIRONMENT

To respond effectively to the everchanging funding environment, an institution must have the organizational capacity to carry out three discrete functions: *information securing, product or proposal development, and program support and monitoring.* Each function carries a subset of tasks critical to document submittal and project management. The following lists of functions and related tasks is augmented by commentary to assist organizations in carrying out the designated functions.

Function: Information Securing

The institution should have the capability to:

1. Systematically collect and analyze data relative to assessing and responding to the general funding environment. The data base should permit the analysis of executive and legislative initiatives (at the state and federal level) and court and agency decisions relevant to program management and priority setting of funding offices.
2. Identify and analyze current and past priorities of government funding offices at both the state and federal level.
3. Identify the status of appropriations bills relevant to given program offices and the fiscal constraints affecting strategies of private funding organizations; and identify the level of appropriations available to any given funding office and the policies governing allocation of the funds.
4. Collect, store, and retrieve data relevant to documenting the need for specific programs the institution anticipates will be compatible with its program development goals. Data should be stored in a form conducive to retrieval, before receipt of the request for proposals, and should provide a permanent and updated source of information for all future submittals.
5. Secure and analyze review ratings accorded past proposals and adjust proposal characteristics in response to commentaries provided by reviewers.
6. Collect, store, and retrieve data relevant to institutional capabilities in given areas, as well as data relevant to other institutions and individuals

that might, through collaboration, complement the institution's delivery capability in anticipated high priority program development areas.

7. Develop a tentative list of programs that could provide a viable source of funding one year hence, and assign personnel to track the progress of these high priority programs. Information obtained should provide the basis for developing draft proposals and identifying persons to participate in the development of a proposal, when solicitation is formally announced.

Task Commentary

1. *Collecting and Analyzing General Funding Climate Data.* Demographic trends, lobbying activities, and voter influence all contribute to the form of legislation and the accompanying budget appropriations for funding offices and grant solicitations. For example, the growing interest in gerontology, reflected in the growth of the budget of the Administration of Aging, DHEW (from $30 million in 1972 to $420 million in 1977), resulted directly from the influence of the previously cited factors. In assessing the environment to project the future, one must recognize that legislation offers a degree of promise and permanency that presidential and gubernatorial pronouncements and bureaucratic decrees cannot. Since it takes from two to two-and-one-half years for a need to be transformed into federal legislation, planning on the basis of needs alone must be flexible enough to reflect new developments regarding both authorization and appropriation status.

Sources of data necessary to carry out this task include:* *Statistical Abstract of the United States*—an annual summary of social, economic, and political statistics of the United States (prepared by the Department of Commerce); *County and City Data Book* (Statistical Abstract Supplement); *The Congressional Record*—coverage of hearings relevant to specific areas of interest, and publications and reports of government agencies; and the *Index* for the Government Printing Office and reports issued by independent agencies, government offices, special interest groups, and professional organizations, both state and federal, documenting the status of current or projected needs. Information should be indexed and stored for rapid retrieval to support document development as well as long-range planning efforts. The collections of data available from local funding agency and government offices, and studies carried out by local organizations that indicate local trends, should also be incorporated in the information resource pool.

2. *Identifying and Analyzing Funding Office Priorities.* Institutions should be able to identify the priorities of federal, state, and private sources of funding prior to formal requests for proposals. At the federal level, the *Catalogue of Federal Domestic Assistance* and the publications of individual program offices

---

*Addresses and other means for securing materials are provided in Appendices A, C and D.

provide institutions with the initial means to estimate the receptivity of program officers to proposed ideas. Personal contacts with program officers, before proposal solicitation and the setting of Rules and Regulations, are also instrumental to the future development of proposals. Priorities within given funding offices can change significantly from year to year, and such changes often provide opportunities for institutions that are not reflected in the program descriptors in the *Catalogue.* The Right to Read program's initial status within the now defunct Bureau of Cooperative Research is an example. The opportunities for securing funds from several different program offices to address the issues of women's equity, the needs of bilingual populations, and children with special learning needs represent other examples.

Since most states do not have formal communications equivalent to the *Federal Register,* the institution must get and stay on mailing lists and establish informal communication mechanisms to secure information for ascertaining state priorities and proposal solicitation schedules. Strategies for gaining access to offices that govern the proposal solicitation process, usually at the state capitol, must also be developed by the institution.

Annual reports of foundations are valuable sources of information for determining foundation priorities. Efforts to determine the priorities of both local and national foundations can be facilitated greatly by The Foundation Center, an independent nonprofit organization dedicated to the collection, analysis, and dissemination of information on foundations. As of 1978, the Center had regional offices in eighteen states. Publications of the Center also provide updated information.* In approaching foundations, however, the importance of knowing current priorities and earning familiarity and respect, either through past program efforts or personal contacts, has increased as the value of foundation portfolios has decreased.

3. *Tracking the Status of Appropriations Bills and Funding Constraints.* Although some major newspapers trace the progress of federal and state appropriations bills through the legislative mazes, newsletters of professional associations, reports by private funding information publications, and staff in program offices are usually able to inform potential submitters of the status of a given bill and the implications for programs sponsored by their offices. Due to the workloads of program staff and the constant barrage of requests from potential submitters, however, staff assistance should be reserved for issues related directly to the scope of a given proposal. Another valuable source of information regarding the status of legislation, one that is often overlooked, is the staff of elected state or federal representatives. Since the job of representatives is to serve constituents, and since aiding constituents to secure an award is compatible with representatives' political needs, staffs are generally extremely helpful in providing relevant information. Remember, however, that the indiscriminate use of the services of these offices can cast the submitter in the role of an aggravant rather than a possible contributor to the goals of a given office. Requests for

---

*See Appendix B for a listing of sources of foundation information.

assistance must be chosen carefully and must be related directly to the needs of all parties.

Increasingly, the levels of funding allocated to projects can be ascertained from information in the *Federal Register* or program announcements distributed by state agencies. Should the range of funding be indeterminate, based on information provided in solicitation documents, individual program awards in the previous year can be valuable guides in setting the level of funding requested for an individual project. Within the context of proposal development, it is appropriate to ask the program officers, government, or foundation for the range of funding anticipated for individual projects. In many cases, grants may be categorized according to the level of funding requested. The determination of program office policies in this regard is critical, as the criteria for evaluation may differ between small and large grants. In the case of foundations, decisions on small grants may be discretionary for a foundation officer whereas larger grants may require trustee action. The impact of the magnitude of the request on both the review of the proposal and the timing of awards is significant.

4. *Collecting, Storing, and Retrieving Program Relevant Data.* Although the scope of programs for which an institution seeks assistance may vary considerably, most institutions can identify high priority areas of need that future proposals will address. The evidence attesting to the need for such programs generally is available before development of a response to a specific funding request. Collecting and storing data documenting high priority needs reduces the difficulty of data collection and analysis tasks at the time of document development.

Data relevant to a particular institution's mission and a particular submittal may be present but not locatable at the time of submittal. Therefore, needs and institutional data must be secured in a central location in a form conducive to rapid recall. This frees the developer from the time-consuming task of collecting documentary data at the time of submittal, and permits the identification of specific program priorities relevant to the particular pool of needs governing the institution's submittal. In addition to the more obvious sources of data (such as, attendance records, achievement scores, levels of income, unemployment rates, survey results, and reports of local and/or professional associations), which may be secured from institutional archives and census data, needs assessments accompanying earlier proposal submittals (provided they are not outdated) serve as additional sources.

5. *The Use of Past Proposal Ratings.* Most funding agencies will provide submitting institutions with reviewers' reports for proposals previously submitted by the institution that failed to secure approval. If a proposal was not funded the first time it was submitted, many institutions write off the agency or the program as an inappropriate funding source. Such actions fail to recognize that proposals that failed to receive support (assuming they reflected the concerns of the submitting institution and the needs of the receiving agency) often provide strong starting points for second submittals. Thus, reviewers' reports can be valuable guides for redrafting the proposal.

The task of developing a follow-up proposal is significantly easier than developing the original. Therefore, all submitted proposals and reviewers' comments should remain in the institutional archives and serve as a technical data bank to guide future proposal development in the same program area. All funded proposals must, by law, be made available to the public; thus, they represent an additional source of technical information for institutions willing to pursue the matter with appropriate agency officers.

6. *Collecting, Storing, and Retrieving Institutional Support Data.* A significant number of proposal requests call for the demonstration of institutional commitment and/or capability to carry out services in a given area. Whether commitment or capability is measured in terms of past performance, personnel qualifications, physical facilities, or administrative support, such data requests occur frequently enough to justify preparing proposal segments or "boiler plates" prior to responding to a particular request. This data, including resumés for staff central to the institution's efforts, should require only minor editorial rewriting, consistent with the criteria governing the specific submittal, at the time of document development.

A complementary resource file of institutions and individuals having working relationships with the submitting institution may be used, when appropriate, to lend credibility to the proposal. Such a resource file, if updated periodically, also provides data that may be useful in developing future collaborative relationships and in implementing the funded project.

7. *Medium Range Planning.* The all-too-common approach of developing individual proposals in response to solicitations, as they become known, is detrimental to the competitive position of the submitting institution and the development and implementation of coherent programs. The institution suffers competitively from the time restrictions of responding to a solicitation after the formal notice of availability.* It suffers programmatically from an inability to develop an individual program within the context of the institution's total program development. By identifying probable funding opportunities and ascertaining interests and priorities of departments or units within the institution, well in advance of anticipated solicitation or closing dates, the institution can make maximum use of available expertise. If proposal development proceeds within the context of institutional program development, both the quality of the proposal and the chances of successful implementation will be increased. Draft proposals allow inputs from other affected parties and decrease the likelihood of conflict between institutional units and those parties at the time of submittal or implementation. The submitting institution must continue to monitor the relevant program offices and make the accompanying adjust-

---

*The U.S. Office of Education, for example, adopted a revised policy in October 1977, establishing at a single time closing dates for receipt of proposals under most USOE programs well in advance of announcement dates. Evidence suggests, however, that institutions that regard proposal development as only one of their activities will continue to develop and submit at the last minute, despite such advance notice of proposal due dates.

ments to the proposal. This approach requires only a technical rewrite to complete the proposal on receipt of the formal invitation to submit.

Function: Product or Proposal Development

The institution should possess:

1. Policies for adjusting individual staff assignments to permit full-time commitments (under specified conditions and for specified periods of time) to the development of the proposal document.
2. Established procedures for securing technical assistance (either from inside or outside the institution) to aid in writing the final document.
3. The ability to assign support staff, as needed, to perform information gathering tasks, related to the proposal's content, and tasks related to the production and submittal of the document.
4. The ability to identify individuals within the institution who possess expertise pertinent to most proposal submittals (e.g., preparation of milestone charts, evaluation design, and program budgeting) and the accompanying mechanisms to define clearly the roles and responsibilities of these individuals.
5. Clearly delineated procedures for securing institutional clearance, including provisions for assisting the document developer in clearing the necessary checkpoints required for processing the written document.
6. Clearly defined policies and procedures for determining whether or not it is in the institution's best interests to compete for funding in response to specific opportunities.
7. Organizational mechanisms that provide for ongoing communication with community groups or other organizations central to the realization of program priorities established by the submitter. These mechanisms should also establish procedures to involve group representatives in the development of programs and submittal of proposals.

Task Commentary

1. *Establishing Policies for Adjusting Staff Assignments.* Most educational institutions and human service agencies, unlike organizations whose operations focus on securing grants and contracts, have organization structures that often impede the effective development of proposals. In these institutions and agencies, proposal writing may be one of many responsibilities, and temporary at that. The person responsible for proposal development often finds several demands competing for his or her time. One strategy to alleviate this pressure is to develop clearly defined institutional policies that permit the temporary assignment of specified individuals, under specified conditions, to the development of proposals. Such assignments assume greater functional value when the organizational structure permits these responsibilities to be allocated to personnel

already on the institution's payroll. Many of the information gathering tasks then represent ongoing activities of the institution.

2. *Developing Procedures for Securing Technical Assistance.* The conceptualization and identification of strategies appropriate for addressing a given problem call for quite a different set of abilities than does the technical writing of the document in conformity to the guidelines provided by the funding agency. Sound conceptualization presented convincingly but without accompanying technical quality, drastically reduces the odds of securing funding. Consequently, it is essential that the institution identify either staff or outside personnel who can write the final document in a form acceptable to the primary developer and consistent with the funding agency's criteria for review. Either by allocating monies for consultants or by specific staff assignments, persons should be available to consult with the developer and anticipated project staff, at the inception of the writing task, and to write the final draft from materials provided by involved personnel. This individual must not be perceived as both a developer and technician, unless the institution is fortunate enough to have a staff member who possesses the skills required of both. It is certain disaster to develop and submit a technically proficient proposal that violates every program tenet of those who ultimately will be responsible for operation of the project and every priority of the institution providing auspice.

3. *Identifying and Assigning Support Staff.* Anyone who has developed a proposal is aware of the frustrating delays that accompany the writing of the document, which result directly from what may be called "administrivia." Telephoning staff, locating data, identifying typists, duplicating materials, delivering the proposal to secure signatures, filling out federal or state forms, and calculating budget figures consume inordinate amounts of time in bringing a proposal to the point of submittal. Although the demands created by some of these tasks may be alleviated by the presence of data banks discussed earlier, the nonwriting demands placed on those responsible for developing the document still merit the provision of technical assistance. Any institution wishing to maximize writers' skills must provide them with assistance in developing the project. Such assistance need not constitute professional or program staff; however, familiarity with the clearance procedures of the submitting institution and the forms accompanying proposal submittal, and the ability to communicate effectively with all participants, are prerequisite to effective assistance.

4. *Setting Procedures for Optimal Use of Professional Staff.* Many institutions, particularly large ones with a broad range of programs, fail to utilize effectively the skills of organization staff. This failure stems from two factors: the institution is unaware of the specific proposal-relevant skills of staff or, being aware, has established neither policies nor conditions to enable these individuals to be called on when their skills are needed. Program budget specialists, evaluators, systems planners, and media specialists can contribute to the quality of a given proposal. Experience suggests that early identification of individuals with skills that may contribute to the development of a given proposal, followed by the provision of time for the individual to work with the

developer in the writing, generally will secure such assistance. Regardless of whether such skills are brought to the development of the document by informal or formal requests for assistance, it is imperative that expectations be clearly delineated and that both the developer and the assisting staff recognize that help offered must be given. There is little room for staff, central to program development, to withdraw or not follow through, once the development calls for their participation.

5. *Communicating Policies for Institutional Approval and Proposal Submittal.* The written communication of clearly established policies governing the submittal of proposals by the institution provides both institutional officers and staff with specific expectations of one another. Such expectations, coupled with provisions to facilitate the submittal of proposals (e.g., providing the developer technical assistance in the development of budgets, filling out federal forms, and typing and reproduction services), can be accepted by staff as functional procedures as opposed to obstacles to be hurdled in submitting proposals. The communication of policies governing submittal should, therefore, provide the developer with the procedures to be followed in securing institutional approval and identify the bugetary constraints (fringe benefits, indirect costs, formulae for calculating salary, etc.) These policies should also provide those responsible for proposal development with a clear statement of assistance available from administrative offices in facilitating the submittal. The delineation and communication of policies and procedures must be standard operating procedure for the institution, not a response to specific requests. This approach significantly decreases the chances for misunderstandings and/or disputes at the time of proposal submittal. Last minute negotiations over the acceptability of proposals or the procedures to be followed at the time of submittal assure the ill will of both staff and administration, a state hardly conducive to future successful development efforts by affected personnel.

6. *Establishing Policies and Procedures to Govern Determination of Feasibility of Submittal.* An institution's eligibility to compete for funding is certainly a necessary condition, but hardly a sufficient reason to submit. For no other reason than that the costs associated with the submittal of a single proposal may be significant (ranging from $50 to thousands of dollars for major competitions), an institution should be able to assess the feasibility of submitting. The decision to submit must consider: the fits between institutional capabilities and proposal specifications; agency and institutional priorities; the relationship between the competition that will be encountered and the demands that will be made on staff to develop the proposal; and the impact of the project on fiscal and programmatic operations, should the effort be successful. In order for the institution to compete for funding in a cost effective manner conducive to effective project implementation, procedures should be firmly established to determine: the identification of institutional capability; the receptivity of both administration and staff to program priorities; the identification of funding agency allocation policies; the nature of the competition; the availability of staff to participate in the development of the document; the attractiveness

of the current opportunity as opposed to projected opportunities; the programmatic and personnel obligations that will be assumed, either formally or informally by the institution, should funding be secured; the implications for future personnel practices and program development priorities; and finally the costs that will be incurred in making a competitive bid, and those associated with securing funding should the bid be successful (e.g., cost-sharing associated with project operations that may not be recoverable through the terms of the grant or contract). The development of policies and procedures to address the previous issues requires the presence of organizational structures that provide program and fiscal officers with the means to communicate systematically with all parties affected by proposal submittal. It also necessitates the development of guidelines that will inform the deliberations on a given submittal. If the institution is not large enough to justify separate organizational units responsible for coordinating all externally funded activities, provisions should be made to establish temporary systems or units (that is, task forces, standing committees, and designated officers and staff) that meet regularly and possess the authority to address these issues. An institution cannot deal effectively with these issues, time and time again, in response to individual staff initiatives concerning individual opportunities. To adopt such an approach is to assure conflict and render the institution incapable of developing a funding program that represents much more than the negotiation of individual interests that appear in response to specific opportunities.

7. Establishing Mechanisms to Assure Ongoing Communication with Community Groups and Other Relevant Organizations. One pattern discernible in both federal and state programs is the increased emphasis on the importance of community participation in program development. Program announcements and Rules and Regulations increasingly are delineating the roles for community personnel and the manner of their selection. Programs addressing the needs of low income and/or disadvantaged groups place the greatest emphasis on community participation in both program development and operation tasks. Programs authorized under Title I of the Elementary and Secondary Education Act, the Emergency School Assistance Act, the Bilingual Education Act, the Indian Education Act, and the Education of the Handicapped Act (administered by the U.S. Office of Education) and the Head Start Program (administered by the Administration for Children, Youth and Families) represent only a few. Given the many demands confronting an institution at the time of responding to a proposal request, identifying appropriate community representatives and establishing roles for them in the development and operation of programs can be virtually insurmountable tasks for the developer. Moreover, the development of collaborative relationships between community representatives and institutions requires a modest level of mutual trust before energies can focus on program and proposal development. Such trust often cannot be established within the time limits set by the solicitation. Given the additional authority and trust variables influencing collaborative submittals, any institution that anticipates the need for citizen involvement or institutional collaboration should establish, within their regular organizational structure, advisory units that include community or institutional representatives. In addition to strengthening the links between institutions and those whom they serve, these units provide a means to address the immediate needs created by a given proposal request.

Before responding to a given request, institutions should be able to identify the appropriate cooperating parties, the roles individuals will play in the development of the proposal, and the policies that will govern the participation of all parties in the program. Often the institutional structures to carry out these tasks already exist in the form of community advisory councils, parent-teacher groups, or advisory boards. When such structures do exist, the task then is to define their roles so that the institution can address the proposal development constraints to collaboration previously identified.

Function: Program Support and Project Monitoring

The institution should possess:

1. Policies and procedures for identifying and communicating the relationship between the roles and expectations held of project staff, as opposed to regular staff.
2. Policies and procedures for payment of project staff on a regular and timely basis. This should include paying essential staff for short periods of time when payments are not authorized by the grant (e.g., periods between notification of award and authorization of project start-up, between start of federal fiscal year and institutional calendar year, and between termination of initial year of funding and start-up date for continuation award).
3. Mechanisms for rapid processing of salary or stipend requests for staff or participants, and the means to purchase and secure materials quickly. These mechanisms may be necessitated by late notification of funding or special needs of staff or participants, which cannot be met by regular but time-consuming bureaucratic procedures of the institution.
4. The means to provide fiscal management assistance, in the form of regular updated budget print-outs, and staff sufficient to develop interim and final fiscal reports and monitor on-going budgetary actions.
5. Mechanisms to report project progress periodically to institutional representatives and interested parties, as well as mechanisms to identify and resolve institutional-project stress.
6. Support structures to work with project staff in identifying strategies for seeking support for project continuation (both internally and externally).

Task Commentary

1. *Delineating Project Personnel Roles and Responsibilites.* The importance of clearly defining the roles and responsibilites of project staff for project

implementation was discussed in the previous chapter. An equally important set of assignment considerations that is often overlooked, however, is the identification and communication of project staff expectations as they relate to the total functioning of the institution. Personnel who are fully committed to carrying out project related responsibilities often feel like second class citizens within an institution because they owe their employment to "soft money." The failure of the institution to recognize and use their skills, which may contribute to the institution's general program delivery capability, or the failure to reward individuals for contributions to the total program may confirm staff's perception of their "second class" status. Give these legitimate concerns, appropriate institutional officers should negotiate with these individuals concerning: the expectations held of them vis-a-vis the general operations of the institution; the factors that will enter into decisions regarding their future status within the institution; and the expectations they legitimately hold of the institution, both during the period of project operation and at termination of the award. The frequency of stress due to differing expectations held of staff by project and institutional administration makes it imperative that the relationships between project assignments and regular institutional assignments, and the resulting expectations of project staff and institutional officers, be firmly established at the time of initial appointment and assignment.

2. *Establishing Policies and Procedures to Assure the Predictability of Compensation.* A major obstacle confronted by many institutions both in implementing and continuing annually funded programs is the failure of the terms of awards to conform with fiscal procedures of the institution. In addition, the fiscal management procedures of the receiving institution may not be appropriate to the financial and support needs of project staff and/or participants. Late payment, and interruptions and errors in payment to staff, indirectly contribute to the reduced effectiveness of any project. The inability to pay and therefore maintain staff between funding periods may also contribute to flawed program development. The common failings of institutional fiscal management mechanisms in adjusting to constraints often set by externally funded programs, and the needs of project staff and participants, require institutions to develop reserve or contingency funds from which a project may draw, up to specified maximum, to meet payroll needs. The development of strategies for addressing the dislocations that may stem from the different fiscal requirements of the participating parties is more important than immediately apparent. The disruptions in operations, which may occur if such strategies are lacking, will only confirm staff feelings of second class status and will unnecessarily raise issues of institutional motivations.

3. *Establishing Mechanisms to Meet Emergency Pay Needs.* For many programs, the ability to transform a request for payment rapidly to available funds assumes a level of importance that cannot be appreciated by individuals accustomed to deferred payment and extended billing as a way of life. Whether the need is for materials critical for tomorrow's activities, stipends to meet living expenses of participants, or a check to meet the needs of a subcontractor of essential services who has become impatient with the slow payment procedures

of the institution, the institution must be able to respond. Although petty cash accounts are often used to meet this need, it is recommended that other procedures, which provide the security and accountability often lacking in the maintenance of petty cash accounts, be developed.

4. *Providing Fiscal Management Assistance.* Educational and human service institutions historically have fallen short of acquiring the level of efficiency necessary to record the fiscal transactions of externally funded programs appropriately and adequately. Most project directors do not possess the necessary background for effective fiscal management and auditing of significantly funded projects. Therefore, the receiving institution must possess both the organizational mechanisms and support personnel essential to effective grant accounting. Staff and/or procedures to develop monthly expenditure reports, time and effort reports, and the development and submittal to appropriate grant accounting offices of interim and final fiscal reports that conform to funding agency specifications are minimal requirements. Project directors, ideally, should be provided grant accounting formats and technical assistance to enable project staff to record expenditures against line items, as a validity check on the accounting provided by designated offices within the organization. Additionally, it is necessary to identify personnel responsible for communicating with the funding agency regarding policies for the appropriate documentation of expenses, transfers between line items, no cost extensions, budget amendments, the schedule and format for the submittal of required reports, and related fiscal and program matters. Such personnel are essential to the effective fiscal management of the project. If the institution's size does not permit the differentiation of roles between program and fiscal personnel, efforts should be made to secure consultation assistance. Such assistance enables the institution to develop a set of procedures to be followed by project directors or other appropriate personnel in the fiscal management of individual projects.

5. *Establishing Mechanisms for the Periodic Reporting of Program Progress.* Projects have a tendency to develop their own identify, which may not be consonant with the initial expectations of the developer or institution, or to operate in isolation from the larger institutional program. Institutions should be able, therefore, to provide technical assistance to a director that enables the project to be perceived as part of the institutional mainstream. Such assistance should facilitate the gathering of data central to the continued development of the project and should provide opportunities for periodic assessment of project progress. Such information serves several purposes: project directors and institutional representatives can assess the relationship between project progress and institutional needs in a relatively nonthreatening environment; adjustments in both institutional practices and project strategies can be made early enough to avoid future conflict; and all parties assume, through their participation in such meetings, a vested interest in the success of the project. The service function of a technical assistance or advisory center (as an integral part of the institution's organizational structure) should never appear to usurp the power of directors or other legitimately concerned individuals but only contribute to the successful implementation of a project. The systematic collection and analysis

of data relevant to a project's operation also makes the submittal of interim and final program reports to the funding agency a much simpler task.

If the technial assistance center concept is expanded slightly, it can provide a base for institutional research to identify and analyze those factors within the institution that contribute to the success or failure of projects. It thereby provides a data base for developing institutional strategies that address the constraints to effective project implementation.

6. *Identifying Strategies for Continued Project Support.* There is an unfortunate tendency for institutions to postpone consideration of strategies for securing project support, beyond the initial period of funding, until the last possible moment. The failure to consider continuation immediately after program inception causes the institution to lose the competitive advantage that is a natural by-product of initial funding. Relationships with the funding agency conducive to the early securing of continuation-relevant information, personnel and organizational structures for planning for program development, staff capable of investing time in the development of a new proposal document, and the several benefits derived from a good track record are a few of the future funding advantages that accrue to an institution through past awards.

Given these advantages, the funded institution should incorporate plans for the development of subsequent proposals into the management plan for the operation of the project. Tasks include: the assessment of alternative funding sources (including the initial sponsor); the securing of data relevant to proposal development (often provided by the day-to-day activities of the current award); and the identification of additional sources of institutional capability (either directly supported by the initial grant or derived from contacts with other individuals and institutions that stem from current project activities).

If the securing of future external funding is not viable, attention should be given to strategies that permit the coadaptation of the project or the adoption of the program by the host institution. Although the latter goal is more difficult, both goals require the developer to identify strategies that result in: visible demonstration of the effectiveness of the project; visible support by those directly affected by the project; support for the project by persons possessing the status to influence those in positions of authority; and recognition by persons, who possess both the power and authority to influence the allocation of funds, of the value of continuation. Although the previous comments do not do justice to the complexity of affecting change, the importance of clearly defined strategies to perpetuate the project beyond the initial termination date set by the grant of contract should be clear. Whether continuation is sought through additional funding or through incorporating the project's goals and activities in the ongoing programs of the institution, strategies must be set long before the date signalling a new competition or the termination of the old program.

SUMMARY

This chapter has identified the major variables that contribute to the state of the funding environment at any particular time. In pursuing this task, those factors that contribute to the shaping of the larger social and political environment have been related to particular trends that contributed to the funding dynamics of the later 1970s. Recognizing that the ability of an institution to secure funding is determined by its awareness of the funding environment, and its ability to respond to that environment, attention focused also on the identification of strategies that will develop an institution's capacity to secure funding systematically and implement programs successfully.

Finally, at the risk of oversimplification, the funding world has been depicted as comprising three major elements: institutions and organizations responsible for determining program and appropriation priorities; institutions and organizations that set the terms and judge the appropriateness of individuals or institutions responding to these priorities; and finally institutions and individuals which seek to meet their own needs or needs of their clients by responding to terms set by those who judge the appropriateness of individual submittals. It is this world one must master in seeking to implement programs by securing a grant or contract.

ENDNOTES

1. Norman C. Thomas. *Education in National Politics* (New York: David McKay Co., 1975), p. 32.
2. Ruth C. Clusen, "The Three Branches of Government," *Washington 76* (Washington, D.C.: District of Columbia Office of Bicentennial Programs, 1976), p. 7.
3. Interview with Allen Schmieder, Program Officer, Teacher Center Program, Washington, D.C., June 1977.
4. Jimmy Carter, quoted in Rufus E. Miles, Jr., *A Cabinet Department of Education, Analysis and Proposal* (Washington, D.C.: American Council on Education, 1977), p. 136.
5. Jimmy Carter, *State of the Union Message,* January 19, 1978 (excerpts from detailed but undelivered version).
6. R.E. Miles, *A Cabinet Department of Education,* p. 1.
7. Ibid., p. 2.
8. Ibid., p. 3.
9. Ibid.
10. Interview with George Kaplan, Officer, Institute for Educational Leadership, Washington, D.C., February 2, 1978.
11. *Federal Register* 42, no. 137 (18 June 1977): 35318.
12. Carol Easton, "The CETA Saga" in *The Grantsmanship Center News* 26, (September/December 1978): 12.
13. Mills v. Board of Education.
14. *The Unfinished Revolution: Education for the Handicapped,* National Advisory Committee on the Handicapped (Washington, D.C.: Government Printing Office, 1976), p. 4.

15. P.L. 94-142, Education for All Handicapped Children Act.
16. U.S., Comptroller General, *Project Head Start: Achievements and Problems,* MWD-75-51, May 20, 1975.
17. U.S., General Accounting Office, *Administration of the Science Education Project, Man: A Course of Study (MACOS),* Report #MWD-76-26, 1975.
18. *Project Head Start,* p. 1.
19. Rep. John Conlan, quote in "NSF: How Much Responsibility for Course Content, Implementation?" *Science* 190 (October–December 1975): 644.

Postscript

This work has advocated constructing a conceptual framework that will allow participants in the world of grants and contracts to cope rationally with what appears at times to be an irrational process. In reviewing the text, I was reminded of the introduction to a novel about the development of a storm, a novel that, in retrospect, must have influenced the choice of metaphors used to illustrate elements of the funding process.

> Every theory of the course of events in nature is necessarily based on some process of simplification of the phenomena and is to some extent therefore a fairy tale.[1]

In developing this work, however, the risk of oversimplification, with the accompanying distortions of reality, was considered a lesser risk than that assumed by focusing on the technical skills prerequisite to securing funding without considering the factors that make up the funding environment. To address the skills necessary for securing funding, without providing the skills and understandings needed to cope with the many jobs required of a person in the development of proposals and the management of projects, was considered both immoral and impractical. Virtue and pragmatism, an odd couple, provided a strong rationale for the approach followed.

The proposition has been offered that, without an understanding of the interdependency of events leading to the formulation of government and foundation programs, the solicitation and awarding of grants and contracts, and the multititude of variables affecting project implementation in a fluid social and political environment, the chances for successful project operation are drastically reduced. One premise that contributed to this approach, which is clearly challengeable, is that programs and projects are designed to improve the conditions of a particular segment of the population or the effectiveness of educational or human service institutions. I chose consciously to proceed with this premise recognizing that one of the major dilemmas that may confront many institutions in the immediate future will be their reliance on federal or state awards to conduct "business as usual," rather than to improve the delivery capability of the institution or to meet the special needs of clientele expecting and deserving special attention.

A second premise that influenced this work was that the funding process is far more complex than immediately apparent to the untrained observer. The motivations and needs of those who participate in the process, from legislation formulation or foundation priority setting to the setting of program guidelines and the development of proposals and implementation of projects, are sufficiently dissonant to introduce conflict into the funding process. It has been proposed that the negotiation of these varying needs, by the several organizational units and the individuals located in these units, energizes the system and creates the dynamics of funding. The very complexity of the phenomenon led to the tendering of a conceptual framework to address the phenomenon; in providing this single framework, the risk of oversimplification was introduced. Clearly, I have risked being subjected to the ridicule that must have been cast on the elderly lady in the following anecdote:

> After delivering a lecture on the solar system, philosopher-psychologist William James was approached by an elderly lady who claimed she had a theory superior to the one described by him.
>
> "We don't live on a ball rotating around the sun," she said. "We live on a crust of earth on the back of a giant turtle."
>
> Not wishing to demolish this absurd argument with the massive scientific evidence at his command, James decided to dissuade his opponent gently.
>
> "If your theory is correct, madam, what does this turtle stand on?"
>
> "You're a very clever man, Mr. James, and that's a good question, but I can answer that. The first turtle stands on the back of a second, far larger, turtle."
>
> "But what does this second turtle stand on?" James asked patiently.
>
> The old lady crowed triumphantly, "It's no use, Mr. James—it's turtles all the way down."[2]

The major difference between the framework set forth in this work and that of the elderly lady is that I prefer the construct of conflict to that of turtles.

Using the solar system as a point of reference, an attempt was made to provide the reader with the means to identify at least the major galaxies within the funding universe and to chart their movements and relationships. The reader has not been seduced, however, into believing that the constellation of events comprising the funding system is so certain or predictable that projections can be formulated with the certainty of the astronomer. Such a temptation would be particularly unfortunate since many of the characteristics of the funding world appear at times to be derived from the theater of the absurd. The funding system will always provide plenty of room for Yossarian of Heller's *Catch 22* to romp.

Should there be any doubt about this last observation, let me include a recent excerpt from a National Science Foundation notice:

> Important Notice to Presidents of Universities and Colleges and Heads of Other NSF Grantee Institutions:
>
> Subject: Revised Submission Procedures for Final Fiscal and Technical Reports
>
> The National Science Foundation has revised its procedures for submitting final NSF grant reports so as to maintain uniformity with the requirements of other Federal Agencies and the provisions of Office of Management and Budget Circular No. A-110.
>
> NSF Important Notice No. 62 issued on May 24, 1976 was intended to simplify the submission of final NSF grant reports. It required that grantee institutions submit Final Fiscal Reports, Final Technical Reports, and Summaries of Completed Project as a single package to NSF's Division of Grants and Contracts.
>
> The provisions of Circular No. A-110 can be interpreted, however, as not requiring submission of all three reports in a single package. Henceforth, therefore, the Final Technical Report need not be submitted along with the Final Fiscal Report and Summary of Completed Report.[3]

What is important to note in closing is that despite the complexity of the process, and despite the elements of the absurd that enter the funding process, the proposal and project provide perhaps the single greatest opportunity to affect an institution's behavior and direct energies creatively to resolving social problems or addressing issues that otherwise might never be confronted directly. It is the opportunity to address apparently unresolvable dilemmas that provides both the frustrations and challenges characteristic of the funding world. Nonparticipation is not a choice open to those seeking to better the condition of persons who rely on the programs of educational and human service institutions to deliver vital services.

ENDNOTES

1. Sir Napier Shaw, quoted by George R. Steward in frontpiece to *Storm*. New York: (Random House, 1941).
2. Bernard Nietschmann, "When the Turtle Collapses, the World Ends," *Natural History* 83 (June 1974): 34-43.
3. National Science Foundation. "Important Notice to Presidents of Universities and Colleges and Heads of Other NSF Grantee Institutions" (April 1977).

APPENDIX *A*

Locating Sources of Federal Funding through Government Publications

The use of U.S. Government Printing Office literature on funding provides a relatively inexpensive way to locate sources of funding appropriate to an institution's needs.

Catalogue of Federal Domestic Assistance (CFDA)

The *Catalogue of Federal Domestic Assistance (CFDA)*, published annually, is the most comprehensive listing of federal programs available anywhere. It explains the types of assistance each program provides, the purpose of the program, who is eligible, and how to apply. Seven different indices provide alternative cues for locating programs. The three most widely used indices are: the simple *subject* index, the *agency* index, and the *functional* index. The subject index is self-explanatory. The agency index lists programs by the agency administering them. Since agencies administer programs of similar content, this index can provide a shortcut for locating possible funding sources. Read the descriptions of all the programs the particular agency of interest is funding. The functional index is useful in identifying the general nature of assistance available in a broad program area.

The programs listed in *CFDA* are identified by a numerical code of five digits, placing them in an organizational context and identifying the page on which the necessary information can be found. To illustrate, the program entitled "Special Programs for the Aging—Research and Demonstration" has the number 13.636. Thirteen (13) identifies the federal agency responsible for the program (in this case, the Department of Health, Education, and Welfare). The third digit (6) refers to the office administering the program (the Office of Human Development). The last two digits refer to the particular program.

Since these code numbers are used by various federal and nonfederal publications to identify programs, a knowledge of the numbering system avoids confusion in identifying program references in other publications.

312 The Dynamics of Funding

Within the *Catalogue,* program listings contain the following pertinent information:

Authorization—Identifies the law authorizing the federal program.

Objectives—Cites the goals and provides a description of the program. In addition, there are two other sections, "Use and Use Restrictions" and "Program Accomplishments," that acquaint the reader with the substance of the program.

Eligibility Requirements—Identifies potential applicants.

Financial Information—Provides an approximate range of funding to match against a submitting institution's expected program support needs.

Regulations, Guidelines and Literature—Lists all relevant literature on the program.

Information Contacts—Identifies the regional or local offices responsible for administering the program; the Headquarters Office in Washington, D.C., is also listed with address and telephone number.

Related Program—Identifies similar programs that might be of interest to the potential submitter.

A sample program description illustrates the full range of information that can be secured from this information source:

TABLE A.1 13.562 Education for Gifted and Talented Children and Youth (Gifted and Talented)

FEDERAL AGENCY: OFFICE OF EDUCATION, DEPARTMENT OF HEALTH, EDUCATION, AND WELFARE

AUTHORIZATION: Education Amendments of 1974, Title IV Section 404, Public Law 93-380; 20 U.S.C. 821.

OBJECTIVES: To support State and local planning, development, operation and improvement of program and projects designed to meet the special educational needs of the gifted and talented at preschool, elementary, and secondary levels; development and dissemination of information pertaining to such education; inservice training of educational personnel working with gifted and talented and their supervisors; leadership training, including internships; and model or exemplary projects.

TYPES OF ASSISTANCE: Project Grants (Contracts)

USES AND USE RESTRICTIONS: The Commissioner is authorized to contract with public or private agencies or organizations for education of gifted and talented children and youth, and for model projects. Grants may be made to State educational agencies (or consortia thereof) and local educational agencies to assist them in planning, development, operation, and improvement of programs and projects designed to meet the special educational needs of gifted and talented children at preschool, elementary, and secondary school levels.

TABLE A.1. (cont.)

Grants may be made to State educational agencies (and consortia) to assist them in programs for training personnel engaged in or preparing to engage in educating gifted and talented children. Grants may be made to institutions of higher education and other appropriate non-profit institutions to provide training to leadership personnel for the education of gifted and talented children and youth and for internships. JOINT FUNDING: This program is considered particularly suitable (eligible) for joint funding with other closely related Federal financial assistance programs in accordance with the provisions of OMB Circular No. A-111. For programs that are not identified as particularly suitable or eligible for joint funding, applicant may consult the headquarters or field office of the appropriate funding agency for further information on statutory or other restrictions involved.

ELIGIBILITY REQUIREMENTS:

Applicant Eligibility: Applications for grants may be submitted by State and local educational agencies, institutions of higher education, and non-profit institutions or agencies. Contracts may be awarded to public or private agencies and organizations.

Beneficiary Eligibility: Gifted and talented children and youth; personnel engaged or preparing to engage in educating gifted and talented children or as supervisors of such personnel; and other leadership personnel.

Credentials/Documentation: Costs will be determined in accordance with FMC 74-4 for State and local agencies.

APPLICATION AND AWARD PROCESS:

Preapplication Coordination: The standard application forms as furnished by the Federal agency and required by FMC 74-7 must be used for this program.

Application Procedure: Applications should be sent to U.S. OE Applications Control Center, Room 5673, ROB No. 3, 7th and D Streets, S.W., Washington, DC; mailing address: U.S. OE Applications Control Center, 400 Maryland Avenue, S.W., Washington, DC 2020. This program is subject to the provisions of OMB Circular No. A-110.

Award Procedure: Applications are processed and assigned to field readers for review. Recommendations are made to the Director, Office of Gifted and Talented concerning approval or disapproval and the suggested funding level. A funding recommendation is made to the Commissioner of Education.

Deadlines: As announced in the Federal Register.

Range of Approval/Disapproval Time: Approximately 120 days.

Appeals: Appeals may be made to deputy Commissioner, Bureau of Education for the Handicapped.

Renewals: Renewals are made only through reapplication on an annual basis.

ASSISTANCE CONSIDERATIONS:

Formula and Matching Requirements: There are no matching requirements.

Length and Time Phasing of Assistance: The award period is for 12 months beginning from July 1 through June 30 of the following year.

POST ASSISTANCE REQUIREMENTS:

Reports: Progress reports and final reports as required by grant document.

Audits: Post-Audit plus periodic audits during life of project.

Records: Records are to be retained as required by grant document.

314 The Dynamics of Funding

TABLE A.1. (cont.)

FINANCIAL INFORMATION:
Account Identification: 75-0270-0-1-503.
Obligations: (Grants and contracts) FY 76 $612,000; TQ $1,948,000; FY 77 $2,560,000; and FY 78 est $2,560,000.
Range and Average of Financial Assistance: $6,000 to $200,000; $48,301.
PROGRAM ACCOMPLISHMENTS: In fiscal year 1976, 53 projects were supported; In fiscal year 1977, 76 projects were supported. In fiscal year 1978, it is estimated that 66 projects will be supported.
REGULATIONS, GUIDELINES, AND LITERATURE: Regulations published — the Federal Register, May 6, 1976, Vol. 41, Number 89, pp. 18660-18673.
INFORMATION CONTACTS:
Regional or Local Office: Not applicable.
Headquarters Office: Dr. Dorothy Sisk, Director, Gifted and Talented Staff, Office of the Deputy Commissioner, Bureau of Education for the Handicapped, U.S. Office of Education, 400 Maryland Ave., S.W., Washington, DC 20202. Telephone: (202) 245-2482.
RELATED PROGRAMS: 13485, Strengthening State Departments of Education-Grants for Special Projects; 13.486, Strengthening State Departments of Education-Grants to States; 13.519, Supplementary Educational Centers and Services, Guidance, Counseling and Testing; 13.525, Emergency School Aid Act-Basic Grants to Local Educational Agencies; 13.561, Education for the Use of the Metric System of Measurement; 45.115, Promotion of the Humanities-Youth Programs.

The *Catalogue* can be ordered from the Superintendent of Document, U.S. Government Printing Office, Washington, D.C. 20402, for about $18.00. Many libraries have the *Catalogue* in loose-leaf construction to allow easy photocopying.

Code of Federal Regulations

The *Code of Federal Regulations (CFR)* is the government's official publication of the Rules and Regulations for all federal agency programs. Guidelines for every program of federal assistance are compiled in four volumes. Most educational and social service programs are included in Title 45 "Public Welfare." Updated and published every fall, the *CFR* can also be ordered from the U.S. Government Printing Office.

Federal Register

The *Code of Federal Regulations* is regularly updated by the daily government publication, the *Federal Register (FR)*. Proposed rule changes, notice of due dates, criteria for selection of applicants, Proposed and Final Rules and Regulations, and other information essential to a funding search are all published first in the *Federal Register.*

Since a program's regulations are often revised or amended each year, it is unwise to depend on the *CFR* alone. Use of both the *CFR* and the *FR* provides the complete, current regulations for any given program. A yearly subscription to the *Federal Register,* which is published daily, can be purchased from the Government Printing Office.

If a daily scanning of the *Federal Register* is not possible, an alternative strategy to secure up-to-date information on a particular program is to contact the program office directly. Information about the expected *FR* publication dates of Intent to Publish Rules and Regulations, Proposed Rules & Regulations, Final Rules and Regulations, or Announcement of a Closing Date for Receipt of Applications is usually available from a program officer.

Commerce Business Daily

This daily publication provides a synopsis of all U.S. Government agency proposal procurement, sales, and contract awards. Requests for proposals (RFPs) are announced through this publication. As the *CBD* carries contract rather than grant notices, it is more useful to organizations competing for major awards than for the average school system or community agency.

Congressional Directory

Although not directly related to the location of funding sources, the data on members of the Senate and House (listed by state and district) and the identification of committee assignments of representatives and senators enables potential submitters to assess the impact individual representatives may have on the funding process.

United States Government Manual

Like the *Directory*, this publication provides valuable background information to guide the efforts of the potential submitter. Descriptions and charts of federal agencies and names of officials enable the reader to obtain a profile of the federal government and follow up on potential leads with appropriate officials.

The latest edition of *A Compilation of Federal Education Laws* provides an institution with most legislation authorizing individual programs. For recent laws that are not contained in the latest edition, staff in offices of local congressmen generally provide the most reliable source of information and will obtain copies of pertinent legislation for interested institutions or individuals. Alternately, single copies of individual bills can be obtained by sending a self-addressed mailing label to the following:

House Document Room
U.S. Capitol Building
Room H-226
Washington, D.C. 20515

or

Senate Document Room
U.S. Capitol Building
Room S-325
Washington, D.C. 20510

Application Kits

The program office will also send, on request, an application packet that includes all the materials needed to write a proposal. If the application packet is not yet available, they will place you on a mailing list. Addresses and telephone numbers of program officers are given in the *Catalogue of Federal Domestic Assistance.*

These application kits provide a submitting institution with all the information needed to meet minimal requirements for proposal submittal and review. Most application kits contain: the most recent Rules and Regulations, proposal due date, excerpts from authozing legislation, and federal forms and instructions for completion.

American Education is published ten times a year by the Office of Education, U.S. Department of Health, Education, and Welfare. The publication of this periodical, which the Secretary of HEW has determined "is necessary in the transaction of the public business required by law, of this Department"[*] provides a valuable overview of Office of Educational activities. This department also publishes an annual *Guide to OE-Administered Programs.* The range of information provided by this guide is illustrated by the following excerpt on p. 317.

---

[*]*American Education.* Office of Education, U.S. Department of Health, Education, and Welfare. Washington, D.C. 20202

TABLE A.2. Excerpt from *Guide to OE-Administered Programs*

TYPE OF ASSISTANCE	AUTHORIZING LEGISLATION	PURPOSE	APPROPRIATION (dollars)	WHO MAY APPLY	WHERE TO APPLY
GROUP I: TO INSTITUTIONS, AGENCIES, AND ORGANIZATIONS PART A — For Elementary and Secondary Education Programs					
1. Bilingual education basic programs (OMB Cat No. 13.403)[1]	Elementary and Secondary Education Act, Title VII	To develop and operate programs for children ages 3-18 with limited English-speaking ability	85,725,000 (includes inservice training component	Local education agencies or institutions of higher education (they may apply jointly)	OE Application Control Center (information from OE Office of Bilingual Education)
2. Bilingual education support services (OMB Cat No. 13.403)	Elementary and Secondary Education Act. Title VII	To operate regional centers providing assistance to bilingual education teachers in local districts (training resource centers), develop bilingual curriculum materials (material development centers), or evaluating and printing such materials (assessment dissemination centers)	12,000,000	Local educational agencies or institutions of higher education (they may apply jointly): state education agencies may apply for training resource centers	OE Application Control Center (information from OE Office of Bilingual Education)
3. Community schools (OMB Cat. No. 13.563)	Education Amendments of 1974. Special Projects Act, Sec. 405	To assist state and local education agencies in establishing community schools: to train personnel to plan and operate community education programs	3,553,000	State and local education agencies, higher education institutions	OE Bureau of Occupational and Adult Education
4. Education and the Arts (omb Cat. No. 13.566)	Education Amendments of 1974. Special Projects Act, Sec. 409	To encourage the establishment of arts education programs at elementary and secondary levels	1,750,000	State and local education agencies	OE Arts and Humanities Staff. Office of the Commissioner
5. Educational innovation and support (OMB Cat. No. 13.571)	Elementary and Secondary Education Act. Title IV-C	To improve leadership resources of state and local education agencies: to support innovative and exemplary projects, nutrition and health service and dropout prevention	184,521,852[2]	State and local education agencies	OE Division of State Educational Assistance Programs
6. Heritage Studies (OMB Cat. No. 13549)	Elementary and Secondary Education Act. Title IX	To develop intercultural understanding among individuals living in a pluralistic society: to promote mutual understanding among various U.S. ethnic groups	2,300,000	Public or private nonprofit education agencies. institutions or organizations	OE Application Control Center (information from OE Ethnic Heritage Studies Branch)
7. Follow Through (OMB Cat. No. 13.433)	Community Services Act (P.L. 93-644). Title V	To extend into primary grades educational gains made by deprived children in Head Start of similar preschool programs	59,000,000	Local education or other agencies nominated by state education agencies in accordance with OE criteria	OE Application Control Center (information from OE Division of Follow Through)

317

APPENDIX B

Researching Foundations

Two major sources of information for researching foundations are *The Foundation Directory* and *The Foundation Grants Index* published annually by The Foundation Center, an independent nonprofit organization located in New York City with regional cooperating libraries in fifty states. (Addresses of national and regional collections are listed on the final page of this index.)

The Foundation Directory provides the names, addresses, and telephone numbers of foundations that account for more than 80 percent of all foundation grants in the country. Name and location data is complemented by names of donors, statements of purpose, financial data (assets, expenditures, total grants, number of grants awarded, highest and lowest awards), names of officers and trustees, and general grant application information. Indices and Appendices to the Directory complement the data found in the body of the work.

The Foundation Grants Index provides an annual cumulation of grant information and recipient and key-word subject indices derived from reports of individual foundations to the Center. Section one of the Index contains grants listed by state; within each state section, foundations are alphabetically listed. Each recipient entry is given a sequential identification number. A hypothetical entry in the *Index* reveals the range of information provided:
Codes for additional information are:

LM — program, geographic, or other limitation set by the foundation
RP — type of recipient
PG — population group to receive benefit from the activity
PH — phase of activity
LO — site(s) of activity other than recipient location
SD — source of grant data

320   The Dynamics of Funding

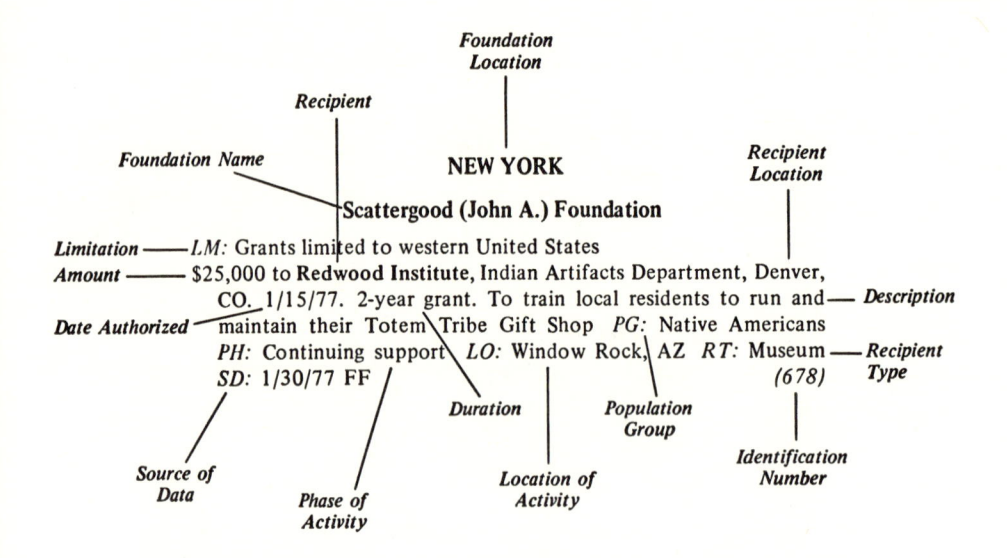

```
                                    Foundation
                                    Location
                      Recipient         |
                          |             |
   Foundation Name        |         NEW YORK              Recipient
                          |                                Location
                     Scattergood (John A.) Foundation
Limitation ——— LM: Grants limited to western United States
Amount ——— $25,000 to Redwood Institute, Indian Artifacts Department, Denver,
              CO. 1/15/77. 2-year grant. To train local residents to run and — Description
Date Authorized — maintain their Totem Tribe Gift Shop  PG: Native Americans
              PH: Continuing support   LO: Window Rock, AZ  RT: Museum —— Recipient
              SD: 1/30/77 FF                                   (678)       Type
                                    Duration     Population
                                                  Group
       Source of                                           Identification
         Data        Phase of       Location of              Number
                     Activity        Activity
```

The Foundation Grants Index, 1977. New York, The Foundation Center, 1978. (Distributed by Columbia University Press, 136 South Broadway, Irvington, New York 10533. $20.00). Reprinted by permission.

The source of grant data, which is generally the date the information was released, may be followed by:

FF — information supplied directly by granting foundation on Form 102 (see Appendix E)

NR — news release

NL — news letter

FS — financial statement

AR — IRS Form 990 AR

R — foundation's latest published report as of date recorded

Section two contains an alphabetical listing of domestic and foreign recipients, their locations, and their locations, and their grant ID numbers.

Section three contains an alphabetical listing of Key Words and Phrases, which refer to the grant description or type of recipient, followed by the ID number. These key words are chosen by the foundations. As foundations may categorize their interests in different ways, the same type of grant may appear under several different key words and phrases.

Section four contains an alphabetical listing of the subject categories of the grants, and each category contains an alphabetical listing of the location of the grant followed by the ID number.

Section five contains an alphabetical listing of the granting foundations and their addresses.

Updates of the *Foundation Grants Index* appears in *Foundation News*, the bimonthly journal published by the Council on Foundations, Inc.

Additional support materials available from the Center include listings of grants made to individuals, computor print-outs by subject area, and papers and pamphlets that address specific aspects of proposal writing and foundation operations.

Further information may be obtained by writing tax Center Offices and/or cooperating collections listed below.

Foundation Center National Libraries

The Foundation Center
888 Seventh Avenue
New York, New York 10019

The Foundation Center
1001 Connecticut Avenue, N.W.
Washington, D.C. 20036

Foundation Center Field Offices

The Foundation Center—San Francisco
312 Sutter Street
San Francisco, California 94108

The Foundation Center—Cleveland
Kent H. Smith Library
739 National City Bank Building
629 Euclid Avenue
Cleveland, Ohio 44114

National Cooperating Collection

Donors Forum of Chicago
208 South LaSalle Street
Chicago, Illinois 60604

Regional Cooperating Collections

ALABAMA
Birmingham Public Library
2020 Seventh Avenue, North
Birmingham 35203

Auburn University at Montgomery
  Library
Montgomery 36117

ALASKA

University of Alaska, Anchorage
  Library
3211 Providence Drive
Anchorage 99504

ARIZONA

Tucson Public Library
Main Library
200 S. Sixth Avenue
Tucson 85701

ARKANSAS

Westark Community College Library
Grand at Waldron
Fort Smith 72913

Little Rock Public Library
Reference Department
700 Louisiana Street
Little Rock 72201

CALIFORNIA

Edward L. Doheny Memorial Library
University of Southern California
Los Angeles 90007

San Diego Public Library
820 E Street
San Diego 92101

COLORADO

Denver Public Library
Sociology Division
1368 Broadway
Denver 80203

CONNECTICUT

Hartford Public Library
Reference Department
500 Main Street
Hartford 06103

DELAWARE

Hugh Morris Library
University of Delaware
Newark 19711

FLORIDA

Jacksonville Public Library
Business, Science, and Industry Department
122 North Ocean Street
Jacksonville 32202

Miami-Dade Public Library
Florida Collection
One Biscayne Boulevard
Miami 33132

GEORGIA

Atlanta Public Library
10 Pryor Street, S.W.
Atlanta 30303
(also covers Alabama, Florida, South Carolina, and Tennessee)

HAWAII

Thomas Hale Hamilton Library
University of Hawaii
Humanities and Social Science Division
2550 The Mall
Honolulu 96822

IDAHO

Caldwell Public Library
1010 Dearborn Street
Caldwell 83605

ILLINOIS

Sangamon State University Library
Shepherd Road
Springfield 62708

INDIANA

Indianapolis–Marion County Public Library
40 East St. Clair Street
Indianapolis 46204

IOWA

Des Moines Public Library
100 Locust Street
Des Moines 50309

KANSAS

Topeka Public Library
Adult Services Department
1515 West Tenth Street
Topeka 66604

KENTUCKY
Louisville Free Public Library
Fourth and York Street
Louisville 40203

LOUISIANA
New Orleans Public Library
Business and Science Division
219 Loyola Avenue
New Orleans 70140

MAINE
University of Southern Maine
Center for Research and Advanced Study
246 Deering Avenue
Portland 04102

MARYLAND
Enoch Pratt Free Library
Social Science and History Department
400 Cathedral Street
Baltimore 21201
  (also covers District of Columbia)

MASSACHUSETTS
Associated Foundation of Greater Boston
294 Washington Street, Suite 501
Boston 01208

Boston Public Library
Copley Square
Boston 02117

MICHIGAN
Henry Ford Centennial Library
15301 Michigan Avenue
Dearborn 48126

Purdy Library
Wayne State University
Detroit 48202

Michigan State University Library
Main Library—Reference Department
East Lansing 48824

Grand Rapids Public Library
Sociology and Education Department
Library Plaza
Grand Rapids 49502

MINNESOTA
Minneapolis Public Library
Sociology Department
300 Nicollet Mall
Minneapolis 55401
  (also covers North and South Dakota)

MISSISSIPPI
Jackson Metropolitan Library
301 North State Street
Jackson 39201

MISSOURI
Clearinghouse for Midcontinent
  Foundations
University of Missouri, Kansas City
School of Education Building
52nd Street and Holmes
Kansas City 64110

Kansas City Public Library
311 East 12th Street
Kansas City 64106
  (also covers Kansas)

The Danforth Foundation Library
222 South Central Avenue
St. Louis 63105

Springfield–Greene County Library
397 East Central Street
Springfield 65801

MONTANA
Eastern Montana College Library
Reference Department
Billings 59101

NEBRASKA
W. Dale Clark Library
Social Sciences Department
215 South 15th Street
Omaha 68102

NEVADA
Clark County Library
1401 East Flamingo Road
Las Vegas 89109

Washoe County Library
301 South Center Street
Reno 89505

NEW HAMPSHIRE
The New Hampshire Charitable Fund
One South Street
Concord 03301

NEW JERSEY
New Jersey State Library
Reference Section
1985 West State Street
Trenton 08625

NEW MEXICO
New Mexico State Library
300 Don Gaspar Street
Santa Fe 87501

NEW YORK
New York State Library
State Education Department
Education Building
Albany 12224

Buffalo and Erie County Public Library
Lafayette Square
Buffalo 14203

Levittown Public Library
Reference Department
One Bluegrass Lane
Levittown 11756

Rochester Public Library
Business and Social Science Division
115 South Avenue
Rochester 14604

Onondaga County Public Library
335 Montgomery Street
Syracuse 13202

NORTH CAROLINA
North Carolina State Library
109 East Jones Street
Raleigh 27611

The Winston-Salem Foundation
229 First Union National Bank Building
Winston-Salem 27101

NORTH DAKOTA
The Library
North Dakota State University
Fargo 58105

OKLAHOMA
Oklahoma City Community Foundation
1300 North Broadway
Oklahoma City 73103

Tulsa City-County Library System
400 Civic Center
Tulsa 74103

OREGON
Library Association of Portland
Education and Psychology Department
801 S. W. Tenth Avenue
Portland 97205

PENNSYLVANIA
The Free Library of Philadelphia
Logan Square
Philadelphia 19103
(also covers Delaware)

Hillman Library
University of Pittsburgh
Pittsburgh 15213

RHODE ISLAND
Providence Public Library
Reference Department
150 Empire Street
Providence 02903

SOUTH CAROLINA
South Carolina State Library
Reader Services Department
1500 Senate Street
Columbia 29211

SOUTH DAKOTA
South Dakota State Library
State Library Building
322 South Fort Street
Pierre 57501

TENNESSEE
Memphis Public Library
1850 Peabody Avenue
Memphis 38104

TEXAS
The Hogg Foundation for Mental Health
The University of Texas
Austin 78712

Dallas Public Library
History and Social Sciences Division
1954 Commerce Street
Dallas 75201
  (also covers Arkansas, Louisiana,
  New Mexico, and Oklahoma)

El Paso Community Foundation
El Paso National Bank Building,
  Suite 1616
El Paso 79901

Minnie Stevens Piper Foundation
201 North St. Mary's Street
San Antonio 78205

UTAH

Salt Lake City Public Library
Information and Adult Services
209 East Fifth Street
Salt Lake City 84111

VERMONT

State of Vermont Department of Libraries
Reference Services Unit
111 State Street
Montpelier 05602

VIRGINIA

Richmond Public Library
Business, Science, & Technology
  Department
101 East Franklin Street
Richmond 23219

WASHINGTON

Seattle Public Library
1000 Fourth Avenue
Seattle 98104

Spokane Public Library
Reference Department
West 906 Main Avenue
Spokane 99201

WEST VIRGINIA

Kanawha County Public Library
123 Capitol Street
Charleston 25301

WISCONSIN
Marquette University Memorial Library
1415 West Wisconsin Avenue
Milwaukee 53233
  (also covers Illinois)

WYOMING
Laramie County Communt College
  Library
1400 East College Drive
Cheyenne 82001

PUERTO RICO
Consumer Education and Service Center
Department of Consumer Affairs
Minillas Central Government Building
  North
Santurce 00908
  (covers selected foundations)

MEXICO
Biblioteca Benjamin Franklin
Landres 16
Mexico City 6, D.F.
  (covers selected foundations)

APPENDIX C

Locating Federal and Foundation Funding Information through Nongovernmental Publications

The complexity of the funding system and the influence of individual legislative and/or agency decisions on specific programs limits the ability of the formal communications of government agencies or foundations to meet the information needs of institutions. Private and professional organizations, therefore, have found a market for services that assist institutions and individuals in identifying, interpreting, and responding to changes in the funding environment. The following publications are particularly helpful in this respect and are valuable complements to federal sources of information.

Federal Education Program Guide

This directory of education programs and administrators contains detailed organizational charts, as well as the names, addresses, and phone numbers of officers and staff associated with individual programs. Federal program descriptions drawn from the *Catalogue of Federal Domestic Assistance* are also presented. The format and clarity of the information enables the potential submitter to identify programs of potential interest quickly and to follow up on the information with program officers. (Published annually.)

Other news services provided by the publisher of this directory include:

Education Daily—Covers all federal involvement in education, and significant developments at the state and local level. Computerized Quarterly and Cumulative annual indexes. (Published every business day.)

Higher Education Daily—The daily news service for administrators in postsecondary education (indexed). College-level counterpart to Education Daily.

Education and Work—A bi-weekly newsletter on career education and the partnership of educators and employers.

Report on Education Research—A bi-weekly publication focusing on federal programs, funding, and education research policy.

Report on Education of the Disadvantaged—A bi-weekly news service about early childhood education, Head Start, day care, and all federal programs for preschool education.

Education of the Handicapped—Bi-weekly news about special education, federal programs, funding, policy, and trends.

School Law News—A bi-weekly report on legal developments, court decisions, student's rights, teacher's rights, privacy, school board liability, and desegregation.

Equal Opportunity in High Education—Bi-weekly news about Title IX, race and sex discrimination, and affirmative action in postsecondary education.

Further information may be secured by writing:

>Education News Services Div.
>Capitol Publications, Inc.
>Suite G-12T
>2430 Pennsylvania Avenue, N.W.
>Washington, D.C. 20037

The Federal Funding Guide for Elementary & Secondary Education

Although limited to elementary and secondary education programs, this publication contains a range of information related to Federal funding, in addition to program descriptions. Highlights of recent legislation, directories of personnel, and an overview of pending legislation are complemented by up-to-date information on individual program priorities, the history of funding in individual program areas, and an overview of the legislation relevant to individual programs. The program descriptions are complete and clear, and include the name, address, and telephone number of a contact person. (Published annually.)

Other news services provided by the publisher include:

Education Funding News—Covers the status of evolving legislation and appropriations, summarizes programs and all announcements of grants, contracts, and requests for proposals that appeared in the *Federal Register* and *Commerce Business Daily* during the previous week.

Congressional Boxscore—Published periodically, this publication describes briefly the major legislation introduced in Congress that is of interest to schools; all information necessary to trace the bill in the legislative process is provided. Further information may be obtained by writing:

Education Funding Research Council
75 National Press Building, N.W.
Washington, D.C. 20045

Contract & Grants Annual

Covers many of the same areas as the two preceding annual publications, with one important distinction; coverage is extended to the full range of activity in the human resources areas.

Other services that complement the *Annual* include:

Federal Funding for Social Research & Demonstration—This bi-weekly publication carries articles on program developments, summaries of program announcements, closing dates for application, and related information particularly relevant to human resource areas.

Human Resource Consultant—Reports on research, evaluation, and development opportunities in human resources areas; analyses of trends in the fields of manpower development; and human service program delivery are also provided.

Further information may be obtained by writing to:

Responsive Procurement Exchange
1204 Half Street, S.W.
Washington, D.C. 20024

The Grantsmanship Center News

Published six times a year by the Grantsmanship Center, this periodical provides perhaps the most comprehensive treatment of the full range of events that shape the funding environment. In addition to information directly related to the submittal of proposals to both foundations and government agencies, this publication traces legislative, legal, and political developments of relevance to the fundraiser. "Background" articles make *News* the *Time* or *U.S. News & World Report* of the funding world.

The Grantsmanship Center, which is "committed to enhancing the quality of human service programs by improving the planning and management skills of private nonprofit and public agencies" through the distribution of reprints of articles and the offering of training programs, provides a wide range of services of value to individuals seeking to secure grant or contract support for education and human service programs. Further information may be obtained by writing:

The Grantsmanship Center
1015 West Olympic Blvd.,
Los Angeles, CA 90015

The above publications are only a few of the many valuable private sources of information available to institutions seeking external funding. In addition, professional associations involved with particular subject areas provide information of particular interest to member institutions through newsletters, reports, and periodicals.

It should also be noted that private and professional organizations increasingly are providing workshops, consultant services, "hot-lines," and so forth to equip subscribing or member institutions to compete in the quest for federal, state, or foundation dollars. Many of the organizations previously cited offer a full range of services in these areas.

APPENDIX *D*

Department of Health Education, and Welfare Regional Headquarters Offices

Although the authority of regional offices of DHEW rises and falls under different administrations, which prohibits identifying their influence on the administration of specific programs, these offices are generally a valuable source of information regarding program status and relevant program developments. Regional offices are located in:

I. MASSACHUSETTS
JFK Federal Office Bldg.
Government Center
Boston, MA 02203

II. NEW YORK
Federal Building
26 Federal Plaza
New York, NY 10007

III. PENNSYLVANIA
3535 Market Street
Philadelphia, PA 19108

IV. GEORGIA
50 Seventh St., N.E.
Atlanta, GA 30323

V. ILLINOIS
300 S. Wacker Drive
Chicago, IL 60606

VI. TEXAS
1114 Commerce St.
Dallas, TX 75202

VII. MISSOURI
601 E. 12 St.
Kansas City, MO 64106

VIII. COLORADO
Federal Office Bldg.
1961 Stout St.
Denver, CO 80202

IX. CALIFORNIA
50 Fulton St.
San Francisco, CA 94102

X. WASHINGTON
Arcade Plaza Bldg.
1321 Second Ave.
Seattle, WA 98101

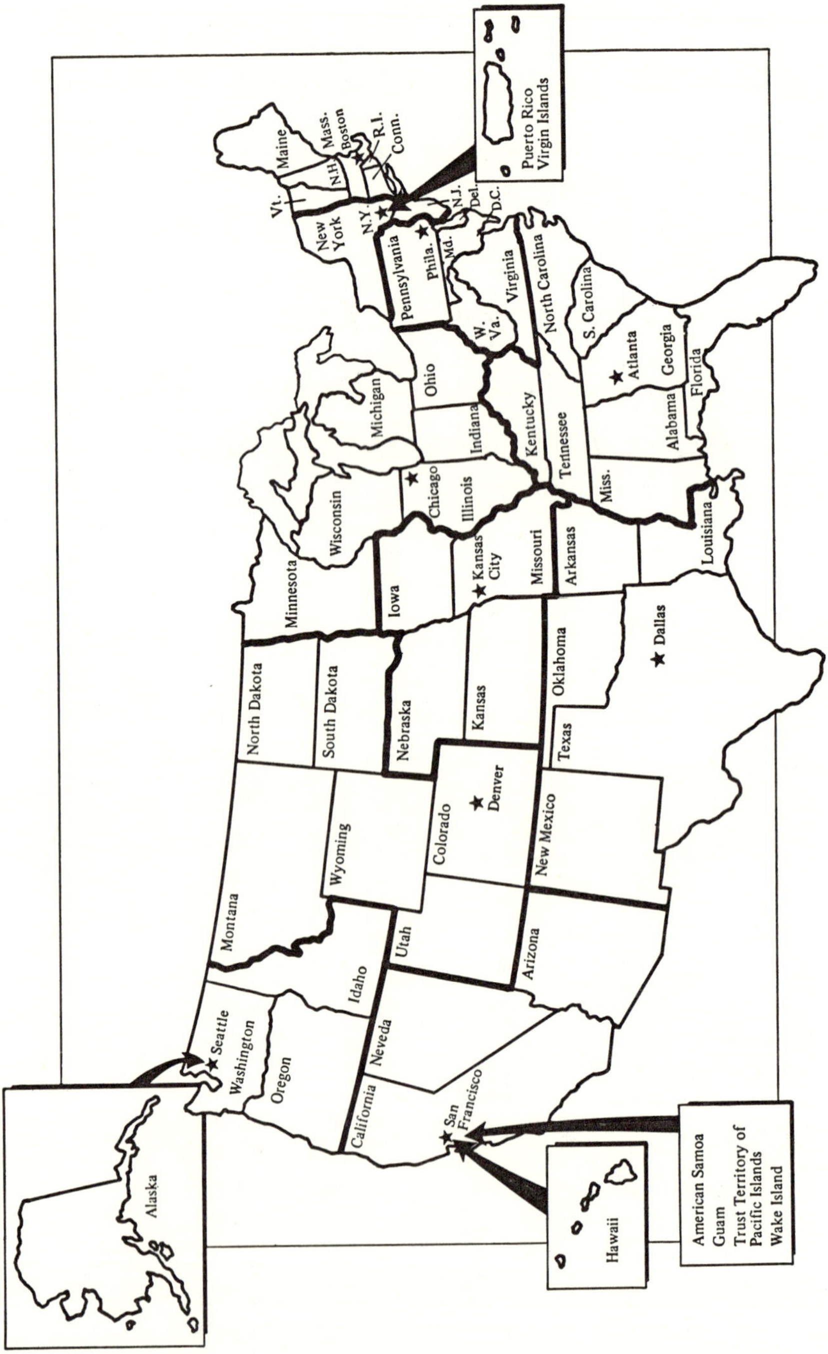

Puerto Rico
Virgin Islands
Maine
Vt.
N.H.
Mass.
Boston
R.I.
Conn.
New York
N.Y.
N.J.
Del.
D.C.
Md.
Pennsylvania
Phila.
Virginia
W. Va.
North Carolina
S. Carolina
Atlanta
Georgia
Florida
Ohio
Michigan
Indiana
Kentucky
Tennessee
Alabama
Miss.
Chicago
Illinois
Wisconsin
Louisiana
Arkansas
Missouri
Kansas City
Iowa
Minnesota
Oklahoma
Dallas
Texas
North Dakota
South Dakota
Nebraska
Kansas
Denver
Colorado
New Mexico
Wyoming
Montana
Utah
Arizona
Idaho
Nevada
Seattle
Washington
Oregon
California
San Francisco
Alaska
Hawaii
American Samoa
Guam
Trust Territory of Pacific Islands
Wake Island

APPENDIX E

Federal Assistance Forms and Instructions for Completion

All proposals for federal assistance must be accompanied by standard forms developed by the government in accordance with Federal Management Office and Office of Management and Budget (OMB) circulars. Although the federal government is making a concerted effort to standardize all forms across agencies, specific program and agency forms will show some variation for the immediate future.

Instructions for Application for Federal Assistance are provided in "application kits" provided by the funding agency. In addition to General Instructions (Standard Form 424), which pertain to all HEW grant programs, there are also Supplemental Instructions which relate to the specific grant program for which application is being made. These instructions are to be used in lieu of or along with the standard instructions.

The five Parts or Sections contained in the Instructions for Application are as follows:

Part I — Applicant/Recipient Data
Part II — Project Approval Information
Part III — Budget Information
Part IV — Program Narrative (the proposal text developed by the submitter)
Part V — Assurances
  1. Assurance of Compliance with the Department of Health, Education, and Welfare Regulation under Title VI of the Civil Rights Act of 1964

2. Assurance of Compliance with the DHEW Regulation under Title VI of the Civil Rights Act of 1964
3. Assurance of Compliance of Title IX of the Education Amendments of 1972
4. Protection of Human Subjects Assurance/Certification/ Declaration.

Following find copies of the forms and Instructions for Application contained in most federal proposal application kits with the exception of the Assurance forms. The Supplemental Instructions are designed for applications to the Gifted and Talented Program, U.S. Office of Education.

Appendix E   339

FIGURE E.1. *Instructions for Application for Federal Assistance, Prototypes from Education for the Handicapped–Gifted and Talented Program.*

DEPARTMENT OF HEALTH, EDUCATION, AND WELFARE
OFFICE OF EDUCATION
WASHINGTON, D.C. 20202

FORM APPROVED
OMB NO. 51-R1149

EDUCATION FOR THE HANDICAPPED – GIFTED AND TALENTED PROGRAM
INSTRUCTIONS FOR APPLICATION FOR FEDERAL ASSISTANCE (Nonconstruction Programs)

GENERAL

This form shall be used to apply to the Gifted and Talented Program of the Office of Education (OE). This form shall be used also to request supplemental assistance, to propose changes or amendments, and to request continuation or refunding, for approved grants originally submitted on this form. No grant will be awarded unless a completed application has been received (Pub Law 93-380, Section 404).

Submit the original and two copies of the forms.

PART I

Part I of this application consists of the standard face page for Federal applications and the concomitant instructions. The Gifted and Talented Program is not presently included as a program under OMB Circular No. A-95, the regulations for facilitating coordinated planning under the Intergovernmental Cooperation Act of 1968; therefore clearinghouse notification is not mandated. However applicants should be aware that in various States, State law requires review of applications for Federal assistance under various programs not covered by OMB Circular No. A-95. Implementation of such laws is enforced through State rules and regulations, and applicants are urged to ascertain the existence of such laws and to acquaint themselves with applicable State procedures. Clearinghouses are the proper source of information on additional review requirements. Applicants are encouraged to check with the appropriate Federal Regional Office to obtain the name(s) and address(es) of the clearinghouses.

Local education agencies must submit their applications to their respective State Education Agency (see instruction for Part II, Item 2). The following supplemental instructions for the items given below are to be used in lieu of or along with the standard instructions for the items:

Item 5. If the applicant organization has been assigned a HEW entity number consisting of the IRS employer identification number prefixed by "1" and suffixed by a two-digit number, enter the full HEW entity number in item 5.

If the payee will be other than the applicant, enter in the remarks section "Payee:", the payee's name, department or division, complete address, and employer identification number or HEW entity number. If an individual's name and/or title is desired on the payment instrument, the name and/or title of the designated individual must be specified.

Item 6. Preprinted.

Item 7. If this application is for the "Intern Program," "Training Institute for Gifted and Talented" and/or "Graduate Training Program for Leadership Personnel," enter these titles as appropriate.

OE FORM 9048, 8/77   REPLACES OE FORM 9048, 1/77, WHICH IS OBSOLETE

Item 8. If applicant is a consortium of States, enter "Con S," if a consortium of universities, enter "Con "

Item 9. Preprinted.

Item 11. For example, if the project is for a local education agency's gifted program, enter the estimated number of gifted and talented youth that will benefit from the project.

Item 20. Preprinted.

Item 23. If the applicant is a consortium of States or universities, the State or university assuming fiscal responsibility should certify by having its authorized representative sign.

PART II

Negative answers will not require an explanation unless the Federal agency requests more information at a later date. Provide supplementary data for all "Yes" answers in the space provided in accordance with the following instructions:

Item 1 - Provide the name of the governing body establishing the priority system and the priority rating assigned to this project.

Item 2 - Local education agencies must submit their applications to their respective State education agency. Attach a copy of the covering letter for documentation purposes.

Item 3 - Attach the clearinghouse comments for the application in accordance with the instructions contained in Office of Management and Budget Circular No. A-95. If comments were submitted previously with a preapplication, do not submit them again but any additional comments received from the clearinghouse should be submitted with this application.

Item 4 - Furnish the name of the approving agency and the approval date.

Item 5 - If the State has a comprehensive plan for the education of the gifted and talented explain the scope of the plan. Give the location where the approved plan is available for examination and state whether this project is in conformance with the plan.

Item 6 - Show the population residing or working on the Federal installation who will benefit from this project.

Department of Health, Education, and Welfare. Office of Education.

Item 7 - Show the percentage of the project work that will be conducted on federally-owned or leased land. Give the name of the Federal installation and its location.

Item 8 - Describe briefly the possible beneficial and harmful impact on the environment of the proposed project. If an adverse environmental impact is anticipated, explain what action will be taken to minimize the impact. Federal agencies will provide separate instructions if additional data is needed.

Item 9 - State the number of individuals, families, businesses, or farms this project will displace. Federal agencies will provide separate instructions if additional data is needed.

Item 10 - Show the Federal Domestic Assistance Catalog number, the program name, the type of assistance, the status and the amount of each project where there is related previous, pending or anticipated assistance. Use additional sheets, if needed.

PART III

General Instructions

Sections A, B, C, and D should provide the budget for the first budget period (usually a year) and **Section E** should present the need for Federal assistance in the subsequent budget periods. All applications should contain a breakdown by the object class categories shown in Lines a-k of Section B.

Section A. Budget Summary

Lines 1-4, Columns (a) and (b).

Enter the name of each activity as applicable (i.e., State grant, LEA grant, intern program, Training Institute for Gifted and Talented, and/or Graduate Training Program for Leadership Personnel) on each line in Column (a) and the catalog number on each line in Column (b).

Lines 1-4, Columns (c) through (g).

For **new applications**, leave Columns (c) and (d) blank. For each line entry in Columns (a) and (b), enter in Columns (e), (f), and (g) the appropriate amounts of funds needed to support the project for the first funding period (usually a year).

For **continuing grant program applications**, submit these forms before the end of each funding period. Enter in Columns (c) and (d) the estimated amounts of funds which will remain unobligated at the end of the grant funding period. Enter in Columns (e) and (f) the amounts of funds needed for the upcoming period. The amount(s) in Column (g) should be the sum of amounts in Columns (e) and (f).

For **supplemental grants and changes to existing grants**, do not use Columns (c) and (d). Enter in Column (e) the amount of the increase or decrease of Federal funds and enter in Column (f) the amount of the increase or decrease of non-Federal funds. In Column (g) enter the new total budgeted amount (Federal and non-Federal) which includes the total previous authorized budgeted amounts plus or minus, as appropriate, the amounts shown in Columns (e) and (f). The amount(s) in Column (g) should **not** equal the sum of amounts in Columns (e) and (f).

Line 5 - Show the totals for all columns used.

Section B. Budget Categories

In the column headings (1) through (4), enter the titles of the same programs, functions, and activities shown on Lines 1-4, Column (a), Section A. When additional sheets were prepared for Section A, provide similar column headings on each sheet. For each activity, fill in the total requirements for funds (both Federal and non-Federal) by object class categories.

Lines 6a-h. - Show the estimated amount for each direct cost budget (object class) category for each column with program, function or activity heading as follows:

Line 6a - "Personnel" must show salaries and wages only. Fees and expenses for consultants must be included on Line 6h.

Line 6b - Leave this line blank if fringe benefits applicable to direct salaries and wages are treated as part of the indirect cost rate.

Line 6c - Indicate travel of employees only. Travel of consultants, trainees, etc. should not go on this line, nor should local transportation (i.e., where no out-of-town trip is involved).

Line 6d - Indicate the cost of nonexpendable personal property. Such property means tangible personal property having a useful life of more than one year and an acquisition cost of $300 or more per unit. A grantee may use its own definition of nonexpendable personal property provided that such definition would at least include all personal property as defined above. NOTE: No such property costing more than $1,000 per unit is an allowable cost.

Line 6e - Show all tangible personal property except that which is on Line 6d.

Line 6f - Use for (1) procurement contracts (except those which belong on other lines such as equipment and supplies and (2) subgrants or other assistance-like payments to secondary recipient organizations such as affiliates, cooperating institutions, delegate agencies, political sub-divisions, etc. Line 6f must not include payments to individuals such as stipends and allowances for trainees, consulting fees, benefits, etc.

Line 6g - Present funding will not allow for new construction. Minor alterations and renovations are allowable costs.

Line 6h - All direct costs not clearly covered by Lines 6a through 6g must be included here. Examples are computer use charges, non-salary and wage payments to individuals (stipends, tuition and fees, dependency allowances and trainee travel cost), space or equipment rental, required fees, consulting fees and travel, communication costs, rental of space, utilities and custodial services, printing materials, and local transportation.

Line 6i - Show the totals of Lines 6a through 6h in each column.

Line 6j - Show the amount of indirect cost. Refer to FMC 74-4.

Line 6k - Enter the total of amounts on Lines 6i and 6j. For all applications for new grants and continuation grants, the total amount in column (5), Line 6k, should be the same as the total amount shown in Section A, Column (g), Line 5. For supplemental grants and changes to grants, the total amount of the increase or decrease as shown in Columns (1)-(4), Line 6k should be the same as the sum of the amounts in Section A, Columns (e) and (f) on Line 5. When additional sheets were prepared, the last two sentences apply to the first page with summary totals.

Line 7 - Enter the estimated amount of income, if any, expected to be generated from this project. Do not add or subtract this amount from the total project amount. Show under the program narrative statement the nature and source of income. The estimated amount of program income may be considered by the Federal grantor agency in determining the total amount of the grant.

Section C. Source of Non-Federal Resources

Lines 8-11 - Enter amounts of non-Federal resources that will be used on the grant. If in-kind contributions are included, provide a brief explanation on a separate sheet. (See Attachment F, FMC 74-7.)

Column (a) - Enter the program titles identical to Column (a), Section A. A breakdown by function or activity is not necessary.

Column (b) - Enter the amount of cash and in-kind contributions to be made by the applicant as shown in Section A. (See also Attachment F, FMC 74-7.)

Column (c) - Enter the State contribution if the applicant is not a State or State agency. Applicants which are a State or State agencies should leave this column blank.

Column (d) - Enter the amount of cash and in-kind contributions to be made from all other sources.

Column (e) - Enter totals of Columns (b), (c), and (d).

Line 12 - Enter the total for each of Columns (b)-(e). The amount in Column (e) should be equal to the amount on Line 5, Column (f), Section A.

Section D. Forecasted Cash Needs

Line 13 - Enter the amount of cash needed by quarter from the grantor agency during the first year.

Line 14 - Enter the amount of cash from all other sources needed by quarter during the first year.

Line 15 - Enter the totals of amounts on Lines 13 and 14.

Section E. Budget Estimates of Federal Funds Needed for Balance of the Project

Lines 16-19 - Enter in Column (a) the same grant program titles shown in Column (a), Section A. A breakdown by function or activity is not necessary. For new applications and continuing grant applications, enter in the proper columns amounts of Federal funds which will be needed to complete the program or project over the succeeding funding periods (usually in years). This Section need not be completed for amendments, changes, or supplements to funds for the current year of existing grants.

If more than four lines are needed to list the program titles submit additional schedules as necessary.

Line 20 - Enter the total for each of the Columns (b)-(e). When additional schedules are prepared for this Section, annotate accordingly and show the overall totals on this line.

Section F. Other Budget Information. (Additional sheets may be attached)

Line 21 - Use this space to explain amounts for individual direct object cost categories that may appear to be out of the ordinary or to explain the following details:

PERSONNEL SALARIES FOR 6a. Include a statement which shows the total commitment of time and the total salary to be charged to the project for each key member of the project staff cited in Part IV, 5a.

TRAVEL FROM 6c. Foreign travel should be separately identified and justified. No foreign travel will be authorized under the grant unless prior approval is obtained.

EQUIPMENT FROM 6d. List items of equipment in the

following format: Item, Number of Units, Cost per Unit, Total Cost.

CONTRACTUAL FROM 6f. Indicate the name of the agency or organization that will receive each proposed contract. This should be supported by Part IV, 3d.

OTHER FROM 6h. (a) Give the total number of consultants that will work on the project and their costs (fees and travel).

(b). For training programs or such functions or activities also give: (1) Costs for stipends in terms of number of weeks times number of trainees (by degree level) times average stipend; (2) Costs for tuition and fees in terms of number of trainees times average tuition times average fees; (3) Costs for dependency allowances: number of weeks times number of dependents times weekly allowance for each dependent; and (4) Costs of travel for students: number of students for whom travel allowances are requested times the average round-trip fare claimed per student.

(c) Give the total direct cost for any or ALL new training activities not previously funded by the OE if this is a continuation application.

(d) Give costs for pupil transportation.

Line 22 - Enter the type of indirect rate (provisional, predetermined, final or fixed) that will be in effect during the funding period, the estimated amount of the base to which the rate is applied, and the total indirect expense. For State grants, see Section 160.b7(e) of the attached Regulations.

Line 23 - Provide any other explanations required herein or any other comments deemed necessary.

PART IV – PROGRAM NARRATIVE

Prepare the program narrative statement in accordance with the following instructions for all new grant programs. Requests for continuation or refunding and changes on an approved project should respond to Item 5b only. Requests for supplemental assistance should respond to Item 5c only.

Note that the program narrative should encompass each activity for which funds are being requested (see Sections A and B in Part III). Relevant regulations (attached) should be carefully examined for criteria upon which evaluation of an application will be made and the program narrative must respond to such criteria under the related headings below. See Sections 160b.3 and 160.b.6 in the attached regulations for general requirements, educational and programmatic criteria, and specific criteria for each program activity (i.e., Section 160b.24 for State and local grants; 160b.32 for training of State and local educators; 160b.46 for leadership personnel training).

1. OBJECTIVES AND NEED FOR THIS ASSISTANCE.

Describe the problem and demonstrate the need for assistance and state the principal and subordinate objectives of the project. Supporting documentation or other testimonies from concerned interests other than the applicant may be used. Any relevant data based on planning studies should be included or footnoted. Model projects should present available data, or estimates for need in terms of gifted and talented children in the geographic area involved.

2. RESULTS OR BENEFITS EXPECTED.

Identify results and benefits to be derived.

3. APPROACH.

  a. Outline a plan of action pertaining to the scope and detail of how the proposed work will be accomplished for each grant program, function or activity, provided in the budget. Cite factors which might accelerate or decelerate the work and your reason for taking this approach as opposed to others. Describe any unusual features of the project such as design or technological innovations, reductions in cost or time, or extraordinary social and community involvement.

  b. Provide for each grant program activity quantitative quarterly projections of the accomplishments to be achieved in such terms as the number of gifted and talented children served or personnel trained. When accomplishments cannot be quantified by activity or function, list them in chronological order to show the schedule of accomplishments and their target dates.

  c. Identify the kinds of data to be collected and maintained and discuss the criteria to be used to evaluate the results and successes of the project. Explain the methodology that will be used to determine if the needs identified and discussed are being met and if the results and benefits identified in item 2 are being achieved.

  d. List organizations, cooperators, consultants, or other key individuals who will work on the project along with a short description of the nature of their effort or contribution.

4. GEOGRAPHIC LOCATION.

Give a precise location of the project or area to be served by the proposed project. Maps or other graphic aids may be attached.

5. IF APPLICABLE, PROVIDE THE FOLLOWING INFORMATION:

  a. Present a biographical sketch of the program director with the following information; name, address, phone

Appendix E 343

number, background, and other qualifying experience for the project. Also, list the name, training and background for other key personnel engaged in the project.

b. Discuss accomplishments to date and list in chronological order a schedule of accomplishments, progress or milestones anticipated with the new funding request. If there have been significant changes in the project objectives, location approach, or time delays, explain and justify. For other requests for changes or amendments, explain the reason for the change(s), If the scope or objectives have changed or an extension of time is necessary, explain the circumstances and justify. If the total budget has been exceeded, or if individual budget items have changed more than the prescribed limits contained in Attachment K to FMC 74-7, explain and justify the change and its effect on the project.

c. For supplemental assistance requests, explain the reason for the request and justify the need for additional funding.

344 The Dynamics of Funding

OMB Approval No. 29-R0218

FEDERAL ASSISTANCE

1. TYPE OF ACTION (Mark appropriate box)
- [ ] PREAPPLICATION
- [x] APPLICATION
- [ ] NOTIFICATION OF INTENT (Opt.)
- [ ] REPORT OF FEDERAL ACTION

2. APPLICANT'S APPLICATION
- a. NUMBER
- b. DATE Year month day 19
- Leave Blank

3. STATE APPLICATION IDENTIFIER
- a. NUMBER
- b. DATE ASSIGNED Year month day 19

SECTION I—APPLICANT/RECIPIENT DATA

4. LEGAL APPLICANT/RECIPIENT
- a. Applicant Name :
- b. Organization Unit :
- c. Street/P.O. Box :
- d. City :
- e. County :
- f. State :
- g. ZIP Code :
- h. Contact Person (Name & telephone No.) :

5. FEDERAL EMPLOYER IDENTIFICATION NO.

6. PROGRAM (From Federal Catalog)
- a. NUMBER 1 3 • 5 6 2 A
- b. TITLE Gifted and Talented Program

7. TITLE AND DESCRIPTION OF APPLICANT'S PROJECT

8. TYPE OF APPLICANT/RECIPIENT
A—State
B—Interstate
C—Substate District
D—County
E—City
F—School District
G—Special Purpose District
H—Community Action Agency
I—Higher Educational Institution
J—Indian Tribe
K—Other (Specify):
Enter appropriate letter ☐

9. TYPE OF ASSISTANCE
A—Basic Grant D—Insurance
B—Supplemental Grant E—Other
C—Loan
Enter appropriate letter(s) **A**

10. AREA OF PROJECT IMPACT (Names of cities, counties, States, etc.)

11. ESTIMATED NUMBER OF PERSONS BENEFITING

12. TYPE OF APPLICATION
A—New C—Revision E—Augmentation
B—Renewal D—Continuation
Enter appropriate letter ☐

13. PROPOSED FUNDING
a. FEDERAL	$ .00
b. APPLICANT	.00
c. STATE	.00
d. LOCAL	.00
e. OTHER	.00
f. TOTAL	$ .00

14. CONGRESSIONAL DISTRICTS OF:
- a. APPLICANT
- b. PROJECT

16. PROJECT START DATE Year month day 19

17. PROJECT DURATION Months

18. ESTIMATED DATE TO BE SUBMITTED TO FEDERAL AGENCY ▶ Year month day 19

15. TYPE OF CHANGE (For 12c or 12e)
A—Increase Dollars F—Other (Specify):
B—Decrease Dollars
C—Increase Duration
D—Decrease Duration
E—Cancellation
Enter appropriate letter(s) ☐☐

19. EXISTING FEDERAL IDENTIFICATION NUMBER

20. FEDERAL AGENCY TO RECEIVE REQUEST (Name, City, State, ZIP code) U.S. Office of Education, Application Control Center, Washington, D.C. 20202

21. REMARKS ADDED ☐ Yes ☐ No

SECTION II—CERTIFICATION

22. THE APPLICANT CERTIFIES THAT ▶
a. To the best of my knowledge and belief, data in this preapplication/application are true and correct, the document has been duly authorized by the governing body of the applicant and the applicant will comply with the attached assurances if the assistance is approved.
b. If required by OMB Circular A-95 this application was submitted, pursuant to instructions therein, to appropriate clearinghouses and all responses are attached:
(1) ☐ (2) ☐ (3) ☐
No response ☐ ☐ ☐
Response attached ☐ ☐ ☐

23. CERTIFYING REPRESENTATIVE
- a. TYPED NAME AND TITLE
- b. SIGNATURE
- c. DATE SIGNED Year month day 19

SECTION III—FEDERAL AGENCY ACTION

24. AGENCY NAME

25. APPLICATION RECEIVED Year month day 19

26. ORGANIZATIONAL UNIT

27. ADMINISTRATIVE OFFICE

28. FEDERAL APPLICATION IDENTIFICATION

29. ADDRESS

30. FEDERAL GRANT IDENTIFICATION

31. ACTION TAKEN
- ☐ a. AWARDED
- ☐ b. REJECTED
- ☐ c. RETURNED FOR AMENDMENT
- ☐ d. DEFERRED
- ☐ e. WITHDRAWN

32. FUNDING
a. FEDERAL	$ .00
b. APPLICANT	.00
c. STATE	.00
d. LOCAL	.00
e. OTHER	.00
f. TOTAL	$ .00

33. ACTION DATE ▶ Year month day 19

35. CONTACT FOR ADDITIONAL INFORMATION (Name and telephone number)

34. STARTING DATE Year month day 19

36. ENDING DATE Year month day 19

37. REMARKS ADDED ☐ Yes ☐ No

38. FEDERAL AGENCY A-95 ACTION
a. In taking above action, any comments received from clearinghouses were considered. If agency response is due under provisions of Part I, OMB Circular A-95, it has been or is being made.
b. FEDERAL AGENCY A-95 OFFICIAL (Name and telephone no.)

424-101 (OE FORM 9048, 8/77)

STANDARD FORM 424 PAGE 1 (10-75)
Prescribed by GSA, Federal Management Circular 74-7

OMB Approval No. 29-R0218

PART II
PROJECT APPROVAL INFORMATION

ITEM 1.
Does this assistance request require State, local, regional, or other priority rating?

☐ Yes ☐ No

Name of Governing Body _____
Priority Rating _____

ITEM 2.
Does this assistance request require State, or local advisory, educational or health clearances?

☐ Yes ☐ No (Attach Documentation)

Name of Agency or
Board _____

ITEM 3.
Does this assistance request require clearinghouse review in accordance with OMB Circular A-95?

☐ Yes ☐ No

(Attach Comments)

ITEM 4
Does this assistance request require State, local, regional, or other planning approval?

☐ Yes ☐ No

Name of Approving Agency _____
Date _____

ITEM 5
Is the proposed project covered by an approved comprehensive plan?

☐ Yes ☐ No Location of Plan _____

Check one:
☐ State
☐ Local
☐ Regional

ITEM 6
Will the assistance requested serve a Federal installation?

☐ Yes ☐ No

Name of Federal Installation _____
Federal Population benefiting from Project ____

ITEM 7
Will the assistance requested be on Federal land or installation?

☐ Yes ☐ No

Name of Federal Installation _____
Location of Federal Land _____
Percent of Project _____

ITEM 8
Will the assistance requested have an impact or effect on the environment?

☐ Yes ☐ No

See instructions for additional information to be provided.

ITEM 9
Will the assistance requested cause the displacement of individuals, families, businesses, or farms?

☐ Yes ☐ No

Number of:
Individuals _____
Families _____
Businesses _____
Farms _____

ITEM 10
Is there other related assistance on this project previous, pending, or anticipated?

☐ Yes ☐ No

See instructions for additional information to be provided.

HEW-608T

GENERAL INSTRUCTIONS

This is a multi-purpose standard form. First, it will be used by applicants as a required facesheet for pre-applications and applications submitted in accordance with Federal Management Circular 74–7. Second, it will be used by Federal agencies to report to Clearinghouses on major actions taken on applications reviewed by clearinghouses in accordance with OMB Circular A–95. Third, it will be used by Federal agencies to notify States of grants-in-aid awarded in accordance with Treasury Circular 1082. Fourth, it may be used, on an optional basis, as a notification of intent from applicants to clearinghouses, as an early initial notice that Federal assistance is to be applied for (clearinghouse procedures will govern).

APPLICANT PROCEDURES FOR SECTION I

Applicant will complete all items in Section I. If an item is not applicable, write "NA". If additional space is needed, insert an asterisk "*", and use the remarks section on the back of the form. An explanation follows for each item:

Item

1. Mark appropriate box. Pre-application and application guidance is in FMC 74–7 and Federal agency program instructions. Notification of intent guidance is in Circular A–95 and procedures from clearinghouse. Applicant will not use "Report of Federal Action" box.

2a. Applicant's own control number, if desired.

2b. Date Section I is prepared.

3a. Number assigned by State clearinghouse, or if delegated by State, by areawide clearinghouse. All requests to Federal agencies must contain this identifier if the program is covered by Circular A–95 and required by applicable State/areawide clearinghouse procedures. If in doubt, consult your clearinghouse.

3b. Date applicant notified of clearinghouse identifier.

4a–4h. Legal name of applicant/recipient, name of primary organizational unit which will undertake the assistance activity, complete address of applicant, and name and telephone number of person who can provide further information about this request.

5. Employer identification number of applicant as assigned by Internal Revenue Service.

6a. Use Catalog of Federal Domestic Assistance number assigned to program under which assistance is requested. If more than one program (e.g., joint-funding) write "multiple" and explain in remarks. If unknown, cite Public Law or U.S. Code.

6b. Program title from Federal Catalog. Abbreviate if necessary.

7. Brief title and appropriate description of project. For notification of intent, continue in remarks section if necessary to convey proper description.

8. Mostly self-explanatory. "City" includes town, township or other municipality.

9. Check the type(s) of assistance requested. The definitions of the terms are:

   A. Basic Grant. An original request for Federal funds. This would not include any contribution provided under a supplemental grant.

   B. Supplemental Grant. A request to increase a basic grant in certain cases where the eligible applicant cannot supply the required matching share of the basic Federal program (e.g., grants awarded by the Appalachian Regional Commission to provide the applicant a matching share).

   C. Loan. Self explanatory.

Item

   D. Insurance. Self explanatory.

   E. Other. Explain on remarks page.

10. Governmental unit where significant and meaningful impact could be observed. List only largest unit or units affected, such as State, county, or city. If entire unit affected, list it rather than subunits.

11. Estimated number of persons directly benefiting from project.

12. Use appropriate code letter. Definitions are:

    A. New. A submittal for the first time for a new project.

    B. Renewal. An extension for an additional funding/budget period for a project having no projected completion date, but for which Federal support must be renewed each year.

    C. Revision. A modification to project nature or scope which may result in funding change (increase or decrease).

    D. Continuation. An extension for an additional funding/budget period for a project the agency initially agreed to fund for a definite number of years.

    E. Augmentation. A requirement for additional funds for a project previously awarded funds in the same funding/budget period. Project nature and scope unchanged.

13. Amount requested or to be contributed during the first funding/budget period by each contributor. Value of in-kind contributions will be included. If the action is a change in dollar amount of an existing grant (a revision or augmentation), indicate only the amount of the change. For decreases enclose the amount in parentheses. If both basic and supplemental amounts are included, breakout in remarks. For multiple program funding, use totals and show program breakouts in remarks. Item definitions: 13a, amount requested from Federal Government; 13b, amount applicant will contribute; 13c, amount from State, if applicant is not a State; 13d, amount from local government, if applicant is not a local government; 13e, amount from any other sources, explain in remarks.

14a. Self explanatory.

14b. The district(s) where most of actual work will be accomplished. If city-wide or State-wide, covering several districts, write "city-wide" or "State-wide."

15. Complete only for revisions (item 12c), or augmentations (item 12e).

STANDARD FORM 424 PAGE 3 (10–75)

Appendix E   347

Item		Item	
16.	Approximate date project expected to begin (usually associated with estimated date of availability of funding).	19.	Existing Federal identification number if this is not a new request and directly relates to a previous Federal action. Otherwise write "NA".
17.	Estimated number of months to complete project after Federal funds are available.	20.	Indicate Federal agency to which this request is addressed. Street address not required, but do use ZIP.
18.	Estimated date preapplication/application will be submitted to Federal agency if this project requires clearinghouse review. If review not required, this date would usually be same as date in item 2b.	21.	Check appropriate box as to whether Section IV of form contains remarks and/or additional remarks are attached.

APPLICANT PROCEDURES FOR SECTION II

Applicants will always complete items 23a, 23b, and 23c. If clearinghouse review is required, item 22b must be fully completed. An explanation follows for each item:

Item		Item	
22b.	List clearinghouses to which submitted and show in appropriate blocks the status of their responses. For more than three clearinghouses, continue in remarks section. All written comments submitted by or through clearinghouses must be attached.	23b.	Self explanatory.
		23c.	Self explanatory.
23a.	Name and title of authorized representative of legal applicant.	Note:	Applicant completes only Sections I and II. Section III is completed by Federal agencies.

FEDERAL AGENCY PROCEDURES FOR SECTION III

If applicant-supplied information in Sections I and II needs no updating or adjustment to fit the final Federal action, the Federal agency will complete Section III only. An explanation for each item follows:

Item		Item	
24.	Executive department or independent agency having program administration responsibility.	35.	Name and telephone no. of agency person who can provide more information regarding this assistance.
25.	Self explanatory.	36.	Date after which funds will no longer be available.
26.	Primary organizational unit below department level having direct program management responsibility.	37.	Check appropriate box as to whether Section IV of form contains Federal remarks and/or attachment of additional remarks.
27.	Office directly monitoring the program.		
28.	Use to identify non-award actions where Federal grant identifier in item 30 is not applicable or will not suffice.	38.	For use with A-95 action notices only. Name and telephone of person who can assure that appropriate A-95 action has been taken—If same as person shown in item 35, write, "same". If not applicable, write "NA".
29.	Complete address of administering office shown in item 26.		
30.	Use to identify award actions where different from Federal application identifier in item 28.		
31.	Self explanatory. Use remarks section to amplify where appropriate.	*Federal Agency Procedures—special considerations*	
32.	Amount to be contributed during the first funding/budget period by each contributor. Value of in-kind contributions will be included. If the action is a change in dollar amount of an existing grant (a revision or augmentation), indicate only the amount of change. For decreases, enclose the amount in parentheses. If both basic and supplemental amounts are included, breakout in remarks. For multiple program funding, use totals and show program breakouts in remarks. Item definitions: 32a, amount awarded by Federal Government; 32b, amount applicant will contribute; 32c, amount from State, if applicant is not a State; 32d, amount from local government if applicant is not a local government; 32e, amount from any other sources, explain in remarks.	A.	*Treasury Circular 1082 compliance.* Federal agency will assure proper completion of Sections I and III. If Section I is being completed by Federal agency, all applicable items must be filled in. Addresses of State Information Reception Agencies (SCIRA's) are provided by Treasury Department to each agency. This form replaces SF 240, which will no longer be used.
		B.	*OMB Circular A-95 compliance.* Federal agency will assure proper completion of Sections I, II, and III. This form is required for notifying all reviewing clearinghouses of major actions on all programs reviewed under A-95. Addresses of State and areawide clearinghouses are provided by OMB to each agency. Substantive differences between applicant's request and/or clearinghouse recommendations, and the project as finally awarded will be explained in A-95 notifications to clearinghouses.
		C.	*Special note.* In most, but not all States, the A-95 State clearinghouse and the (TC 1082) SCIRA are the same office. In such cases, the A-95 award notice to the State clearinghouse will fulfill the TC 1082 award notice requirement to the State SCIRA. Duplicate notification should be avoided.
33.	Date action was taken on this request.		
34.	Date funds will become available.		

STANDARD FORM 424 PAGE 4 (10-75)

OMB Approval No. 29-R0218

PART III - BUDGET INFORMATION

SECTION A - BUDGET SUMMARY

GRANT PROGRAM, FUNCTION OR ACTIVITY (a)	FEDERAL CATALOG NO. (b)	ESTIMATED UNOBLIGATED FUNDS		NEW OR REVISED BUDGET		
		FEDERAL (c)	NON-FEDERAL (d)	FEDERAL (e)	NON-FEDERAL (f)	TOTAL (g)
1.		$	$	$	$	$
2.						
3.						
4.						
5. TOTALS		$	$	$	$	$

SECTION B - BUDGET CATEGORIES

6. OBJECT CLASS CATEGORIES	GRANT PROGRAM, FUNCTION OR ACTIVITY				TOTAL (5)
	(1)	(2)	(3)	(4)	
a. PERSONNEL	$	$	$	$	$
b. FRINGE BENEFITS					
c. TRAVEL					
d. EQUIPMENT					
e. SUPPLIES					
f. CONTRACTUAL					
g. CONSTRUCTION					
h. OTHER					
i. TOTAL DIRECT CHARGES					
j. INDIRECT CHARGES					
k. TOTALS	$	$	$	$	$
7. PROGRAM INCOME	$	$	$	$	$

HEW-608T

OMB Approval No. 29-R0218

SECTION C - NON-FEDERAL RESOURCES

(a) GRANT PROGRAM	(b) APPLICANT	(c) STATE	(d) OTHER SOURCES	(e) TOTALS
8.	$	$	$	$
9.				
10.				
11.				
12. TOTALS	$	$	$	$

SECTION D - FORECASTED CASH NEEDS

	TOTAL FOR 1ST YEAR	1ST QUARTER	2ND QUARTER	3RD QUARTER	4TH QUARTER
13. FEDERAL	$	$	$	$	$
14. NON-FEDERAL					
15. TOTALS	$	$	$	$	$

SECTION E - BUDGET ESTIMATES OF FEDERAL FUNDS NEEDED FOR BALANCE OF THE PROJECT

(a) GRANT PROGRAM	FUTURE FUNDING PERIODS (years)			
	(b) FIRST	(c) SECOND	(d) THIRD	(e) FOURTH
16.	$	$	$	$
17.				
18.				
19.				
20. TOTALS	$	$	$	$

SECTION F - OTHER BUDGET INFORMATION (attach additional sheets if necessary)

21. DIRECT CHARGES:

22. INDIRECT CHARGES:

23. REMARKS:

PART IV - PROGRAM NARRATIVE (attach per instructions)

HEW-608T

Glossary and Acronyms

The following definitions and acronyms represent a sampling of reference points commonly used in discussing the workings of the federal government and the evolution of funding opportunities. The selection is limited to those terms that are used in the narrative and that are, for the most part, essential for communicating with those who participate in the administration and development of federal programs and projects.

Allocation: The designation of appropriated monies for specific programs or types of activity carried out by individual program offices.

Appropriation: Congressional action setting aside funds earmarked for a particular federal agency or program.

Authorization: Legislation enacted by Congress that sets up a federal program or agency either indefinitely or for a given period of time. Such legislation may set a maximum amount that can be appropriated, but does not usually provide budget authority.

Block Grants: Allocation of federal funds that may address several needs or problem areas identified by authorizing legislation; precise distribution of funds is determined by receiving agency.

Continuing Resolution: Congressional authority action to agencies to continue operations in the event that action on appropriations is not completed by the beginning of the fiscal year.

Cost Sharing: That portion of the project costs that the grantee assumes.

Discretionary Money: Money appropriated to a government agency to fund project grants that are selected on a competitive basis. Project grants are funded at the discretion of the federal agency.

Entitlement Programs: Programs for which the federal government is obligated to make payments to eligible programs and/or participants, according to legislatively prescribed criteria. Examples are Social Security, G.I. Bill, Medicare.

Federal Contracts: Procurement or purchase by the federal government of an identifiable product or services under specific terms to the best economic advantage of the government.

Fiscal Year: An accounting period for the federal government that begins October 1 and ends September 30. The fiscal year is designated by the calendar year in which the fiscal period ends.

Formula Grants: Federal grants, for which states and state agencies apply, made on the basis of a distribution formula prescribed by legislation and usually based on factors such as population, per capita income, and enrollment. Examples are Head Start, Title I, ESEA.

Guidelines: The requirements, recommendations, and suggestions of a funding agency for applications for assistance; do not have the force of law.

In-Kind Contribution: Nonmonetary assistance to the project by the applicant organization that otherwise would be covered through direct or indirect costs covered by the funding agent.

Matching Funds: Dollar equivalent of total request from funding agent that is donated to the project by the applicant organization in the form of cash or services.

Project or Categorical Grants: Federal funds for specific projects that are applied for by individuals and private and public organizations and institutions through a competitive selection basis. Various types of project grants include:

Construction Grants: Grants for support of building, expanding, or modernizing facilities.

Demonstration Grants: Grants made for "model" idea or approach to demonstrate its feasibility.

Planning Grants: Grants made to support planning and set-up activities preparatory to performing research or accomplishing other objectives.

Research Grants: Grants made in support of discovery of new theories, revision of accepted theories in light of new facts, or the application of such new or revised theories.

Service Grants: Grants made for delivery of services to a specific area or community, either for purposes of organizing and establishing the services or expanding already existing services.

Training Grants: Grants made to support instructional activities.

Request for Proposals (RFPs): Procurement announcements by the federal government, for goods and services exceeding $5,000, that are published in the *Commerce Business Daily* or *Federal Register.*

Rules and Regulations: Federal guidelines, published in the *Federal Register* by the executive departments and agencies of the federal government, that implement a legislative act and govern the individual grant programs.

Supplemental Appropriations: Additional funds for programs that were not covered in the regular appropriations bill, usually due to lack of authorizing legislation.

Unsolicited Proposals: Proposals to an agency either for project grants or contracts for which there are no identifiable grant programs. Federal agencies normally set aside funds for this purpose.

Acronyms

ACYF	Administration for Children, Youth, and Families
ADAMHA	Alcohol, Drug Abuse, and Mental Health Administration
BEH	Bureau of Education for the Handicapped
CETA	Comprehensive Employment and Training Act
CFDA	*Catalogue of Federal Domestic Assistance*
CFR	Code of Federal Regulations
DHEW or HEW	Department of Health, Education, and Welfare
EPDA	Education Professions Development Act
ESAA	Emergency School Aid Act
ESEA	Elementary and Secondary Education Act
FR	*Federal Register*
FY	Fiscal Year
DOL	Department of Labor
DOT	Department of Transportation
GAO	General Accounting Office
GPO	Government Printing Office
IHE	Institution of Higher Education
LEA	Local Educational Agency
LEAA	Law Enforcement Assistance Administration
NDEA	National Defense Education Act
NEA	National Endowment for the Arts
NEH	National Endowment for the Humanities
NIE	National Institute of Education
NIH	National Institutes of Health
NIMH	National Institute of Mental Health
NSF	National Science Foundation
OCD	Office of Child Development
OE or USOE	United States Office of Education
OHDS	Office of Human Development Services
OMB	Office of Management and Budget
P.L.	Public Law
S.	Senate Bill
U.S.C.	United States Code
USOE	United States Office of Education

Bibliography

BOOKS

Bailey, Stephen K. *Education Interest Groups in the Nation's Capital.* Washington, D.C.: American Council on Education, 1976.

Bailey, Stephen K., and Mosher, Edith K. *ESEA: The Office of Education Administers a Law.* Syracuse: Syracuse University Press, 1968.

Bendiner, Robert. *Obstacle Course on Capital Hill.* New York: McGraw-Hill, 1964.

Bruner, Jerome. *The Process of Education.* Cambridge: Harvard University Press, 1960.

Castetter, William B., and Heisler, Richard S. *Developing and Defending a Dissertation Proposal.* Philadelphia: University of Pennsylvania, Graduate School of Education, Center for Field Studies, 1977.

Chin, Robert, and Benne, Kenneth D. "General Strategies for Effecting Changes in Human Systems" in *Creating Social Change,* edited by Gerald Zaltman, Philip Kotler, and Ira Kaufman. New York: Holt, Rinehart & Winston, 1972.

Commager, Henry Steele. *Documents of American History.* New York: Appleton-Century-Crofts, 1968.

Corrigan, R. E., Associates. *A System Approach for Education.* Anaheim R. E. Corrigan Associates, 1969.

Corwin, Ronald G. *Reform and Institutional Survival.* New York: John Wiley & Sons, 1973.

CPM in Construction: A Manual for General Contractors. Washington, D.C.: Associated General Contractors of America, 1965.

Federal Education Program Guide. Edited by James Fauntleroy. Washington, D.C.: Capital Publications, Fall 1976.

Fenno, Richard. *National Politics and Federal Aid to Education.* Syracuse: Syracuse: Syracuse University Press, 1962.

Fenton, Edwin. *Developing a New Curriculum: A Rationale for the Holt Social Studies Curriculum,* New York: Holt Rinehart & Winston, 1967.

Gephart, William J.; Ingle, Robert B.; and Saretsky, Gary. *Similarities and Differences in the Research and Evaluation Process.* Pamphlet of *Phi Delta Kappa,* April 1973.

Goodlad, John, and Anderson, Robert H. *The Nongraded Elementary School.* Edited by William B. Spaulding. New York: Harcourt, Brace and World, 1959.

Grantsmanship: Money and How to Get It. Orange, N.J.: Academic Media, 1973.

Hall, Mary. *Developing Skills in Proposal Writing,* Second Edition. Corvallis, Oreg.: Continuing Education Publications, September 1977.

Hanna, Lyle. *Preparing Proposals for Government Funding.* Englewood Cliffs, N.J.: Prentice-Hall, 1969.

Hostrop, Richard W. *Managing Education for Results.* Homewood, Ill.: ETC Publications, 1973.

Krathwohl, David R. *How to Prepare a Research Proposal,* Second Edition, Syracuse, N.Y.: Syracuse University Press, 1977.

Machiavelli, Niccolo. *The Prince and the Discourses.* New York: Modern Library, 1940.

Mager, Robert F. *Preparing Instructional Objectives.* Belmont, Calif.: Fearon Publishers, 1962.

Martino, Joseph. *Technological Forecasting for Decision Making.* New York: American Elsevier Publishing, 1972.

Miles, Rufus E., Jr. *A Cabinet Department of Education.* Washington, D.C.: American Council on Education, 1976.

Moynihan, Daniel P. *Maximum Feasible Misunderstanding: Community Action in the War on Poverty.* New York: The Free Press, 1969.

Munger, Frank J., and Fenno, Richard F., Jr. *National Politics and Federal Aid to Education.* Syracuse, N.Y.: Syracuse University Press, 1961.

Owens, Robert G. *Organizational Behavior in Schools.* Englewood Cliffs, N.J.: Prentice-Hall, 1970.

Parsons, Talcott. *The Social System.* Glencoe, Ill.: The Free Press, 1951.

Putting Together: A Guide to Proposal Development. Chicago: Board of Education, City of Chicago, 1975.

Report of the National Advisory Commission on Civil Disorders. New York: Bantam Books, 1968.

Sarason, Seymour B. *The Culture of the Schools and the Problem of Change.* Boston: Allyn and Bacon, 1971.

Silberman, Charles E. *Crisis in the Classroom.* New York: Random House, 1970.

Summerfield, Harry L. *Power and Process: The Formulation and Limits of Federal Educational Policy.* Berkeley: McCutchan Publishing, 1974.

Taylor, Peter A., and Cowley, Doris M. *Readings in Curriculum Evaluation.* Dubuque, Iowa: William C. Brown, 1972.

The 1977 Federal Funding Guide for Elementary and Secondary Education. Washington, D.C.: Education Funding Research Council, 1977.

Thomas, Norman C. *Education in National Politics.* New York: David McKay, 1975.

Weiss, Carol. *Evaluating Action Programs.* Boston: Allyn and Bacon, 1972.

ARTICLES

Arnold, Mark R. "The Good War That Might Have Been." *The New York Times Magazine,* 29 September 1974, pp. 56-64.

Cicirrelli, Victor G.: Evans, John W.; and Schiller, Jeffrey S. "A Reply to the Report Analysis." *Harvard Educational Review* (February 1970): 105-129.

Cronin, Thomas E., and Thomas, Noman C. "Educational Policy Advisors and the Great Society." *Public Policy* 18 (1970): 659-86.

Davies, Don. "Reflections on EPDA." *Theory into Practice* 13 (June 1974): 210-217.

Dixon, John. "Conference Report: The Dartmouth Seminar." *Harvard Educational Review* 39 (Spring 1969):

Evans, John W. "Evaluating Social Action Programs." *Social Science Quarterly* 50, No. 3 (December 1969): 568-581.

Grant, Vance W. "Trends in Public School Systems." *American Education* (August-September 1973).

Halperin, Samuel. "ESEA: Decennial Views of the Revolution; I. The Positive Side." *Phi Delta Kappan* (November 1975).

Herbers, John. "Integration: A Vocally Pessimistic White House," *The New York Times,* 8 March 1970, Section 4, p. 1.

Hull, Ronald. "The Degradation of an Education Research Group: A Case Description." *Educational Researcher* (June 1976).

Johnson, Thomas. "Causal Modeling in Educational and Social Program Evaluation," paper presented at the American Educational Research Association, Washington, D.C., April 1975. Reprinted. Bethesda, Md.: ERIC Document Reproduction Service, ED 1108 603, 1975.

Light, Richard, and Smith, Paul. "Choosing a Future; Strategies for Designing and Evaluating New Programs." *Harvard Educational Review* 4 (February 1970): 1-28.

MacMillan, Charles B. "Organizational Change in Schools: Bedford-Stuyvesant." *The Journal of Applied Behavioral Science* 11 (October 1975): 137-452.

Mann, Dale. "For the Record." *Teachers College Record* 77 (February 1976): 313-322.

———. "The Politics of Training Teachers in Schools." *Teachers College Record* 77 (February 1976): 323-338.

Sarason, Seymour. "Educational Policy and Federal Intervention in the Days of Opportunity." *Journal of Education* 158 (November 1976): 3-24.

Sky. Theodore. "Rulemaking and the Federal Grant Process in the United States Office of Education." *Virginia Law Review* 62 (October 1976): 1017-1043.

Wayson, William. "ESEA: Decennial Views of the Revolution; II. The Negative Side." *Phi Delta Kappan* (November 1975).

GOVERNMENT AND MISCELLANEOUS PUBLICATIONS

Abt Associates. *Innovation and Change: A Study of Strategies in Selected Projects Supported by the National Center for the Improvement of Educational Systems.* 5 vols. Boston: Abt Associates, 1972.

Adkins, John F.; McHugh, James R.; and Seay, Katherine. *Desegregation: The Boston Orders and Their Origin.* Boston: Boston Bar Association, 1975.

Berman, Paul; Greenwood, Peter W.; McLaughlin, Milbrey Wallin; and Pincus, John. *Federal Programs Supporting Educational Change.* 5 vols. Santa Monica: Rand Corporation, April 1975.

Carter, Jimmy. State of the Union Message, January 19, 1978 (excerpts from detailed but undelivered version).

Cicirrelli, Victor G.; Evans, John W.; and Schiller, Jeffrey S. *The Impact of Head Start: An Examination of the Effects of Head Start on Children's Cognitive and Affective Development.* Contract B: 89-4536, April 1969.

Cicirrelli, Victor G.; Merrow, John; Taylor, Ann; and McCann, Walter. *The Role of Evaluation in Federal Education Training Programs.* Cambridge: Center for Education Policy Research, 1971.

Clusen, Ruth C. *Washington 76.* Washington, D.C.: District of Columbia Office of Bicentennial Programs, 1976.

Commonwealth of Massachusetts. Chapter 636 of the Acts of 1974, Amendments to the Racial Imbalance Act of 1965.

Commonwealth of Massachusetts, Department of Education, Massachusetts Research Center. *Balancing the Public Schools.* Bureau of Educational Information Services, 1974.

Conant, James. "Social Dynamite in Our Large Cities." Speech delivered before the Conference on Unemployed Out-of-School Youth in Urban Areas, Washington, D.C., May 24, 1961.

Education of All Handicapped Children Act (PL 94-142).

"Facts About the Phase II Desegregation Plan in Boston: 1975-76 Academic Year." Report compiled by the Citywide Coordinating Council, Boston, 1975.

A Foundation Goes to School: The Ford Foundation Comprehensive School Program, 1960-1970. New York: The Ford Foundation, 1972.

Gilbert, Neil, and Specht, Harry. *The Model Cities Program, A Comparative Analysis of Participating Cities: Process, Product, Performance and Prediction.* Washington, D.C.: U.S. Government Printing Office, 1973.

Kaagan, Stephen S. "Executive Initiative Yields to Congressional Debate: A Study of Educational Renewal 1971-1972." Ph.D. dissertation, Harvard University, 1973.

Kaplan, George R. *From Aide to Teacher: The Story of the Career Opportunities Program.* OE-12010. Washington, D.C.: U.S. Government Printing Office, 1977. (Report of program sponsored by the Office of Education, U.S. Department of Health, Education, and Welfare.)

National Advisory Council on Education Professions Development. *Windows to the Bureaucracy.* Report dated March 31, 1971.

Peat, Marwick, Mitchell and Co. *A Study of Late Funding of Elementary and Secondary Education Programs.* Final Report prepared for the U.S. Office of Education, Office of Planning, Budgeting, and Evaluation. Washington, D.C., February 1976.

Report of the Masters in Tallulah Morgan, et al, Versus John Kerrigan, et al, 1st submitted to the Parties March 31, 1975.

Smith, Othanel B.; Cohen, Saul B.; and Pearl, Arthur. *Teachers for the Real World.* Washington, D.C.: American Association of Colleges for Teacher Education, 1969.

The Unfinished Revolution: Education for the Handicapped. National Advisory Committee on the Handicapped. Washington, D.C.: Government Printing Office, 1976.

U.S. Commission on Civil Rights. *Racial Isolation in the Public Schools.* Washington, D.C.: Government Printing Office, 1967.

U.S. Comptroller General. *Project Head Start: Achievements and Problems.* Report #MWD-75-51. May 20, 1975.

U.S. Congress, 95th Session. Hearings Before the Subcommittee on Elementary, Secondary, and Vocational Education of the Committee on Education and Labor, on H.R. 15.

U.S. Congress. *A Compilation of Federal Education Laws,* as amended through December 31, 1974. Washington, D.C.: Government Printing Office, 1975.

U.S. *Congressional Record,* Samuel Halperin quoted in, "ESEA: Five Years Later." Washington, D.C.: Government Printing Office, September 9, 1970.

U.S. Department of Health, Education, and Welfare. National Center for Educational Statistics. *The Condition of Education.* Washington, D.C.: Government Printing Office, 1975.

U.S. Department of Health, Education, and Welfare. National Center for Educational Statistics. *Equality of Education Opportunity.* Reported by James Coleman. Washington, D.C.: Government Printing Office, 1966.

U.S. Department of Health, Education, and Welfare. *Report of the Task Force on Timing of DHEW Appropriations for Educational Programs.* Washington, D.C.: Government Printing Office, 1967.

U.S. Department of Health, Education, and Welfare, Office of Education. "Rules and Regulations: Emergency School Aid Act." *Federal Register* 40, no. 114, June 12, 1975. 14166-83.

U.S. District Court, District of Massachusetts, *Tallulah Morgan* et al., *Versus John J. Kerrigan et al., Memorandum of Decision and Remedial Orders,* June 5, 1975.

U.S. General Accounting Office. *Administration of the Science Education Project, "Man: A Course of Study."* MACOS. Report #MWD-76-26. 1975.

U.S. General Services Administration, National Achievement Records Service, Office of the Federal Register. *1977/78 United States Government Manual.* Washington, D.C.: General Services Administration, Office of the Federal Register, 1977.

U.S. Office of Education, Bureau of Education for the Handicapped. *Informal Memorandum on Research Questions Related to Evaluation Methodologies to Test the Effectiveness of Programs and Projects for Handicapped Children.* Washington, D.C.: Government Printing Office, September 1977.

U.S. Office of Education. *Educational Programs that Work.* San Francisco: Far West Laboratory for Educational Research and Development, 1976.

U.S. Office of Education, Office of Planning, Budgeting, and Evaluation. Internal Briefing Paper, 1975.

U.S. Office of Education. *Teacher Centers.* Washington, D.C.: Government Printing Office, 1977.

Widmer, Jeanne L. *What Makes Innovation Work in Massachusetts.* Boston: Department of Education, Bureau of Curriculum Services, n.d.

Index

Abstract of proposal document:
  characteristics of, 172-173
  checklist for, 175
  common flaws of, 175
  function of, 172
  samples of, 173-174
Activity development, strategy for, 197-199
Administrative Procedures Act, 62, 63, 64n, 83
Adult education, 118-124
Advocacy group actions, 280-282
Agency constraints, 116, 121-124, 130, 143, 164, 169, 231
  criteria for, 119-124
Agency definition, 10-11, 26, 53, 61-62, 89
  variables affecting, 39-41
Agency needs, consonance with institutional needs, 92-93, 95, 116-117, 121-123
Agenda-setting process, 275
Allen, James E., 57, 66
Analysis:
  decision-tree, 117-143
  discrepancy, 145
  network, 144-145, 152
  systems model, 146
  tasks, 95-97, 117-118
Antipoverty program, 6
APA (see Administrative Procedures Act)
Appendices:
  characteristics of, 229-230
  checklist for, 231
  common flaws of, 230-231
  functions of, 229
Appropriation, level of, 59, 237
Appropriation-setting process, 59-61
Assessment tasks, 95-97

Bailey, Stephen K., 3
Basic Skills and Educational Quality Act, 276-278

BEEO (*see* Bureau of Equal Educational Opportunity)
Bilingual education, 120-124, 177-178, 192-193
Bilingual Model for Adult Education, 120-124
Boston, response to Racial Imbalance Act, 28-29, 31-34, 39-47
Boston School Committee, 29, 32-34, 43, 47
Brown v. Board of Education of Topeka, 29
Budget:
  characteristics of, 221-222
  common flaws of, 228
  defined, 220-221
  development
    political elements in, 106
    tasks for, 104-107
  functions of, 221
  negotiations, and project implementation, 237-240
  program, allocation of, 251-252
  sample formats, 222-227
  submittal checklist for, 228
Bureau of Equal Educational Opportunity, 28-29, 31-34, 39-47
Busing, 34, 40

Carter, Pres. Jimmy, 276, 278, 279, 283
Causal model, 98-99
CETA (*see* Comprehensive Employment and Training Act)
"Change agent" programs, 18
Chapter 636 (*see* Racial Imbalance Act)
Circular A-95, 282-284
Civil Rights Acts, 4, 29-30, 32
Collective assessment, 11-12
Commissioner of Education, 35, 36, 37, 62, 63, 83, 277
  functions of office, 84-85
Community Education Program, 165-169

The Dynamics of Funding

Community relations, conclusions about, 247-248
Comprehensive Employment and Training Act (1973), 278-280
Conant, James, 35
Conflict resolution, 18-22
Congressional Budget Act (1974), 60, 283-284
Conlan, Cong. John B., 285
Constituent groups:
  needs of, 274
  pressures on Congress, 57
Constitution, Fourteenth Amendment to, 33
Constraints:
  agency and institutional, 116, 121-124, 130, 143
  time, 144
Context evaluation, 205
Control-monitor phase, 145-146
Cooperative Research Act (1964), 57, 66, 76, 77
Cooptation, 256
Corrigan Associates, 146-147
Costs, allocation of (*see* Budget development)
Courts, and the handicapped, 280-282
Crisis in the Classroom, 37

Data gathering, analysis and assessment tasks, 95-97, 116-118
Decision making, time lines governing, 84-85
Decision-tree analysis, 117-143
  application of, 118-143
De facto segregation, 29, 30
Definition setting, variables affecting, 39-41
De jure segregation, 29, 32
Department of Education, Federal, proposed, 276-278
Desegregation, 27-34
  in Boston, history of, 31-34, 50
  societal and legislative definition in, 29-34
Design factors, in funding process, 233-234
Discrepancy analysis evaluation, 145 207
Dunkirk Bilingual Program 210-212

Eagleton, Sen. Thomas, 66, 83
Economic Opportunity Act (1964), 4, 35
Economic Stimulus Appropriations Request, 279

Education for All Handicapped Children Act (1975), 281
Educational Amendments of 1974, 28, 31-34, 40 (*see also* Racial Imbalance Act)
Educational Professions Development Act (1967), 35, 36, 37, 80n
Education Amendments:
  of 1972, 36
  of 1974, 57, 62, 66-67, 281
  of 1976, 37, 58
Education renewal, concept of, 36
Elementary and Secondary Education Act (1965), 3, 4, 5, 31, 35, 57, 58
  1974 Amendments, 5
  Title I, 31, 43, 278
  Title III, 258
Emergency School Assistance Act (1974), 30, 31, 34
  project management plan, 158-159
  systems approach to, 153-158
Emergency School Assistance Program (1970), 30
EPDA (*see* Educational Professions Development Act)
ESAA (*see* Emergency School Assistance Act)
ESEA (*see* Elementary and Secondary Education Act)
Evaluation tasks, 101-103
Executive-initiated actions, 275-278
External review process, 235-236

Federal District Court, in desegregation program, 31, 33
Federal education programs, advance funding of, 60
Federal Register, 61-64 passim, 117n, 125
  Community Education Program in, 165-169
Fenton, Edwin, 110
Final report, 103
Financial management, conclusions about, 246-247
Ford, Pres. Gerald R., 66, 283
Foundation review process, 236
Funded projects, implementation of, 64, 233-268
Funding:
  late
    legislative response to problems, 248-249
    and project implementation, 242-248
  second tier of, 237

Funding agency request, local agency response to, 41-44
Funding decision, 236-237 (*see also* Budget)
Funding environment:
 characteristics of
  general, 272-274
  organizational, 274-287
 and executive-initiated actions, 275-278
 forecasting for, 272-275
 and General Accounting Office reports, 284-287
 importance of personal contacts to, 273-274
 and information securing, 291-296
 institutional strategies for responding to, 291-304
 and judicial and advocacy group actions, 280-282
 and legislative actions, 278-280
 and Office of Management and Budget actions, 282-284
 and program support, 300-303
 and project monitoring, 300-303
 and proposal development 296-300
 proposal document and, 287-290
 responding to, 271-304
 submitting institution and, 290-291
Funding system:
 agency definition in, 10-11, 26, 53, 61-62
 assumptions governing response to, 12
 characteristics of, 8-12
 collective assessment in, 11-12
 conflict and, 13-22
 dynamics of, 25-51
 elements shaping project development, 12-13
 evolution of, 8-12
 generalizations about, 38-39
 historical overview, 1-6
 initial precipitating events, 8-12
 institutional definition in, 11, 12, 19-22, 89
 legislative definition in, 10, 26, 29-38
 model, 8-22, 45
  applications of, 25-51
 operational definition in, 11, 12
 and problem definition, 8-12, 26, 54-55
 project development, 12-18, 26-27
 proposal and, 6-8
 and school desegregation, 27-34
 societal recognition and definition in, 10, 26, 29-38
 and Teacher Centers, 27-28, 34-38
 variables affecting definition setting, 39-41
 variables affecting program definition, 25-26
 working hypotheses, 17

Garrity, Judge W. Arthur, Jr., 29, 32, 33
General Accounting Office reports, 284-287
General Counsel, Office of, 80, 82-83
General Education Procedures Act, 1974 Amendments, 64
General Education Provisions Act, 60, 62, 83, 246n
GEPA (*see* General Education Provisions Act)
G.I. Bill of Rights, 2
Goals, multiplicity of, 273-274
Grants and Procurement Office, 83-84
Great Society, 4, 5, 80

Head Start program, 47-50, 284-287
History of funding, 1-6
House Appropriations Sub-Committee, 38
Howe, Harold, II, 35
Hull, Ronald, 262-263
Humphrey, Vice Pres. Hubert, 281
Hypotheses, 99, 102

Idaho, State of, 173-174, 181-182
Ideographic dimension, 15-16, 28
IHE (*see* Institution of higher education)
Implementation (*see* Project implementation)
Impoundment, 60-61
Information securing, 291-296
Initial design, 147-150
Input evaluation, 205
Inquiry, mode of, 93, 109-113
Institutional constraints, 116, 121-124, 143
Institutional definition, 11, 12, 19-22, 89
 variables affecting, 39-41, 96-97
Institutional factors:
 in funding process, 233-234
 in program slippage, 255-263
Institutional needs, consonance with agency needs, 92-93, 95, 116-117, 121-123

Institutional strategies, and funding environment, 291-303
Institutional support for funded project, 253-254
Institution-community collaboration, 254-255
Institution of higher education, 39-40, 118, 121
Internal review process, 235-236

Jefferson, Thomas, imaginary letter to, 170-171
Job descriptions, 103-104
Johnson, Pres. Lyndon, B., 3, 4, 29, 36, 276
Judicial actions, 280-282

Kennedy, Pres. John F., 3, 4, 29, 36, 281, 288
Kerner Commission Report, 30

Labor and Educational Committee, 57, 59
Labor and Public Welfare Committee, 57-58, 63
LEA (see Local education agency)
Leadership, generalizations and recommendations about, 267-268 (see also Project management)
Legislative activities, 278-280
Legislative definition, 10, 26, 53-55
 in desegregation program, 29-34
 in Teacher Center Program, 34-38
Legislative process, in birth of program, 55-59
Local education agency, 40, 50, 60, 69, 107, 118, 125, 151
 response to funding agency request, 41-44
Long-term desegregation plan, 34, 39-41, 44-47 (see also Racial Imbalance Act)

Macchiavelli, Niccolo, 26
McFarland, Stanley J., 38
MacMillan, Charles B., 260-261
Magnet schools, 28, 40
Man: A Course of Study, 284-287
Management (see also Project implementation; Project management):
 financial, conclusions about, 246-247
 generalizations and recommendations on, 265-267
 objectives, 188

personnel, conclusions about, 247
system, 290-304
Mann, Dale, 18
Marland, Sid, 57
Massachusetts:
 Bureau of Equal Education Opportunity, 28-29, 31-34, 39-47
 Commission Against Discrimination, 33
 Department of Education, Bureau of Adult Services, 118-124
 General Court, 33
 Racial Imbalance Act, 28-29, 31-34, 39-47
 State Board of Education, 32, 33, 43
 Supreme Judicial Court, in desegregation program, 31
Memorandum of Decision and Remedial Orders, 44
Methodologies, criteria for, 207
Methods and procedures (see Program activities)
Milestone chart, 100-101, 145, 146, 198, 215, 218
Mode of inquiry, 93, 109-113
Model:
 bilingual, for adult education, 120-124
 causal, 98-99
 decision-making, 117
Mondale, Sen. Walter, 37
Morgan v. Hennigan, 33
Morgan v. Kerrigan, 29
Morrill Act (1862), 1-2
Morse, Samuel, 1
Mosher, Edith F., 3
Moynihan, Daniel P., 3
Munger, Frank J., 3
Mutual adaptation, 256

National Advisory Commission on Civil Disorders, 30
National Defense Education Act (1958), 3, 34, 35
National Defense Training Act (1958), 2-3
National Defense Training Program (1940), 2
National Education Association, 37, 57, 277
 Director of Governmental Relations, 37-38
National Reading Improvement Act (1977), 57, 66, 76, 276
 Rules and Regulations, 125 142
National Reading Improvement Program, 67-68, 76

National Science Foundation, 3, 285–286
  Institutes for Teachers, 34
  Training Program Proposal, 201–203
NDEA (see National Defense Education Act)
Network analysis, 144–145, 152
Nixon, Pres., Richard M., 31, 35–36, 57, 60–61, 283–284
Nomothetic dimension, 15–16, 27
Nonimplementation, 256

OCD (see Office of Child Development)
OEO (see Office of Economic Opportunity)
Office of Child Development, 47, 285–286
Office of Civil Rights, 32, 84–85
Office of Economic Opportunity, 4, 47
Office of Education, 36–37, 63, 66, 83, 85, 124
  Bureau of Educational Personnel Development, 35
  Division of Adult Education, 118
  Division of Educational Personnel Training, 35
Office of Human Development, 85, 285
Office of Legislation, 83–84
Office of Management and Budget, 36, 60–61
  actions of, 282–284
Office of Regulations, 78
Office of Rules and Regulations, 82–83
Old Deluder Satan Act (1647), 2
OMB (see Office of Management and Budget)
Operational definition, 11, 12, 96
  budget as, 220–221
Ordinance of 1787, 2
Organizational characteristics, 274–287
Organizational charts, 103–104

Parsons, Talcott, 15
Participant, qualifications and availability of, 252–253
Peat, Marwick, Mitchell & Co., 243, 244, 248
Performance objectives, 145, 188
Perkinson, Jean, 367
Personal contacts, importance of, 273–274

Personnel management, conclusions about, 247
Phase I (see Short-Term Plan to Reduce Racial Imbalance)
Phase II (see Long-term desegregation plan)
Planning phase, 145
Problem definition, 12, 26, 54–55
Problem statement:
  characteristics of, 179–180
  checklist for, 186
  common flaws of, 183–186
  function of, 179
  questions and hypotheses in, 185
  samples of, 180–183
Procedural factors, in funding process, 233–235, 263–264
Procedures, methods and (see Program activities)
Process evaluation, 205, 208–209
Process objectives, 188
Product evaluation, 205, 208
Product objectives, 188
Program activities:
  characteristics of, 195–199
  checklist for, 204
  common flaws of, 203–204
  functions of, 195
  samples of, 199–203
Program budget, allocation of, 251–252
Program conceptualization, 91, 96, 98, 234
Program definition, variables affecting, 25–26
Program development, 12–13, 233–268 (see also Project implementation; Project management)
Program evaluation:
  characteristics of, 205–207
  checklist for, 213
  common flaws of, 213
  functions of, 204–205
  samples of, 207–212
  tasks, 101–103
Program formulation, 264–265
Program implementation (see Project implementation)
Program management (see Project management)
Program objectives:
  characteristics of, 187–189
  checklist for, 194
  common flaws of, 193–194
  functions of, 186–187
  samples of, 190–193
Program office, 78–82

Program planning conclusions, 245–246
Program renewal, 12
Program slippage, 255–263
Program-specific factors, 234
Program summary, 100, 172 (*see also* Abstract)
Program support, funding environment and, 300–303
Project development, 12–18, 26–27
  elements shaping, 12–13
  event and characteristic overview, 14–15
Project governance (*see* Project management)
Project governance tasks, 103–104
Project implementation:
  and budget allocation, 251–252
  budget negotiations in, 237–240
  conclusions about, 245–248
  design and institutional factors affecting, 249–255
  and funding decision, 236–237
  institutional support for, 253–254
  institution-community collaboration in, 254–255
  late funding and, 242–249
  leadership for, 267–268
  and management, 265–267
  participants and, 252–253
  procedural factors affecting, 234–235
  and program formulation, 264–265
  and program slippage, 255–263
  proposal review in, 235–236
  response to conditions of, 263–268
  staff and, 252–253
  and start-up commitments, 240–242
Project initiation (*see* Project implementation)
Project management:
  characteristics of, 214–215
  checklist for, 220
  common flaws of, 220
  defined, 213
  functions of, 214
  samples of, 215–219
Project monitoring, funding environment and, 300–303
Project operation (*see* Project management)
Proposal, 1, 5, 6
  and funding system, 6–8
  research, 164
  review of, 235–236, 282–284
Proposal development:
  activities, identification and ordering of, 150–153
  characteristics of process, 158–159
  funding environment and, 296–300
  planning for, 144
  systems management approach to, 144–147
    application of, 147–158
Proposal document (*see also* Proposal request; Proposal writing)
  abstract of, 172–175
  and accountability concerns, 101
  agency and institutional needs in, 92–93, 95
  analysis tasks for, 95–97, 117–118
  and appendices, 229–231
  assessment of need (*see* Problem statement)
  assessment tasks for, 95–97
  background to, 175–179
  and budget, 220–229
    development tasks, 104–107
  components of, 169–172
  data gathering tasks for, 95–97, 116–117
  final report, 103
  format of, 163–169
  formulation and development tasks for, 97–101
  and funding environment, 287–290
  goals of, 93–95, 97–101
  hypotheses behind, 99, 102
  introduction to
    characteristics of, 175–176
    checklist for, 179
    common flaws of, 178
    functions of, 175
    samples of, 176–178
  management and assessment tasks for, 101–107
  methods and procedures (*see* Program activities)
  and mode of inquiry, 93
  nature of, 90–91
  objectives of, 93–95, 97–101
  problem statement (*see* Problem statement)
  and program activities, 195–204
  and program conceptualization, 91, 96, 98
  and program evaluation, 204–213
  and program management (*see* Project management)
  program objectives, 186–194
  project governance tasks, 103–104
  and project management, 213–220
  structure of, 91–95

Proposal document (cont.)
  style of, 163-169
  writing of, 107-109, 163-231 (see also Proposal writing)
  linked with content, 109-112
Proposal format (see Proposal document)
Proposal request, 53-87
  analysis of, 116-118
  response to, 115-160
Proposal-specific factors, 234
Proposal writing (see also Proposal document; Proposal request)
  general-specific conflict, 108-109
  process, 107-112
  skills for, 7-8, 89-92

Racial Imbalance Act (1965), 28-29, 31-34, 39-47 (see also Educational Amendments of 1974)
Racial Isolation in the Public Schools, 30
Rand Corporation, The, 250, 256-257, 260
Reading Academy, 76
Reading Improvement Program, 130 (see also National Reading Improvement Act; Reading Improvement Projects)
Reading Improvement Projects, 125-127
  Rules and Regulations, 131-142
Regulation setting:
  private domain and, 77-78
  process, 62-63
  public domain and, 63-65
Regulations, Office of, 78
Relevance analysis (see Decision-tree analysis)
Rescission, 60-61
Research design, factors relevant to, 243
Research proposal, 164
  characteristics of, 196-197
Review process, 235-236
Ribicoff, Sen. Abraham, 278
Richardson, Elliott, 57
Right to Read Office, 57, 66, 76, 80
Right to Read program, 57, 61, 66-77, 83, 86
  Proposed Rules and Regulations, 68-75
Rules and Regulations, 47-48, 53-55, 62-87, 108
  for Community Education Programs, 165-169

Emergency School Assistance Act, systems approach to, 153-158
National Reading Improvement Act, 124-142
Office of, 82-83
Reading Improvement Projects, 131-142

Sarason, Seymour, 7
Scheduling phase, 145
School desegregation (see Desegregation)
Science and Technology Committee, 285-286
Second tier funding, 237
Short-Term Plan to Reduce Racial Imbalance, 33, 34, 39-44 (see also Racial Imbalance Act)
Silberman, Charles, 37
Slippage (see Program slippage)
Smith-Hughes Act (1917), 2
Social definition (see Societal definition)
Social system, classes of phenomena in, 15-16
Societal definition, 10, 26
  in desegregation program, 29-34
  in Teacher Center Program, 34-38
"Southern Strategy," 31
Special Projects Act, 276, 277
Staff:
  leadership, 267-268
  participation (see Project management)
  qualifications and availability, 252-253
Start-up commitments, 240-242
Strategy development meeting, 147-150
Subcommittee on Education, 57
Submitting institution, and funding environment, 290-291
Supreme Court, desegregation ruling (1954), 4, 29, 30
System Approach for Education, A, 146-147
Systems management approach, 144-147
  application of, 147-158
Systems model analysis, 146

Task commentaries, 292-303
Task Force on Education Manpower, 35
Task Force on Government Reorganization, 276

Teacher Center Program, 27-28, 50
  societal and legislative definition, 34-38
Teachers for the Real World, 35
Teacher Renewal Program, 80n
Teague, Cong. Olin, 285
Time-Action-Budget Plan, 201
Time constraints, 144
Title I (*see* Elementary and Secondary Education Act)
Training Institute Project, 183

U.S. Department of Education, proposed, 276-278
U.S. Department of Health, Education and Welfare, 32, 36, 50
U.S. District Court, District of Massachusetts, 44
U.S. House of Representatives:
  Appropriations Committee, 59
  Labor and Education Committee, 57, 59
  Ways and Means Committee, 59
U.S. Senate:
  Education Committee, 59
  Labor and Public Welfare Committee, 57-58, 63
  Subcommittee on Education, 57
USOE (*see* Office of Education)

War on Poverty, 4-6 passim
Washington, D.C., 31, 273
Washington, State of, 174
Widmer, Jeanne, 260

Youth Employment and Demonstration Projects Act (1977), 278-280